The Cambridge Companion to Gershwin

George Gershwin is often described as a quintessentially American composer. This *Cambridge Companion* explains why, engaging with the ways in which his music was shaped by American political, intellectual, cultural, and business interests. As a composer and performer, Gershwin embraced technological advances and broke new ground in music business practices. In the decades preceding World War II, he captured the mechanistic pulse of modern life with his concert works and lay the groundwork for the Great American Songbook with his Broadway shows and film music. With his brother Ira, and his cousins Henry and B. A. Botkin, Gershwin explored various ethnic and cultural identities and contemplated their roles in US culture. His music confronted race during the Jim Crow era and continues to engage with issues of race today. This interdisciplinary exploration of Gershwin's life and music describes his avowed pursuit of an "American" musical identity and its ongoing legacy.

ANNA HARWELL CELENZA is the Thomas E. Caestecker Professor of Music at Georgetown University, where she also serves as core faculty in the American Studies Program. She is the author/editor of many scholarly books, including the award-winning *Jazz Italian Style: From Its Origins in New Orleans to Fascist Italy and Sinatra* (Cambridge, 2017). She has published numerous articles on a range of composers, from Franz Liszt and Gustav Mahler to Duke Ellington, Billy Strayhorn, and Louis Armstrong.

Cambridge Companions to Music

Topics

The Cambridge Companion to Ballet
Edited by Marion Kant

The Cambridge Companion to Blues and Gospel Music
Edited by Allan Moore

The Cambridge Companion to Choral Music
Edited by André de Quadros

The Cambridge Companion to the Concerto
Edited by Simon P. Keefe

The Cambridge Companion to Conducting
Edited by José Antonio Bowen

The Cambridge Companion to Eighteenth-Century Opera
Edited by Anthony R. DelDonna and Pierpaolo Polzonetti

The Cambridge Companion to Electronic Music
Edited by Nick Collins and Julio D'Escriván

The Cambridge Companion to Film Music
Edited by Mervyn Cooke and Fiona Ford

The Cambridge Companion to French Music
Edited by Simon Trezise

The Cambridge Companion to Grand Opera
Edited by David Charlton

The Cambridge Companion to Hip-Hop
Edited by Justin A. Williams

The Cambridge Companion to Jazz
Edited by Mervyn Cooke and David Horn

The Cambridge Companion to Jewish Music
Edited by Joshua S. Walden

The Cambridge Companion to the Lied
Edited by James Parsons

The Cambridge Companion to Medieval Music
Edited by Mark Everist

The Cambridge Companion to Music in Digital Culture
Edited by Nicholas Cook, Monique Ingalls and David Trippett

The Cambridge Companion to the Musical, third edition
Edited by William Everett and Paul Laird

The Cambridge Companion to Opera Studies
Edited by Nicholas Till

The Cambridge Companion to the Orchestra
Edited by Colin Lawson

The Cambridge Companion to Percussion
Edited by Russell Hartenberger

The Cambridge Companion to Pop and Rock
Edited by Simon Frith, Will Straw and John Street

The Cambridge Companion to Recorded Music
Edited by Eric Clarke, Nicholas Cook, Daniel Leech-Wilkinson and John Rink

The Cambridge Companion to the Singer-Songwriter
Edited by Katherine Williams and Justin A. Williams

The Cambridge Companion to the String Quartet
Edited by Robin Stowell

The Cambridge Companion to Twentieth-Century Opera
Edited by Mervyn Cooke

Composers

The Cambridge Companion to Bach
Edited by John Butt

The Cambridge Companion to Bartók
Edited by Amanda Bayley

The Cambridge Companion to the Beatles
Edited by Kenneth Womack

The Cambridge Companion to Beethoven
Edited by Glenn Stanley

The Cambridge Companion to Berg
Edited by Anthony Pople

The Cambridge Companion to Berlioz
Edited by Peter Bloom

The Cambridge Companion to Brahms
Edited by Michael Musgrave

The Cambridge Companion to Benjamin Britten
Edited by Mervyn Cooke

The Cambridge Companion to Bruckner
Edited by John Williamson

The Cambridge Companion to John Cage
Edited by David Nicholls

The Cambridge Companion to Chopin
Edited by Jim Samson

The Cambridge Companion to Debussy
Edited by Simon Trezise

The Cambridge Companion to Elgar
Edited by Daniel M. Grimley and Julian Rushton

The Cambridge Companion to Duke Ellington
Edited by Edward Green

The Cambridge Companion to Gershwin
Edited by Anna Harwell Celenza

The Cambridge Companion to Gilbert and Sullivan
Edited by David Eden and Meinhard Saremba

The Cambridge Companion to Handel
Edited by Donald Burrows

The Cambridge Companion to Haydn
Edited by Caryl Clark

The Cambridge Companion to Liszt
Edited by Kenneth Hamilton

The Cambridge Companion to Mahler
Edited by Jeremy Barham

The Cambridge Companion to Mendelssohn
Edited by Peter Mercer-Taylor

The Cambridge Companion to Monteverdi
Edited by John Whenham and Richard Wistreich

The Cambridge Companion to Mozart
Edited by Simon P. Keefe

The Cambridge Companion to Arvo Pärt
Edited by Andrew Shenton

The Cambridge Companion to Ravel
Edited by Deborah Mawer

The Cambridge Companion to the Rolling Stones
Edited by Victor Coelho and John Covach

The Cambridge Companion to Rossini
Edited by Emanuele Senici

The Cambridge Companion to Schoenberg
Edited by Jennifer Shaw and Joseph Auner

The Cambridge Companion to Schubert
Edited by Christopher Gibbs

The Cambridge Companion to Schumann
Edited by Beate Perrey

The Cambridge Companion to Shostakovich
Edited by Pauline Fairclough and David Fanning

The Cambridge Companion to Sibelius
Edited by Daniel M. Grimley

The Cambridge Companion to Richard Strauss
Edited by Charles Youmans

The Cambridge Companion to Michael Tippett
Edited by Kenneth Gloag and Nicholas Jones

The Cambridge Companion to Vaughan Williams
Edited by Alain Frogley and Aiden J. Thomson

The Cambridge Companion to Verdi
Edited by Scott L. Balthazar

Instruments

The Cambridge Companion to Brass Instruments
Edited by Trevor Herbert and John Wallace

The Cambridge Companion to the Cello
Edited by Robin Stowell

The Cambridge Companion to the Clarinet
Edited by Colin Lawson

The Cambridge Companion to the Guitar
Edited by Victor Coelho

The Cambridge Companion to the Harpsichord
Edited by Mark Kroll

The Cambridge Companion to the Organ
Edited by Nicholas Thistlethwaite and Geoffrey Webber

The Cambridge Companion to the Piano
Edited by David Rowland

The Cambridge Companion to the Recorder
Edited by John Mansfield Thomson

The Cambridge Companion to the Saxophone
Edited by Richard Ingham

The Cambridge Companion to Singing
Edited by John Potter

The Cambridge Companion to the Violin
Edited by Robin Stowell

780.92
Gershwin

The Cambridge Companion to
GERSHWIN

....

EDITED BY
Anna Harwell Celenza
Georgetown University, Washington DC

CAMBRIDGE
UNIVERSITY PRESS

University Printing House, Cambridge CB2 8BS, United Kingdom

One Liberty Plaza, 20th Floor, New York, NY 10006, USA

477 Williamstown Road, Port Melbourne, VIC 3207, Australia

314–321, 3rd Floor, Plot 3, Splendor Forum, Jasola District Centre, New Delhi – 110025, India

79 Anson Road, #06-04/06, Singapore 079906

Cambridge University Press is part of the University of Cambridge.

It furthers the University's mission by disseminating knowledge in the pursuit of education, learning, and research at the highest international levels of excellence.

www.cambridge.org
Information on this title: www.cambridge.org/9781108423533
DOI: 10.1017/9781108528757

© Cambridge University Press 2019

This publication is in copyright. Subject to statutory exception and to the provisions of relevant collective licensing agreements, no reproduction of any part may take place without the written permission of Cambridge University Press.

First published 2019

Printed and bound in Great Britain by Clays Ltd, Elcograf S.p.A.

A catalogue record for this publication is available from the British Library.

Library of Congress Cataloging-in-Publication Data
Names: Celenza, Anna Harwell.
Title: The Cambridge companion to Gershwin / edited by Anna Celenza.
Description: Cambridge, United Kingdom ; New York, NY : Cambridge University Press, 2020. | Series: Cambridge companions to music | Includes bibliographical references and index.
Identifiers: LCCN 2019011494 | ISBN 9781108423533 (alk. paper)
Subjects: LCSH: Gershwin, George, 1898–1937. | Gershwin, George, 1898–1937 – Criticism and interpretation. | Music – United States – 20th century – Criticism and interpretation.
Classification: LCC ML410.G288 C26 2020 | DDC 780.92–dc23
LC record available at https://lccn.loc.gov/2019011494

ISBN 978-1-108-42353-3 Hardback
ISBN 978-1-108-43764-6 Paperback

Cambridge University Press has no responsibility for the persistence or accuracy of URLs for external or third-party internet websites referred to in this publication and does not guarantee that any content on such websites is, or will remain, accurate or appropriate.

Contents

List of Figures	*page* xi
List of Tables	xii
List of Music Examples	xiii
List of Contributors	xiv
Preface	xvii
Acknowledgments	xx

Part I Historical Context — 1

1 The Unlikely Patriarch
   Michael Owen — 3
2 Hearing Gershwin's New York
   Ellen Noonan — 16
3 Gershwin's Musical Education
   Susan Neimoyer — 29
4 Gershwin in Hollywood
   Jessica Getman — 43

Part II Profiles of the Music — 57

5 *Blue Monday* and New York Theatrical Aesthetics
   Kristen M. Turner — 59
6 Broadway in Blue: Gershwin's Musical Theater Scores and Songs
   Todd Decker — 80
7 The Works for Piano and Orchestra
   Timothy Freeze — 102
8 Harmonizing Music and Money: Gershwin's Economic Strategies from "Swanee" to *An American in Paris*
   Mark Clague — 130
9 Exploring New Worlds: *An American in Paris*, *Cuban Overture*, and *Porgy and Bess*
   Anna Harwell Celenza — 153
10 Complexities in Gershwin's *Porgy and Bess*: Historical and Performing Contexts
   Naomi André — 182
11 Writing for the Big Screen: *Shall We Dance* and *A Damsel in Distress*
   Nathan Platte — 197

Part III Influence and Reception   219

12 The Coverage of Gershwin in Music History Texts
    Howard Pollack   221
13 When Ella Fitzgerald Sang Gershwin: A Chapter from
    the Great American Songbook
    Will Friedwald   235
14 The Afterlife of *Rhapsody in Blue*
    Ryan Raul Bañagale   246
15 Broadway's "New" Gershwin Musicals: Romance, Jazz,
    and the Ghost of Fred Astaire
    Todd Decker   261
16 Gershwin and Instrumental Jazz
    Nate Sloan   275
    Epilogue: The Gershwin I Knew, and the Gershwin I Know
    Michael Feinstein   289

    Guide to Further Reading   298
    Index   301

Figures

1.1	Ira Gershwin, Frances Gershwin, George Gershwin, Arthur Gershwin, Westchester Hills Cemetery, Hastings-on-Hudson, New York (1933). Courtesy of the Ira and Leonore Gershwin Trusts	*page* 4
1.2	George Gershwin, Rose Gershwin, Ira Gershwin, Westchester Hills Cemetery, Hastings-on-Hudson, New York (1933). Courtesy of the Ira and Leonore Gershwin Trusts	5
4.1	Music composer George Gershwin painting the portrait of fellow composer Arnold Schoenberg, 1936. Photo by Gabriel Hackett/Archive Photos/Getty Images	50
9.1	George Gershwin works on a score at the piano in his 72nd Street apartment, New York, New York, 1934. Photo by PhotoQuest/Getty Images	175
10.1	The cast of George Gershwin's *Porgy and Bess* performing on stage, 1935. Photo by Pictorial Parade/Archive Photos/Getty Images	183

Tables

3.1	Composers most frequently represented in Gershwin's concert program collection (arranged in order from most to least heard)	*page* 35
3.2	Better-known composers with only one work in Gershwin's concert program collection	36
3.3	Representative major works listed in Gershwin concert programs	37
6.1	"Production" numbers and published "hits" in five Gershwin scores (musical comedies staged between 1924 and 1930 included among reconstruction recordings)	86
7.1	George Gershwin, Concerto in F, Mvt. 1: formal overview	107
7.2	George Gershwin, *Second Rhapsody*: formal overview	115
7.3	Extant recordings of concerti with George Gershwin as soloist	122
8.1	Performances of *An American in Paris* 1928–1929	144

Music Examples

7.1a)	C. Conrad and J. R. Robinson, "Singin' the Blues"	*page* 104
b)	Transcription of Gershwin's roll recording	104
7.2a)	George Gershwin, Concerto in F, Mvt. 1, R13-1–R14	110
b)	Anton Rubinstein, Piano Concerto No. 4, Mvt. 1, mm. 130–36	111
7.3	George Gershwin, Concerto in F, Mvt. 1: Gradual Synthesis of P and S	112
7.4	George Gershwin, *"I Got Rhythm" Variations*, Piano Solo, $R28^{+10}$–$R28^{+13}$	121
7.5	*Rhapsody in Blue*, m. 302: voicing of final chord	126
16.1	"Fascinating Rhythm," chorus, mm. 1–4	277
16.2	"I Got Rhythm," chorus, mm. 1–4	278
16.3	Transcription of Lester Young's solo on "I Got Rhythm," 1944, Take 2, 00:20–00:25	279
16.4	"Rhythm-a-ning," B section, mm. 17–24	281
16.5a)	Gershwin chord changes, "But Not for Me," chorus, mm. 1–4	282
b)	Coltrane reharmonization, "But Not for Me," chorus, mm. 1–4	282

Contributors

Naomi André is Professor in Afroamerican and African Studies, Women's Studies, and the Residential College at the University of Michigan. Her research focuses on opera and issues surrounding gender, voice, and race. Her work focuses on opera from the nineteenth to the mid-twentieth centuries and explores constructions of gender, race, and identity. Her books include: *Voicing Gender: Castrati, Travesti, and the Second Woman in Early Nineteenth-Century Italian Opera* (Indiana University Press, 2006); *Blackness in Opera*, coedited with Karen M. Bryan and Eric Saylor (University of Illinois Press, 2012); and *Black Opera: History, Empowerment, Engagement* (University of Illinois Press, 2018).

Ryan Raul Bañagale is an Associate Professor of Music at Colorado College. His first book, *Arranging Gershwin: Rhapsody in Blue and the Creation of an American Icon*, was published by Oxford University Press in 2014. He also sits on the editorial board of the *George and Ira Gershwin Critical Edition* and has edited the original jazz-band arrangements of *Rhapsody in Blue*.

Anna Harwell Celenza is the Thomas E. Caestecker Professor of Music at Georgetown University, where she also serves as a core member of the American Studies Program. She is the author of several scholarly books, the most recent being the award-winning *Jazz Italian Style, from Its Origins in New Orleans to Fascist Italy and Sinatra*. In addition to her scholarly work, she has served as a writer/commentator for National Public Radio and published eight award-winning children's books. She is also an active curator, and her most recent exhibition catalogue, *Margaret Bonds and Langston Hughes: A Musical Friendship*, won a 2018 Leab Exhibition Award by the American Library Association.

Mark Clague is an Associate Professor of Musicology at the University of Michigan and the General Editor of the *George and Ira Gershwin Critical Edition*, for which he has edited the composer's *An American in Paris*. He is currently at work on a book for W. W. Norton on the "Star-Spangled Banner."

Todd Decker is a Professor of Musicology and Film & Media Studies at Washington University in St. Louis. He has published four books on commercial popular music in the United States from the 1920s to the present: *Music Makes Me: Fred Astaire and Jazz* (University of California Press, 2011), *Show Boat: Performing Race in an American Musical* (Oxford University Press, 2013), *Who Should Sing "Ol' Man River"?: The Lives of an American Song* (Oxford University Press, 2015), and *Hymns for the Fallen: Combat Movie Music and Sound after Vietnam* (University of California Press, 2017).

Michael Feinstein, founder of the Great American Songbook Foundation in 2007, has built a career over the last three decades as a performer and writer as evidenced from recordings that have earned him five Grammy Award nominations to his Emmy nominated PBS-TV specials and NPR series. He is the

Principal Conductor of the Pasadena Pops and Kravis Center Pops Orchestras. He is also author of the award-winning book *The Gershwin's and Me: A Personal History in Twelve Songs*.

Timothy Freeze currently holds the Pocock Family Distinguished Visiting Professorship at The College of Wooster. He has published research on Gustav Mahler, Viennese operetta, and Aaron Copland and is currently working on critical editions of Gershwin's Concerto in F and *"I Got Rhythm" Variations* for the *George and Ira Gershwin Critical Edition*.

Will Friedwald is a freelance critic and author with a special interest in the Great American Songbook. He writes about music and popular culture for *The Wall Street Journal* and *Vanity Fair*. He also is the author of eight books including the award-winning *A Biographical Guide to the Great Jazz and Pop Singers; Sinatra: The Song Is You; Stardust Melodies; Tony Bennett: The Good Life; Looney Tunes & Merrie Melodies; Jazz Singing: America's Great Voices from Bessie Smith to Bebop and Beyond*; and *The Great Jazz and Pop Vocal Albums*. He has written over 600 liner notes for compact discs, received ten Grammy nominations, and appears frequently on television and other documentaries. He is also a consultant and curator for Apple Music.

Jessica Getman is the Managing Editor of the *George and Ira Gershwin Critical Edition*. Before joining the staff of the University of Michigan, she worked as an editorial assistant for *Music of the United States of America*, a scholarly series of music editions published for the American Musicological Society by A-R Editions. Her research on music and film has been published in the *Journal of the Society of American Music*.

Susan Neimoyer is Visiting Professor of Music Composition and History at Brigham Young University – Idaho. A specialist in twentieth-century American music, her dissertation focused on Gershwin's musical education. Her research in the areas of Gershwin and Canadian singer-songwriter Joni Mitchell has been published in *The Musical Quarterly, Journal of Musicology, American Music*, and the Canadian journal *Intersections*. She is currently preparing an edition of Gershwin's *Lullaby for String Quartet* for the *George and Ira Gershwin Critical Edition*.

Ellen Noonan is Clinical Associate Professor of History and Director of the Archives and Public History Program at New York University. Her award-winning book, *The Strange Career of Porgy and Bess* (University of North Carolina, 2012), examines the opera's long history of invention and reinvention as a barometer of twentieth-century American expectations about race, culture, and the struggle for equality.

Michael Owen is the Historian and Archivist for the Ira and Leonore Gershwin Trusts, where he also curates www.gershwin.com, the official George and Ira Gershwin website. He is the author of *Go Slow: The Life of Julie London* (Chicago Review Press, 2017). He is currently preparing *The Gershwins Abroad*, an annotated version of Ira Gershwin's 1928 travel journal, as a volume for the *George and Ira Gershwin Critical Edition*, for which he is a member of the editorial board, and is at work on a full-length biography of the lyricist.

Nathan Platte is an Associate Professor of Music at the University of Iowa. His publications explore film music of Hollywood's studio era and the collaborative process of film scoring. His books include *The Routledge Film Music Sourcebook* (coedited with James Wierzbicki and Colin Roust), *Franz Waxman's "Rebecca": A Film Score Guide* (co-authored with David Neumeyer) and *Making Music in Selznick's Hollywood*. He is currently completing a critical edition of the film score to *Damsel in Distress* for the *George and Ira Gershwin Critical Edition*.

Howard Pollack is the John and Rebecca Moores Professor of Music at the University of Houston. He has published widely in the field of American music, including the award-winning books *Aaron Copland: The Life and Work of an Uncommon Man*, *George Gershwin: His Life and Work*, *Marc Blitzstein: His Life, His Work, His World*, and *The Ballad of John Latouche: An American Lyricist's Life and Work*.

Nate Sloan is an Assistant Professor of Musicology at the University of Southern California. He is the author of articles on Harold Arlen and Cab Calloway and co-author of *Switched on Pop: How Popular Music Works, and Why It Matters* (Oxford University Press, 2019). He hosts the podcast *Switched on Pop* and is currently preparing a book on the history of the Cotton Club.

Kristen M. Turner is a lecturer at North Carolina State University. Her research centers on staged musical entertainment in the United States at the turn of the twentieth century. Her publications on American operatic culture have appeared in the *Journal of Musicological Research* and the *Journal of the Society for American Music*. The National Endowment for the Humanities and the Society for American Music have supported the research for her forthcoming book on the role of opera in American popular entertainment.

Preface

George Gershwin (1898–1937) is frequently defined as one of the most emblematically American composers of the twentieth century. An intuitive and inquisitive artist, he tapped into the pulse of the 1920s Jazz Age and created a range of works that straddled the supposed boundary between "high brow" and "low brow" cultures. In the decades preceding World War II, Gershwin became an international sensation with his concert works *Rhapsody in Blue* (1924), Concerto in F (1925), and *An American in Paris* (1928). To many listeners at the time, these compositions seemed to capture the mechanistic pulse of modern life, with its soaring skyscrapers, roaring automobiles, and pulsating rhythms. Similarly, his *Cuban Overture* (1932) tapped into the public's growing interest in Latin America. Gershwin's work for Broadway and Hollywood, with collaborators such as his brother Ira and Fred and Adele Astaire, produced a series of sensational revues, light-hearted musical comedies, and satirical political operettas that reflected urban American popular culture of the 1920s and 1930s. In the realm of opera, Gershwin offered two works based on African American characters. The first, *Blue Monday* (1922), was a one-act, black-face "Afro-American Opera" that was roundly rejected by audiences and critics alike. The second, *Porgy and Bess* (1935), marked the acme of Gershwin's compositional career. It is a work that is equally powerful and controversial and since its premiere has garnered both praise and criticism.

Gershwin also dominated the realm of popular music during the 1920s and 1930s, and his numerous tunes for stage and screen became standards in the canon of American popular song. His lyricist for nearly all of these works was his older brother, Ira. A few of their most memorable collaborations include: "I Got Rhythm," "'S Wonderful," "Strike Up the Band," "Oh, Lady Be Good," "Fascinating Rhythm," "Someone to Watch Over Me," "Embraceable You," "Let's Call the Whole Thing Off," and "They Can't Take That Away from Me."

Gershwin's interest and success in both "serious" and "popular" music often led to a muddled reception of his work among contemporary critics, which in turn impeded serious study of his music by scholars for several decades after his death. Consequently, his music is often referred to as quintessentially American without any in-depth exploration of what such a classification actually means and how it has come into existence. For example, how did his music interact with the racial terrain of American culture during the Jim Crow era? And does it continue to engage with issues of race today? How has Gershwin's legacy been shaped by American intellectual, political, and business interests? Did technology play a role in the shaping of an "American" sound? If yes, then how did this influence Gershwin's creative identity? In pursuit of answers to questions such as these, the *Cambridge Companion to Gershwin* offers an interdisciplinary study of Gershwin's life and music that explores, in various ways, his avowed pursuit of an "American" musical identity.

The son of Jewish immigrants from Russia, Gershwin was a product of multicultural New York. Eager to imbibe as wide an array of music influences as possible, he familiarized himself with the various traditions New York had to offer, from the European classics of the concert hall to the Yiddish Theater songs and Klezmer tunes of the Lower East Side, the music of Tin Pan Alley and Broadway, and the African American jazz of Harlem. Over the course of his career, Gershwin was praised and criticized in equal measure for his willingness to borrow and fuse musical elements from various cultural and ethnic realms: classical and jazz, white and black, Jewish and gentile, urban and rural. As the chapters in this volume collectively explain, this "melting pot" mentality affected not only the content of Gershwin's music, but also its reception over the past century. Gershwin regularly tapped into the aesthetic values and popular tastes of his surroundings in an attempt to compose works that would connect with as broad and diverse a public as possible. This approach to composition produced mixed results. Although contemporary audiences embraced most of his works when they first appeared, and many of these compositions (most notably *Rhapsody in Blue*) have stood the test of time, other pieces (such as the blackface hit "Swanee") have understandably received a cooler reception by twenty-first-century audiences. Still, all these works are important if we are to understand fully Gershwin's place in the musical canon; collectively, all of these works contributed to his identity as a composer.

Ever since the premiere of *Rhapsody in Blue*, Gershwin's compositions have been at the center of key developments in the history of jazz, although certain aspects of his style and legacy still sit uncomfortably within it. The question of whether Gershwin's work deserves the appellation of "jazz" at all has occupied musicians and critics since the debut of *Rhapsody in Blue*. Consequently, the contributors to this volume explore Gershwin's fluid status as a composer linked to jazz, popular music, and concert music and in so doing highlight disciplinary tensions that have developed in American scholarship over music, commerce, and race.

Gershwin came of age during the watershed years of recorded sound, and the differing technical innovations and limitations of gramophones, radio, and film noticeably influenced the structure, distribution, and preservation of his music. *The Cambridge Companion to Gershwin* engages with various extra-musical phenomena (i.e. technology, ethnicity, race, religion, politics, and the burgeoning music industry) in its discussions of the composer's life and works. Consequently, the volume is divided into three primary parts: 1) "The Historical Context," which explores Gershwin's life, education, and connections with local communities in New York and Los Angeles; 2) "Profiles of the Music," which offers discussions of his compositional practices as they pertained to specific genres and local stimuli; and 3) "Influence and Reception," which examines various responses to and treatments of Gershwin's music after his death.

Gershwin's compositions do not sit easily in a single musical category. Because he consciously combined classical music, jazz, blues, and popular song – artistic traditions with different performance practices and conventions of musical notation – his compositions do not always speak to a clearly definable audience or evoke a particular moment in American history. Instead, they are shifting entities, whose content, orchestration, performance style, and cultural significance continue to change from one generation to the next.

Acknowledgments

The *Cambridge Companion to Gershwin* is the result of multiple generations of music scholarship. The insights revealed in each chapter are deeply indebted to the groundbreaking contributions made by previous scholars, most notably Richard Crawford, Steven Gilbert, Edward Jablonski, Howard Pollack, David Schiff, Wayne Schneider, and Larry Starr.

Special thanks also go to Harlan Greene and Stephanie Yuhl for their insights concerning Charleston, SC and Gershwin's various visits there, my research assistant at Georgetown University, Leanne Almeida, and the Georgetown students who participated in my "Gershwin's World" seminar in Fall 2018, especially Tory Broadus. Your insights and enthusiasm for the project kept me motivated. Thank you also to my colleagues in the Department of Performing Arts, the American Studies Program, and the Americas Initiative. The administration at Georgetown University offered what is most valuable to a scholar in the humanities: a semester of research leave. For this I am very grateful.

A volume such as this is dependent on the knowledge and insights of great archivists and librarians. Special thanks to the staff of the George and Ira Gershwin Collection at the Library of Congress, the Archives of American Art, the Archives & Special Collections at the University of Nebraska–Lincoln Libraries, the Special Collections Research Center at Syracuse University Libraries, the College of Charleston Special Collections, and the Booth Family Center for Special Collections at Georgetown University. Jessica Getman proved especially helpful, not only in her contribution of a chapter to this book, but also for reading drafts of chapters by other contributors and assisting in the acquisition of permissions for the volume's music examples.

Once again, working with Cambridge University Press has been a wonderful experience, and this is largely due to the enthusiastic support I have received from my editor, and now great friend, Kate Brett. Gratitude also goes to Janice Baiton, Eilidh Burrett, Sunantha Ramamoorthy, and Lisa Sinclair for the copyediting and production of this book.

Finally, I would like to thank my husband, Chris, for all the years of love and encouragement. With each new project, you cheer me on, which makes the research and writing all the more enjoyable.

PART I

Historical Context

1 The Unlikely Patriarch

MICHAEL OWEN

Shortly before the death of his father, George Gershwin told his friend and biographer Isaac Goldberg that the saddest part of knowing that the end was near was the realization "that there is nothing we can do to really help him."[1] One year later, in the spring of 1933, in accordance with Jewish burial traditions, the Jahrzeit of Morris Gershwin's death was commemorated with the unveiling of his tombstone at the Westchester Hills Cemetery, a Jewish reform cemetery in Hastings-on-Hudson, New York. Although the Gershwins were not observant Jews, they did participate in certain traditions of their faith.

As his automobile passed through the gates of the cemetery, George peered out of the window and saw members of his family awaiting his arrival. After walking up the gentle, grass-covered slope toward Morris's tombstone, he was warmly greeted by his mother Rose, his brothers Ira and Arthur and sister Frances, his aunt Kate Wolpin, his uncle Aaron Gershwin, his cousin Gertrude Geller, and his maternal grandmother.

As the ceremony of laying the wreath and placing flowers took place, and reminiscences of the humorous, gentle Morris were exchanged, each person in attendance that day surely took a moment to glance over at George, recognizing this moment as the culmination of more than a decade of events that had not only brought him from the obscurity of New York's Lower East Side to a penthouse apartment on the Upper West Side, but also touched each of them with a dusting of his celebrity.

More than eighty years later, we remain fortunate that someone brought a camera to the cemetery; two images among the thirty-one photographs captured that day illustrate the transformation of the Gershwin family and the moment George Gershwin became its unlikely patriarch. The first photograph (Figure 1.1) is the only known image of George Gershwin together with his three siblings when they were adults. The quartet is grouped tightly together, with George's older brother Ira on the far left, hands in pockets and pipe in mouth, leaning awkwardly toward his sister, as if the photographer had just

4 Michael Owen

Figure 1.1 Ira Gershwin, Frances Gershwin, George Gershwin, Arthur Gershwin, Westchester Hills Cemetery, Hastings-on-Hudson, New York (1933). Courtesy of the Ira and Leonore Gershwin Trusts

asked him to move closer before clicking the camera. Frances is sandwiched between Ira and George, her left hand reaching across her body to clutch her right hand in a protective stance, while Arthur – looking remarkably like George's double – stands to the far right, holding a cigarette while his fingers fiddle nervously. By contrast, George looks composed and in control of the moment. Although the receding hairlines of all three brothers give the impression of additional years, the composer is just four months shy of his thirty-fifth birthday. Gazing steadily into the camera as he stands behind his siblings, George, wearing a flower in his lapel, stretches out his arms to place his hands comfortingly on their shoulders.

The second photograph (Figure 1.2) shows George and Ira on either side of their mother. Again, Ira appears uncomfortable, while George calmly puts his left hand on Rose's shoulder. What is most notable about this image is Rose's deferential attitude toward George; rather than leaning toward her oldest son, which would be the typical position, she clearly recognizes George as her protector. If this change in family dynamics had been unspoken since the success of "Swanee" thirteen years earlier, it was now clear: Morris and Rose Gershwin's second son was the rock that the disparate members of his family clung to for stability.

5 *The Unlikely Patriarch*

Figure 1.2 George Gershwin, Rose Gershwin, Ira Gershwin, Westchester Hills Cemetery, Hastings-on-Hudson, New York (1933). Courtesy of the Ira and Leonore Gershwin Trusts

The Gershwin Family

The personalities of George Gershwin's parents have, over the course of eighty years of Gershwin biographies, typically been encapsulated in anecdotes. The father, Morris, was saddled with adjectives such as "easy-going" and "humorous," yet he also displayed a restlessness that led him on a constant search for the American dream of financial security. The mother, Rose, was characterized as having the more dominant personality: a tough, unsentimental woman "who steered the family through the early years" with steely determination.[2]

The Gershwin line, said the composer's first biographer, was one of "commercial acumen [rather] than artistic dedication."[3] Born in the Russian city of St. Petersburg in 1872, Morris Gershovitz was the son of a successful mechanic and the grandson of a rabbi from a small town near Vilna, in what is now Lithuania. At the age of eighteen, Morris – who apprenticed as a maker of ladies' shoe uppers (a sought-after specialty wherever he might choose to live) – opted to avoid the mandatory military draft instituted by Czar Alexander III and left his family as he journeyed to create a new life for himself in the United States.

The daughter of a furrier, Rosa Bruskin was born around 1875 and, like Morris, was a native of St. Petersburg. She arrived in New York with her parents and two siblings within a few years of Morris's immigration. The couple, who had already known each other in St. Petersburg, soon reunited and were married in July 1895.

Included among Morris's many business ventures after leaving shoemaking were periods as an owner of restaurants and bakeries; a proprietor of Turkish baths, a rooming house, and a summer hotel in Spring Valley; an operator of a cigar and pool room near Grand Central Station and an automobile garage in the Bronx; and a memorable summer as a licensed bookie at Belmont Park racetrack. His preference for living within walking distance of his job led his family to twenty-eight different residences by the time George reached the age of eighteen. The financial instability of Morris's businesses often left his family in need of ready cash, moments that would send Ira off to the pawnshop with his mother's diamond ring.

The economic status of the Gershwin family was hardly that of the poor immigrant Jews who lived in the squalid tenements of New York's Lower East Side. E. Y. (Yip) Harburg, Ira's schoolfriend and fellow-lyricist, knew poverty firsthand, and the life of the Gershwins, exemplified by their "swank" apartment on Second Avenue and East Fifth Street, was not one of need. He recalled that Ira even "had an allowance and money to buy magazines, books and records" and that Morris and Rose were usually comfortable enough to employ a maid.[4] After George's death, his mother took pains to refute the portrayal of the family's financial poverty in the fanciful 1945 Warner Bros. biopic of the composer, *Rhapsody in Blue*. Morris, she averred, "always made enough to take care of the family."[5]

Whether or not the Gershwins had money, Rose "was never the doting type," George wrote in a letter to his biographer. "Although very loving, she never watched every move we made. She was set on having us completely educated, the idea being that if everything else failed we could always become school-teachers." As children, the three brothers were largely left to their own devices, and George admitted that he could usually be found "with the boys on the street, skating and, in general, making a nuisance of myself."[6]

Music was not a part of his world. Any expression of musicality was restricted to Morris's knack of playing melodies on an improvised instrument of paper and comb, and in listening to the Enrico Caruso records that Morris favored, played on the Victrola that Ira was content to crank rather than pursue the piano lessons his aunt Kate briefly gave him. But from that now-fabled moment in 1910 when a used, upright piano was hoisted through the window of their second-floor flat on Second Avenue, life changed for the Gershwin family. George's inherent musical talent blossomed, first as a piano player and song plugger, then as a songwriter. By the end of the decade, George's income provided financial security.

Rise of the Patriarch

The doors of the majestic Capitol Theatre opened on October 24, 1919 with a lavish production that included two songs composed by twenty-one-year-old George Gershwin. One of these, an "American one-step" written with lyricist Irving Caesar to capitalize on the faux-exoticism of popular songs like "Hindustan," was called "Swanee." Sung to little effect and notice in its original setting, when George played "Swanee" at a party for Al Jolson (one of Broadway's most popular performers, whose hit show *Sinbad* was playing across the street at the Winter Garden), the combination of song and artist gave off sparks. Jolson's exuberant performance of "Swanee," on stage and on a Columbia Records disc, became the launching pad for George's career as a popular songwriter.

Jolson's recording, as well as George's piano roll of the song and the published sheet music, each sold in the millions and reportedly garnered the composer ten thousand dollars in royalties in the first year alone. This sudden flush of money transformed Morris's second son from the boy whom his father predicted might become a vagabond into the family's primary breadwinner. Thus began the gradual process of the next decade that relegated Morris to the role of nominal patriarch.

While his father continued to maintain a series of businesses, it was George's fame that pushed the family onto an upwardly mobile path. Only a year after the success of "Swanee," the Gershwins' uptown apartment was abandoned for a significantly better dwelling on East 12th Street in Greenwich Village, and by an even more spacious property on West 110th Street in Morningside Heights in 1922. By the following spring, George had established himself as a Broadway songwriter, with a series of scores for producer George White's popular *Scandals* revues, as well as *Stop Flirting*, a successful show in London starring Fred and Adele Astaire, which its producer, Alex Aarons, hoped would lead to "just the kind of thing we have been wanting for a long time to do."[7] The result was 1924's *Lady, Be Good!*, the first full-length Broadway collaboration of George and Ira Gershwin. George also had larger ambitions that he was convinced could take him beyond the formulaic thirty-two-bar tunes of Tin Pan Alley. These were realized on the evening of February 12, 1924, when the final notes of the first performance of *Rhapsody in Blue* rang out in New York's Aeolian Hall. Representatives of the worlds of music and letters, including conductor Walter Damrosch, violinist Fritz Kreisler, pianist Leopold Godowsky, and writer Carl Van Vechten, were dazzled by a new voice that critic and composer Deems Taylor quickly labeled as "a link between the jazz camp and the intellectuals."[8]

George's blurring of the lines between popular songwriter, classical composer, concert pianist, and celebrity gave him an entrée to high society in the United States and Europe. In the years that followed, he took on many roles, although his position as the financial backbone of his family was, in some ways, the closest to his heart. George's fame provided financial independence for his entire family. Not only did he support them directly, but he also became a financial conduit by facilitating stock market recommendations from newly minted friends on Wall Street. He supplied loans to Morris and Ira for their investments in some of his Broadway shows (productions in which he himself was often an investor). Ira gratefully acknowledged the assistance: "I told him I didn't have $2,500.00 [to invest in *Of Thee I Sing*] ... but maybe I could borrow it. The next day my brother loaned me the money and happily I was able to repay the loan a few months later. My $2,500.00 investment brought me besides the repayment some $11,000.00."[9]

In July 1925, George became the first composer to grace the cover of *Time* magazine, and shortly thereafter he purchased a five-story white granite house on West 103rd Street, a property spacious enough that he could occupy the entire top floor, while his parents and siblings inhabited distinctive lodgings of their own on the lower levels.

Morris, naturally, was proud of George's accomplishments. Rather than being troubled by his son having taken over his role as patriarch, he discovered joy and freedom in his new position as the life of the party when his son entertained friends. Morris's antics were ready-made fodder for the press: "Besides telling stories that amuse the guests because of their unconscious humor," wrote one New York newspaper columnist, "his father entertains by imitating a trumpet." Morris even reportedly stood guard outside his son's door while he was composing. "If Gershwin should stop playing the piano for a few minutes, Papa Gershwin will enter the room, whistle a bit and then say: 'Perhaps that will help you, George?'"[10]

George and Ira loved to relate their father's po-faced comments to anyone within earshot. The song "Embraceable You" from *Girl Crazy* was one of Morris's favorites, said its lyricist: "Whenever possible, with company present, his request to George was: 'Play that song about me.' And when the line 'Come to papa – come to papa – do!' was sung, he would thump his chest, look around the room, and beam."[11] The composer wrote to a friend that, during the composition of the *Second Rhapsody* in 1931, his father "came out with the brilliant suggestion that I should call it

'RHAPSODY IN BLUE #2.' Then, he says, 'You can write #3 and #4, just like Beethoven.'"[12]

Rose, relieved to see her "Georgie" move from a twenty-five-dollar-a-week piano player on Tin Pan Alley to a Broadway and concert hall success, reveled in her son's fame in a distinctive style.[13] George never failed to make sure that his mother dressed in elegant furs and jewels and that she occupied a prominent seat at the premieres of his concert works and Broadway musicals. "At his cocktail parties or midnight affairs at his apartment, she was often an honored guest, moving with dignity and respect (Yiddish accent and all) among the celebrities."[14] He also subsidized her vacations, joking to a friend that he made at least one trip to Miami Beach just "to give mother a whirl. Four people last night thought she was my wife."[15]

After his father's death in 1932, George – between artistic commitments and his ongoing relationship with the composer Kay Swift – focused much of his attention on his mother's health. Rose had suffered from bouts of respiratory ailments since the late 1920s, and she had undergone at least one serious nasal operation. George sent her to Arizona in the hope that the dry air of the southwest would bring her relief, and he accompanied her to a Pennsylvania sanitarium where she sought treatment.[16] Yet nothing seemed to help, he said. "It all seems very hopeless and sad."[17]

George's younger brother and sister, Arthur and Frances, spent most of their lives out of the public eye. Consequently, their relationships with him remain somewhat opaque. At the height of the composer's fame in the mid-1930s, Arthur had yet to find a similar level of professional or personal success. Two years younger than George, Arthur had ambitions to join his brothers in the family songwriting business. After abandoning his musical training not long after George began studying piano ("His principal complaint," wrote Ira, "was that George, when taking a lesson, sat down – whereas he, taking one, had to stand up"), Arthur became a salesman – first of men's clothing, then for a variety of motion picture companies, including Metro-Goldwyn-Mayer, before settling into work as a stockbroker – all the while continuing to dabble at the piano.[18]

When presented with the opportunity, George never failed to offer Arthur a helping hand. In the spring of 1934, when the composer was hosting *Music by Gershwin*, a successful half-hour radio show broadcast over the NBC network, he featured the work of many up-and-coming songwriters (including Harold Arlen, Vernon Duke, and Dana Suesse). On one episode, he extended that generosity to Arthur. He also facilitated the publication of one of his brother's tunes, "Slowly but Surely" (lyrics by Edward Heyman), which appeared shortly after its radio broadcast under the imprint of New World Music, the company that had published

George's own songs since the late 1920s. There was even a story George told one friend – perhaps in jest – that since his current producers were so slow to provide a good story for his next show, he would have to train Arthur to write the books[19] and suggested to his mother that perhaps his brother could oversee the entire production.[20] Toward the end of his life, George continued to express concern over Arthur's future, telling Rose that he hoped a market could be found for his music.

George's youngest sibling, his sister Frances – born in 1906, a decade to the day after Ira, and usually known as "Frankie" – was only a teenager when "Swanee" became a national hit. Nonetheless, she had already acquired her own taste of the theatrical life when, at age ten, she joined the cast of a touring vaudeville act called Daintyland.

George was extremely protective of his sister, even as she grew into a "chestnut-haired flapper."[21] He often reminded her to mind her language in public, and he suggested she would be more lady-like if she kept her skirts below her knees. That said, he actively encouraged her theatrical ambitions and acted as her accompanist at parties and at auditions for roles in musicals, moments when she would interpret his songs "with convincing abandon."[22] Frances had small parts in two Broadway revues (*Merry-Go-Round* 1927 and *Americana* 1928), but her most prominent moment in the Gershwin story came in the spring and summer of 1928, when she took an extended trip to Europe with George and Ira.

George was feted by European society; so too was his sister, who, after being spotted by Cole Porter at a party, was asked to join the cast of his new Paris production, *Les Revue Des Ambassadors*. On the opening night, George played the piano while Frances warbled a medley of Gershwin songs, prefaced by Porter's own specialty number that predicted "an orgy of music written by Georgie."[23]

Although her career as an actress eventually faltered, Frances continued to benefit from her brother's generosity, both artistically and financially. A year after the European journey, George accompanied her performance of his rarely heard art song "In the Mandarin's Orchid Garden" on a CBS radio broadcast. More personally, George acted as chief serenader when his sister married Leopold Godowsky, Jr., in November 1930. Decades later, Frances recalled that her father was more concerned that he and Rose would miss their train to Florida than he was with the details of his daughter's wedding. On the other hand, she continued, "George came in from his apartment; he just walked across with his bathrobe on, his pajamas, and a long cigar in his mouth, and he sat down and was fooling around on the piano ... When the ceremony was over George played the 'Wedding March.'"[24]

George appears to have had the closest relationship with his older brother, Ira. Morris and Rose Gershwin's first child was born in 1896 in the couple's home above Simpson's Pawnshop at the corner of Hester and Eldridge Streets in New York. Ira's scholarly mien was a distinct contrast to that of his scrappy kid brother. While George played in the streets, Ira pursued literature, devoured books and magazines, and kept hand-written journals in which he set down his thoughts about the world around him and his nascent dreams of a career as a writer. Ira's parents – somewhat hampered by their imprecise grasp of the English language – acknowledged their son's easy facility with words, and during George's school days, deputized Ira to visit his brother's teachers to explain his frequent absences.

Once George began to display a facility at the piano, Ira became his ardent admirer and champion. It was Ira who was responsible for his brother's first public appearance as a performer and composer in 1914, in his role as a member of the committee tasked with hiring the entertainment for a function at the Finlay Club, an organization affiliated with the City College of New York. After George was hired as a Tin Pan Alley song plugger, the brothers' shared interest in musical theater was magnified exponentially. Not only did they attend the latest shows together – George avidly studying the music, Ira the lyrics, and both the form itself – but George often brought home copies of the newest published songs and would sit at the piano, Ira standing by him rapt in wonder at his brother's technique.

George, sensing that Ira might be ready to find his own place in the musical theater world, introduced his brother to another rising composer, Vincent Youmans, with whom the "scared stiff" lyricist wrote his first full Broadway score, the successful musical comedy *Two Little Girls in Blue* (1921).[25] Rather than use his own name, George's self-effacing sibling cast himself as one Arthur Francis, whom George described to a producer as "a clever college boy with lots of talent."[26] The pseudonym, which made its first appearance on the sheet music to "Waiting for the Sun to Come Out" in 1920 – the initial published song credited jointly to the brothers – was derived from the given names of his younger brother and sister; thus the fortunes of Arthur and Frances – unbeknownst to the world at large – also became part of the Gershwin story.

After the brothers' partnership was cemented by *Lady, Be Good!*, Ira became George's most trusted collaborator, their push-and-pull method of working highlighting their very dissimilar personalities. If George was lightning in a bottle, Ira was the quiet scholar whose erudite and jewel-like lyrics provided the counterpoint to the composer's unstoppable fount of melodies. The brothers' working relationship was not so much dependent on their being brothers, as it was on an undying mutual respect for each other's abilities.

The Death of a Patriarch

A little more than four years after the unveiling of Morris's tombstone, the Gershwin family returned to the Westchester Hills Cemetery to bury George. The tragedy of George Gershwin's unexpected death on July 11, 1937 was felt around the world; the effect of that loss on the members of his immediate family was multiplied by his status as their lodestone. Now as their automobiles left the cemetery once again, the mourners became lost in their thoughts of the impact George had made on their lives as son, brother, and artistic collaborator. As Ira later explained, his brother "had a great admiration for family," and since his meteoric rise to fame and fortune, he had been the literal glue that bonded his parents and siblings together.[27] With his death, that bond began to fracture as the individual members of the Gershwin family drifted apart, never to fully heal or unite again.

Seven months before George's death, Rose, Frances, and her husband Leo left the chilly climes of New York for a stay with George and Ira at their rented house in sunny Beverly Hills, California. Their visit, George informed a correspondent, "cheered me up immeasurably ... I am myself again."[28] Home movies taken during this time show the visitors gathered around the swimming pool, laughing and joking for the camera, clearly enjoying these moments of familial togetherness. George, eschewing the Hollywood starlets he had been squiring, even took Rose as his date to a dinner hosted by the actor Edward G. Robinson for composer Igor Stravinsky. When Frances and Leo left for Mexico in January, and Rose departed for New York three months later, they could not have suspected it would be the last time they would see George alive.

Life after George

Rose Gershwin outlived her husband by sixteen years; her second son by eleven. As George's sole heir, she became a wealthy woman; she also became a somewhat awkward representative of her late son's legacy. When she passed away in December of 1948, her estate, which included George's, was left to her three surviving children.

Arthur's place in the story of his brother remained that of an enigma. "I'm the Gershwin nobody ever hears about," he once mused regretfully.[29] In the spring of 1938, he gave up his career as a Wall Street stockbroker to make another attempt as a songwriter, hoping in vain that Ira would agree to become the lyrical half of a new Gershwin partnership. That was not to be, and without George's guidance, he floundered. His one moderate success came in the mid-1940s with the song "Invitation to the Blues," the same decade in which his mother's financial investment helped bring about his only Broadway credit, as the composer of *A Lady Says Yes*, which starred Hollywood sex symbol Carole Landis in her lone stage musical. The undistinguished score did little to help the show, which closed after less than one hundred performances. In 1940, he married former Xavier Cugat vocalist Judy Lane; they had one son. Arthur Gershwin died in New York at the age of eighty-one on November 20, 1981.

Paralyzed by the trauma of George's death, Ira decided to make a permanent home in California and retreated behind a veil of business, claiming that his lack of artistic output was the result of the pressure of dealing with his brother's musical estate. His inactivity was also affected by the knowledge that, lacking the drive to work that had come from George and that sparked his own creativity, he had become an empty shell. It took the combination of two high-profile artists, writer Moss Hart and composer Kurt Weill, and the highly successful play-with-music *Lady in the Dark* to bring Ira Gershwin's lyrical voice back to a Broadway stage. His career relaunched, the next fifteen years saw movie successes (the songs "Long Ago and Far Away" and "The Man That Got Away") and stage failures (*The Firebrand of Florence* and *Park Avenue*), and much of the 1950s was spent exploring his memory while writing the witty reminiscence *Lyrics on Several Occasions*. By the beginning of the following decade, Ira eased into a welcome retirement, his hours devoted to crosswords, the racetrack, writing letters, checking his investments, enjoying the company of his Hollywood friends, and keeping alive the memory of his beloved brother.

Most of the mail Ira received from George's fans in the years following his brother's death was separated from the main body of his correspondence. But in 1941, shortly before what would have been his brother's forty-third birthday, Ira opened a letter that he did not put aside, perhaps because it included a comment about Ira himself that the writer claimed George had made to her in the 1920s: "He's everything I'd like to be but never will."[30] A remark such as this surely must have evoked bittersweet memories and thoughts of what might have been. Ira Gershwin passed away at his home in Beverly Hills on August 17, 1983. He was eighty-six years old.

After their wedding, Frances and Leo Godowsky moved to Rochester, New York, where his career with the color photography laboratory at the Eastman-Kodak Company took off. The couple later moved to Connecticut, where they raised four children, and where Frances pursued the visual arts. Her work included paintings of abstract images unique enough to merit a place in gallery exhibitions and on the walls of private collectors around the world. In 1973, she made a brief return to music with the recording *For George and Ira*. It was a fitting tribute, performed by a now-sixty-something woman who had known many of these songs since their creation. Frances Gershwin Godowsky passed away on January 18, 1999, at the age of ninety-two, the last member of the storied Gershwin family.

George Gershwin played *the* pivotal role in the lives of his parents and siblings, yet even they at times wondered if he was ever truly happy. Reflecting on George's life twenty-five years after his passing, Frances concluded that her brother was "lonely inside himself." Although George had often spoken of marrying and having a family, she noted, "there was some unconscious fear which made it impossible for him to lose himself in a personal relationship."[31] Looking at the two photographs taken at Morris's graveside in 1933, one can see that George Gershwin had perhaps found a way "to lose himself" in the company of his parents and siblings. The unlikely patriarch recognized, more than anything else, that his heart belonged to his family.

Notes

1. George Gershwin to Isaac Goldberg (May 6, 1932). Library of Congress, Washington, DC. George and Ira Gershwin Collection.
2. S. N. Behrman, "Troubadour," *The New Yorker*, May 25, 1929.
3. Isaac Goldberg, *George Gershwin: A Study in American Music* (New York: Simon & Schuster, 1931), 52–53.
4. Bernard Rosenberg and Ernest Goldstein, *Creators and Disturbers: Reminiscences by Jewish Intellectuals of New York* (New York: Columbia University Press, 1982), 182.
5. David Ewen, *A Journey to Greatness: The Life and Music of George Gershwin* (New York: Henry Holt, 1956), 29.
6. George Gershwin to Isaac Goldberg (June 30, 1931). Harvard University, Houghton Library, George Gershwin Letters to Isaac Goldberg, 1929–31 (MS Thr 222).
7. Alex Aarons to Ira Gershwin (May 19, 1923). Library of Congress, Washington, DC. Ira and Leonore Gershwin Trusts Archives.
8. Deems Taylor, *New York World*, February 13, 1924, cf. Goldberg, George Gershwin, 151.
9. Ira Gershwin, undated, unpublished note to David Ewen. Ira and Leonore Gershwin Trusts, San Francisco. Lawrence Stewart papers, box 1, folder 31.
10. Sidney Skolsky, "The Times Square Tintypes," *New York Sun*, January 21, 1929.
11. Ira Gershwin, *Lyrics on Several Occasions* (New York: Knopf, 1959), 31.
12. George Gershwin to George Pallay, n.d. [March 1931]. Library of Congress, Washington, DC. Ira and Leonore Gershwin Trusts Archives.
13. Goldberg, *George Gershwin*, 53.
14. David Ewen, "Farewell to George Gershwin," in Merle Armitage (ed.), *George Gershwin:* (London, New York: Longmans, Green & Co., 1938), 205.
15. George Gershwin to Lou Paley (February 22, 1935). Library of Congress, Washington, DC. Ira and Leonore Gershwin Trusts Archives.
16. George Gershwin to Harry Botkin (February 12, 1933). Library of Congress, Washington, DC. Ira and Leonore Gershwin Trusts Archives.
17. George Gershwin to George Pallay (November 9, 1933). Library of Congress, Washington, DC. Ira and Leonore Gershwin Trusts Archives.
18. Gershwin, *Lyrics on Several Occasions*, 179.

19. George Gershwin to Aileen Pringle (August 17, 1931). Library of Congress, Washington, DC. George and Ira Gershwin Collection.
20. George Gershwin to Rose Gershwin (June 10, 1937). Library of Congress, Washington, DC. George and Ira Gershwin Collection.
21. Vernon Duke, *Passport to Paris* (Boston: Little, Brown, 1955), 92.
22. Ibid., 222.
23. William McBrien, *Cole Porter: A Biography* (New York: Knopf, 1998), 118.
24. Vivian Perlis and Libby Van Cleve. *Composers' Voices from Ives to Ellington: An Oral History of American Music* (New Haven: Yale University Press, 2005), 202–03.
25. Ira Gershwin, *Lyrics on Several Occasions*, 119.
26. Ibid., 188.
27. "LDS Evenings with Ira," Ira and Leonore Gershwin Trusts, San Francisco. Lawrence Stewart papers, box 2, folder 19.
28. George Gershwin to Julia Van Norman (January 9, 1937). Library of Congress, Washington, DC. George and Ira Gershwin Collection.
29. Earl Wilson, *New York Post*, June 27, 1960.
30. Helen Lee Brock to Ira Gershwin (September 13, 1941). Library of Congress, Washington, DC. Ira and Leonore Gershwin Trusts Archives.
31. Frances Gershwin Godowsky, "George Gershwin Was My Brother," *Reader's Digest Music Guide*, July 1962.

2 Hearing Gershwin's New York

ELLEN NOONAN

In 1898 both George Gershwin and the modern city of New York were born. On January 1, Kings and Richmond counties, along with parts of Queens and Westchester counties, officially consolidated with the island of Manhattan to create the five boroughs of New York that we know today. George Gershwin (listed on his birth certificate as Jacob Gershwine) followed nine months later, entering the world at 242 Snedicker Avenue in Brooklyn on September 26. Gershwin grew to manhood in and with a burgeoning city full of noise, invention, and endless entertainments, whose disparate ethnic neighborhoods retained a character all their own even as they were being knit together in new ways.

Early twentieth-century New York City proved the perfect incubator for Gershwin's natural gifts. It was a distinctive moment in the city's history. Consolidation and unprecedented levels of immigration brought the city's population to 3.4 million by 1900, making it twice as large as any other American city. By 1910, New York's population had ballooned to nearly five million, 40 percent of whom were foreign born. New York's infrastructure and economic development boomed on a similar scale, as the city constructed subways, bridges, and roads that in turn spurred real-estate development and industrial and commercial growth. While Progressive-era reformers and urban planners struggled to bring order, the streets of New York's neighborhoods remained crowded and often unruly. They also remained segregated. The city's black population stood at 60,000 in 1900 and rose to 327,000 by 1930, an increase largely due to an influx of African Americans who fled the violence and economic oppression of the South. De facto segregation confined this growing group of New Yorkers to a handful of neighborhoods, most famously Harlem, which rose to national prominence in the 1920s as a cultural mecca.

A crucial part of New York's booming early twentieth-century economy was its leisure and commercial culture. In an era before radio or television, working- and middle-class people, young and old, flocked to amusements in the penny arcades, theaters, cabarets, and nickelodeons that flourished in many neighborhoods. Making and consuming music was a face-to-face endeavor in Gershwin's New York, which was filled with music created by amateurs and professionals who gathered in parlors, school auditoriums, concert halls, cabarets, theaters, and dance halls. And New York's commercial culture became American commercial culture, with the city serving as the originator of music and stage productions that toured the country, supplying the shared national cultural experience that radio and movies would eventually supplant. In Harlem, ragtime and jazz were part of a cultural flowering that also included literature, visual art, theater, dance, and political movements for self-determination, all of which influenced American identity for decades to come. In short, New York offered George Gershwin access to a panoply of musical and cultural expressions and a robust professional infrastructure of performance and distribution opportunities. In this city – freewheeling, bigger, and more culturally influential than any other – George Gershwin grew up listening to the music and soundscapes around him and seized the opportunities to make the sounds of modern America his own.

Gershwin's parents, Morris and Rose, emigrated from St. Petersburg, Russia to New York City as young people and married in 1895. They were an early part of the massive wave of Jewish immigrants to New York City during this era. The city's Jewish population more than doubled between 1900 and the beginning of World War I, and in many ways the family's experience paralleled that of other Jewish immigrants.[1] Many Russian Jewish immigrants came from urban areas, and as such possessed some industrial or artisan skills that could be adapted to suit the jobs available in New York's industrial and commercial economies. While Morris was working as a foreman in a shoe factory at the time of George's birth, his subsequent jobs (including a string of restaurants, Turkish baths, bakeries, a cigar store, pool parlor, and bookmaking stall at the Brighton Beach Race Track) were more entrepreneurial, and mostly short-lived.[2] The turn toward small business ownership was also not unusual for Jewish immigrants – historian Selma Berrol estimates that "as early as 1908 there was a pronounced shift from manual to white collar jobs in the East European Jewish community."[3] Morris Gershwin's tendency to go into business with his brothers was also a common immigrant strategy of using family and social connections to find jobs, housing, and other opportunities. Small business ownership tended to be the route out of the working class for Jewish immigrants, while it was not until their children's generation, born in America, that they began the move into professions such as law, medicine, education, and the arts.[4]

Although the Gershwins moved frequently, they always resided in one of the city's major Jewish neighborhoods on the Lower East Side, in East Harlem, or in Brownsville/East New York in Brooklyn. Ira estimated that the family lived in twenty-eight different residences between 1896 and

1916. This kind of residential mobility was not uncommon among Jewish immigrant families, with landlords often offering a month's free rent to new tenants, and rental housing enabled greater financial flexibility and the capacity to ride out hard times.[5] In Brooklyn, the Gershwins were part of a swelling population of Jewish immigrants working in the factories that sprang up in Brownsville and East New York during the 1890s. The neighborhood grew even more when construction of the subway began in 1904, and bridges built across the East River (Williamsburg in 1903, Manhattan in 1909) rendered the borough less isolated from the rest of the city. These infrastructure developments spurred the growth of Jewish neighborhoods in other parts of the city, including East Harlem, where the Gershwins moved when George was still a child.[6] By 1910, the upper Manhattan area from Madison Avenue east to Third Avenue, from 100th to 125th streets, had become a largely Jewish neighborhood, which was home to the second largest concentration of East European Jews in the United States.[7]

If New York's early twentieth-century neighborhoods were ethnically distinct, one shared constant was noise, indoors and out. Regardless of social class, it was the very nature of apartment building life to hear your neighbors. Windows, thin walls and floors, shared hallways, airshafts – all provided avenues for the sounds of others to infiltrate domestic space. Duke Ellington captured the porous aural boundaries of apartment building life when he described the inspiration behind his composition *Harlem Air Shaft*: "You get the full essence of Harlem in an air shaft. You hear fights, you smell dinner, you hear people making love. You hear intimate gossip floating down. You hear the radio. An airshaft is one great big loudspeaker."[8] As phonographs and radios became more common household items in the early 1920s, New Yorkers began to hear those sounds through walls and windows and in hallways and stairwells. For example, in 1921, the neighbors of Mrs. Richard T. Wilson of 130 West 57th Street took her to court over the noise of her frequent late-night music parties. Part of the neighbors' complaint was that the music "was of a jazz character" and one described it as "Ragtime. I should say cacophony." Although Mrs. Wilson belonged to one of the city's rarefied social circles, a *New York Times* article on the case noted that her neighbors' plight was a common one: "Practically everybody in the city, rich, poor and those in between, must have felt what was or amounted to a personal interest in the case of Mrs. Richard T. Wilson ... The same quarrel has arisen innumerable times before."[9]

Outdoors, human and mechanical sources – shouting peddlers, recorded music, delivery wagons, trolleys, elevated trains, construction equipment, automobiles – combined to banish tranquility from the streets where George Gershwin grew to adulthood. More than one Gershwin chronicler has waxed nostalgic about the urban noises that shaped the composer's musical sensibilities. Isaac Goldberg (Gershwin's first biographer, and the only one to write his life story while he was still alive), for example, identified urban sounds as "the rhythms that sound not only from his first hits but from his most ambitious orchestral compositions," ambient urban noise such as:

> The clatter of rollers over asphalt ... The din of the elevated overhead ... The madness of the traffic below ... the cracked tones of the hurdy-gurdy ... The blare of the automatic orchestra as the merry-go-round traced its dizzy circles through Coney Island's penny paradises ... The plaintive wail of the street singer across the obbligato of a scraping fiddle ... These were the earliest rhythms to which young George awoke.[10]

In a 1927 interview, Gershwin himself, with some grandiosity, identified New York and New Yorkers as embodying "the soul of the American people." A soul that "spoke to me on the streets, in school, at the theater. In the chorus of city sounds I heard it."[11]

While the sounds of urban life served as inspiration for composers like Gershwin and Ellington, the nature and volume of noise brought by the modern age was at best a nuisance to many New Yorkers, and at worst a problem that threatened health and productivity. In 1896, novelist William Dean Howells described the noise of elevated trains in decidedly less romantic terms:

> No experience of noise can enable you to conceive of the furious din that bursts upon the sense, when at some corner two cars encounter on the parallel tracks below, while two trains roar and shriek and hiss on the rails overhead, and a turmoil of rattling express wagons, heavy drays and trucks, and carts, hacks, carriages, and huge vans rolls itself between and beneath the prime agents of the uproar.[12]

The first elevated trains were in place in Manhattan by 1880, and while an improvement over horse-drawn streetcars in speed and range, their bulk and noise were less than ideal. They also immediately proved inadequate to serve the city's exploding population, and in 1888 the city embarked on building an underground subway system. Brooklyn had its own transit system, in the form of streetcars that converged on downtown Brooklyn and over the Brooklyn Bridge to Park Row in lower Manhattan, but they went no further.[13] The first of what would become New York City's interlocking subway lines, the IRT, opened to great fanfare on October 27, 1904. It covered twenty-two route miles from lower Manhattan to 145th Street. When the first train emerged aboveground onto the elevated tracks at Manhattan Valley (between 122nd and 135th

Streets) during its ceremonial run, it was greeted by cheering uptown crowds that could well have included Gershwin and his family, since they lived in East Harlem at the time. But the IRT could not keep up with the city's growth any better than the elevated trains had. Ridership doubled between 1905 and 1908, exceeding the system's planned maximum capacity by one-third.[14] Eventually, the subways became the physical manifestation of the consolidation that the city achieved politically in 1898. Public transportation enabled greater mobility for workers and opened up farther flung neighborhoods to residential and industrial development, all of which stimulated the city's already vigorous commercial amusement economy. Gershwin lived through this dramatic transformation in transportation – the demise of horse-drawn streetcars, the creation of the city's iconic underground subway, and the rise of automobiles on the streets.

Moving public transit largely underground (some elevated trains remained) did not immediately make the city's streets quieter. Reformers sought anti-noise legislation as a way to guarantee New Yorkers their right to an environment free of noise. A 1909 ordinance targeted peddlers and hucksters directly, an early salvo aimed toward a larger goal of clearing the streets of pushcart vendors altogether (which the city achieved by the 1930s). But the calls of street peddlers were hardly the city's greatest noise offenders. By the 1920s, the increased number of automobiles and trucks on New York's streets produced a greater volume of noise than the elevated trains. These new sounds posed a difficult adjustment for human ears. While the number of motorized vehicles had been growing during the first decades of the twentieth century, as early as 1922 New Yorkers were complaining about the noise made by electroacoustic loudspeakers. The worst offenders were radio retailers, who installed such speakers over their shop doors as a form of advertising.[15]

New York's streets also rang with the sounds of unsupervised children, in a way that is hard to imagine today. Many young people worked on city streets, calling out to passersby hawking newspapers, gum, or offering their services as bootblacks.[16] For those lucky enough to be in school, they still spent their non-school hours outdoors because there was a lack of indoor space for them, and because their parents were busy with work and housekeeping. As one observer put it, "the streets were the true homes of the [city's] small Italians, Irish, and Jews."[17] According to a 1914 study, 95 percent of New York City's children played in the streets, and the Gershwin boys were among them. Goldberg, presumably informed by George and Ira, noted that "Ma Gershwin, though very loving, never pestered her children with excessive surveillance."[18] The block was the basic unit of social organization for city kids, and they devised their own games that required little equipment. As long as they did not end up in the arms of the police, abandon younger siblings, or disgrace themselves or their families, they were largely left alone to govern themselves. But in one sense, the children were not completely unsupervised. As historian David Nasaw observes, urban streets were filled with adults – peddlers, prostitutes, policemen, delivery wagon drivers, stoop sitters, corner loungers – and "the presence of adults in the street – and the tenements overhead – protected the children at play."[19] Gershwin's childhood occurred during a singular era of urban freedom for the young; the children of earlier generations would have been put to work, and subsequent generations of middle-class children had their non-school hours increasingly structured by organized sports and other supervised activities and camps.[20]

George Gershwin was, by his own account, a leader of the pack on the streets of Manhattan and Brooklyn. He described himself as "the rough-and-ready, the muscular type and not one of your sad, contemplative children."[21] On the Lower East Side, "he reveled in games of 'cat' and hockey; here he achieved his first pre-eminence as the undisputed roller-skate champion of Seventh Street." But Goldberg also describes George as having been "a 'hard' kid" and recounts: "Certainly his parents held no high hopes for his future. He was, frankly, a bad child. He was guilty of petty pilfering; he ran the gamut of minor infractions. With a little less luck, he might have become a gangster."[22] Not surprisingly, this "hard kid" did not excel as a student at PS 20 and later PS 25. Unlike Ira, who was destined for the academically elite Townsend Harris High School and then City College of New York, George briefly attended Commerce High School before dropping out at age fifteen. This was not uncommon for a child of immigrants, including those from Jewish families, most of whom left school by eighth grade in order to contribute to the family economy.[23]

Both George and Ira, like all of early twentieth-century New York City's young people, partook of the city's low-cost public amusements, in the form of penny arcades and nickelodeons. A penny arcade is at the center of one of the most iconic and oft-repeated stories from George's childhood:

> One of my first definite memories goes back to the age of six. I stood outside a penny arcade listening to an automatic piano leaping through Rubinstein's *Melody in F*. The peculiar jumps in the music held me rooted. To this very day I can't hear the tune without picturing myself outside that arcade on One Hundred and Twenty-fifth Street, standing there barefoot and in overalls, drinking it all in avidly.[24]

While George presented this story as one of musical awakening at a tender age, it is not difficult to see the appeal that such establishments held for all children. Located along commercial thoroughfares like 125th Street, 14th

Street, and the Bowery, New York's penny arcades were invitingly decorated and brightly lit, ringing with the sounds generated by mechanical amusements and visitors engaging in sporting games. Arcades offered coin-operated machines where patrons could watch short films, learn their fortune or horoscope, hear music or comedy routines, or partake of a kinetoscope or "peep show." These "peep shows" explicitly targeted young men and boys, promising films with titles such as *How Girls Undress*. A key part of the penny arcades' appeal lay in the mechanical aspect of their entertainments (which for music included player pianos and phonographs), and in their democratic accessibility – conveniently located and inexpensive, no cultural sophistication (or even knowledge of English) was required to appreciate the entertainment on offer.[25]

From the penny arcade evolved the nickelodeon, a venue solely dedicated to showing moving pictures and so-named for the customary five cent entrance fee. For that nickel, audiences would see a selection of short films, usually accompanied by songs and vaudeville skits (often tailored to the ethnic makeup of a neighborhood audience).[26] Between 1900 and 1908, the number of nickelodeons in New York City jumped tenfold, from fifty to nearly 500. A theater operator's handbook from 1910 described the ideal location for a storefront nickelodeon as "a densely populated workingmen's residence section, with a frontage on a much-traveled business street."[27] Open from early morning to late at night, nickelodeons were extensions of the city's noisy and unruly street life. Describing the barkers who enticed audiences with the latest film fare, one contemporary observer described "their megaphones are barking before the milkman has made his rounds," and historian Kathy Peiss describes how working-class crowds "audibly interacted with the screen and each other, commenting on the action, explaining the plot, and vocally accompanying the piano player."[28] Ira recalled having "been a moviegoer since the time the shoe store on Grand Street became a nickelodeon."[29]

While some of the defining anecdotes of George Gershwin's childhood involved the streets and public amusements of New York City, another iconic story of his development as a musician centered on the family's acquisition of an upright piano. In George's own words: "No sooner had it come through the window and been backed up against the wall than I was at the keys. I must have crowded out Ira very soon, for the plan originally had been to start him on the instrument."[30] Many New Yorkers made and listened to music at home. Owning a piano had long been a marker of respectability, and sales of pianos in the United States rose steadily in the first decade of the twentieth century.[31] Pianos also connected New Yorkers to the popular music of the day, as they purchased sheet music for tunes propagated via the vaudeville stage.[32] Many of those early twentieth-century pianos were manufactured by German immigrant workers at the Steinway factory in Manhattan or at one of the more than forty piano manufacturers in the Mott Haven section of the Bronx, making the borough the capital of piano and player-piano manufacturing nationwide.[33] But learning to play the piano proficiently took time and skill, and in 1898 (the year of George's birth) the Aeolian Company put the first player piano, or pianola, on the market. Player pianos had a playing mechanism built into them and their owners purchased pre-recorded "rolls" for the piano to play. Popular in the years preceding radio and improved phonograph recording technologies, player pianos brought into the home music that was too difficult for most amateur players to master.[34]

In 1914, Gershwin left amateur musicianship behind and entered the world of professional working musicians when he quit school to take a job as a "song plugger" for the Jerome H. Remick music publishing company.[35] It was a job unlikely to have been available to fifteen-year-old piano prodigies anywhere else, and one that brought the teenaged Gershwin into contact with the city's best piano players, establishing professional connections that would expand his musical horizons and influence his own compositions. By 1910 New York was the undisputed capital of American popular music, host to many of the country's most profitable music publishing firms.[36] Music publishing was a core segment of New York City's cultural economy, and its center was Tin Pan Alley, a collection of publishing houses originally located on West 28th Street between Fifth and Sixth Avenues.

The sight-reading and improvisatory skills that served Gershwin well as a song plugger also opened up the professional avenue of recording piano rolls for the player-piano industry. Gershwin began this work in 1915, earning five dollars per roll. The makers of piano rolls, like the piano manufacturers, were part of New York's cultural economy, located in the Bronx and near Newark, New Jersey, both an easy commute for Manhattan piano players. Gershwin's early piano-roll recordings included ragtime and tunes from Broadway and Yiddish musical theater.[37] Gershwin's gifts as a piano player on daily display at Remick quickly came to the attention of other professional musicians, including several African Americans. Arranger Will Vodery was impressed enough with the young Gershwin to secure him an additional job as pianist at Fox's City Theater, a vaudeville house on 14th Street. Eubie Blake recalled hearing from James P. Johnson and Luckey Roberts about a white pianist at Remick who was "good enough to learn some of those terribly difficult tricks that only a few of us could master."[38] Gershwin, in his turn, greatly admired a group of black "stride" pianists (which included Blake, Johnson, Roberts, Willie

"The Lion" Smith, and Fats Waller) for their style of embellishing and improvising around syncopated melodies.

Just as every other aspect of New York City life was expanding and creating new forms, so too was nightlife in the first decades of the twentieth century, and George Gershwin was a frequent visitor to the city's burgeoning array of cafes, restaurants, dance halls, vaudeville theaters, and cabarets. This expanding nightlife scene opened up many new spaces in which music was performed, heard, and danced to. It also created spaces where middle- and upper-class women were able to socialize in public in unprecedented ways. Restaurants began providing musical entertainment to their customers, and hotel roof gardens did the same. By 1911, cabarets and cafes with music and dancing began to multiply, and with them opportunities for audiences of all social classes to mingle in intimate social spaces that put them, in the words of one historian, "in handshaking proximity" to the performers.[39] The ratification of the 18th amendment to the US constitution in 1919 outlawed the sale and consumption of alcohol, which, paradoxically, accelerated the growth of New York's nightlife rather than curbed it. New Yorkers, like other urbanites across the United States, flouted Prohibition's strictures – by the end of the 1920s, New York's police commissioner estimated that the city contained 32,000 illegal drinking establishments.[40] Nightclubs flourished, and entrepreneurs opened clubs featuring black entertainers to draw white audiences newly fascinated with black music and dance. Widespread extra-legal drinking hastened existing trends toward social mixing in commercial entertainments and gave rise to increased social visibility and space for those considered "outside" polite society, namely gays and lesbians and African Americans.[41]

Gershwin was a celebrated composer by the 1920s, but his wide-ranging musical appetites drove him to seek out a variety of musical styles beyond the theaters and nightclubs of Times Square. He was a regular audience member in the Yiddish theaters that populated Second Avenue on the Lower East Side, particularly when a musical was playing. Gershwin's connection to the Yiddish theater stretched back to his childhood, when a Yiddish musical theater composer played cards with Morris Gershwin, and young George ran errands for Yiddish theater actors and even appeared onstage as an extra.[42] Located in the neighborhoods where Jewish immigrants settled (starting on the Bowery and Grand Street in the 1890s, then expanding to Second Avenue and into Brooklyn and the Bronx), Yiddish theaters provided portrayals of immigrant life and occasions to gather for entertainment and escape; some of the fare was translated from English, giving immigrants entrée to American culture. By the 1920s the Yiddish theater's operettas, melodramas with music, and musical comedies mixed jazz and ragtime with traditional Jewish musical styles, building bridges between the ethnic community and mainstream Broadway forms.[43]

Gershwin also sought out African American music in New York, an interest that took him to Harlem and the more established cultural precincts where black composers were slowly gaining a foothold during the 1920s. Verna Arvey, the wife of African American classical composer William Grant Still, noted that Gershwin "was certain to be present at any concert or show in which a Negro was doing something new in music ... He admired Ethel Waters's singing very much and ... attended the performance of William Grant Still's *Levee Land* at New York's Aeolian Hall."[44] African American artists also broke into the world of musical theater. In 1921 the musical *Shuffle Along*, with music by Noble Sissle and Eubie Blake, proved a surprise hit and helped white producers and critics see black performers and subjects as possessing economic viability and artistic merit. It paved the way for a wave of black musical revues during the 1920s and boosted the careers of performers like Ethel Waters and Florence Mills and composers like James P. Johnson.

By the time of Gershwin's adulthood, Harlem had become Manhattan's primary black neighborhood, although during his childhood most of the borough's African Americans lived in two West Side neighborhoods, known as the Tenderloin and San Juan Hill. By the early 1920s there were around 300,000 African Americans living in New York City and most were living in Harlem (though they still represented no more than 30 percent of the total Harlem population).[45] Harlem's music scene revved up in the wee hours of the morning, and Gershwin frequently made his way there to be part of the audience.[46] After black performers had finished their paying gigs with commercial bands downtown, they returned uptown to play at nightclubs and rent parties. The combos in most clubs and dance halls were small – a piano, drummer, and banjoist or harmonica player, or perhaps just a piano – and the style was lively and improvised.[47] Harlem also possessed larger clubs with more elaborate revues, and by the 1920s almost a dozen of these were segregated (allowing white patrons only), catering to the sensibilities of white New Yorkers who were fascinated by black culture but not interested in social contact with African Americans.

Gershwin was an inveterate party-goer; the sounds of his adult world included frequent evenings of tinkling glasses, swirling conversation, laughter, and piano playing (by himself and others) and his identity as a pianist was central to his experiences of New York parties. Reminiscences and biographies abound with stories of Gershwin attending a party only to sit down at the piano and play for hours. While Gershwin played gratis, as a guest, for African American pianists such parties could provide a welcome source of income. Famed stride pianist Willie "The Lion" Smith recalls how Gershwin opened the door for those paid opportunities by inviting him, Fats Waller, and James P. Johnson to a Park Avenue party being held in his honor to celebrate the debut of *Rhapsody in Blue*. Gershwin was, as usual, installed at the piano, and Smith worried that

> he was going to stay seated at the piano all night himself and hog all the playing. We three were standing at the bar getting up our courage and the more we imbibed the more anxious we became to get at those keys. I finally went over and said to Gershwin, "Get up off that piano stool and let the real players take over, you tomato." He was good-natured fellow and from then on the three of us took over the entertainment.[48]

For black pianists, these parties paid handsomely ("fifty dollars apiece and all the food and liquor we could consume") and sometimes prompted career breakthroughs, as when the head of the CBS radio network heard Waller play and immediately found an opening for him on the air.[49] But in an era of racial segregation, even the most talented African American musicians were still subject to sometimes insulting treatment from white hosts and guests.[50]

Gershwin also attended parties in Harlem, drawn by what he could learn from the black pianists playing at them. Waller recalled that Gershwin and other white composers

> were uptown incessantly, making the rounds and drinking in all there was to be seen and heard ... penetrating even the lowest of the lowdown clubs. He invaded the rent-parties and socials and was often to be seen sitting on the floor, agape at the dazzling virtuosity and limitless improvisation that clamored around him.[51]

Harlem's rent parties charged admission and were designed to help the host pay that month's rent. They offered food and liquor, sometimes for an additional fee, and entertainment from some of Harlem's finest musicians. Smith remembered that he and other prominent stride pianists "never stopped and we were up and down Fifth, Seventh, and Lenox all night long hitting the keys," usually earning ten or twenty dollars per party (often booking as many as three a night) plus all the liquor they could drink. The parties were a proving ground for Harlem's pianists, a free-wheeling space for improvisation and competition where they sharpened their already formidable skills.[52]

Historical turning points are not always identifiable in the moment when they occur, but 1898 was surely one in the history of America's most prominent city and one of its foremost twentieth-century composers. The year gave birth to modern New York, which, over the next three decades nurtured George Gershwin as no other place on earth could have done. It was the center of American musical and theatrical production, with a growing, diverse population brought together via public space, public amusements, and public transit. As a child whose experiences were largely confined to the Jewish immigrant neighborhoods where his family lived, Gershwin had freedom to explore the streets, penny arcades, and nickelodeons of a city launching itself into the modern cultural age. Starting in his teenaged years, Gershwin was a working, endlessly curious musician whose professional passions took him across Manhattan into music publishing houses, nightclubs, theaters in Times Square and on Second Avenue, and parties for both the rich and the struggling. It was the professional regard of the city's African American pianists that gained him entry to Harlem's after-hours clubs and rent parties, and his admiration of their talent that enabled them to cross racial lines into the Park Avenue apartments of the rich and famous. Early twentieth-century New York possessed unmistakable cultural dynamism and social boundaries that were real but not irredeemably rigid. Gershwin embraced his native city's gifts, and from that pairing came the enduringly New York sound of his music.

Notes

1. Annie Polland, Daniel Soyer, and Deborah Dash Moore, *Emerging Metropolis: New York Jews in the Age of Immigration, 1840–1920* (New York: NYU Press, 2013), xiii.
2. Edward Jablonski, *Gershwin Remembered* (Portland, OR: Amadeus Press, 1992), 4–5.
3. Selma Berrol, "School Days on the Old East Side: The Italian and Jewish Experience," *New York History* 57/2 (April 1976), 210.
4. Polland et al., *Emerging Metropolis*, 118, 120, 121, 134.
5. Ibid., xix; David Nasaw, *Children of the City, at Work and at Play* (New York: Anchor Press/Doubleday, 1985), 28.
6. Polland et al., *Emerging Metropolis*, 130; Ira Gershwin, ". . . But I Wouldn't Want to Live There," *Saturday Review* (October 18, 1958), 27.
7. Polland et al., *Emerging Metropolis*, 131.
8. Emily Thompson, *The Soundscape of Modernity: Architectural Acoustics and the Culture of Listening in America, 1900–1933* (Boston, MA: MIT Press, 2004), 131.
9. Ibid.
10. Isaac Goldberg, *George Gershwin: A Study in American Music* (New York: Simon & Schuster, 1931), 53–54.
11. George Gershwin, "Jazz Is the Voice of the American Soul," *Theatre Magazine*, March 1927.
12. William Dean Howells, *Impressions and Experiences* (New York: Harper and Brothers, 1896), 258–59.
13. Clifton Hood, *722 Miles: The Building of the Subways and How They Transformed New York* (New York: Simon & Schuster, 1993), 51–55; Mike Wallace, *Greater Gotham: A History of New York City from 1898 to 1919* (New York: Oxford University Press, 2017), 226–27.
14. Hood, *722 Miles*, 93, 95; Wallace, *Greater Gotham*, 235.
15. Thompson, *The Soundscape of Modernity*, 118, 125, 145.
16. Wallace, *Greater Gotham*, 526–27.
17. Nasaw, *Children of the City*, 19.
18. Goldberg, *George Gershwin*, 53.
19. Nasaw, *Children of the City*, 20.
20. Ibid., 19, 38, 32, 24–25.
21. Goldberg, *George Gershwin*, 53.
22. Ibid., 53, 56–57.

23. Polland et al., *Emerging Metropolis*, 123, 214; Berrol, "School Days on the Old East Side," 206.
24. Goldberg, *George Gershwin*, 54.
25. David Nasaw, *Going Out: The Rise and Fall of Public Amusements* (New York: Basic Books, 1993), 155, 154, 157–58; Kathy Peiss, *Cheap Amusements: Working Women and Leisure in Turn-of-the-Century New York* (Philadelphia, PA: Temple University Press, 1986), 145.
26. Peiss, *Cheap Amusements*, 146, 149; Nasaw, *Going Out*, 165; Polland et al., *Emerging Metropolis*, 240.
27. Lewis Erenberg, *Steppin' Out: New York Nightlife and the Transformation of American Culture, 1890–1930* (Westport, CT: Greenwood Press, 1981), 69.
28. Peiss, *Cheap Amusements*, 146, 149.
29. Ira Gershwin, ". . . But I Wouldn't Want to Live There," 48.
30. Goldberg, *George Gershwin*, 56.
31. Cynthia Adams Hoover and Edwin M. Good, "Piano," *Grove Music Online* (2014). www.oxfordmusiconline.com/grovemusic/view/10.1093/gmo/9781561592630.001.0001/omo-9781561592630-e-1002257895.
32. Artis Wodehouse, "Tracing Gershwin's Piano Rolls," in Wayne Schneider, ed., *The Gershwin Style: New Looks at the Music of George Gershwin* (Oxford University Press, 1990), 209.
33. Wallace, *Greater Gotham*, 278, 314.
34. Edwin M. Good, Cynthia Adams Hoover, and Michael Chanan, "Designing, Making, and Selling Pianos," in James Parakilas (ed.), *Piano Roles: Three Hundred Years of Life with the Piano* (New Haven: Yale University Press, 2002), 60–61; Wodehouse, "Tracing Gershwin's Piano Rolls," 201.
35. Howard Pollack, *George Gershwin: His Life and Work* (Berkeley, CA: University of California Press, 2007), 61.
36. Wallace, *Emerging Metropolis*, 409.
37. Wodehouse, "Tracing Gershwin's Piano Rolls," 211–13, 217.
38. Charles Schwartz, *Gershwin: His Life and Music* (New York: Bobbs-Merrill Company, 1973), 32; Pollack, *George Gershwin*, 63.
39. Erenberg, *Steppin' Out*, 75, 115, 124, 138; George Chauncey, *Gay New York: Gender, Urban Culture, and the Making of the Gay Male World, 1890–1940* (New York: Basic Books, 1994), 307.
40. Daniel Okrent, *Last Call: The Rise and Fall of Prohibition* (New York: Scribner, 2010), 208.
41. Michael Lerner, *Dry Manhattan: Prohibition in New York City* (Cambridge, MA: Harvard University Press, 2007), 131; Chauncey, *Gay New York*, 309–10.
42. Schwartz, *Gershwin*, 24; Pollack, *George Gershwin*, 43–44.
43. Polland et al., *Emerging Metropolis*, 219; Nahma Sandrow, "Yiddish Theater," in Kenneth T. Jackson and Nancy Flood (eds.), *The Encyclopedia of New York City* (New Haven, CT: Yale University Press, 2010), 1426; Nahma Sandrow, "Popular Yiddish Theater: Music, Melodrama, and Operetta," in Edna Nahshon (ed.), *New York's Yiddish Theater: From the Bowery to Broadway* (New York: Columbia University Press in association with the Museum of the City of New York, 2016), 80.
44. Verna Arvey, "George Gershwin through the Eyes of a Friend," in Robert Wyatt and John Andrew Johnson (eds.), *The George Gershwin Reader* (New York: Oxford University Press, 2004), 23.
45. David Levering Lewis, *When Harlem Was in Vogue* (New York: Oxford University Press, 1981), 26.
46. Arvey, "George Gershwin through the Eyes of a Friend," 23; Samuel A. Floyd, Jr., "Music in the Harlem Renaissance: An Overview," in Samuel A. Floyd (ed.), *Black Music in the Harlem Renaissance: A Collection of Essays* (New York: Greenwood Press, 1990), 21.
47. Willie "The Lion" Smith (with George Hoefer), *Music on My Mind: The Memoirs of an American Pianist* (New York: Da Capo Press, 1975), 159; Floyd, "Music in the Harlem Renaissance," 3; Eileen Southern, *The Music of Black Americans: A History*, 3rd edn (W.W. Norton, 1997), 349.
48. Smith, *Music on My Mind*, 226; Floyd, "Music in the Harlem Renaissance," 21–22.
49. Ed Kirkeby (in collaboration with Duncan P. Schiedt and Sinclair Traill), *Ain't Misbehavin': The Story of Fats Waller* (New York: Dodd, Mead & Company, 1966), 165.
50. Smith, *Music on My Mind*, 226–27.
51. Kirkeby, *Ain't Misbehavin'*, 53.
52. Smith, *Music on My Mind*, 154–55; Floyd, "Music in the Harlem Renaissance," 21.

3 Gershwin's Musical Education

SUSAN NEIMOYER

From the time of its creation George Gershwin's concert music was viewed with skepticism by classically trained musicians. His signature mixture of popular and art music elements – taboo among his contemporaries unless "folk" elements were significantly modified – was seen as evidence of a lack of taste, skill, and originality. Their view of Gershwin's music as "half-baked" or lacking in proper technique was exacerbated by his habit of marketing himself as an "unschooled naif."[1] Many of Gershwin's contemporaries struggled to have their works performed while his popularity grew, leading some to question the extent of his musical education.[2] As Virgil Thomson's scathing review of *Porgy and Bess* in 1935 indicates, Gershwin's commercial success was seen as evidence of glaring deficits in his musical knowledge:

> I do not wish to indicate that it is in any way reprehensible of [Gershwin] not to be a serious composer. I only want to define something that we have all been wondering about for some years. It was always certain that he was a gifted composer . . . I think, however, that it is clear by now that Gershwin hasn't learned his business. At least he hasn't learned the business of being a serious composer, which one has always gathered to be the business he wanted to learn.[3]

Gershwin called himself "a man without traditions."[4] Although most early twentieth-century American composers eschewed tradition, ranging from Dane Rudhyar's "spiritual dissonance" to Aaron Copland's exploration of jazz rhythms, Gershwin's approach was viewed cynically – his concert works labeled as tainted products of an uneducated outsider. Larry Starr crystallizes this disparity most succinctly: "There was simply no preexisting model for the kind of American composer that Gershwin became; he had to invent himself each step of the way, and it stands to reason that his remarkable success in doing so was met with skepticism and resentment by those personally invested in more traditional musical paths."[5]

The unconventional educational path Gershwin pursued was integral to his self-invention. Taking a more holistic view, this path – comprising both formal and experiential learning – was closer to that followed by jazz musicians of his day. The unique blend of written and oral tradition

Gershwin pursued shaped his distinctive musical style and practice, resulting in a catalog that demonstrates that he was better educated than has long been recognized, and perhaps more than he was consciously aware.

Legend paints Gershwin as an autodidact who had so little technical knowledge of music that he was unable to name the compositional devices he used. He seems to have consciously promoted this image, both to the press and to his less-intimate associates. He told his first biographer, Isaac Goldberg, that at the time he wrote the *Rhapsody in Blue* he knew "about as much harmony as could be found in a ten-cent manual."[6] To another reporter he claimed that while writing the Concerto in F he had to go out and buy "four or five books on musical structure" to figure out what a concerto was.[7] This part of the myth was perpetuated by Ira Gershwin: "It seems to me the bravest thing [George] ever did was the *Concerto in F*. He undertook to write a composition form he did not know about, and which he had to study."[8] Russian émigré composer Vladimir Dukelsky (who wrote popular music under the pseudonym Vernon Duke) recalled similar sentiments in a 1947 article, where he quoted Gershwin as saying: "Oh, I didn't study much ... I guess I'm just a natural-born composer," and this classic statement:

> I used to do all kinds of things – harmony and counterpoint, I mean – did them correctly, too, but didn't even know what I was doing! It was pure instinct ...
> I once wrote a whole 32-bar chorus in canon and if someone told me it was a canon I'd laugh right in his face ... You see, I never knew why I was doing all these things – I thought they were just parlor tricks.[9]

One can only speculate on Gershwin's reasons for publicly, or perhaps selectively, minimizing his formal education. Documentary evidence such as exercise manuscripts and written contemporary accounts demonstrate that the comparative breadth of Gershwin's musical knowledge lay closer to college-educated composers than to Broadway songwriters, some of whom did not read music and relied on musical secretaries to write down their compositions. In a filmed interview, Gershwin's sister, Frances Gershwin Godowsky, observed: "I think he was very sorry that he never finished school. He had a great feeling for learning."[10] He had dropped out of high school at age fifteen to work as a Tin Pan Alley song plugger. Formal studies were pursued in piecemeal fashion as they fitted into his busy work schedule, nearly all with private teachers. Perhaps the intermittent nature of those studies led Gershwin to believe himself more ignorant than he actually was.[11]

Gershwin's comparatively spotty formal education seems not to have been an indicator of his overall attitude toward learning. Although detractors portray him as a lazy dilettante who claimed authorship of music ghost written by others,[12] his closest associates paint a different picture. His brother, Ira Gershwin, said he could not recall a time in George's life when, "despite all his musical creativity, he didn't find time to further his academic studies."[13] His close friend Kay Swift described his passion for learning in this way:

> I don't think that he was out of focus at any time ... He could bring a whole big sweep into whatever was going on. Sometimes it was listening to music, and he was wonderful at that – terrific. It was an exciting thing to see anything new with him [that] he loved.[14]

These descriptions, combined with anecdotes recounted in various Gershwin biographies, point away from laziness and toward the way jazz musicians of his day learned their craft. Ethnomusicologist Paul Berliner's groundbreaking study, *Thinking in Jazz*, demonstrates that because jazz is based in oral tradition, its practitioners learn in a manner different from their classically trained counterparts.[15] This was particularly true for Gershwin's generation.

Berliner describes a learning pattern for which the student is individually responsible. It begins with life-changing musical experiences that lead to self-directed study on an instrument, followed by formal education including private lessons (where the student is exposed to both jazz and classical music), mentoring from working professionals, and musical employment at an early age. Formal studies in music theory come later, when the student perceives the need.[16] Because these steps take place according to personal initiative, the order in which they occur varies with each individual.

Not surprisingly, Gershwin's learning process matches the pattern Berliner describes. The jazz/pop music world of the 1920s was the milieu in which Gershwin operated. Some of the initial steps Berliner outlines, such as early, life-changing interactions with music, occurred before Gershwin's family became aware of his interest. The formal part of his education began at age twelve, when his family bought a piano for Ira and discovered that it was George who had an affinity for music. The deftness Ira describes in George's playing indicates that he had already undergone a laborious self-teaching process:

> I remember being particularly impressed by his swinging, lightning fast left hand, and by harmonic and rhythmic effects I thought as proficient as those of most of the pianists I'd heard in vaudeville ... How? When? We wanted to know. George made it sound very simple. Whenever he had the chance, he'd been fooling around and experimenting on a player piano at the home of a schoolmate around the corner.[17]

Learning to realize the left-hand patterns Ira describes from a player piano would have required countless hours of slowly pedaling the piano roll through the playing mechanism, placing his fingers on the depressed keys as the roll progressed, and memorizing the patterns. Berliner observes that such laborious self-teaching methods were common among the jazz musicians of Gershwin's generation.[18]

Gershwin took private piano lessons for several years, yet publicly downplayed that training. In 1926 he told an interviewer:

> I have always had an aptitude for the piano. I never played like a beginner, neither have I played very serious things, and yet pianists like Godowsky have told me that I am a fine pianist. My technique is not like that of so-called great pianists. I developed an original method, for altogether I have studied only about five years.[19]

That "original method" would have been acquired of necessity through his earliest full-time musical employment, at age fifteen, as a "song plugger" for Tin Pan Alley song publisher Jerome H. Remick. Although he concurrently studied piano with Charles Hambitzer, his most expert teacher, the skills required at Remick's probably lay outside Hambitzer's pedagogical focus, which introduced Gershwin to the music of Bach, Chopin, Liszt, and Debussy.[20] Gershwin worked ten- to twelve-hour days, six days a week, including evenings when he and other pluggers would frequent cafés and other establishments to demonstrate items in Remick's catalog. In that role he was expected to sight-read well and instantaneously transpose music to suit the singing range of each performer.[21]

Gershwin's three years at Remick's was an apprenticeship that served him well. Playing so many hours daily put his hands in terrific shape and gave him the technical ability to tackle more advanced piano literature in his private lessons. By his own admission, Gershwin got bored quickly at Remick's, so he experimented with the music he was expected to sell, developing improvisational skills that benefited his budding compositional skills almost without his being aware of it.[22] His sister Frances said he became one of Remick's preferred song pluggers: "People would come in and want to hear certain songs, and they'd all say 'Go to Gershwin's room … You'll hear the song the way it really is [meant to be performed].'"[23]

Gershwin's employment at Remick's further taught him to recognize superior-quality music (through having to promote poorly written music).[24] Biographers identify the first time Gershwin heard songs by Jerome Kern as a major turning point in his early career. Recognizing the exceptional quality of Kern's songs, he studied every one he could find.[25] This led Gershwin into a pattern of self-directed study, which eventually embraced the classics, that he would follow for the rest of his life. According to Oscar Levant, Gershwin not only collected scores but also recordings of classical and contemporary music as they became available:

> Like many other musicians, George found that he could get even more from phonograph records of his favorite works than he could from their scattered performances in public. Among the albums I recall which gave him particular pleasure were Stravinsky's "Symphonie des Psaumes," the first symphony of Shostakovitch [sic.], the Milhaud violin concerto, the "Lyrische Suite" of Berg and the complete Schoenberg quartets ... Somewhere, somehow, he had acquired a liking for the records of Honegger's lively operetta *Les Aventures du Roi Pausole*. On the other hand, he admired greatly certain records of Duke Ellington's orchestra ... Among modern works he studied in score were Stravinsky's "Les Noces," the third piano concerto of Prokofieff, the Debussy piano preludes – for which he had great fondness – and various orchestral works by this composer and Ravel.[26]

Berliner points out that self-guided study was expected; in the jazz world one learns one musical principle at a time, each from a different working professional, rather than at the feet of one inspired teacher.[27] When one views Gershwin's work and study habits through the lens of this piecemeal learning model, behaviors his critics derided take on a different appearance. Moving from one job to the next, one teacher to the next, or one interest to the next was commonplace in the musical world Gershwin negotiated.[28] When he briefly studied with Henry Cowell, Wallingford Riegger, or approached Maurice Ravel or Nadia Boulanger for lessons, Gershwin was trying to learn that "one musical principle" instead of "trying to overcome some of his many shortcomings" or satisfy the needs of an insatiable ego.[29]

Gershwin as "Intensive Listener"

Gershwin claimed to have a "habit of intensive listening" – something more than a casual immersion in sound: "I had gone to concerts and listened not only with my ears, but with my nerves, my mind, my heart. I had listened so earnestly that I became saturated with the music ... Then I went home and listened in memory. I sat at the piano and repeated the *motifs*."[30] Although it is tempting to accuse Gershwin of exaggeration, this was an expected skill in the jazz/pop world of his day. According to jazz trumpeter Art Farmer: "[W]hen I was learning, you heard people play things that sounded nice, and you thought about what you were playing ... You thought about how you sounded and how you would like to sound, and you went home, and you worked on it. If you couldn't learn by what you heard ... it was your own fault."[31]

Kay Swift's description of Gershwin's "terrific" listening abilities comes into specific relief when considering jazz pioneer Eubie Blake's recollection of Gershwin's pianistic reputation:

> Soon after I came to live in New York – about 1916 ... James P. Johnson and Luckey Roberts ... told me of this very talented "ofay" [white] piano player at Remick's publishing house. They said he was good enough to learn some of those difficult tricks that only a few of us could master. They said this boy could play almost as well as they could, and if you ever heard James P. or Luckey play, you'll know how good that is.[32]

Samuel Floyd stated that during the 1910s and 1920s, "[f]or white musicians, the process of learning black music was osmotic" – they learned by listening.[33] Thus, gaining a sense of Gershwin's listening habits becomes vital to understanding his educational process. While not all of his listening activities can be documented, biographers note that he familiarized himself with the playing styles of major jazz, ragtime, and novelty piano artists.[34] This meant frequenting Harlem clubs and "rent parties," since these venues were the province of great jazz pianists like James P. Johnson, Willie "The Lion" Smith, Thomas "Fats" Waller, Luckey Roberts, and Duke Ellington.[35] Johnson and Roberts likely knew of Gershwin's abilities by having heard him participate in one or more of the "cutting contests" that were an integral part of those venues. This was affirmed by Ed Kirkeby, who noted that:

> [B]y 1920 [Fats Waller] had met and knew well, some of the leading lights of Tin Pan Alley. Irving Berlin, Paul Whiteman, and George Gershwin – especially the last – were uptown incessantly, making the rounds and drinking in all there was to be seen and heard. Gershwin wrote down the jazz forms that came to him from the horns, drums and pianos, penetrating even the lowest of the low-down clubs. He invaded the rent parties and socials and was often to be seen sitting on the floor, agape at the dazzling virtuosity and limitless improvisation that clamored around him.[36]

Gershwin frequented black clubs throughout his life, first in New York and later in Los Angeles. As expected, the jazz elements he heard seeped into his music – although he seems to have deliberately reserved them primarily for his concert music.

Gershwin's Concert Attendance

The "Gershwin myth" holds that he had little to no exposure to classical music before writing *Rhapsody in Blue*, which suddenly thrust him into the world of "serious" music. This notion is defrayed only minimally by references to his piano studies with Charles Hambitzer, or to his theoretical studies in his early twenties with Edward Kilenyi, Sr. However, a scrapbook Gershwin kept between 1912 and 1920 held in the Gershwin Collection at the Library of Congress (referred to hereafter as the LC Gershwin Collection) demonstrates that his exposure to classical music began as early as 1912, at age thirteen or fourteen.[37] When Ira Gershwin donated the scrapbook in 1962, his introductory notes stated that although the collection of programs is not comprehensive, it accurately represents the kinds of concerts George attended.[38]

A summary of the data from this collection of concert programs (Tables 3.1–3.3) suggests that Gershwin's concert attendance may have been guided by someone who knew classical repertoire well.

Charles Hambitzer seems the most logical candidate, given the repertoire represented in the program collection. Fellow Hambitzer student, Mabel Pleshette Schirmer, recalled that Hambitzer assigned "a lot of Chopin," whose works appear most often in the program collection.[39] The second most frequently represented composers are Beethoven and Liszt. Two concerts given by Leo Ornstein (February 17 and April 3, 1913), who was "the single most important figure on the American modern-music scene in the 1910s," also point to Hambitzer.[40] Only someone so well informed would have recognized Ornstein as an up-and-coming innovator.[41] The overall content of

Table 3.1 *Composers most frequently represented in Gershwin's concert program collection (arranged in order from most to least heard)*

Frédéric Chopin (1810–1849) – 31
Ludwig van Beethoven (1770–1827) – 14
Franz Liszt (1811–1886) – 13
Richard Wagner (1813–1883) – 9
Pyotr Ilyich Tchaikovsky (1840–1893) – 7
Anton Rubinstein (1829–1894) – 5
Edvard Grieg (1843–1907) – 4
Franz Josef Haydn (1732–1809) – 4
Camille Saint-Saëns (1835–1921) – 4
Franz Schubert (1797–1828) – 4
Johannes Brahms (1833–1897) – 3
Felix Mendelssohn (1809–1847) – 3
Henri Vieuxtemps (1820–1881) – 3
Georges Bizet (1838–1875) – 2
Ferrucio Busoni (1866–1924) – 2 (transcriptions of works by J.S. Bach)
Antonín Dvořák (1841–1904) – 2
Wolfgang Amadeus Mozart (1756–1791) – 2
Leo Ornstein (ca. 1893–2002) – 2
Sergei Rachmaninoff (1873–1943) – 2
Robert Schumann (1810–1856) – 2
Carl Maria von Weber (1786–1826) – 2

Table 3.2 *Better-known composers with only one work in Gershwin's concert program collection*

Jacques Arcadelt (1507–1568) – Belgium
Johann Sebastian Bach (1685–1750) – Germany
Mily Balakirev (1837–1910) – Russia
Emmanuel Chabrier (1841–1894) – France
Archangelo Corelli (1653–1713) – Italy
Alexander Glazunov (1865–1936) – Russia
Reinhold Glière (1875–1956) – Russia
Mikhail Glinka (1804–1857) – Russia
Leopold Godowsky (1870–1938) – Poland
Charles Gounod (1818–1893) – France
George Frideric Handel (1685–1759) – Germany/England
Engelbert Humperdinck (1854–1921) – Germany
Mikhail Ippolitov-Ivanov (1859–1935) – Russia
Ruggiero Leoncavallo (1857–1919) – Italy
Edward MacDowell (1860–1908) – United States
Pietro Mascagni (1863–1945) – Italy
Giovanni Pierluigi da Palestrina (1525–1594) – Italy
Giacomo Puccini (1858–1924) – Italy
Jean-Phillippe Rameau (1683–1764) – France
Nikolai Rimsky-Korsakov (1844–1908) – Russia
Gioachino Rossini (1792–1868) – Italy/France
Christian Sinding (1856–1941) – Norway
Franz von Suppé (1819–1895) – Austria
Arnold Schoenberg (1874–1951) – Austria/United States
Giuseppe Tartini (1692–1770) – Italy
Giuseppe Verdi (1813–1901) – Italy

these programs further reflects Hambitzer's stated determination to make sure Gershwin got "a firm foundation in the standard music first."[42] Viewed in a pedagogical light, the concert programs exhibit a selection of works that would be covered in a basic music appreciation course.

Surprisingly, not one Broadway show playbill appears in this collection. With the exception of an occasional patriotic song such as "The Battle Hymn of the Republic," which seems to have been a favorite in this era, every concert – including the few performed by students or community groups – features serious art music written by European or American composers. The almost exclusive content of nineteenth-century music, including many transcriptions, reflects the tastes of a bygone era. Although most concerts included works that would not now be programmed due to their obscurity or perceived "lightness," they were generally balanced with lengthier, familiar "serious" works such as sonatas, tone poems, or symphony or concerto movements. Gershwin apparently favored professional over amateur concerts, especially those featuring internationally renowned performers such as pianists Josef Lhevinne, Leo Ornstein, and Leopold Godowsky; violinist Efram Zimbalist;

Table 3.3 *Representative major works listed in Gershwin concert programs*

Bach, J. S.	Toccata and Fugue in E Major
Beethoven	Rondo a Capriccio, Op. 129
	Sonata in F Minor, Op. 57 ("Appassionata")
	Sonata Op. 81
	Sonata Op. 110
	String Quartet, Op. 18, No. 4
	Symphony No. 3 ("Eroica")
	Symphony No. 7
Brahms	*Variations on a Theme of Paganini*
	Zigeunerlieder
Chopin	Ballades (nos. 1 and 3)
	10 etudes
	4 impromptus
	6 nocturnes
	2 polonaises
	2 waltzes
	Sonata [no. 3] in B Minor
	Scherzo [no. 2] in B flat Minor
Grieg	Piano Concerto in A Minor
Haydn	*Finale* from Quartet No. 8
	Symphony No. 13
Liszt	Sonata in B Minor
	Les Préludes
	Legende (St. Francis Walking on the Waves)
	Hungarian Rhapsody No. 6
	Rhapsody No. 12
Mendelssohn	Piano Concerto No. 1
	Symphony No. 4
Rachmaninoff	Piano Concerto No. 2
Rimsky-Korsakov	*Scheherezade*
Schoenberg	*Pierrot Lunaire*
Schubert	Quintet in A Major, Op. 114
	Symphony No. 8 ("Unfinished")
Schumann	*Kinderscenen*
	Vogel als Prophet
Tchaikovsky	*Andantino in modo di canzona* from Symphony No. 4
	Piano Concerto No. 1
Vieuxtemps	Violin Concerto No. 2
Wagner	Prelude to *Die Meistersinger*
	"Siegfried's Rhine Journey" from *Götterdamerung*

conductor Pierre Monteux; and ensembles like the New York Philharmonic, the New York Symphony, and the Kneisel Quartet.

Gershwin attended concerts with incredible regularity, suggesting he had a voracious musical appetite. He often attended two or three concerts per week, sometimes more than one per day. Although the impressive array of performers and concerts represented in the program collection could only occur in a city like New York, it is informative that Gershwin was introduced to classical music as early as he was to ragtime and jazz. Concurrent exposure to both concert and popular music partially explains his rejection of the highbrow–lowbrow boundaries that separated the seemingly incompatible worlds he negotiated. As Ira Gershwin wrote, the idea that George had little exposure to classical music prior to writing *Rhapsody in Blue* is a myth:

> There are a few musicologists who still would like to believe that George "graduated" from Broadway to Carnegie Hall. However, these concert programs he saved in his early teens show that George had more than passing interest in the more serious side of music.[43]

Gershwin's Studies in Music Theory

Gershwin pursued formal studies in music theory several times. From 1917/18 to early 1923, he studied basic harmony, form, and orchestration with Edward Kilenyi, Sr. During the summer of 1921 he completed courses in basic orchestration and nineteenth-century music literature at Columbia University.[44] Between 1923 and 1925 he took an indeterminate number of lessons with Rubin Goldmark. During the spring of 1924 he pursued a self-directed study in simple form.[45] From 1926 to 1927 Gershwin briefly studied counterpoint, first with Wallingford Riegger, later with Henry Cowell. Finally, his studies with Joseph Schillinger took place between 1932 and 1936.

Gershwin's studies with Kilenyi and Schillinger are the most extensively documented phases of his formal education. Folders containing manuscripts from both periods of study are available in the LC Gershwin Collection. The most extensive scholarly work done thus far has covered the "Kilenyi period" of Gershwin's studies in the late 1910s and early 1920s.[46] Extensive work on the "Schillinger period" has yet to be undertaken.

The material covered in Gershwin's private lessons with Kilenyi is roughly equivalent to the first two years of theory courses now required in undergraduate music programs: four-part harmony, chromatic harmony, basic and chromatic modulation, introductory form, and basic orchestration and instrumentation. The theory exercises assigned and graded by Kilenyi (held in the LC Gershwin Collection) show these lessons to have been thorough and detailed. Gershwin was an excellent student. Kilenyi wrote two accounts of Gershwin's studies with him,[47] and they reveal important details of Gershwin's studies, including the textbooks and curriculum covered. Kilenyi's approach to teaching harmony was quite contemporary; the primary text of Gershwin's lessons was *The Materials Used in Musical Composition* by Percy Goetschius – a book reflecting post-Romantic and

Modernist harmonic practices, so widely used that it was colloquially known as "the Bible of Harmony."[48] Kilenyi supplemented Gershwin's instruction in chromatic harmony with Arnold Schoenberg's *Harmonielehre*, which emphasizes music's horizontal plane and argues that harmony results as "an accident of the voice leading."[49] From this argument Kilenyi concluded that "fresh, new, lush or strange chromatic harmonies"[50] could be created "not from going into many keys, but from writing 'stufenreich' (stepwise)."[51]

Kilenyi included free composition assignments in Gershwin's curriculum, one of which was assumed to have been the *Lullaby* for String Quartet.[52] Ira Gershwin called it an "exercise for strings" and placed its composition "about 1919," during George's studies with Kilenyi.[53] However, Kilenyi stated that George never wrote a complete string quartet for him. The string exercise he recalled was "not at all a full movement. Not even a beginning!"[54] Gershwin also supposedly showed the *Lullaby* to Rubin Goldmark to demonstrate his readiness for advanced coursework – a hint Goldmark reportedly ignored.[55] And Gershwin used its primary theme as the basis of the arietta "Has Anyone Seen My Joe" in *Blue Monday* (1922). Whatever its origins, the *Lullaby* demonstrates that Gershwin developed the ability to create extended-length works prior to writing *Rhapsody in Blue*. Little else can be accurately written of its origins because the original manuscript has been lost. The only known manuscript sources are piano sketches of the quartet's principal theme and the *Blue Monday* sketch of the aria based on it.[56] The string parts were later commissioned by Ira, which were copied from the now-lost original score.

Kilenyi saw his role in Gershwin's formal education as preparatory, anticipating that Gershwin would go on to study counterpoint and advanced composition with a "great musical personality." In "Gershwiniana," Kilenyi said he recommended that Gershwin study with Ernest Bloch, because Bloch's musical sensibilities lay close to Gershwin's:

> Years later his association with Henry Cowell proved that my idea of having George study with Bloch was correct. I would not have advised him to study with Cowell or with anyone else who would have damagingly and without success treated him as if he had been an average student or a little more than a beginner.[57]

Unlike other teachers with whom Gershwin studied in ensuing years, Kilenyi recognized that Gershwin's professional path would be different from many of his contemporaries: "[The] only correct and fitting method should have been an individual one created and applied to Gershwin's special need. It should have been inspiring and without shackling him with pedantic disciplinary methods."[58]

The teacher Gershwin found best suited to his "special need" was Russian music theorist Joseph Schillinger, with whom other composer/arrangers in the jazz/pop music world, including Glenn Miller, studied. Gershwin's focus with Schillinger appears to have been counterpoint, although one must learn Schillinger's entire system in order to incorporate his theories in any practical way. Steven Gilbert and Wayne Shirley each recognized the influence of Schillinger's teaching in Gershwin's later works, such as "geometric expansion" in the *Variations on "I Got Rhythm"* (1933) or "rotated versions of [a] theme" in *Porgy and Bess* (1935).[59] Paul Nauert has also explored Gershwin's use of the Schillinger system in these works and others.[60] Nonetheless, this period in Gershwin's education needs more scholarly analysis. Doing so, however, will require gaining fluency in every aspect of the Schillinger method to interpret and analyze the exercises, many of which were written on graph paper.

Kilenyi served as an occasional resource for Gershwin for the rest of his life. Because Kilenyi began working as a music director and conductor in the film industry during the silent film era and then continued in Hollywood until retiring in the early 1960s, Gershwin sought his help in preparing to conduct performances of his own works.[61] He also occasionally asked Kilenyi for feedback and recommendations for solving compositional problems in some of his concert works, most notably the *Second Rhapsody* for Piano and Orchestra.[62]

It is curious that despite so much documentary evidence to the contrary, the myth that Gershwin was self-taught persists. Perhaps this myth's enduring nature testifies to the strength of the public image Gershwin initially created, which was seized upon by critics who sought to minimize his achievements after his death, when he could no longer defend himself. Was Gershwin self-taught or unschooled? No, but his educational path was unconventional in comparison to that of his classically trained contemporaries. When Gershwin's music education is viewed holistically, its individual components are essentially the same as he would have received through systematic study in a music school: practicing for instrumental mastery, listening and exposure to a wide variety of music, study and mastery of music theory. Only the proportions of those elements differ between Gershwin's self-directed studies and formal systematic curricula.

The education Gershwin acquired was appropriate to his professional and artistic goals, which lay in the nebulous, controversial area between traditional art music and popular music. In the early twenty-first century, composers regularly mix classical and popular musical styles in their "serious" works without having the legitimacy of their music questioned. Gershwin's pioneering contributions, both musically and educationally, are part of what made that reality possible. Clearly, he was a century ahead of his time.

Notes

1. Roy Harris to Aaron Copland (1928), cf. Carol J. Oja, *Making Music Modern: New York in the 1920s* (Oxford: Oxford University Press, 2000), 242.
2. Carol J. Oja, "Gershwin and the Modernists of the 1920s," *The Musical Quarterly* 78/4 (Winter 1994), 646–68.
3. Virgil Thomson, "George Gershwin," *Modern Music* 13/1 (November–December 1935), 15–16.
4. Isaac Goldberg, *George Gershwin: A Study in American Music*, reprint and supplemented by Edith Garson (New York: Frederick Ungar Publishing, 1958; 1st edn, Simon & Schuster, 1931), 273.
5. Larry Starr, *George Gershwin* (New Haven, CT: Yale University Press, 2011), 8.
6. Goldberg, *George Gershwin*, 63.
7. Howard Pollack, *George Gershwin: His Life and Work* (Berkeley, CA: University of California Press, 2006), 347.
8. Deena Rosenberg, *Fascinating Rhythm: The Collaboration of George and Ira Gershwin* (Ann Arbor, MI: University of Michigan Press, 1991), 124.
9. Vernon Duke, "Gershwin, Schillinger, and Dukelsky: Some Reminiscences," *The Musical Quarterly* 33/1 (January 1947), 109.
10. *Gershwin Remembered*, prod. and writ. Peter Adam, dir. Clark Peters, BBC-TV Program Development, Co., 1987, videocassette.
11. David Ewen, "The Stature of George Gershwin," *American Mercury* (June 1950), 716–24.
12. Charles Schwartz, *Gershwin: His Life and Works* (Indianapolis, IN: Bobbs-Merrill, 1973), 52–57, 380; Joan Peyser, *The Memory of All That: The Life of George Gershwin* (New York: Simon & Schuster, 1993), 10.
13. Edward Jablonski, *George Gershwin: A Biography* (New York: Doubleday, 1987), 106.
14. *Gershwin Remembered*, videocassette.
15. Paul Berliner, *Thinking in Jazz: The Infinite Art of Improvisation* (Chicago: University of Chicago Press, 1994).
16. Susan Neimoyer, "*Rhapsody in Blue*: The Culmination of George Gershwin's Musical Education," Ph.D. dissertation, University of Washington (2003), 27.
17. Ira Gershwin, "Foreword," in *The George and Ira Gershwin Song Book* (New York: Simon & Schuster, 1960), cf. Rosenberg, *Fascinating Rhythm*, 11.
18. Berliner, *Thinking in Jazz*, 28.
19. "Gershwin, King of the Jazz Composers at 26, Says Piano Made Good Boy of Him," *The Brooklyn Daily Eagle* (July 19, 1925), 90.
20. Goldberg, *George Gershwin*, 61.
21. Ibid., 74–75.
22. Jablonski, *Gershwin*, 16.
23. *Gershwin Remembered*, videocassette.
24. Goldberg, *George Gershwin*, 74–80.
25. Rosenberg, *Fascinating Rhythm*, 28–29.
26. Oscar Levant, *A Smattering of Ignorance* (New York: Doubleday, Doran and Co., 1940), 189–90, 199–200.
27. Berliner, *Thinking in Jazz*, 51–52.
28. Schwartz, *Gershwin*, 56; Goldberg, *George Gershwin*, 81.
29. Schwartz, *Gershwin*, 54, 125–29.
30. Goldberg, *George Gershwin*, 67.
31. Berliner, *Thinking in Jazz*, 59.
32. Robert Kimball, liner notes in George Gershwin, Ira Gershwin, and DuBose Heyward, *Porgy and Bess*, Houston Grand Opera, cond. Sherwin Goldman, prod. Thomas Z. Shepherd, RCA CD RCD3-2109, 1976, compact disc, 16–17.
33. Samuel A. Floyd, Jr., ed., *Black Music in the Harlem Renaissance: A Collection of Essays* (New York: Greenwood Press, 1990), 21.
34. Rosenberg, *Fascinating Rhythm*, 22, 118.

35. Floyd, *Black Music in the Harlem Renaissance*, 21.
36. Ed Kirkeby, *Ain't Misbehavin'* (New York: Dodd, Mead and Co., 1966), 53.
37. George Gershwin, "First Scrapbook [1909?]–[1920]," Library of Congress, Washington. DC, Gershwin Collection, Box 100, Book 32. For a complete listing of the Scrapbook programs see Appendix 1a in Neimoyer, "*Rhapsody in Blue*: A Culmination," 276–86.
38. Ira Gershwin, introductory notes in Gershwin, "First Scrapbook" dated April 20, 1962.
39. Jablonski, *Gershwin*, 10.
40. Oja, Making Music Modern, 11–24.
41. Edward Kilenyi, Sr., "Gershwiniana: Recollections and Reminiscences of Times Spent with My Student George Gershwin," 1963, unpublished typescript, call number ML410.G288K54, Library of Congress, Washington, DC. Kilenyi Collection, 24–25.
42. Goldberg, *George Gershwin*, 61.
43. Ira Gershwin, letter dated April 20, 1962, Gershwin scrapbook.
44. Pollack, *George Gershwin*, 32.
45. George Gershwin, Notebook: March–April 1924, Library of Congress, Washington, DC. Gershwin Collection, Box 58, Folder 10.
46. Susan Neimoyer, "George Gershwin and Edward Kilenyi, Sr.: A Reevaluation of Gershwin's Early Musical Education," *The Musical Quarterly* 94/1 and 2 (Spring/Summer 2011), 9–62.
47. Edward Kilenyi, Sr., "George Gershwin As I Knew Him," *The Etude* 68/10 (October 1950), 11–12, 64; and "Gershwiniana."
48. Berliner, *Thinking in Jazz*, 73.
49. Arnold Schoenberg, *Theory of Harmony*, trans. Roy E. Carter (Berkeley, CA: University of California Press, 1978), 343–44.
50. Kilenyi, "Gershwiniana," 85
51. Edward Kilenyi, Sr., "Arnold Schönberg's 'Harmony,'" *New Music Review and Church Music Review* 14/6 and 7 (1915), 324–28, 360.
52. Jablonski, *Gershwin*, 42–43; Pollack, *George Gershwin*, 33–34.
53. Letter from Ira Gershwin to Harold Spivacke dated March 8, 1967. Gershwin Collection, Library of Congress, Washington, DC. Box 50, Folder 7.
54. Kilenyi, "Gershwiniana," 74.
55. David Ewen, *George Gershwin: His Journey to Greatness*, expanded and updated edn (New York: Prentice Hall, 1970), 58–59; Pollack, *George Gershwin*, 34.
56. Gershwin Collection, Library of Congress, Washington, DC. Box 50, Folder 6; Box 1, Folder 33.
57. Kilenyi, "Gershwiniana," 81–82.
58. Ibid.
59. Steven E. Gilbert, *The Music of George Gershwin* (New Haven, CT: Yale University Press, 1995), 174–75; Wayne D. Shirley, "'Rotating' *Porgy and Bess*," in Wayne Schneider (ed.), *The Gershwin Style: New Looks at the Music of George Gershwin* (Oxford: Oxford University Press, 1999), 21–34.
60. Paul Nauert, "Theory and Practice in *Porgy and Bess*: The Gershwin-Schillinger Connection," *The Musical Quarterly* 78/1 (Spring 1994), 9–33.
61. Kilenyi, "Gershwiniana," 36, 43–45.
62. Ibid., 58–60.

4 Gershwin in Hollywood

JESSICA GETMAN

George Gershwin encountered Hollywood in the early years of the talkies, as sound technology advanced quickly, public opinion about the role of music in film fluctuated rapidly, and studios experimented with how best to employ composers and songwriters. Entering the world of movie musicals by way of a successful Broadway career was in turns exciting and uncomfortable. Gershwin enjoyed living in Los Angeles but chafed against the reduced artistic control he was afforded. First visiting Los Angeles for fourteen weeks in 1930 to write the score for Fox's *Delicious* (1931), and then returning in the last year of his life to compose RKO's *Shall We Dance* (1937) and *Damsel in Distress* (1937), in addition to Samuel Goldwyn's *The Goldwyn Follies* (1938), Gershwin's interaction with Los Angeles and the people who lived and worked there brings into focus both the vitality of a city invigorated by a growing film industry and the tragedy of a promising life cut short.

Gershwin died on July 11, 1937, at the age of 38, at Cedars of Lebanon Hospital in Los Angeles. The previous months had been alternately exhilarating and marred by mysterious health issues – headaches and vertigo among them – for which doctors could find no source. Between February and July 1937, his health steadily worsened, and on the evening of July 9, he fell into a coma. Doctors operated, but he passed away the morning of the surgery. This was a devastating (and devastatingly rapid) end for a man who only a few months earlier had written to his friend Mabel Schirmer that "California has many very delightful advantages," including warm, dry weather that complemented the pool at his home nicely.[1] To his sister, he wrote that he was already planning more symphonies, operas, and chamber works.[2] Gershwin came to enjoy Los Angeles during his final trip, but he intended his work in film to extend only as long as it took to fund his orchestral projects.

Gershwin and the Movie Musical

Hollywood powered through the sound revolution only a few years prior to *Delicious*. Between 1925 and 1928, both Warner Bros. and Fox experimented with "talking pictures," with the former studio investing in AT&T's Western

Electric sound-on-disc technology (the Vitaphone system), and the latter promoting a sound-on-film system (Movietone). From these new technologies emerged the first viable talkies, and films that included an audio track took the industry by storm; notable entries include Warner Bros.'s *Don Juan* (1926) and *The Jazz Singer* (1927), Fox's *Mother Knows Best* (1928), and Disney's *Steamboat Willie* (1928). In May 1928, the primary Hollywood studios – Loew's/MGM, Paramount, and United Artists – came to a simultaneous agreement to standardize the industry with sound-on-film technology, an arrangement that included the installation of audio technology in theaters across the country.[3]

Talkies between 1927 and 1931 leaned heavily toward music, featuring songs similar to those produced by Tin Pan Alley in the previous decade. Studios hired their own large orchestras, composers, arrangers, and conductors to provide these new soundtracks, pulling in Tin Pan Alley talent (such as Irving Berlin, Arthur Freed, and Gershwin's *Blue Monday* [1922] collaborator Buddy DeSylva), and purchasing music publishing companies in order to both capitalize on the economic potential of the new songs and to reduce music licensing fees.[4] But this initial fascination with song on screen was short-lived, as the preference of producers and critics shifted toward realism. At the end of 1930, a decline in ticket sales indicated that audiences, as well, were done with Broadway on screen. Between 1930 and 1931, only twenty-one of the 990 feature films coming out of Hollywood were musicals.[5]

This was the situation into which Gershwin and his brother Ira were first hired for film by Fox in 1930. Rumors had been circulating since 1928 that Gershwin was heading to Hollywood, and despite the delay in contract, and the decline of song on screen in the interim, Gershwin and Ira together pulled in $100,000 for the job, which included fourteen weeks of work in Los Angeles. This amount was perhaps less than what Gershwin had expected – DeSylva, Lew Brown, and Ray Henderson had received $150,000 for the 1929 *Sunny Side Up*, and Gershwin himself was paid $50,000 simply for Paul Whiteman's use of *Rhapsody in Blue* in the 1930 film *King of Jazz* – but this was a "notable victory" since the value of composition in Hollywood had declined precipitously in just a few years.[6]

Gershwin arrived in Los Angeles in November 1930, spending the first half of his fourteen-week residency writing the film's songs with Ira and the second half working on the *New York Rhapsody*, an orchestral sequence developed in conjunction with his *Second Rhapsody* for solo piano and orchestra (1931).[7] He and Ira resided in Beverly Hills for the duration, working both there and at Fox's Movietone City. They enjoyed an active social life, and Gershwin found himself often at dinner parties with the Hollywood elite, enduring "picture talk." In order to complete the score, however, he ultimately retreated to the Beverley Hills residence and limited his activities to swimming, hiking, and playing tennis with a narrow set of friends.[8]

The music of *Delicious* responds to the public's new aversion to song-for-the-sake-of-song and its preference for verisimilitude; the film has little underscoring, and the music, when present, is usually diegetic. The film pushes this restriction only twice: during the dream sequence, in which the fantasy allows for the irrational presence of an underscore (real life is rarely accompanied by a full orchestra), and during the *New York Rhapsody* scene, as Heather, an illegal immigrant in New York, runs from the authorities; her distress encourages the audience to accept the orchestral score as emotional excess. Otherwise, songs and musical numbers in the film have a direct narrative purpose, with their sources visible or inferred.[9]

While Gershwin approached this first film project with a degree of humility, noting his lack of familiarity with the medium, and while he agreed with the studio that "music must not interfere with the story, but help it," he was dismayed with the final product, complaining to a friend that "imagination in producing it & cutting it was lacking."[10] He was away from Hollywood for the final months of production, having returned to New York after his fourteen weeks in Los Angeles were up, and he did not return to oversee the score's recording. The artistic authority he had earned on Broadway was not afforded to him in this setting, and the studio, for instance, cut his *New York Rhapsody* from about fifteen minutes down to seven, and recorded it in such a way that it would be less prominent than the sound effects. Still, the picture was popular and financially successful. It also provided a vehicle for Gershwin's work on his *Second Rhapsody*, allowing him to fulfill a request from Serge Koussevitzky of the Boston Symphony Orchestra, the group that later premiered the work, with Gershwin as soloist, in January 1932.[11]

Return to Los Angeles

After finishing *Delicious*, Gershwin did not return to the film industry, or to Los Angeles, for several years. Between 1932 and 1936, he composed *Cuban Overture* (1932) and *Variations on "I Got Rhythm"* (1934), wrote two 1933 Broadway shows (*Pardon My English* and *Let 'Em Eat Cake*), and produced what is considered one of the hallmark American operas, *Porgy and Bess* (1935). During this time, the movie musical again rose to prominence in Hollywood, with big names like Fred Astaire and Ginger Rogers, Jeanette MacDonald, Shirley Temple, and Busby Berkeley taking the lead. Sound technology had advanced to such a level that it was possible to prerecord musical numbers, play them back during filming, and then dub dance sounds into the final soundtrack after the fact, increasing the aural quality of the film.[12]

By 1936, there were again rumors that Gershwin was returning to Los Angeles, slated to write for a Vincente Minnelli revue. Although he and Ira ended up lending "By Strauss" to Minnelli's *The Show Is On* (1936) at Broadway's Winter Garden Theatre, the two instead signed in June 1936 with RKO for the Astaire–Rogers film that eventually became known as *Shall We Dance* (1937).[13] This time, they netted only $55,000 for sixteen weeks of work – a fee comparable to that earned by Jerome Kern ($50,000, with a percentage of the profits) for RKO's *Swing Time* (1936) – but their contract also stipulated that RKO had the exclusive right to sign a second film from the brothers at $70,000. This option was quickly exercised when it became clear that work on *Shall We Dance* was going well, resulting in the 1937 film *A Damsel in Distress* (1937), with Astaire joined not by Rogers, but by Joan Fontaine.[14]

The Gershwin brothers arrived in Los Angeles on August 10, 1936, after driving a Buick cross-country (and having to replace the engine in Colorado Springs). They took a beautiful house on North Roxbury Drive in Hollywood – spacious with a "fine workroom" and a Steinway.[15] In the transition, RKO had expressed concern that Gershwin's songs might be too highbrow for the industry, leading to Gershwin's famous telegraph: "Incidentally rumors about highbrow music ridiculous. Am out to write hits."[16] Blurred boundaries between high and low art, however, had been part of Gershwin's brand since his 1924 success with *Rhapsody in Blue*, a perception reinforced by his recent "folk opera" *Porgy and Bess*. This tension between high and low art, a common plot device in Hollywood, became a central force in *Shall We Dance* and *A Damsel in Distress*; the former pits jazz against ballroom dance and ballet, and the latter, jazz against the English madrigal. As Howard Pollack has observed, this clash between the refined and the popular "shadowed Gershwin particularly closely, perhaps because the film industry needed this handle to help understand and market the composer."[17]

The Gershwins finished their music for *Shall We Dance* in December; the score again provided vocal numbers while also featuring orchestral music by George. "Let's Call the Whole Thing Off" and "They Can't Take That Away from Me" both premiered in this film, as did "Hoctor's Ballet" (the film's lavish production number performed by Harriet Hoctor) and "Walking the Dog" (posthumously re-orchestrated and published as *Promenade*). Though Gershwin was able to spend more time on the production set on this occasion, he still found the difference between the authority he was afforded as a composer on Broadway and in Hollywood disconcerting; he felt that the creative team, for instance, misused some of the songs by holding reprises to a minimum.[18] On top of this, the studio made him rewrite "Hoctor's Ballet" at the behest of Astaire and other studio executives, leading to several major revisions. At one point, RKO demanded that he include one of the film's primary songs in the ballet; at another, they had jazz orchestrator Fud Livingston create a new arrangement of the number on his own. Finally, displeased with the result of Livingston's work, Gershwin, orchestrator Robert Russell Bennet, and RKO's music director Nathaniel Shilkret stayed up all night to create one last, successful version.[19] Despite this turmoil, the critics generally appreciated the score, and "They Can't Take That Away from Me" was nominated for an Academy Award for "Best Original Song." Audiences, however, were ambivalent, with the film netting much less than half of Astaire and Rogers's previous film.[20] Ira Gershwin commented that he and George were proud of the "sophisticated" score, but admitted that "maybe that was a mistake, to put so many smart songs in one picture."[21]

Once they had completed the score for *Shall We Dance*, the Gershwin brothers moved forward to the next task quickly, working between January and May 1937 on P.G. Wodehouse's own screen adaptation of his 1919 novel *A Damsel in Distress*. Gershwin felt this second score was superior to the previous, and that the songs provided greater variety, with one seemingly influenced both by Gilbert and Sullivan and by English ballads ("The Jolly Tar and the Milkmaid"), and another based on "a short contrapuntal exercise originally called 'Back to Bach'" ("Sing of Spring"). This film produced some popular hits as well, including "A Foggy Day (In London Town)" and "Nice Work If You Can Get It."[22] Unfortunately, Fred Astaire and Joan Fontaine did not pair well, and Fontaine struggled in her role; the film was ill received, and Astaire's first RKO film without Ginger Rogers actually lost money (to the tune of $65,000).[23] Still, George and Ira Gershwin came out well, and Samuel Goldwyn signed them to write for his lavish 1938 *Goldwyn's Follies*. After a week's vacation, they began working in May 1937, though Gershwin made it through only five of the planned nine numbers before his death.[24]

California Life

When Gershwin moved to Los Angeles, he left behind a robust network of family and friends in New York with whom he exchanged letters, but his celebrity meant that he was not for want of company. He entertained and attended parties with major figures in film and music, including Charlie Chaplin, Harold Arlen, Yip Harburg, Marlene Dietrich, Igor Stravinsky,

Oscar Levant, Moss Hart, and Frank Capra, among others.[25] Performances before friends were common among the talented crowd in these private settings. Stravinsky, for instance, performed a few pieces with violinist Samuel Dushkin at a soiree in 1937 at which Gershwin was present, and descriptions of Gershwin presiding at the piano during parties are numerous. (Rouben Mamoulian recalled that "George loved playing the piano for people and would do at the slightest provocation."[26]) The Gershwins' home in Los Angeles was a popular gathering place, and he, Ira, and Ira's wife, Leonore (or "Lee"), were known for entertaining their friends at their home, which featured a swimming pool and tennis court, as well as Gershwin's dog, a terrier named Tony. Gershwin, his brother, and his sister-in-law were known for their leftist political leanings, having supported labor, anti-fascist, and socialist causes. In fact, during McCarthyism, Gershwin's music was labeled posthumously subversive.[27]

Gershwin enjoyed the California sun, taking long hikes and indulging in golf and tennis. Overall, felt that Hollywood had improved since his previous visit, commenting in a letter to his publisher Max Dreyfus that his social life was more enjoyable, as he had the opportunity to talk shop and associate with screen- and songwriters "in a way that [was] practically impossible in the East."[28] He also enjoyed poker parties with Irving Berlin and Jerome Kern, and noted that "Hollywood has taken on a new color since our last visit six years ago ... the feeling around is very *gemütlich.*"[29]

Gershwin's friendships with notables like Berlin and Kern became legendary, especially as his early death prompted the celebrities in his circle – guided by impresario Merle Armitage – to publish their memories of him.[30] His tennis matches with Arnold Schoenberg are an oft-noted part of his life in Los Angeles. Both men were dedicated to the sport, and their friendship resulted, as reported by Oscar Levant, in a "standing invitation for the older man to use the Gershwin court on a regular day each week."[31] Schoenberg prioritized his tennis sessions at the Gershwin home, often bringing friends and not missing a week even for the birth of his son.[32] While the two composers wrote very different music, they admired each other's work. Schoenberg commented after Gershwin's passing (defending Gershwin's work against those who did not believe he was a "serious composer") that Gershwin's music was holistic and meaningful in a way that much art music at the time was not:

> His melodies are not products of a combination, nor of a mechanical union, but they are units and could not therefore be taken to pieces. Melody, harmony and rhythm are not welded together, but cast ... But I know he is an artist and

a composer; he expressed musical ideas; and they were new – as is the way in which he expressed them.[33]

While acknowledging the loss dealt to American music at Gershwin's death, Schoenberg lamented: "I lose also a friend whose amiable personality was very dear to me."[34]

Gershwin also pursued romance during his year on the West Coast. His on-again, off-again affair with the married Katherine ("Kay") Swift has been widely reported; it spanned about a decade, stretching past her 1934 divorce from the prominent banker James Warburg, but ending shortly before Gershwin moved to Hollywood in 1936. Though Gershwin had continued to have affairs with other women throughout their relationship (he had dated actress Aileen Pringle during his first visit to Los Angeles, for instance), Swift was a central figure in his life and very dear to him.[35] The break was painful, especially after Gershwin learned that Swift planned to marry another man, but he approached his sojourn in California as an opportunity for personal growth, writing to his psychoanalyst, Gregory Zilboorg: "Now, as to my future, I believe I have matured to a point where I can & will make decisions. A great change has come over me & I think I can at last have an opportunity to find my true level."[36] Gershwin dated several famous women that year in Hollywood, including Ginger Rogers and French actress Simone Simon, but he was most taken with Paulette Goddard, star of Charlie Chaplin's 1936 *Modern Times* – and secretly Chaplin's wife.[37] Gershwin considered her "the most glamorous & enchanting girl in the west," and, according to Harold Arlen, debated whether he should settle down with her.[38] The fact that she would not leave her marriage with Chaplin wounded his ego, and the two called off their affair shortly before his death.[39]

Like Schoenberg, Gershwin was also a painter, and his interest in art continued while he was in Los Angeles. After he arrived, he decided that the new house could "use some paintings," and had his assistant in New York (Zenna Hannenfeldt) ship him several works from his New York residence. As part of this package he considered including Picasso's *Absinthe Drinker* (1901), Rousseau's *L'Île de la Cité* (1890–1900), and his own *Portrait of Grandfather*.[40] He also continued painting while in Los Angeles, and, true to form, painted those friends whom he admired, including Jerome Kern and Arnold Schoenberg (Figure 4.1).[41] In all, California seemed to please Gershwin very much, and in a November 1936 letter to his friend Julia Van Norman, he proclaimed: "I've learned & felt more in 8 months out here than I thought possible for me ... Right now I am having a swell time."[42]

Figure 4.1 Music composer George Gershwin painting the portrait of fellow composer Arnold Schoenberg, 1936. Photo by Gabriel Hackett/Archive Photos/Getty Images

Despite the richness of his Hollywood life, music remained Gershwin's focus. On February 10 and 11, 1937, the Los Angeles Philharmonic performed the first all-Gershwin concert on the West Coast. The program included *An American in Paris, Rhapsody in Blue*, and the Concerto in F, as well as excerpts from *Porgy and Bess* performed by Todd Duncan. Gershwin was at the piano for the orchestral works (under the baton of Alexander Smallens), but he conducted the *Porgy and Bess* portion of the concert himself.[43] His pleasure over the pre-concert hype bubbled into a letter to Mabel Schirmer the day before the concert: "They tell me they've seen nothing like the excitement for a concert in years."[44] His agent, Arthur Lyons, had rented a room at the Trocadero nightclub on the Sunset Strip for the after party, inviting 250 guests and booking two orchestras, one Russian and one American.[45] Gershwin also performed in other concerts in Seattle and San Francisco during this time, taking advantage of his West Coast residence.[46]

Amidst it all, Gershwin continued to dream. He assured his sister, Frances ("Frankie") Godowsky, that his priority was to continue composing art music; what he really wanted to do was work on "symphonies, chamber music, and opera."[47] He shared with his friends and family that he wanted to write a string quartet; Armitage recalled that he wanted to base it on melodies he had heard while researching *Porgy and Bess* on Folly Island (on the South Carolina coast). Gershwin dreamed of renting a cabin away from the crowd in Coldwater Canyon (Los Angeles) once he was done with the films, so that he could get the music for this quartet written down.[48] He was considering a symphony, too, as well as another collaboration with the Theatre Guild in Boston, which had put together the first production of *Porgy and Bess*. He hoped to write a second opera with DuBose Heyward, a "cowboy opera" that indulged his burgeoning interest in the American southwest, and perhaps yet another with Lynn Riggs – author of *Green Grow the Lilacs* (1931), a play eventually musicalized as Rodgers and Hammerstein's *Oklahoma!* (1943) – set in New Mexico.[49] Of course, despite all these options, he and his brother also planned to return to New York for a while after the Goldwyn picture was finished, and perhaps to take another trip to Europe.[50]

Death and Remembrance

The symptoms of Gershwin's illness – ultimately diagnosed as a brain tumor that had degenerated and formed a large cyst – were easy to dismiss at the time. One of the most cited, and most obvious, of these effects was his brief blackout in February, 1937, during his performance of the Concerto in F with the Los Angeles Philharmonic. He had a slight dizzy spell at the podium while rehearsing *Porgy and Bess* before the performance, and then fumbled on the piano twice while playing the concerto in concert.[51] Upon reflection, friends also noted increased moodiness and irritability in the days leading to his death – strange from a man known for his energy, confidence, and charm – and he had complained, variously over the previous few months and years, of headaches, stomach issues, fatigue, and olfactory hallucinations. After the concert blackout, he had a medical check-up at the behest of family and friends, but no cause was found. Symptoms worsened until June, when he tried to throw his valet, Paul Mueller, out of a moving car. He was eventually directed to a neurologist and was admitted to Cedars of Lebanon Hospital (now Cedars-Sinai in Los Angeles) on June 23 for more in-depth study.

Preliminary tests provided no clear results, and Gershwin and his doctors decided to forego the only recommended procedure – a painful lumbar puncture. The doctors concluded that his malady was "mostly like hysteria."[52] He deteriorated quickly, suffering from severe headaches and light sensitivity (photophobia), as well as a loss of fine motor control. He was moved, on July 4, to the home of Yip Harburg and given a full-time nurse.[53] On Friday, July 9, he suffered a seizure while in the bathroom and fell into a coma; his friend George Pallay, who was present at the time with Ira, claimed that "his eyes seemed to swell."[54] He was admitted to Cedars of Lebanon for a final time that evening.

The hospital's Dr. Carl Rand determined that Gershwin did, indeed, have a brain tumor, and that immediate surgery was necessary. The esteemed Dr. Harvey Cushing was approached, but because he had recently retired, he recommended his student, Dr. Walter Dandy. Dandy was on vacation, however, yachting on the Chesapeake for the weekend. Pallay and another Gershwin friend, Emil Mosbacher, attempted to retrieve him, but Gershwin deteriorated too quickly to wait for his arrival. The local Dr. Howard Naffziger from the UCLA Medical School was flown down from Lake Tahoe (where he, too, was vacationing), and he and Rand performed the surgery just after midnight on July 11, with Rand presiding. The surgeons found a large cyst on the right temporal region of Gershwin's brain that had shifted past the midline and damaged the brain tissue. The cyst, as well as the tumor that caused it, were removed. When the surgery was finished, Gershwin's friends and family were told not to expect a recovery, and they returned home at about six in the morning to wait. The doctors had explained that if Gershwin pulled through, he would likely be paralyzed on the left side, unable to play the piano, and susceptible to recurring tumors. Gershwin's condition worsened, and he died at 10:35am on Sunday, July 11, 1937.[55] Dandy, who had access to the medical details, reported that the tumor was sudden and severe and that Gershwin would have suffered greatly even if he had lived: "I believe that it was the best outcome for him, since for a brilliant man a recurring tumor would be a terrible, slow death."[56]

Gershwin's case has been a repeated topic of medical study in the intervening decades. For a long time, the medical community believed Gershwin had a glioblastoma multiforme – an aggressive malignant tumor. Researchers have more recently begun to explore other options, including the possibility that the tumor was more slow-moving and that Gershwin might have had a better prognosis had the cancer been diagnosed sooner. Medical science was simply not advanced enough at the time to image Gershwin's brain with the precision necessary to locate the tumor before the cyst formed.[57]

Gershwin's death was a shock, not only to his inner circle, but also to the world. The *New York Times* headline the next day read "George Gershwin, Composer, Is Dead: Master of Jazz Succumbs in Hollywood at 38 After Operation for Brain Tumor," and the obituary memorialized him as "a composer of his generation," who wanted most to "interpret the soul of the American people."[58] He was laid to rest in New York following simultaneous funerals at Temple Emamu-El in Manhattan and Temple B'nai B'rith in Los Angeles. Both services included famous faces – on the East Coast, George Cohan, Walter Damrosch, Vernon Duke, W.C. Handy, and Paul Whiteman were present; and on the West Coast, Richard Rogers and Oscar Hammerstein II. Tributes were quickly arranged, including the August 1937 memorial concert in New York that drew a crowd of over twenty thousand and featured Gershwin's music performed by such dignitaries as Ethel Merman and Ferde Grofé with the New York Philharmonic. The September memorial concert at the Hollywood Bowl, broadcast around the world, presented Fred Astaire, Oscar Levant, and more.[59] Gershwin's paintings and drawings were exhibited at the Marie Harriman Gallery in New York between December 18, 1937, and January 4, 1938.[60] Merle Armitage's offering, a book of memories and personal thoughts solicited from among Gershwin's friends and colleagues, many of whom were celebrities and cultural luminaries, went a long way toward solidifying Gershwin's legend as a composer of rare genius. Both Hammerstein and Irving Berlin wrote poems in his honor. Berlin's read: "I could dwell on the talent that placed him / In the class where he justly belongs, / But this verse is a songwriter's tribute / To a man who wrote wonderful songs."[61]

Ira Gershwin's burden was particularly great; not only had he lost a brother with whom he was especially close (and a colleague with whom he produced much of his best work), but he was also responsible for tying up their business dealings and centralizing George's creative materials. *The Goldwyn Follies*, for instance, was left undone, and Ira had to negotiate with Goldwyn over the extra work it would take to complete the film. Ira traveled back to Los Angeles for a few more weeks of work after the funeral and teamed up with Oscar Levant and Vernon Duke to finish the soundtrack. It was through this collaboration that George and Ira's "Love Is Here to Stay" was completed, subsequently becoming a favorite in the Great American Songbook. The film itself was met with generally positive reviews, and the soundtrack was nominated for an Academy Award for "Best Score," though the entire project lost over $700,000. Kay Swift helped Ira collect George's stray musical sketches, and – in some cases – was able to complete fragmented material from memory.[62] Ira and his wife settled in Los Angeles, purchasing the home next to the one they had rented with George on North Roxbury Drive.[63]

Notes

1. George Gershwin to Mabel Schirmer (September 18, 1936). Cf. Robert Wyatt and John Andrew Johnson, eds., *The George Gershwin Reader* (New York: Oxford University Press, 2004), 257.
2. Robert Kimball, Alfred Simon, and Bea Feitler, *The Gershwins* (New York: Atheneum, 1973), 214.
3. James Wierzbicki, *Film Music: A History* (New York: Routledge, 2008), 90–105; Douglas Gomery, *The Coming of Sound* (London: Taylor & Francis, 2004), 87.
4. Wierzbicki, *Film Music*, 113–16; Howard Pollack, *George Gershwin: His Life and Work* (Berkeley: University of California Press, 2007), 482.
5. Wierzbicki, *Film Music*, 119–21.
6. Pollack, *George Gershwin*, 308, 482.
7. James Wierzbicki, "The Hollywood Career of Gershwin's Second Rhapsody," *Journal of the American Musicological Society* 60/1 (Spring 2007), 133–86.
8. Pollack, *George Gershwin*, 484–85.
9. Ibid., 486–87.
10. Ibid., 487, 489.
11. Ibid., 484–89; Wierzbicki, "The Hollywood Career of Gershwin's Second Rhapsody," 147.
12. Pollack, *George Gershwin*, 667, 677.
13. Ibid., 668–69.
14. Ibid., 666–67.
15. Wyatt and Johnson, *The George Gershwin Reader*, 252–53, 254–55.
16. Pollack, *George Gershwin*, 667.
17. Ibid., 671, 680.
18. Ibid., 675–76.
19. Ibid., 674–75.
20. Richard B. Jewell, "RKO Film Grosses, 1929–1951: The C.J. Tevlin Ledger," *Historical Journal of Film, Radio and Television* 14/1 (January 1, 1994), 44.
21. Pollack, *George Gershwin*, 677.
22. Ibid., 677, 680–81.
23. Jewell, "RKO Film Grosses, 1929–1951," 44.
24. Pollack, *George Gershwin*, 684–87.
25. Merle Armitage, ed., *George Gershwin: Man and Legend* (New York: Duell, Sloan and Pearce, 1958), 60–62; Pollack, *George Gershwin*, 116.
26. Wyatt and Johnson, *George Gershwin Reader*, 259–60; Rouben Mamoulien, essay in *George Gershwin*, ed. Merle Armitage (New York: Longmans, Green & Co., 1938), 53.
27. Wyatt and Johnson, *George Gershwin Reader*, 252; Pollack, *George Gershwin*, 209.
28. Edward Jablonski, *Gershwin Remembered* (Portland: Amadeus Press, 1992), 147–48.
29. Ibid.
30. Merle Armitage, ed., *George Gershwin* (New York: Longmans, Green & Co., 1938).
31. Oscar Levant, *A Smattering of Ignorance* (New York: Doubleday, Doran & Co., 1941), 186–87.
32. Walter H. Rubsamen, "Schoenberg in America," *The Musical Quarterly* 37/4 (1951), 474.
33. Arnold Schoenberg, essay in *George Gershwin*, ed. Armitage, 97–98.
34. "Remarks by Arnold Schoenberg (Live)," Radio Tributes & Memorials to George Gershwin: Historical Live Broadcasts, July 1937, CD (Cambria, 2015).
35. Pollack, *George Gershwin*, 111–13.
36. George Gershwin to Gregory Zilboorg (February 19, 1937). George and Ira Gershwin Collection 1895–2008, ML31.G38, Music Division, Library of Congress.
37. Pollack, *George Gershwin*, 115–16.
38. George Gershwin to Emily Paley (March 16, 1937). George and Ira Gershwin Collection 1895–2008, ML31.G38, Music Division, Library of Congress.
39. Pollack, *George Gershwin*, 115–16.
40. George Gershwin to Zenna Hannenfeldt (September 2, 1936). George and Ira Gershwin Collection 1895–2008, ML31.G38, Music Division, Library of Congress.

41. Pollack, *George Gershwin*, 198.
42. Ibid., 210–11.
43. "Two All-Gershwin Concerts Slated at Philharmonic," *Los Angeles Times*, January 24, 1937; "Sponsoring Board Announced: Women's Committee Will Give Help to Gershwin Concerto," *Los Angeles Times* (February 1, 1937); Isabel Morse Jones, "Gershwin Analyzes Science of Rhythm: Swing Music Fundamental Because It Follows Mathematical Rules, Says Noted Pianist and Composer," *Los Angeles Times* (February 7, 1937).
44. Wyatt and Johnson, *George Gershwin Reader*, 257–58.
45. Ibid.
46. Jones, "Gershwin Analyzes Science of Rhythm"; Wyatt and Johnson, *George Gershwin Reader*, 256–57.
47. Kimball, Simon, and Feitler, *The Gershwins*, 214.
48. Armitage, *George Gershwin*, 77.
49. Pollack, *George Gershwin*, 690–91.
50. Wyatt and Johnson, *George Gershwin Reader*, 262.
51. Levant, *A Smattering of Ignorance*, 198.
52. Davide Bagatti, "Music and Medicine: The Tragic Case of Gershwin's Brain Tumor and the Challenges of Neurosurgery in the First Half of the 20th Century," *World Neurosurgery* 85 (January 2016), 299.
53. Bagatti, "Music and Medicine," 298–99; Pollack, *George Gershwin*, 212; Wyatt and Johnson, *George Gershwin Reader*, 264–65; Gabriel Segal to Gregory Zilboorg (October 12, 1938), George and Ira Gershwin Collection 1895–2008, ML31.G38, Music Division, Library of Congress.
54. George A. Pallay to Irene Gallagher (July 1937). George and Ira Gershwin Collection 1895–2008, ML31.G38, Music Division, Library of Congress.
55. Ibid.; Gabriel Segal to Gregory Zilboorg, 12 October 1938; Pollack, *George Gershwin*, 212–13; Bagatti, "Music and Medicine," 299–302.
56. Pollack, *George Gershwin*, 213.
57. Bagatti, "Music and Medicine," 299–303.
58. "George Gershwin, Composer, Is Dead: Master of Jazz Succumbs in Hollywood at 38 After Operation for Brain Tumor," *New York Times* (July 12, 1937).
59. Pollack, *George Gershwin*, 214–15.
60. Nancy H. Yeide, "The Marie Harriman Gallery (1930–1942)," *Archives of American Art Journal* 39/1–2 (1999), 3, 6.
61. Irving Berlin, poem [16 May 1938], in Armitage, *George Gershwin*, 78.
62. Wyatt and Johnson, *George Gershwin Reader*, 281–82; Pollack, *George Gershwin*, 686–92.
63. Martha Groves, "In Beverly Hills, the Real Estate Ethos Is 'Buy and Demolish,'" *Los Angeles Times* (September 28, 2013).

PART II

Profiles of the Music

5 *Blue Monday* and New York Theatrical Aesthetics

KRISTEN M. TURNER

The New York of George Gershwin's childhood was awash in entertainment choices: vaudeville, variety, revues, operetta, musical comedies, Yiddish theater, dramatic plays, operas, symphony concerts, and more. In 1927, Gershwin wrote:

> Having been born in New York and grown up among New Yorkers, I have heard the voice of that soul. It spoke to me on the streets, in school, at the theater ... Old music and new music, forgotten melodies and the craze of the moment, bits of opera, Russian folk songs, Spanish ballads, chansons, ragtime ditties combined in a mighty chorus in my inner ear. And through and over it all I heard, faint at first, loud at last, the soul of this great America of ours.[1]

Gershwin evocatively describes a soundscape that pulses with all kinds of music that are ostensibly at different points in the cultural hierarchy, but that he portrays as equally compelling parts of his personal musical environment. He recognizes no difference between opera and folksongs, chansons and ragtime, old and new music. While some early twentieth-century critics asserted strict distinctions between high and low culture and maintained that one should have little to do with the other, the reality was rather different. American audiences expected to hear references to highbrow and lowbrow culture on vaudeville bills and in musicals, plays, and comedies. Ingenious mixtures of musical and theatrical conventions often provided the mass appeal to productions that otherwise were simply a repackaging of a few familiar plot tropes.

Gershwin scholars and critics looking back on his career often focus on Gershwin's modernity, his skillful use of jazz in his concert repertoire, and marvel at his ability to cross the divide between popular and classical music. Many people interpret Gershwin as essentially an art music composer who happened to work in musical theater. The over-representation in musicological scholarship that privileges Gershwin's "classical" works such as *Rhapsody in Blue*, Concerto in F, and *Porgy and Bess* compared to his songs and musicals demonstrates the bias of the field toward the long compositions that are routinely performed in concert music spaces and analytical approaches that are grounded within the classical repertory.[2] But viewing Gershwin as primarily a theatrical composer provides a different vantage point on his career, and one, I argue, that is truer to the development of his compositional voice. Gershwin's pluralistic style is not a disruption to previous practice. Rather, his work reflects an outlook shared by many early twentieth-century musical theater composers. They strove to write music that transgressed stylistic boundaries and included numbers from multiple genres to appeal to audiences and producers who valued musical versatility and flexibility. While it is a truism that all artists build on what came before them, in Gershwin's case, this observation seems to have been obscured in favor of a narrative that privileges the ways in which Gershwin's career was unusual, instead of how it worked within an aesthetic framework rooted in the New York theater scene of his youth. This frame of reference must include the training and musical aesthetics of the theater composers working in New York City before World War I, the features that impresarios believed characterized a successful production, and the effect of racialized ideas about music and American identity. Many of Gershwin's biographers situate his first opera, *Blue Monday* (1922), as the last of his substantial early compositions before his artistic and critical breakthrough with *Rhapsody in Blue* in 1924. But *Blue Monday* is also the summation of the influences he absorbed from his education and cultural environment. Written for white singers in blackface, this work injects classical sensibilities into a piece of popular entertainment with musical inspirations from a variety of sources that cross racial and cultural divides.

Although Gershwin tended to downplay his formal training, Susan Neimoyer has demonstrated that Gershwin had an excellent and thorough private musical education, which provided him with ample tools to write concert and theatrical music. His student notebooks and accounts by his teachers attest that he was well acquainted with tonal theory and orchestration. Moreover, in addition to his lessons, much of Gershwin's training occurred through a sort of communal apprenticeship to the jazz and ragtime performers in New York who provided him with examples to follow as a composer and pianist.[3] While Neimoyer characterizes Gershwin's combination of private lessons and aurally based informal study as unusual for white composers, it seems to have been a common way for black composers to receive their musical instruction at the turn of the twentieth century. Some black Broadway composers such as Will Marion Cook and J. Rosamond Johnson attended conservatories, but most African Americans had little access to formal, institutional training. Will Vodery, for example, the African American composer who helped Gershwin find work early in his career and later arranged *Blue Monday*, received his only institutionalized education through music classes offered at his Philadelphia high school. In his late teens, he probably studied privately with Louis Koemmennich, once a teacher with the University of Berlin who had relocated to Philadelphia, and Hugh A. Clarke, professor of music at the University of Pennsylvania. In addition to this classical training, Vodery started arranging songs for black vaudeville musicians as a teenager and, like Gershwin, basically grew up in the theater business with access to mentorship from ragtime composers and popular performers.[4]

Composers with little formal education, as exemplified by George M. Cohan and Irving Berlin, were the exception among the most important white theatrical composers active prior to World War I. Many Broadway figures including Victor Herbert, Ivan Caryll, Julian Edwards, and Reginald De Koven received their schooling at prestigious European conservatories and wrote art music while also composing musical comedies and operettas that combined characteristics of many different kinds of music. Gershwin's reluctance to acknowledge his own expertise may have been a strategy to associate himself with Berlin's story and ingratiate himself with critics and reporters who were always looking for a good rags-to-riches narrative. Other people in his network, especially Isaac Goldberg, confirmed the impression that he was an autodidact by minimizing Gershwin's musical background. In his hagiographic biography, Goldberg paints a compelling image of Gershwin toiling in what Goldberg describes as the "slavery in the galleys" of a song plugger's studio learning how to compose through observation and osmosis.[5] Goldberg presents Gershwin as a self-taught genius in the nineteenth-century romantic tradition of the great man, whose art springs from an internal, natural force.[6]

Gershwin's high-profile search for new teachers later in his career is reminiscent of a similar play for credibility that motivated many pre-World War I musicians to publicize their work with European teachers. American critics and audiences distrusted the abilities of a classical composer or performer trained in the United States. For a composer who had earlier positioned himself as someone who had learned the craft from on-the-job training, publicly pursuing more instruction was a way for Gershwin to move the narrative to a place where he might be taken seriously as a classical composer. After securing the commission for Concerto in F, for example, Gershwin announced (or perhaps joked) that he had bought some theory books, so he could read up on concerto form.[7] His obvious interest in art music was not entirely a publicity stunt, but a person can have more than one motivation for their actions.

The musical scene in New York changed significantly during the 1920s, which may be one reason Gershwin wished to publicize his search for a music teacher in the classical tradition. The aspirational critical rhetoric before the War that posited a distinct difference between popular and classical music, not just stylistically, but also socially and culturally, was becoming fact.[8] Particularly by the early 1930s, the segregation of the popular and classical audiences was such that composers who once moved rather easily between the two worlds had more and more difficulty straddling this divide. The career of Vernon Duke, a composer whom Gershwin admired and who also worked in multiple musical spheres, is an instructive example. Duke not only developed contrasting styles for his popular songs and his "serious" music, but he also used a different name when presenting these works to the public. For his operas, ballets, and instrumental pieces he composed under his given name, Vladimir Dukelsky, using Duke only for works he deemed popular, such as his musicals and film scores. Gershwin, therefore, had examples of at least two possible approaches for his career. As a young composer and pianist, he was exposed to people who routinely transgressed genre boundaries in their pieces to produce a flexible musical style that functioned in multiple realms. Or, he could have followed the lead of composers he met in the 1920s, like Duke, who compartmentalized their work to conform to conventional divisions between highbrow and lowbrow music. Obviously, he chose the former path.

Musical Eclecticism and Theatrical Aesthetics

During the first part of the twentieth century, Gershwin worked within an entertainment economy that was dominated by musical comedies, operettas, and vaudeville. Composers, impresarios, and performers routinely worked in all three genres, blurring the lines between each type of entertainment. Powerful syndicates based in New York controlled the booking in the majority of the theaters in the country and sent out hundreds of shows and vaudeville acts every season to travel the nation.

Scholars who study Broadway musical theater before the 1930s often make a distinction between operettas and musical comedies based upon how similar the work is to conventional operas. Operettas (or comic operas as they were usually called at the time) generally feature a relatively rational plot and musical coherence, European or pseudo-European characters and settings, as well as a musical style and level of technical difficulty that is similar to that of opera. Musical comedies combine flamboyant song and dance numbers, Tin Pan Alley songs, and plots with American characters and settings, although many stories contain a trip abroad on the flimsiest of excuses to provide a note of exoticism.[9] These categories are clearer in retrospect, however, than they were in the moment. Generally, the genre designation seemed to derive from the marketing needs of the premiering theater, the composer, the producer, or the stars. Critics and impresarios thought technically difficult operatic musical numbers were "high class," while Tin Pan Alley songs or pieces that overtly drew upon the musical and theatrical traditions of minstrelsy were "popular." Producers evaluated a show partly based upon the amount and quality of the "high class" and "popular" music present in the production, and valued scores and even individual songs with a pleasing combination of both.

A similar inclination to combine high and low culture existed in Yiddish theater. Yiddish impresarios and writers emulated the melodramas, operettas, farces, and extravaganzas popular among English-speaking audiences, while at the same time retaining elements of Jewish music and culture. European opera, Eastern European folk music, *klezmer*, ragtime, and Tin Pan Alley songs, as well as Jewish sacred music influenced the sound of Yiddish theater.[10] Although Gershwin never wrote for a Yiddish production, he attended many Yiddish shows and knew the leading composers and impresarios who specialized in the genre. According to Walter Rimler, when Gershwin was sixteen he was "asked to collaborate with ... Sholom Secunda [composer of "Bei mir Bist du Schön"] on a Yiddish operetta ... But Secunda considered him too young and inexperienced, and the plan fell through."[11] Indeed, Goldberg contends that Gershwin's use of blue notes was as much an influence from "Polish pietists" as it was "the folk song of the Negro."[12]

The advantage of Gershwin's eclectic musical background was that it provided him with the tools to write the sort of genre-crossing scores popular at the beginning of his career. Hundreds of musical comedies that were at once formulaic and highly variable were produced between 1900 and 1920 in New York City. Unlike the integrated, plot-driven pieces that became popular in the 1930s and 1940s, these works were a chaotic amalgamation of exotic or urban locales, ridiculous plot twists, lavish dance numbers, and songs of every type. Musicals typically contained numbers with influences that ranged from European transplants such as operatic arias and Viennese waltzes to homegrown ragtime Tin Pan Alley songs and minstrel-style parodies. In a handwritten autobiographical note, Will Marion Cook described his music in these terms when remembering a rehearsal for his first musical, *Clorindy*: "First I started in with the verse of 'Hottes' Coon [in Dixie]' which they learned and wowed in five minutes ... Then the development of the operatic part – full of rhythm and modulations, peculiar cadences ... didn't make sense to their acute and alert ears."[13] Thomas Riis characterizes the score for *In Dahomey* (most of which was written by Cook and Alex Rogers) as one that does not have stylistic unity. Cook included what Riis describes as "stirring operatic effects in his choruses" along with elements from ragtime, black folk music, and Romantic-period concert music.[14]

The song reigned supreme in these early musical comedies. Shows were designed around the needs of the stars and the music, not the story. Very often, the plot was merely an excuse to move from song to song. For example, Charles Dillingham, one of the most important New York City producers before World War I, kept track of the level of applause and number of encores after each song.[15] Those that did not measure up to his expectations were replaced. Whether the new song made much sense with the plot was irrelevant. As Jeffrey Magee points out, many productions from the 1910s relied on vaudeville performers who essentially transplanted their independent acts, or at least their personas, from vaudeville into musicals.[16] Stars frequently interpolated their own signature songs into a musical without regard to the circumstances of the narrative. Because of concerns that would have sounded familiar to nineteenth-century opera composers, some powerful Broadway composers such as Victor Herbert and Irving Berlin began including "no interpolations" clauses in their contracts to maintain some measure of control over the content of their scores.[17]

In this context, it is no surprise that Gershwin became suspicious of the classifications that musicians and critics tended to apply to music. He complained that "'classical music' ... means as many things as there are people who say it ... From any sound critical standpoint, labels mean nothing at all. In other words, ideas are the things that count, not mere labeling of form."[18] According to musicologist Larry Starr, "to speak of a rapprochement between cultivated and vernacular in Gershwin's art" is misguided: "his music tells us in the clearest possible way that, while the schism might be our perception, it is not his aesthetic reality ... [Gershwin] never believed in the validity of the schism to begin with."[19] Starr acknowledges, however, that Gershwin's stylistic versatility was essential to his success as a theatrical composer and moreover that Gershwin was clearly aware that critics and audiences thought there was a difference between high and low art; classical and popular music. Whether he believed in the distinction or not, Gershwin, like other composers, often wrote music that included markers of different styles in one piece.

The musical career and agility of Victor Herbert may have been one example Gershwin emulated whether consciously or not in his approach to his music and career. Herbert wrote in every major genre: musical comedies, operettas, opera, extravaganzas, popular song, orchestral pieces, concerti, etc. He was a composer, cellist, and conductor, as well as one of the most important figures on Broadway when Gershwin first entered the field. During a revealing written exchange between Herbert and his producer Charles Dillingham over revisions to one of his operettas, Herbert disclosed that he accepted that the perception existed that there was a difference between popular and classical music. Yet, he argued that multiple factors such as lyrical content or the context in which a piece was performed went into this distinction in addition to musical style. The clash between Herbert and Dillingham is instructive because it not only illustrates Herbert's ideas about genre, but also the economic and artistic pressures that contributed to a show's development. These same forces influenced Gershwin's work.

On December 5, 1903, Dillingham asked Herbert to replace a number in his latest work, *Babette*, starring Fritzi Scheff.

> The Pierrot song that Mme Scheff has in the second act does not receive a single encore and we are taking it out as soon as you can give us something to replace it. What we want in the middle of this act is a stirring song for the star, for ... she, of course, is our drawing card. I would suggest a stirring march song, and something that will show off her voice and yet not interfere with the big number in the last act.[20]

This letter precipitated an argument between the two men that lasted over a month. Dillingham begged Herbert to write a number that would disrupt the primarily operatic style of the score, but Herbert denied that he could write such a piece without the proper lyrics. All the while, Herbert disputed Dillingham's basic premise that a "stirring march song" (by which he meant a "popular" number) would solve the problems Dillingham had identified.

After receiving Dillingham's first letter, Herbert replied in a terse telegram "Need popular lyrics to write popular songs. Send me a few as soon as possible."[21] Apparently, Herbert sent something to Dillingham fairly quickly, which he rejected explaining:

> I would say that you have got an entirely wrong idea about the music of "Babette". You say that the last number you sent is "very brilliant". It is brilliant, but, like the rest of the music, it lacks popular features. The business is unsatisfactory, partly because the book of the second act is not up to the mark, and partly because the music is too high-class ... You know that I think the music is the best ever composed in America, and it has made a great impression with the boxes and first twenty rows of the orchestra which are filled every night, but nobody comes in the gallery or balcony.[22]

Herbert, seemingly insulted, wrote back,

> Both the "Wizard" and the "Serenade" [earlier shows] were declared to be "too heavy" by the papers when they were first performed. If I had to follow the advice

of every empty headed, uneducated, unmusical newspaper-scribbler, my lot would be a sad one. I have told you repeatedly, and you ought to know yourself, that a "popular" song must have "popular" words.[23]

Dillingham persists in his request and clarifies that popular music is a repertoire that "all the bands are playing ... and everybody is whistling."[24] On January 20, Herbert followed up with: "Of course I understand what you mean and what you want, and I am perfectly willing to write a song for Miss Scheff that can be whistled, hummed, organ-ized, band-aged etc. etc. but you forget that I have told you a dozen times! (at least!) that a song of that character must have popular and witty lyrics!"[25]

In these letters, Dillingham claims "high-class" music only attracts the wealthy audience members who can afford box seats or the best spots in the orchestra section and begs Herbert for music that will bring in other patrons in order to fill the whole theater. While Dillingham professes to value Herbert's "high class" music, he thinks that the imbalance between popular and more classical-style music in *Babette* is hurting the show and, most importantly, the bottom line. Herbert, on the other hand, rejects the idea that a song with a catchy melody will provide Dillingham with what he wants. While he never says this explicitly, the subtext of his objections seems to be that Dillingham has reduced the show into a series of almost unrelated numbers rather than a score that is greater than its individual parts. Herbert repeatedly insists that the lyrics are crucial (perhaps even more important than musical style) in controlling whether an audience will think a piece of music is "popular." Additionally, Herbert suggests in his January 20 letter that a popular song is one that can be arranged for other instrumentations (the organ or the band). Considering that operatic music was routinely arranged in a similar manner, this reinforces Herbert's contention that popular style is about more than musical elements. Gershwin's reluctance to acknowledge a divide between classical and popular music seems aligned with Herbert's argument that genre distinctions are less a matter of notes and more a matter of audience perception, which is controlled as much by lyrics and theatrical context as by the musical style. As in Herbert's case, producers expected Gershwin's early songs, musicals, and revues to attract a wide audience, and they counted on musically pluralistic scores to do the job. Gershwin had to adapt to these demands.

Ragtime's Example and Jazz as American Music

While art music and Tin Pan Alley songs were significant influences on the musical comedies that Gershwin heard while he was maturing as a composer, African American music played an equally important role in musical theater and his compositional style. Jazz was the pre-eminent black musical genre by 1925 when the success of *Lady Be Good!* and *Rhapsody in Blue* had secured Gershwin's reputation as one of the best young composers in New York. Gershwin's approach to jazz and his uneasiness about the music as both a black and an American musical style were similar to the anxieties about ragtime circulating among white musicians and critics before World War I. While acknowledging the connection between black people and jazz, Gershwin repeatedly denied that jazz was primarily a black musical genre, instead asserting that it reflected an American national identity that was larger than any one racial or ethnic category. His stance replicates the conversations about ragtime occurring in the musical press before 1920.

During the early twentieth century, ragtime underwent a transformation from a genre marked as black to a type of music that symbolized American vitality. In the racially polarized environment of the times, the term "American" music, as it was used in the print media, really meant music accepted by white people as representative of a white America. At the turn of the twentieth century, musicians and critics alike generally understood ragtime as a black genre born in the South.[26] Thus, while it originated in the United States among American citizens, critics identified ragtime as black music, not American music. As an anonymous author in the black newspaper *The Freeman* explained in 1897, ragtime was a "movement now very popular with Negro specialists."[27] While today many people think of ragtime as piano solos written by composers such as Scott Joplin, at the time, ragtime had a much more expansive meaning that encompassed syncopated music for piano or dance bands, as well as popular songs with texts written in black dialect called coon songs.[28] Black and white singers (so-called coon shouters) performed this repertoire in vaudeville and musical comedies. White singers generally appeared in blackface because to do otherwise would have been interpreted as a cross-racial performance unacceptable to many white people in Jim Crow America. Theater managers and critics evaluated white singers based upon how closely they could replicate a stereotypical image of African American musicians. In reports from 1902 to the United Booking Office, owned by vaudeville impresarios B.F. Keith and Edward Albee, for instance, managers reported that the famous coon shouter Tom Moore was "a white man who sings coon songs nearer like a negro than any one we have had" and was the "best singer of coon songs, outside of [Ernest] Hogan."[29]

Ragtime was controversial in black and white communities. For many white critics, ragtime's rhythms were too "hot" and primitivistic. To them the popularity among young white people of black music associated with dancing and hedonism indicated an unacceptable coarsening of musical culture. In 1901, the president of the American Federation of Musicians complained: "The ragtime craze has lowered the standard of American music as compared with other countries. We have duty as well as business to look after, and we will not give way to a popular demand that is degrading."[30] Meanwhile, for some black critics, ragtime undermined African American claims to musical respectability and by extension their quest for political and cultural equality. In one heated article from the *Negro Music Journal*, the author refused to accept ragtime as black music, charging instead that the style was a fraud enacted by white people hoping to discredit the black race:

> White men also perpetrate so-called music under the name of "rag-time" representing it to be characteristic of the Negro music. This is also a libelous insult. The typical Negro would blush to own acquaintance with the vicious trash that is put forth under Ethiopian titles. If *The Negro Music Journal* can only do a little missionary work among us, and help banish this "rag-time" epidemic, it will go down in history as one of the greatest musical benefactors of the age.[31]

Other black critics and musicians disagreed. They were happy to associate blackness with ragtime as a modern genre developed by African Americans and thus uniquely suited to black musical aesthetics. James Reese Europe, composer and the conductor/founder of the Clef Club Orchestra, consistently promoted his organization's ragtime as "a kind of symphony music that no matter what else you think, is different and distinctive, and lends itself to the playing of the peculiar compositions of our race."[32] He asserted that "music breathes the spirit of a race and, strictly speaking, it is a part only of the race which creates it."[33] Europe's belief in the innate musicality of African Americans was shared by most musicians and critics of the time period.

The overwhelming success of Irving Berlin's 1911 Tin Pan Alley song "Alexander's Ragtime Band" marked a significant change in the reception of ragtime by white audiences and critics. White writers crowned Berlin the "King of Ragtime" and began to downplay the African American musicians who had previously dominated the genre. Many white singers stopped blacking up to perform the music. The iconography of sheet music covers changed from the overt racism of minstrelsy-style visual stereotypes in favor of images of white performers associated with a particular piece. In this context, the widespread practice of "ragging the classics" (i.e. arrangements of famous classical pieces using syncopated rhythms) changed from a method of musically representing respectability through a demonstration of black musicians' familiarity with white art music, to a way of "whiting" African American music. By washing ragtime through pieces by white classical composers, the style could be wiped of some of its association with black music and, in the racial logic of the early twentieth century, become Americanized. Although black musicians, such as James Reese Europe, still insisted that ragtime was a black art form, the rhetoric used by white people about the genre indicates that for many of them ragtime had become increasingly divorced from blackness. Instead, they called the music simply "American" or American "folk" music – a designation which allowed them to suggest an intimate connection to American identity without having to confront race directly. The Act II finale of Irving Berlin's first musical, *Watch Your Step* (1914), is an example of this process. In this long choral number, Berlin takes quotations from six well-known operas and incorporates them into ragtime dances. Meanwhile, an actor playing Giuseppe Verdi begs the chorus not to ruin the melodies by ragging them. The chorus rejects his entreaties, singing that they must modify those old European melodies to fit the needs of the new energetic and youthful American nation. When Berlin promoted the show, he amplified the message in his music by declaring "rag-time is the one distinctive American contribution to the musical materials of the world."[34]

By the time Gershwin began composing, he would have heard "ragged" music all over New York. Perhaps, then, it should come as no surprise that his first composition, "Ragging the Traumerei" (1913) is an example of "ragging the classics." It is striking, however, that from the beginning of his compositional career, he was thinking about ways to combine classical and popular styles.[35] "The Real American Folksong (is a Rag)" (1917), the first song by George Gershwin with lyrics by his brother Ira, demonstrates that the Gershwins understood the cycle of cultural appropriation followed by claims of nationalism that arguably began in minstrelsy.[36] Gershwin's musical setting is not a traditional rag, as the verse is in 6/8, but the cut-time chorus features the syncopated rhythms typical of ragtime.[37] This metrical change follows the text. The song opens with "Near Barcelona the peasant crooned / The old traditional Spanish tunes / The Neapolitan street song sighs" – effectively placing folk music within European rural traditional cultures with the text and lilting melody. The rest of the lyrics, which Ira called "too much like an essay" read like an artistic manifesto.[38] They go on to assert that American folksongs are superior to other folk traditions because they are rhythmically exciting, reflecting the energy of the American people and the youth of the nation itself. "With folk songs plaintive and others gay / In their own peculiar way. American folk songs, I feel, / Have a much stronger appeal ... For it's inoculated / With a syncopated / Sort of meter, / Sweeter / than a classic strain; ... The real American folk song is like a Fountain of Youth."[39] The change to cut time in the chorus reorients the music toward ragtime and away from what, in this context, is the dowdy meter of 6/8. Ragtime reflected the young, vigorous, and healthy image that many people, including George Gershwin, had of America. Ira's lyrics accurately describe ragtime's journey from a genre at first vilified or at least dismissed by critics to one celebrated for its American qualities. There is no overt mention of ragtime as black music, only the insistence that rags are American music.

Framed in similar terms to the anxiety over ragtime twenty years earlier, jazz was, if anything, an even more controversial subject in the early 1920s. The so-called "Jazz Problem" affected composers and critics alike as they struggled to describe this new style, its proper cultural position, and its artistic worth. Opinions ranged from views similar to those held by violinist Franz Drdla, who thought that "jazz is the characteristic folk music of modernity," to Anne Shaw Faulkner, who warned her readers of "jazz music and its evil influence on the young people of to-day."[40] As in ragtime, African American critics were divided between praising jazz as a black art form and denouncing it for its musical impurity or stylistic characteristics that left jazz open to racist critiques of the music and the people associated with it. African American critic J. Cogdell's complaints about jazz echoed those of some white writers when he described what he saw as jazz's vulgarity. He warned that the music would corrupt its listeners and castigated the genre for its wholesale appropriation of musical styles.

> Our prohibited instincts riot disgustingly here like thirsty men in a desert oasis; we revel in "jazz." This "lets off steam" but it deplorably cheapens our instincts and corrupts the true spirit of music. Jazz is essentially a capitalistic production, it steals its melodies from all sources, the Masters, the Negroes, the Orient, with naïve greed and unconcern, then proceeds to ruin them. It is as noisy and rapacious as the system that creates it.[41]

Cogdell's comments, couched in a critique of capitalism, is a condemnation of jazz's transgressive exuberance. Critics agreed that the style could not be contained as it sprawled from popular to art music; its performers and composers were black and white, Christian and Jewish; it was found in dance halls and in musical theater productions; it ranged from improvisatory band charts to scored symphonic compositions. Cogdell dismissed jazz for its impurities and its enthusiastic appropriation of the Masters (art music), the Negroes, and the Orient (by which he meant Jewish musicians). Jazz challenged not just artistic paradigms, but also cultural, racial, and social structures.[42]

When he talked about jazz later in his career, George Gershwin used rhetoric that was similar in approach to that used by him and his brother in "The Real American Folksong (is a Rag)." While Gershwin defended jazz against racist propaganda, he also tried to separate jazz from black antecedents by focusing on its transformation from black folk music to a style that connected to all Americans through its rhythmic energy and modernity. In several essays, he repeatedly made a clear distinction between black music and American music.

> In speaking of jazz there is one superstition, and it is a superstition which must be destroyed. This is the superstition that jazz is essentially Negro. The Negroes, of course, take to jazz, but in its essence it is no more Negro than is syncopation, which exists in the music of all nations. Jazz is not Negro but American. It is the spontaneous expression of the nervous energy of modern American life.[43]

Gershwin recognized that the development of jazz reception and music was comparable to that of ragtime, for in the same article he writes: "The more one studies the history of jazz during the last fifteen years the more one realizes that it is following precisely the same course that all dances of the past have followed. Beginning with crudity and vulgarity, it has gradually been freeing itself and moving towards a higher plane."[44] In 1927, Gershwin wrote that jazz might seem to be a black form of music, but that did not take away from its American nature, which he was careful to say was not "negroid" but rather was "black and white. It is all colors and all souls unified in the great melting pot of the world."[45]

Gershwin's early compositions demonstrate a knowledge of American folk songs, a growing commitment to jazz, and an interest in classical music. He composed many Tin Pan Alley songs, some of which exhibited influences from various combinations of Americana, jazz, and European music including "We're Six Little Nieces of Our Uncle Sam" (1917 or 1918, featuring quotations from patriotic songs paired with musical exoticism reminiscent of *The Mikado* by Gilbert and Sullivan), "Little Sunbeam" (1918, which contains bold harmonies that Gershwin marked a "Debussyian vamp"), "Yan-Kee" (1920, a bluesy parody inspired by Puccini's *Madame Butterfly*), "Yankee Doodle Blues" (1922, a humorous song with hints of the blues along with extended quotations from "Yankee Doodle"), and "Mischa, Jascha, Toscha, Sascha" (1921). This last piece was a novelty song performed, according to Ira, "by the writers at the slightest provocation."[46] Ira's text pays tribute to four Russian-born Jewish violinists (Mischa Elman, Jascha Heifetz, Toscha Seidel, and Sascha Jacobsen) who were stalwarts in the flourishing New York party scene that George also frequented. Dena Rosenberg argues that the text represents the Gershwins' ideas about highbrow and lowbrow music.[47] The brothers contrast classical music (stiff but important) with popular music (syncopated and American). "For though we play the high-brow stuff, / We also like the syncopations / Of Uncle Sammy . . . We're only human / And like to shake a leg to jazz . . . High-brow He-brow may play low-brow / In his privacy. / But when concert halls are packed, / Watch us stiffen up and act."[48] The music is equally witty. For example, open fifths – the intervals that violinists use to tune their instruments – accompany the moment the four violinists' names are sung. A parody of "Humoresque" by Dvořák and a few bluesy chords liven up the otherwise rather straightforward Tin Pan Alley-style accompaniment. At the same time, Gershwin also composed two concert pieces – *Novelette in Fourths* (1919), which he recorded on a piano roll, and *Lullaby* (1919) for string quartet. Just a few years later, he composed art music that included jazz influences, effectively washing jazz through white compositions and helping to validate his contention that jazz was American not black music. Although *Rhapsody in Blue* is the most famous early example of the juxtaposition of classical music and jazz in Gershwin's output, it was a slightly earlier piece that sent him down the path of truly combining the two styles – the one-act opera *Blue Monday*.

Blue Monday: A Way Forward by Looking Back

Gershwin wrote *Blue Monday*, a one-act opera with lyrics by B.D. DeSylva, to open the second act of the 1922 production of *George White's Scandals*.[49] George White was a dancer turned impresario who organized yearly editions of revues he called *Scandals* between 1919 and 1939. DeSylva and Gershwin, who wrote the music for the *Scandals* produced between 1920 and 1924, originally pitched the idea of a one-act blackface opera to White relatively early in the compositional process for the 1922 show, but White rejected the concept. Not long before the show went into rehearsals, however, White changed his mind. DeSylva and Gershwin claimed they wrote the entire opera in only five days.

Although some scholars speculate that the success of *Shuffle Along* (1921), the first African American musical on Broadway since 1910, was the impetus for *Blue Monday*, there are many antecedents for opera performed as part of popular entertainment. Edward Jablonski reports that Gershwin called the work a "vaudeville opera."[50] This designation acknowledges the long history of operatic performance in vaudeville, revues, and as part of other types of musical theater. Opera was presented in many different guises in popular entertainment. Minstrel shows frequently contained operatic parodies. Twenty to thirty minutes of opera arias, choruses, and sometimes even condensed versions of operas closed most all-black vaudeville shows at the turn of the twentieth century. Many pianists, violinists, harpists, and singers performed operatic excerpts, arrangements, and arias in short vaudeville acts. For example, Valerie Bergere and Company presented a one-act play "taken from the opera *Carmen*" on the Keith–Albee vaudeville circuit in 1905 and 1906.[51] Gustave Kerker's *Burning to Sing or Singing to Burn*, a comedic one-act opera, first appeared on American vaudeville bills in 1904, and was still being performed as late as 1925. Skits featuring references to famous opera singers and impresarios were also a staple of vaudeville and the pre-War *Ziegfeld Follies*. Newly composed operatic works destined for vaudeville were often played for laughs and poked fun at operatic musical conventions and the peculiarities of wealthy but shallow opera lovers. An exception was *The Patriot* by Julian Edwards, a one-act "grand" opera about a fictional attempt on George Washington's life at Valley Forge which was performed on the vaudeville circuit in 1908 and 1909. *Blue Monday* breaks new ground because of its tragic ending and jazz, rather than ragtime, influences. At about twenty-five minutes, *Blue Monday* was too long (and too serious) for an otherwise upbeat revue that ran over three hours. Although the work received positive critical notice after the out-of-town tryout in New Haven, White cut *Blue Monday* from the *Scandals* following its New York premiere on August 28, 1922.

Set in Harlem, the libretto tells the story of a working-class African American woman (Vi) who shoots and kills her lover (Joe) in a fit of jealous rage thinking that he has received a telegram from another woman. In fact, the telegram informed him that his mother had died three years previously, but Vi had been misled by Tom, a gambler she rejected earlier in the opera, who told her that the message was from a rival. The working-class characters, the setting in a black neighborhood, and the use of jazz harmonies combined with operatic elements clearly presages *Porgy and Bess*. Will Vodery arranged *Blue Monday* and added the inscription "An Afro-American Opera" to his copy of the score. One reviewer, Gordon Whyte, was particularly complimentary of Vodery's arrangement, writing: "Whoever scored the orchestration is a master ... At times it is symphonic in structure and the instrumentation is never muddled and always cleverly thought out."[52] Vodery, who arranged the score for *Shuffle Along*, had worked in musical theater and vaudeville since at least 1904. In 1922 he was one of the most important arrangers in New York. His description of the work accounts for not only the race of the characters, but also subtly asserts jazz as a black musical style and the lives of African Americans as a suitable subject for art music. The caption is rather poignant because Vodery knew black composers, including Will Marion Cook and H. Lawrence Freeman, who had tried to get their operatic work taken seriously for years with little success.[53]

Blue Monday is an opera because of formal distinctions: it is continuous and includes recitative. In other ways, however, the work features the same stylistic variety and overt references to highbrow and lowbrow music that were common in musicals. One reviewer described *Blue Monday* as "a little bit of 'La Boheme' with the Liebestod of 'Tristan' to close, burlesqued almost beyond recognition, but was remarkably swung."[54] The reference to *Tristan und Isolde* may have been a rather sloppy comparison to an opera with a tragic ending, since there is little in *Blue Monday* that is reminiscent of Wagner's music. Allusions to *Pagliacci* by Ruggero Leoncavallo, however, are clear enough. Both pieces have an opening prologue that primes the audience for the drama to come. The two works also share some plot points including a gossip who provokes the lead character's jealousy by repeating an overheard conversation and the murder at the end. Gershwin also included quotations from Felix Mendelssohn's "Wedding March" in a short section that was cut prior to the first performance.[55]

The prologue opens with a timpani solo, immediately evoking a connection between drumming and the black characters. Constantly changing emotional affect, the prologue careens from jazzy melodic figures that Gershwin would return to in *Rhapsody in Blue* to dramatic passages that support Joe's announcement that the piece would be "in operatic style and like the white man's opera the theme will be love! Hate! Passion! Jealousy." A bluesy Tin Pan Alley song (the titular "Blue Monday") sung by Sam the janitor follows the prologue. In quick succession, Gershwin stylistically evokes, in only about twenty-five minutes, an aria, a spiritual, an upbeat Broadway dance, and melodrama.[56] Gershwin quoted himself in two sections when he recycled the melody from his *Lullaby* (1919) in the prologue and in the centerpiece of the work, Vi's aria "Has Anyone Seen My Joe." Between each number, the opera is held together with a connective tissue of reprises of earlier themes, jazz licks, recitative, and anticipatory passages that add to the sense of heightened (even overheated) drama that infuses the work. Jablonski described Joe's aria, "I'm Going to See My Mother," dismissively as a "mammy song," but other writers have described it as a spiritual with its simple, heartfelt melody and thin texture.[57] Joe forgives Vi for shooting him with a reprise of "I'm Going to See My Mother" as he prepares himself for a reunion in the hereafter. The work ends with Vi's operatic flourish of despair when she realizes she has killed Joe over her baseless suspicions. The spiritual-like qualities of the music, enhanced by Vodery's soaring orchestration (complete with chimes), brings the opera to a melodramatic close.

Blue Monday's kaleidoscopic score fits right into the already almost schizophrenic combination of many different musical and theatrical styles typical of a revue. In some ways, *Blue Monday* resembles the stand-alone

Act II finales that appeared in some early musical comedies, because it is long, stylistically varied, and tells a coherent story. In this case, the ragtime melodrama that closes Act II of Irving Berlin's *Stop! Look! Listen!* (1915) is a plausible comparison. *Blue Monday* is also reminiscent of the operatic burlesques that included Tin Pan Alley-style songs as well as overt musical and textual references to specific works performed by Weber and Fields at the beginning of the century, including Victor Herbert's *The Magic Knight* (1906).

The critical reaction to the opera was generally positive. Out of nine reviews, only one writer hated the work. Charles Darnton thundered that it was "the most dismal, stupid and incredible black-face sketch that has probably ever been perpetrated. In it a dusky soprano finally killed her gambling man. She should have shot all her associates the moment they appeared and then turned the pistol on herself."[58] But others enjoyed *Blue Monday* and were ready to anoint it an American opera – a designation that had eluded composers such as George Bristow, William Henry Fry, and many others for generations. By the early 1920s, the anxiety among some critics about the lack of an American operatic style was becoming intense. Set against this context, it is remarkable that a New Haven critic called *Blue Monday* the "first real American opera ... a genuinely human plot of American life, set to music in the popular vein, using jazz only at the right moments, the sentimental song, 'The Blues,' and above all a new and free ragtime recitative."[59]

Although some critics mentioned that the characters in *Blue Monday* were supposed to be African American, only one (Charles Darnton's negative commentary) pointed out that the singers were blacked up. The other reviews either described the work as being about "colored people" without specifying the actual race of the singers, or ignored the issue altogether. This willful blindness to race was not unusual. Blacking up was so common that critics often did not comment upon it. Many white people at the time were completely oblivious to the racism inherent in blackface, instead seeing it as merely a mask little different from other types of costumes.[60]

Just as earlier composers had effectively "whited" ragtime by combining it with influences from classical music, Gershwin accomplished the same thing with *Blue Monday* and jazz. Another way of looking at *Blue Monday* and his later classical works is that Gershwin was injecting elements of blackness into classical music. Gershwin's statements contending that jazz was an American musical style and minimizing the genre as a black art form, however, demonstrate that in the early 1920s, he seemed to be more interested in introducing whiteness into jazz. He boasted, for instance, that with *Rhapsody in Blue* he had "succeeded in showing that jazz is not merely a dance; it comprises bigger themes and purposes."[61] Gershwin was not the only person to write music that tried to straddle the divide between jazz and classical music. Both Edmund Jenkins and John Powell composed symphonic jazz pieces well before Gershwin, but it was his music that caught the sustained attention of critics and, perhaps more importantly, Paul Whiteman.

Many reviewers emphasized that Paul Whiteman's Palais Royale Orchestra was one of the best things about the 1922 *Scandals*. The band provided the accompaniment for many of the numbers and performed some instrumental solos. Critic Charles Pike Sawyer reported that "the greatest hit of the evening was Paul Whiteman and his orchestra, which 'jazzed' Schubert and Beethoven symphonies to applause that was loud and long."[62] The 1922 *Scandals* was the first time that Gershwin and Whiteman worked together. This engagement kicked off a professional relationship that would be important to both of them for years to come. Gershwin wrote *Rhapsody in Blue* for the famous "An Experiment in Modern Music" concert Whiteman organized in 1924. The following year, Whiteman revived *Blue Monday* (renaming it *135th Street*), and he also programmed many Gershwin songs throughout his career. Whiteman's Modern Music concert was just the venue that Gershwin needed to launch his foray into art music. Critics were ready to hear Gershwin's compositions as a promising new development in American music in part because Whiteman had been priming them to hear music similar to Gershwin's as the next logical step in the development of jazz and American classical music with his own concerts and relentless promotion of his style of polished, concert jazz.

In 1924, Gershwin's steadily growing reputation as a young composer with a bright future came to fruition with the success of *Rhapsody in Blue* and his first hit musical, *Lady, Be Good!*. The seeds for both these pivotal works were planted in 1922 with some of the pieces for the *Scandals* of that year. *Blue Monday* contains many hints of Gershwin's skillful combination of jazz and classical music that matured with *Rhapsody in Blue* and later in *Porgy and Bess*. "(I'll Build a) Stairway to Paradise" – the big production number at the end of Act I in the *Scandals* – was also an important precursor to the harmonically complex, bluesy popular songs that would propel the rest of Gershwin's career.

Blue Monday seems to have stimulated Gershwin's desire to write an American opera. In a 1925 interview with Herbert S. Greenhalgh around the time Whiteman revived *Blue Monday*, Gershwin, using the racist and essentialist language common to the 1920s, said that "I shall certainly write an opera and I shall write it for niggers. Blacks sing beautifully. They are always singing; they have it in their blood. They have jazz in their blood, too, and I have no doubt that they will be able to do full justice to a jazz opera."[63] Gershwin's initial attempt at American opera with *Blue Monday*, a piece designed not for the opera house but for the popular stage, demonstrates his ambition to be a composer who bridged divides between popular and classical, highbrow and lowbrow, musicals and operas, European and American national styles. This desire was shared by many early twentieth-century composers because it was at the heart of popular staged entertainments. Although scholars often think of Gershwin as a modernist who sought to bring the vitality of the American city to the staid confines of American art music, his work is grounded not in the conventions of classical music, but that of the theatrical traditions, economic pressures, and racial dynamics of New York City before the Great War. His music was born out of not just a turn to the future, but also a firm grasp of the past.

Notes

1. George Gershwin, "Jazz Is the Voice of the American Soul" (orig. pub. *Theatre Magazine*, March 1927), in Gregory R. Suriano (ed.), *Gershwin in His Time: A Biographical Scrapbook, 1919–1937* (New York: Gramercy Books, 1998), 47–48.
2. Stephen E. Gilbert, *The Music of Gershwin* (New Haven: Yale University Press, 1995); Christopher A. Reynolds, "*Porgy and Bess*: 'An American *Wozzeck*,'" *Journal of the Society for American Music* 1/1 (February 2007), 1–28.
3. Susan E. Neimoyer, "*Rhapsody in Blue*: A Culmination of George Gershwin's Early Musical Education," Ph.D. diss., University of Washington (2003), 34.
4. Mark Tucker, "In Search of Will Vodery," *Black Music Research Journal* 16/1 (Spring 1996), 127–30.
5. Isaac Goldberg, *George Gershwin: A Study in American Music* (New York: Frederick Ungar, 1958), 77.
6. George Newell, "George Gershwin and Jazz," *The Outlook* (February 29, 1928), cf. Suriano (ed.), *Gershwin in His Time*, 55.
7. Edward Jablonski, *Gershwin* (New York: Doubleday, 1987), 98.
8. Carol J. Oja, *Making Music Modern: New York in the 1920s* (New York: Oxford University Press, 2000), 318–60.
9. Gerald Bordman, *American Operetta: From H.M.S. Pinafore to Sweeney Todd* (New York: Oxford University Press, 1992) and *American Musical Theatre: A Chronicle*, 3rd edn (New York: Oxford University Press, 2001); Ethan Mordden, *Make Believe: The Broadway Musical in the 1920s* (New York: Oxford University Press, 1997); Robert W. Snyder, *The Voice of the City: Vaudeville and Popular Culture in New York* (New York: Oxford University Press, 1989); and Larry Stempel, *Showtime: A History of the Broadway Musical Theater* (New York: W.W. Norton, 2010).
10. Irene Heskes, "Music as Social History: American Yiddish Theater Music, 1882–1920," *American Music* 2/4 (Winter 1984), 73–87; Edna Nahshon, ed., *New York's Yiddish Theater: From the Bowery to Broadway* (New York: Columbia University Press, 2016); Nahma Sandrow, *Vagabond Stars: A World History of Yiddish Theater* (New York: Harper & Row, 1977); Mark Slobin, "Music in the Yiddish Theater and Cinema, 1880–1950," in Joshua S. Walden (ed.), *The Cambridge Companion to Jewish Music* (Cambridge: Cambridge University Press, 2015), 215–27.
11. Walter Rimler, *George Gershwin: An Intimate Portrait* (Urbana and Chicago: University of Illinois Press, 2009), 39.
12. Goldberg, *Gershwin*, 41.

13. Handwritten autobiographical note, Writings by Will Marion Cook, Mercer Cook Papers, Box 157–9, folder 6, Moorland-Spingarn Research Center, Manuscript Division, Howard University, Washington, D.C.
14. Thomas L. Riis, ed., *The Music and Scripts of* In Dahomey (Madison, WI: A-R Editions, 1996), xiv.
15. For examples, see Stage Manager's Reports for *The Echo* (1910–1911), *The Old Town* (1911), and *Over the River* (1911), Box 30, Charles Bancroft Dillingham Papers, Manuscripts and Archives Division, The New York Public Library, Astor, Lenox and Tilden Foundations (hereafter Dillingham Papers).
16. Jeffrey Magee, *Irving Berlin's American Musical Theater* (New York: Oxford University Press, 2012), 36.
17. Contract between producer Charles B. Dillingham and Irving Berlin for *Stop! Look! Listen!* Box 32, Dillingham Papers. Correspondence between Dillingham and others concerning the London production of *Watch Your Step.* Box 13, Dillingham Papers. Neil Gould, *Victor Herbert: A Theatrical Life* (New York: Fordham University Press, 2008), 281.
18. Edward Jablonski, "Gershwin on Music," *Musical America* 82/7 (July 1962), 33.
19. Larry Starr, *George Gershwin* (New Haven, CT: Yale University Press, 2011), 159–60.
20. Charles B. Dillingham to Victor Herbert, December 5, [1903], Box 1, Dillingham Papers.
21. Herbert to Dillingham, December 9, 1903, Box 1, Dillingham Papers.
22. Dillingham to Herbert, undated [probably late December 1903], Box 1, Dillingham Papers (emphasis in the original).
23. Herbert to Dillingham, January 13, 1904, Box 1, Dillingham Papers (emphasis in the original).
24. Dillingham to Herbert, January 18, 1904, Box 1, Dillingham Papers.
25. Herbert to Dillingham, January 20, 1904, Box 1, Dillingham Papers (emphasis in the original).
26. Edward A. Berlin, *Ragtime: A Musical and Cultural History* (Berkeley: University of California Press, 1980), 25.
27. "The Stage," *Freeman* (Indianapolis), June 19, 1897, 6.
28. Berlin, *Ragtime*, 1.
29. Report of Providence Show, Week of September 15, 1902 and John J. Keirans, Criticism of First Show, Philadelphia, September 22 [1902], Keith-Albee Manager Reports, September 2, 1902–September 3, 1903, Keith/Albee Collection, The University of Iowa Libraries, Iowa City, Iowa.
30. "War on Ragtime" (orig. pub. *American Musician*, July 1901), in Kip Lornell (ed.), *From Jubilee to Hip Hop: Readings in African American Music* (Upper Saddle River, NJ: Prentice Hall, 2010), 24.
31. "What 'The Concert-Goer' says of the 'The Negro Music Journal,'" *Negro Music Journal* 1/2 (October 1902), 28.
32. "Negro's Place in Music," *Evening Post* (March 13, 1914). Cf. David Gilbert, *The Product of Our Souls: Ragtime, Race, and the Birth of the Manhattan Musical Marketplace* (Chapel Hill: University of North Carolina Press, 2015), 182.
33. Ibid., 183.
34. Julian Johnson, "Irving Berlin – A Restless Success," *The Theatre* 21/168 (February 1915), 97.
35. Howard Pollack, *George Gershwin: His Life and Work* (Berkeley: University of California Press, 2006), 219.
36. See Eric Lott, *Love & Theft: Blackface Minstrelsy and the American Working Class* (New York: Oxford University Press, 1993).
37. Gilbert, *The Music of Gershwin*, 41–45.
38. Deena Rosenberg, *Fascinating Rhythm: The Collaboration of George and Ira Gershwin* (Ann Arbor: University of Michigan Press, 1997), 35.
39. Ira Gershwin, *Lyrics on Several Occasions* (New York: Alfred A. Knopf, 1959), 180–81.
40. "Where the Etude Stands on Jazz," *The Etude*, XLII/8 (August 1924), 517–20. Cf. Stephanie Doktor, "'The Jazz Problem': How U.S. Composers Grappled with the Sounds of Blackness, 1917–1925," Ph.D. diss., University of Virginia (2016), 2; Anne Shaw Faulkner, "Does Jazz Put the Sin in Syncopation?" *Ladies Home Journal* 38/8 (August 1921), 16.
41. J. Cogdell, "Truth in Art in America," *Messenger: New Opinion of the Negro* 5/3 (March 3, 1923) 636 (italics in the original).
42. Scott Appelrouth, "Constructing the Meaning of Early Jazz, 1917–1930," *Poetics* 31 (2003), 117–31.

43. George Gershwin, "Our New National Anthem," *Theatre Magazine* (August, 1925). Cf. Suriano (ed.), *Gershwin in His Time*, 27.
44. Ibid., 27.
45. Gershwin, "Jazz Is the Voice of the American Soul," cf. Suriano (ed.), *Gershwin in His Time*, 48.
46. Gershwin, *Lyrics*, 177.
47. Rosenberg, *Fascinating Rhythm*, 44.
48. Gershwin, *Lyrics*, 178.
49. Leo A. Marsh, *New York Morning Telegraph* (August 30, 1922).
50. Jablonski, *Gershwin*, 50; Pollack, *Gershwin*, 270.
51. H.T. Jordan, Report on Philadelphia Show, December 11, 1905, Keith-Albee Managers' Report Book, September 4, 1905–April 23, 1906, Keith/Albee Collection, The University of Iowa Libraries, Iowa City, Iowa.
52. Gordon Whyte, "Scandals of 1922," *The Billboard* (September 9, 1922).
53. Will Marion Cook, "Clorindy, the Origin of the Cakewalk," in Eileen Southern (ed.), *Readings in Black American Music*, 2nd edn (New York: W.W. Norton, 1983), 229.
54. Charles Pike Sawyer, "Scandals of 1922 Is Most Pleasing," *Post* (August 29, 1922) in Biographical Scrapbook, Book 1, microfilm #93/20013, George and Ira Gershwin Collection, Music Division, Library of Congress, Washington, D.C. (hereafter Gershwin Scrapbook #1).
55. Wayne D. Shirley, "Notes on George Gershwin's First Opera," *I.S.A.M. Newsletter* 11/2 (May 1982), 9.
56. John Andrew Johnson, "Gershwin's *Blue Monday* (1922) and the Promise of Success," in Wayne Schneider (ed.), *The Gershwin Style: New Looks at the Music of George Gershwin* (New York: Oxford University Press, 1999), 111–41.
57. Jablonski, *Gershwin*, 52; Goldberg, *Gershwin*, 122; Johnson, "Gershwin's *Blue Monday*," 120.
58. Charles Darnton, "The New Plays," *World* (New York City), undated, 1922, Gershwin Scrapbook #1.
59. "White's Scandals of 1922 Score Triumph," unknown newspaper or date, New Haven, CT, Gershwin Scrapbook #1.
60. It is outside the scope of this chapter to discuss the complicated reception of blackface among white audiences. See the Appendix in Christopher J. Smith, *The Creolization of American Culture: William Sidney Mount and the Roots of Blackface Minstrelsy* (Chicago: University of Illinois Press, 2014), 217–33 for a critical essay on blackface scholarship.
61. Gershwin, "Jazz Is the Voice of the American Soul." Cf. Suriano (ed.), *Gershwin in His Time*, 49.
62. Sawyer, "'Scandals of 1922' Is Most Pleasing," Gershwin Scrapbook #1. The only program I have discovered from that year's *Scandals*, dated October 9, 1922, does not include a reference to the "jazzed" classical music Sawyer and others described in the reviews of the premiere. The playbill can be found in the Theatrical Productions Collection, George White *Scandals*, Box 1, Museum of the City of New York.
63. Herbert S. Greenhalgh, "When We Have Jazz Opera: An Interview with Mr. George Gershwin," *Musical Canada* 6/10 (October 1925), 13.

6 Broadway in Blue: Gershwin's Musical Theater Scores and Songs

TODD DECKER

George Gershwin composed for the Broadway stage for two decades. Two songs – single numbers in shows featuring several songwriters – bookend this area of Gershwin's output: "Making of a Girl" in the *Passing Show of 1916* and "By Strauss" in the 1936 revue *The Show Is On* (both productions played the Winter Garden Theatre). In the intervening years, Gershwin was the sole credited composer on twenty-two musical shows, and songs by Gershwin were included in nineteen more productions. From 1924 to 1932, Gershwin was a dominant commercial and artistic force on the New York musical stage.

Gershwin was six years old in 1904 when Longacre Square – where Broadway crosses 7th Avenue – was re-named Times Square. The opening of the subway that same year spurred the rapid development of an entertainment district around the system's 42nd Street and Broadway hub. During his early career as a song plugger on Tin Pan Alley – a cluster of popular song publishers on and around West 28th Street – Gershwin witnessed the explosive growth in theater construction just a few blocks to the north in the midtown rectangle loosely bounded by 6th and 8th Avenues and 41st and 54th Streets. He eagerly joined the ranks of Broadway songwriters as soon as he could, aspiring to compose, he remembered in 1931, "production music – the kind Jerome Kern was writing."[1] In 1919, at the age of twenty-one, Gershwin's first full score for a Broadway show, *La-La-Lucille!*, played a modest 104-performance run at Henry Miller's Theatre (today replaced by the Stephen Sondheim). As his career writing for the popular stage took off in the mid-1920s, Gershwin was at the center of Broadway's heyday as an engine of American popular music (just before the emergence of mass media musical formats like network radio and sound film). His final shows faced the harsh effects of the 1929 Stock Market Crash (after which Broadway production activity plummeted).

Gershwin contributed to the full range of musical theater genres on offer between the two world wars. He composed entire scores for revues, musical comedies, and operettas – the three principal types of musical shows. Gershwin's 1935 "folk opera" *Porgy and Bess* (124 performances) – a musical theater work outside Broadway norms for the time (although it opened in a commercial engagement at the Alvin Theatre) – sits squarely in the interwar genre of the black-cast show, the fourth sort of musical typical of the time. (For more on *Porgy and Bess*, see chapters 9 and 10, this volume.) No other Broadway songwriter or composer impacted every kind of Broadway musical show like Gershwin did.

Gershwin's career began with songs interpolated into shows featuring multiple songwriters – a common practice for emerging talents. One of these songs, "Swanee," scored as Gershwin's first commercial hit after Broadway star Al Jolson added it to his specialty act in the *Capitol Revue* (1919). From 1920 to 1924, Gershwin had a recurring job composing songs for *George White's Scandals*, an annual summer season revue that emphasized up-to-date song and dance. Isaac Goldberg, Gershwin's earliest biographer and a helpful period guide to Broadway in the 1920s, noted in 1931 that the *Scandals* provided the young composer with "firmly-entrenched recognition on Broadway."[2] After some early opportunities to compose complete scores for book shows – *Primrose* (1924) for London's West End; *Sweet Little Devil* (1924, 120 performances) for Broadway, in addition to *La-La-Lucille!* – Gershwin hit his stride as a theater composer with *Lady, Be Good!* (1924, 330 performances), a defining musical comedy of the decade. Gershwin wrote eight more musical comedies in the next five years, most all in the mold of *Lady, Be Good!* – set in the present, in fashionable East Coast locales, peopled with vibrant young characters who find love by way of farcical, lightly romantic plots. Gershwin's older brother Ira, who became his principal songwriting partner with *Lady, Be Good!*, was the sole lyricist on all of these but *Sweet Little Devil*, whose lyricist was B.G. DeSylva. Any survey of George's Broadway must include the equal contribution of Ira: this chapter is about both.

In 1925, Gershwin shared composing duties with composer Herbert Stothart on an uncharacteristic project, a romantic operetta about the Russian revolution set in Moscow and Paris titled *Song of the Flame* (219 performances; Stothart and Oscar Hammerstein II wrote the lyrics). But further operettas in this grand style were not in Gershwin's future. Instead, the Gershwin brothers teamed up with bookwriters George S. Kaufmann and Morrie Ryskind to create three satirical, political operettas in the British tradition of Gilbert and Sullivan: *Strike Up the Band* (1930, 191 performances; a 1927 version closed during out-of-town tryouts before reaching Broadway); *Of Thee I Sing* (1932, 441 performances, winner of the Pulitzer Prize for drama); and *Let 'em Eat Cake* (1933, 90 performances, a commercially unsuccessful sequel to *Of Thee I Sing*). Gershwin's final Broadway musical – the 1933 flop *Pardon My English* (46 performances) – has the sardonic edge of musical comedy, but its setting in Germany and several waltzes suggest Broadway operetta. Ira's lyrics consistently reference or mock operetta yet select numbers, such as the love duet "Tonight," would not be out of place in a work that takes itself more seriously. Tensions between "German" and American music, understood to be jazz, play out as well: with the operetta-singing ingénue prevailing romantically over her torch- and blues-singing rival. *Porgy and Bess* followed, after which the Gershwins moved to Hollywood where George died unexpectedly in 1937 after writing songs for two film musicals made by RKO and starring Fred Astaire (*Shall We Dance* and *A Damsel in Distress*, both 1937).

For virtually the entire span of his professional and creative life – even as he carved out a place in the concert hall with works like *Rhapsody in Blue* (1924) and *An American in Paris* (1928) – Gershwin was invested in the collaborative process of making Broadway musicals, a creative sphere with specific challenges within which he was an important commercial and artistic force. This chapter considers Gershwin's work as a composer of scores and songs for the Broadway stage from two complementary angles: form and content. First: form. Successful Broadway shows in Gershwin's time sought to reconcile a formal tension between the whole and the parts: shows succeeded as wholes (an evening's or afternoon's entertainment in a New York theater) but were composed of somewhat autonomous constituent parts (individual songs and performers). It was Gershwin's job, working with a varied group of musical theater professionals, to balance these two imperatives in the musical realm (the primary focus in this consideration of musical theater, a multifaceted art of which music is only a part). Second: content. Gershwin's Broadway songs and scores, like his concert music, were understood to be marked by the sounds of popular syncopated music of the 1920s – at the time called jazz. The content of his shows included many audible and textual links to this music, which was understood to be derived from African American sources but was swiftly being claimed by white Americans. Gershwin's musical comedies did important and subtle cultural work moving jazz into mainstream white mass culture. But before exploring larger questions of form and content, the very accessibility of Gershwin's Broadway shows from the perspective of the present bears consideration.

Gershwin's musicals were built for the moment with no thought for posterity. Specific performers – and those performers' connection with the New York audience – were essential to their effect. In historical terms, this has meant that none of Gershwin's musicals enjoyed enduring afterlives. Only twice have commercial producers attempted to bring a Gershwin musical back to Broadway: a revived *Of Thee I Sing* lasted just 72 performances in 1952; a heavily-revised black-cast version of *Oh, Kay!* failed to find an audience in 1990. (The vibrant revival history of *Porgy and Bess* – brought back to the commercial New York stage five times between 1942 and 2012 – underlines this work's aesthetic distance from Gershwin's other theater scores.) But if Gershwin's musical comedy and operetta scores failed to survive on the commercial stage, many of Gershwin's theater songs endured, forming the core of both the repertory of jazz standards and the so-called great American songbook of pre-rock and roll popular music heard in cabaret and concert and on record. Beginning in the 1980s, a modest trend of "new" Gershwin musicals using select theater and film songs and completely new scripts found success on Broadway. But these "new" musicals – like Gershwin's originals from the 1920s and 1930s – invariably served the commercial requirements of their respective production moments and do not provide any sense for how the shows Gershwin made in his time worked musically, dramatically, or as spectacle. An effective performance of Gershwin's concert works – set down by the composer in standard musical notation – allows us to assess his power as a composer in that realm. How might Gershwin's achievement as a composer of scores and songs for the Broadway stage be understood and re-experienced in similar fashion?

As it happens, a late twentieth-century confluence of scholarship devoted to the popular musical stage, fortuitous archival finds, the height of the compact disc as a recorded music medium, and financial support from the Gershwin family produced a group of ten complete recordings of Gershwin scores for Broadway. This ambitious recovery project – sound-only versions of shows not viable for commercial production – applied the values and priorities of the historical performance movement to works of the American commercial stage. Gershwin's reputation in the concert hall and efforts to bolster his stature as a great American composer surely played into these efforts. Conductor Michael Tilson Thomas, a noted Gershwin interpreter, initiated this cycle of recordings with a 1987 disc for CBS Masterworks, an elite classical label, pairing the operettas *Of Thee I Sing* and *Let 'em Eat Cake*.[3] While orchestrations for the former survived, the latter required reconstruction of the piano-vocal score by John McGlinn and orchestration in historical style by Russell Warner. In the early 1990s, the Leonore S. Gershwin – Library of Congress Recording and Publishing Project released five complete musical scores on the Elektra Nonesuch label, each with liner notes detailing the challenges of reconstructing both musical texts and performance styles: *Girl Crazy* (1930, 272 performances), the 1927 version of *Strike Up the Band*, *Lady, Be Good!*, *Pardon My English*, and *Oh, Kay!* (1927, 256 performances).[4] The death of Leonore S. Gershwin, Ira's widow, prematurely ended this project before the already-recorded 1930 version of *Strike Up the Band!* could be issued (PS Classics released this recording in 2011).[5] In 2001, New World Records – a non-commercial label devoted to American classical and folk music – brought out a box set of *Tip-Toes* and *Tell Me More* (both 1925, 100 and 192 performances).[6] The above Nonesuch and New World releases all feature restored scores supervised by archivist Tommy Krasker. *Tip-Toes* proves an especially important addition to these discs. A complete set of pit orchestra parts for *Tip-Toes* was found in an extensive cache of Broadway scores discovered in a warehouse in Secaucus, New Jersey in the 1980s. The *Tip-Toes* materials, in Krasker's words, offered "one of the very few totally authentic orchestrations from the mid-twenties."[7] The interest, energy, and resources expended on reconstructing Gershwin scores as recordings in the late 1980s and 1990s was facilitated by the historic high point of the compact disc format. Since 2001, this sort of scholarly yet entertaining disc – together with the compact disc itself as a commercially dominant media – has largely disappeared. Indeed, only one further score has been released in the twenty-first century: in 2012, PS Classics issued *Sweet Little Devil* (1924, 120 performances), the musical comedy Gershwin wrote just before *Lady, Be Good!* with lyrics by B.G. DeSylva.[8]

The above body of reconstruction recordings offer invaluable aural introductions to Gershwin's Broadway. (All but *Tip-Toes, Tell Me More, Sweet Little Devil*, and the 1930 *Strike Up the Band* are available on the streaming service Spotify.) Crucially, these discs present Gershwin's theater scores as wholes, helping the listener understand how individual songs – familiar and forgotten – were originally joined into a larger musical theater entertainment. The discs go some distance to revealing the expressive integrity and aesthetic balance that marked these ephemeral Broadway products. Two caveats obtain regarding these recordings: orchestration and singing style. As noted, some original orchestrations survive and can be heard on these discs. However, most of the orchestrations were commissioned expressly for these recordings in a period style. The choice of singers on these discs generally favors musical theater professionals with Broadway experience. Hearing such singers deliver Ira's lyrics as theater songs – articulating for an imagined back row and singing in character – proves especially valuable to dislodging familiar tunes from jazz and pop contexts. (Important musical aspects, often linked to jazz practices, are similarly highlighted by the sensitive insertion of improvised instrumental performance and tap dance.) But Gershwin often composed for specific performers and, in some cases, these performers recorded pop records of songs they were singing onstage. Such period recordings of original stars offer a vital supplement to the reconstruction discs and are referenced below when appropriate: most can be found on the streaming site

YouTube. For the purposes of this introduction to Gershwin and Broadway, the reader is referred to the reconstruction discs as representative of each show. However, any deeper study of these works necessitates a finer-grained assessment of the sources.[9]

Scores and Songs

A new musical playing eight shows a week in a midtown Manhattan theater faced stiff competition in the 1920s. *Lady, Be Good!* opened in December 1924 to a field of nineteen competing shows. At one point in its run, the Gershwins' *Funny Face* (1927, 250 performances) faced off against twenty-four competitors. With the onset of the Great Depression in 1930, the number of new productions plummeted and the construction of new theaters – still going strong in 1928 – stopped cold. When *Of Thee I Sing* opened in December 1931 there were only nine other musicals playing midtown; for much of the summer of 1932, Gershwin's operetta was one of only three musicals still running (the other two survivors were by Jerome Kern). But for most of Gershwin's Broadway career, the musical stage was a vital and expanding commercial arena consistently producing a high volume of product. A run of around 250 performances – about eight months – marked a solid success.

This rapid turnover in new musicals (by later and certainly contemporary Broadway standards) rewarded creators who worked quickly and confidently, as Gershwin did. Shows were made in a matter of weeks around the talents and personas of individual performers. Topicality informed the plots, the jokes, and the singing and dancing. Revues were constructed around comic sketches, often including song and dance, and production numbers and musical specialties. Musical comedies and operettas told two-, sometimes three-act stories through spoken dialogue and sung lyrics. The plots, especially in musical comedies, were often perfunctory. Still, as shown below, a fair amount of the music Gershwin composed in these story-centered genres (and especially in operetta) supported lyrics that set the scene or moved the story forward.

Broadway scores for revues, musical comedies, and operettas alike were made of songs structured around a thirty-two-bar chorus (usually including and repeating the song's title) typically preceded in performance by a freer form verse. Different sets of lyrics for the verse (and sometimes the chorus) helped extend these rather short musical forms into numbers that could also include dancing (usually done to an instrumental arrangement of the chorus). (Operettas generally included some extended stretches of continuous music in varying forms.) Select songs in every musical score were chosen for marketing independently from the show. These separate song commodities had their own commercial lives in the popular music market as sheet music for domestic use and, more and more across the 1920s, also generated income on records and radio, emerging mass media platforms that, together with a show's theatrical run, in turn encouraged sheet music sales. Overtures – rousing medleys of tunes from the score heard before the curtain when up and assembled shortly before opening night – hinted at the anticipated hit songs or, more cynically, tipped the listener to the tunes tapped for sheet music promotion by the show's creators. Not every song in a show was a candidate for such "exploitation," to use an industry term of art. For example, songs sung by the chorus to open acts or scenes were frequently too specific to the show's story and setting to prove suitable for individual sale. Key to song exploitation from show scores were the ballads and rhythm tunes sung by leading characters that featured generic romantic or dance-oriented lyrics: such songs were designed as much for singing out of context as in. But these tunes were sometimes tailored to their original performers' individual talents, in Gershwin's case performers such as Fred and Adele Astaire and Ethel Merman.

And so, to borrow two period terms from Goldberg, successful Broadway composers worked to write both "production" songs "intended for the stage spectacle chiefly" and "hits . . . aimed at the public purse."[10] An appreciation for this division between music for the show in the theater and music meant to translate to the pop music market proves a useful way to think about the compositional challenge faced by Broadway songwriters. The Gershwins were successful creators on the 1920s commercial stage because they could write both kinds of songs. The balance between "production" songs and "hits" in the Gershwins' musical comedies varied (Table 6.1), but both types were crucial. This accounting of the number of discrete songs needed to make a musical comedy suggests the importance of "production" music: writing a Broadway score involved much more than simply writing "hits" that could sell.

Table 6.1 *"Production" numbers and published "hits" in five Gershwin scores*
(musical comedies staged between 1924 and 1930 included among reconstruction recordings)

	"Production" numbers	"Hits" (published)
Lady, Be Good!	7	7
Tell Me More	7	6
Tip-Toes	4	8
Oh, Kay!	4	7
Girl Crazy	7	7

"Production" music at the start of an act or scene used the men and (especially) the women of the chorus to usher the audience into the world of the show and the dramaturgical sphere of the musical as a genre, a theatrical space where singing and dancing require no dramatic excuse. Such numbers also immediately satisfy audience desire for song and dance (and performers who sing and dance as objects of desire; Goldberg described opening choruses as an excuse "to exhibit the female wares").[11] Choruses like "A Wonderful Party" and "Linger in the Lobby" (*Lady, Be Good!*) and "The Moon Is on the Sea" and "A Woman's Touch" (*Oh, Kay!*) alike set the scene, whether a party, a public space, the beach, or a living room. Some such numbers divide the chorus into contrasting groups for a dramatic and musical effect: *Tell Me More*'s "Shopgirls and Mannequins" distinguishes between different female groups within a luxury department store setting, much as a number in a revue might, and sorts the female chorus almost literally into the standard Broadway categories of "ponies" ("girls" who dance and sing) and "clothes-horses" ("girls" who primarily parade in fancy clothes). Male and female choruses play contrasting roles in *Girl Crazy*'s "Bronco Busters": the women excitedly arrive in a Western town from the urban East; the men, residents of the town, boldly declare their cowboy credentials. In *Tip-Toes*'s "Florida," the men of the chorus enter first, selling options on real estate in the state's land boom; the women of the chorus, entering second, turn out to be "brokers too." The real-estate bubble that sets the topical tone for *Tip-Toes* has drawn in everyone and all join in a jerky, blues-inflected dance tune that, in the lyrics, references Irving Berlin's 1911 hit "Everybody's Doing It Now" (a ragtime dance song).

The music and lyrics the Gershwins provided for these book numbers – destined to be heard only in the context of the show – are consistently engaging and clever. "Lady Luck," the scene-setting chorus number for the gaming tables at the Palm Beach Surf Club in *Tip-Toes*, concludes with a lyric and music quote from the Gershwins' own "Oh, Lady Be Good," plugging the title song from the pair's earlier show but also suggesting a continuity across all their shows. In a Broadway context where new musicals played short runs and audiences craved novelty, such moments established a musical comedy world built on frequent theater attendance and a continuity of affect and energy that was attached not to one show only but to the creativity of special talents, such as the brothers Gershwin, whose tunes and shows opened a world understood by audiences to be distinctly "Gershwinian."[12] Gershwin's music for musical comedy chorus is uniformly bright and snappy, with patter verses (many fast notes in even values) and strongly syncopated choruses that administer an energetic kick to the show ("Love Is in the Air," a leisurely strolling tune opening Act II of

Tell Me More, proves an exception). Ira's lyrics often draw subtle but sharp attention to the artificiality of "production" music moments. In "A Wonderful Party," a chorus of excited young people sing "sounds like our entrance cue," a lyric that works as a sly critique of fashionable posing among the Smart Set (the characters are performing for each other) and as a self-reflexive moment (the number is, literally, the chorus' entrance cue). The corporate nature of such lyrics allows for further comic touches that declare in no uncertain terms that song and singers inhabit the stylized world of musical theater. For example, the cowboys in "Bronco Busters" declare exultantly, in a moment of urban fashion awareness unlikely for real Westerners, that their "pants have never been creased." Their chorus climaxes with a robust high note sung "à la Romberg," a reference to well-known operetta composer Sigmund Romberg, that locates these cowboys firmly in the confines of the musical stage. The clarity with which the Gershwins wrote for the voice allowed these lyrics to be comprehended on first hearing – as, indeed, they had to be in the theater and can be on the reconstruction recordings. And Gershwin did not skimp on the music for these choruses. For example, the chorus of "Linger in the Lobby" juxtaposes a melody in triple meter against a duple meter accompaniment, in its own way as rhythmically complicated as *Lady, Be Good!*'s more famous syncopated "hit," "Fascinating Rhythm."

Some production songs include the names of characters or locations in the show. Others come across as less tightly connected to a show's setting and instead as theatrical in a more general sense, as songs whose fundamental nature demands musical theater staging. For example, "Bride and Groom" (*Oh, Kay!*) would function perfectly well in a revue scene on a wedding theme. "End of a String" (*Lady, Be Good!*) and "When Do We Dance?" (*Tip-Toes*) both feature young people dancing in a domestic party setting. The former mines the inherent theatricality of a "cobweb party," a Victorian parlor game where young men and women follow twisted ribbons around a room to find their dancing partners.[13] Ira's lyrics update this quaint game to the current younger generation, about whom there was great concern in the decade: using 1920s slang, the chorus members declare themselves "full of pep" and promise to be "a peppy partner" until three in the morning. In a more functional manner, "When the Debbies Go By" and "My Fair Lady" (*Tell Me More*) and "Dear Little Girl" and "Oh, Kay!" (*Oh, Kay!*) are purpose written to feature a leading performer in an energetic solo backed up by a chorus.

Songs conceived as special material for specific performers fall into a gray area between "production" music and "hits." *Lady, Be Good!* includes four custom-made numbers for Fred and Adele Astaire: "Hang on to Me" (with a lyric about siblings, which the Astaires played in the show); "I'd Rather

Charleston" (another sister–brother number added for London); "Juanita" (a comic Spanish routine for Adele and the show's "boys"), and "Swiss Miss" (an end-of-the-evening excuse for nutty comedy – an Adele specialty – and the pair's signature runaround, a sustained physical gag that had them high-stepping, side-by-side in increasingly larger circles to an oom-pah beat). Only the first two were judged potential "hits" and released as sheet music. To succeed on Broadway, the Gershwins had to be adept at writing special material for whomever was brought into a show, be it the scat-singing pop singer Cliff "Ukulele Ike" Edwards (*Lady, Be Good!*), for whom they wrote the jazz-centric tunes "Fascinating Rhythm" and "Little Jazz Bird" (both published), or comedian Lou Holtz (*Tell Me More*), for whom they crafted a waltz full of Jewish jokes titled "In Sardinia," or the dancer Queenie Smith (*Tip-Toes*), for whom the show's title song provided a chance to show off her signature dancing (neither published). In the case of Ethel Merman, special material for the role of Kate in *Girl Crazy* famously made her a star. Merman/Kate sang three numbers: "Sam and Delilah," a bluesy ballad, immediately followed by "I Got Rhythm," near the end of Act I; "Boy! What Love Has Done to Me," a wry torch song near the close of Act II. "I Got Rhythm" – like "Fascinating Rhythm" – stands alone: a historically successful "hit" that was put over in *Girl Crazy* in a manner that made Merman an instant star.[14] Merman's other two tunes were crafted to fit her character and the show more closely: the "he done her wrong" lyric of "Sam and Delilah" strikes an appropriately non-urban note for *Girl Crazy*'s Nevada setting and a character hailing from the "wilds" of San Francisco; the verse of "Boy! What Love Has Done to Me" deals with Kate's specific problems and includes her name and that of her lover, Slick. All three of Merman's songs were published. Each of the above described numbers was an excuse for a star performer to meet their Broadway audience. In each case, the Gershwins opened a custom-tailored space within a given score where this encounter could take place to the best advantage of all: the performers, the audience, the show, and – in a few cases – the song itself as a commodifiable "hit."

Gershwin's "hits" – extractable songs built for independent, hopefully profitable lives – can be sorted into the two main categories of popular music at the time: ballads and rhythm tunes. The Gershwins' excelled in the making of ballads with an up-to-date attitude: love songs, introduced by leading players, frequently sung as duets but usually also workable as solos, with lyrics that dissected modern love in an often rueful but never sentimental tone. The predictable shapes of musical comedy plots (boy meets girl, complications ensue, boy gets girl) played into the generic address of these ballads and the connection of the lyrics to the specifics of any given show's story is, with a few exceptions, altogether loose.[15]

George's melodies encourage rhythmically vital performance at a moderate tempo in a popular style: these are smart, not sentimental love songs where the words matter. Subtle touches give several of these tunes an unmistakably "blue" edge; for example, the unaltered and lowered third scale degrees alternating in the A phrases of "Looking for a Boy." These ballads are eminently singable by just about anyone: they do not require trained voices, do not have propulsive patter rhythms (as "production" choruses often do), and favor an informal, breezy delivery. In this, the leads in a Gershwin musical comedy often sang less technically challenging music than did the chorus members. The combination of clear-eyed lyrics and lightly rhythmic melodies helped transfer more than a few of these ballads to the pop marketplace and beyond that into the canon of jazz and pop standards.[16]

Rhythm tunes, often with lyrics about the power of rhythm, were central to the Gershwins' "hits." These songs often suddenly and somewhat arbitrarily jumpstarted the proceedings in their shows of origin, more loosely connected to the plots than the ballads (which required love stories to make minimal dramatic sense). With their frequent allusions to jazz and blues, extractable rhythm songs often drew links to popular culture outside the theater, an expected strategy for a song designed to, literally, live beyond the confines of the show in which it was introduced. Given the frequent appearance of racially coded or direct lyrics referencing jazz and blues, rhythm tunes about the power of rhythm are discussed in detail in the following section.

As Goldberg notes, "Not all the fine music [in a show] was printed for the racks of the parlor pianoforte."[17] A curious type of rhythm tune, commonly found in Gershwin's musicals, was not typically seen as a candidate for publication. All five shows discussed here include a frisky male–female rhythm duet, often with sexual undertones, and usually sung by the show's secondary or tertiary couple. These include: "We're Here Because" (*Lady, Be Good!*), "How Can I Win You Now?" and "Baby!" (*Tell Me More*), "Nice Baby! (Come to Papa!)" (*Tip-Toes*), and "Don't Ask" (*Oh, Kay!*). The male solo "Treat Me Rough" (*Girl Crazy*), sung to a bevy of chorus girls, also fits this category. In all these numbers, the implied tempo is brisk and the tune is smartly syncopated – suitable for dancing – but, as several of the titles suggest, the lyrics carry flirtatious content laced at times with sexual innuendo (or as much as Ira, a rather prudish lyricist – compared to Cole Porter, for example – allowed himself). Such numbers – apparently seen as essential to the variety of an evening in the theater – were not, generally, viewed as candidates for publication: only "Baby!" and "Nice Baby! (Come to Papa!)" from the above songs were issued as sheet music. Perhaps this type of song was judged too difficult for amateurs to pull off, implying the need for strong, highly theatrical performance by comic singing actors in the theater to succeed. Whatever the strategy, it was assumed that sheet music buyers did not especially want to take this kind of theater song home for parlor use.

But while "hits" were intentionally made to be commercially transferrable outside their respective shows, they can often be found serving important plot or character functions within a show's score by way of reprises and re-written lyrics. The line between "production" songs and "hits" is far from clear in these examples, which do not suggest integration of music and plot – as found in operettas more generally and in the musical plays of later Broadway decades – so much as an attempt to tie the music in a musical comedy score together as tightly as possible. For example, "Oh, Lady Be Good" is sung multiple times in the eponymous show with sly changes to the title lyric. Initially, the character Watty Watkins addresses the song to Suzie, singing "Suzie be good," when enlisting her in a scheme to impersonate the widow of Jack Robinson. When Suzie refuses, Watty transfers his attentions to a group of willing chorus girls and sings "lady be good." A cute production number ensues. In neither case does the full chorus lyric make much sense, especially the line about the singer being alone in a "great big city" (*Lady, Be Good!* is set among the upper crust of Beacon Hill, Rhode Island). But the song's repeated and earnest if casual plea from man to woman – the yearning yet snappy descending gesture that sets the title – works in both cases. In Act II, the tune returns, this time sung as "wifey be good" by Jack Robinson as a teasing taunt to Suzie (who eventually does impersonate Jack's supposed widow). And so, in the context of the score, "Oh, Lady Be Good" functions multiple ways to tie the musical whole that is *Lady, Be Good!* together. (On the reconstruction recording these connections can be experienced by the listener.) "Fascinating Rhythm" serves a similar function in the same show, its lyric recomposed for the finale as "fascinating wedding" with each of the show's four couples given a moment to consolidate their affections in song – a labor of the lyricist and not the composer. This formal approach – re-written lyrics to an extractable ballad serving plot development during a finale – also occurs in *Tip-Toes*, with "That Certain Feeling," and in *Oh, Kay!*, with the Act I finale's wholesale revision of the lyric of "Maybe" into a choral response to the revelation that "It was Jane!" making noise in the master's bedroom.[18] The above examples draw mostly on the lyricist's art: Ira was tasked with making these moments work. A more musically expressed tying of the score together can be heard in "Tell Me More," which has the chorus respond to a leading character with the useful phrase "tell me more" on several occasions across the score.

The balance between "production" numbers, native to a given show's world, and "hits," designed for standalone success, tips strongly in favor of the former in the case of Gershwin's three operettas. Built on the model of Gilbert and Sullivan's operettas composed for London in the late nineteenth century, the lyrics for almost every song in *Strike Up the Band, Of Thee I Sing,* and *Let 'em Eat Cake* include show-specific content, whether related to the plot and characters or delivering a satirical blow against whatever political or cultural establishment sits in a show's crosshairs. The Gershwins did not write florid extractable love songs typical of Broadway's romantic operettas – such as the hit songs "Serenade" in Rudolf Friml's *The Student Prince in Heidelberg* (1924) or "Lover, Come Back to Me" from Romberg's *The New Moon* (1928). Political operettas offered few openings for non-ironic romance or even flirtation between romantic couples; for example, the romantic leads in *Of Thee I Sing* are most strongly linked by the man's attraction to the woman's wonderful corn muffins. Furthermore, the themes of the Gershwin operettas worked against the making of extractable popular "hits." *Strike Up the Band* is a bitter burlesque of warmongering on the part of American big business and of militarism generally in American culture. *Of Thee I Sing* and *Let 'em Eat Cake* alike present a cynical, frequently incompetent nexus of politics, the media, and sex. The latter show engages with the rise of fascism in Europe and toys with nihilism in its most indicative number, "Down with Everything That's Up." There's some evidence Gershwin and his collaborators recognized the need for an extractable tune or two in the operettas. One of the substantive changes made in the revised *Strike Up the Band* of 1930 – which unlike the 1927 version made it to Broadway – was the addition of two ballads: "Soon" (an easy fit for any musical comedy) and "I've Got a Crush On You" (interpolated from the Gershwin's *Treasure Girl* [1928, 68 performances], which had failed to hold an audience). The tune for "Soon" was heard in the 1927 version of *Strike Up the Band* as part of an extended finale with words relating only to the plot – another bit of evidence that Gershwin approached "production" music with a full investment in its melodic potential.

Black Music in White Shows

Rhapsody in Blue for "jazz band and piano" made a splash on the New York scene in February 1924 in a concert at Aeolian Hall. Ten months later, *Lady, Be Good!* opened at the Liberty Theatre. These two venues hosting Gershwin premieres were located within three blocks of each other on West 42nd Street. Audiences heard the two works as similarly marked by select inclusion of the new syncopated popular music of the day: a music called jazz.

Jazz rapidly displaced ragtime as the urban dance music of choice shortly after the end of World War I in 1919, just as Gershwin was assuming composing duties for *George White's Scandals*. Like ragtime, jazz grew out of and was closely associated with African American migration and the growth of black urban populations in Northern cities. Also, like ragtime, jazz was linked to new social dances innovated by the black working class and taken up by the white middle class. Gershwin's Broadway songs and scores brought jazz song and dance to the New York (and London) musical stage. In this, Gershwin was following the lead of Irving Berlin, who had introduced ragtime themes and rhythms to the Broadway stage in the pre-World War I years.[19] (Indeed, among the first songs Gershwin wrote with lyrics by his older brother Ira was "The Real American Folk Song (is a Rag)," a tune interpolated in the 1918 show *Ladies First*. The topical title and lyric rendered the song decidedly out of date shortly after its premiere.)

Jazz in the 1920s was both an array of musical practices revealed in performance – such as tempo, rhythmic style, choice of instrumentation, or improvised passages – and a set of textual references evident in a song's title, lyrics, melody, harmony, or accompaniment as found in sheet music. Jazz as musical practice and textual reference show up across Gershwin's Broadway scores and songs. Musical personnel provide evidence for occasions when jazz as musical practice was part of a Gershwin show. Popular duo pianists Victor Arden and Phil Ohman were featured in *Lady, Be Good!*, *Tip-Toes*, *Oh, Kay!*, *Funny Face*, and *Treasure Girl* – sometimes onstage – and were known to improvise on tunes from the score during intermission and after final bows "for the fans who refused to go home" (recalled Fred Astaire of *Lady, Be Good!*).[20] *Strike Up the Band* (on Broadway) and *Girl Crazy* both included young white jazz greats such Benny Goodman, Red Nichols, Jimmy Dorsey, Gene Krupa, Glenn Miller, and Charlie and Jack Teagarden on winds and brass, lending the pit orchestra a dance-band quality.[21] Given the intense topicality of musical comedy, jazz and blues references in the text of a Gershwin show – most prominently in Ira's lyrics – can be understood as of a piece with the genre's persistent popular culture references, be it to current events, other Broadway shows, or to advertising (e.g. a laugh line in *Lady, Be Good!* referenced the Camel cigarettes slogan).[22]

Gershwin's Broadway shows are all set within white milieus: department stores, hotel lobbies, posh beachfront estates, a small Nevada town, the halls of political power in Washington DC, and Dresden, Germany. No performer of color played a leading or featured role in any of these shows and the members of the chorus were, similarly, visibly all white. Like most Broadway musicals across the twentieth century, Gershwin's shows staged imaginary worlds devoid of African Americans where the complicated history of racial segregation in the United States is completely set aside – except when African American music or dance were part of the show. When – in this segregated context – were jazz or blues given a nod or directly performed?

The 1920s practice of slumming – white spectators traveling to a black area of town to enjoy African American music and dance, a much-discussed activity in the decade – was never represented onstage in a Gershwin show but was instead, on two occasions, described in song. The verse to "Sweet and Low-Down" (*Tip-Toes*) paints a picture of a "cabaret" the singer recommends: the "pep" to be found there offers a "tonic," tapping into a current notion that jazz could renew the lost vitality of enervated white listeners. The tune's chorus instructs the listener to "grab a cab" and travel to said club located in a vague but class-specific "down" location. Further cues, such as biblical references ("milk and honey") and the racially marked word "shuffling," indicate that the "syncopation" to be found at this "cabaret" derives from African American sources: the "band" blowing "that Sweet and Low-Down" is clearly black (why else travel "down" in the first place?). The A phrases of Gershwin's AABA tune are built on a fourfold iteration of a bouncy, syncopated rhythmic idea followed by the invocation "Blow that Sweet and Low-Down." Ira's lyric, written after George composed the tune, puts the title phrase, preceded by an imperative verb, inside quotation marks, inviting the song's singer to play a part in the musical energy of the club: the singer of "Sweet and Low-Down" calls out to the lyric's imagined band – with a high, held note on the word "blow" – in a speech act that can be understood as both a command ("play that music") and a response ("yes, that's it") signaling recognition on the part of the singer as to what jazz sounds like. The implied drama of the lyric and the tune crosses the color line – white singer/listener commanding and/or affirming black musicians playing in a style understood to be their unique racial gift. In *Tip-Toes*, "Sweet and Low-Down" was, in Ira's words, "sung, kazooed, tromboned, and danced ... at a Palm Beach party."[23] Performed in the Liberty Theatre on 42nd Street – where any visibly black patrons would have been relegated to the balcony in practice if not by law – this number displaced an interracial encounter (white singers and dancers with black music) to an effectively all-white space: in sum, "Sweet and Low-Down" named and enacted onstage the cultural work being done by musical comedy in the midtown theater district by putting black music into white mouths and bodies in an effectively all-white zone.

The song "Little Jazz Bird," a specialty number for Cliff "Ukulele Ike" Edwards in *Lady, Be Good!*, extends a similar if more veiled invitation to white listeners to learn to "syncopate" by slumming: a "songbird" flies into a "cabaret," hears a "jazz band," stays "till after dark," and finds that "singing 'blue'" helps him shed his "troubles." The distance Ira's lyric affects between the bird (understood as a white listener) and black culture is telling: the practice of "singing 'blue'" is kept at a remove and understood as a performance; the word "blue" set apart in quotes, nicely setting the seventh scale degree. "Sweet and Low-Down" and "Little Jazz Bird" typify the rather modest degree to which jazz and blues were mentioned in the Gershwins' musical comedies: their white Broadway audience, more sensitive to the new sounds of jazz than listeners are today, would have caught these small touches well enough.

Rhythm tune "hits" lent themselves particularly well to the sort of brief invocations of black music typical of the Gershwin show with an all-white cast and, given their positioning within the show, these tunes would have marked these musical comedies as especially engaged with current trends in popular culture. Four of the five shows discussed at length here included a rousing jazz-themed rhythm number at the midpoint of Act I, then reprised the tune at the end of the Act I finale, sending the audience into intermission tapping their toes to syncopated dance tunes that bore specific connections to black culture. "Sweet and Low-Down" served this function in *Tip-Toes*. In *Tell Me More*, "Kickin' the Clouds Away" plays the exact same structural role. The song's verse begins with the singer framing the chorus to follow as a "spiritual" (an alternate version reads "Southern spiritual") suitable for every home with a "phonograph." The distance between black and white is here bridged by a popular music commodity – the record – instead of the act of slumming. The accompaniment texture in the sheet music – thick block chords on every beat – supports the notion in the lyric. (This standard textural indicator of the blues also appears in the verse to "I'll Build a Stairway to Paradise," used to end Act I of *George White's Scandals of 1922*.) The chorus lyric to "Kickin' the Clouds Away" promises to make the listener happy – to "kick" away any lingering clouds – and uses the slangy exhortation "Hey! Hey," again in quotes, Ira's distancing way to include a hip phrase without adopting it into his own voice. In "Clap Yo' Hands" (*Oh, Kay!*), Ira drops the quotation marks and moves in rare fashion entirely into black popular music slang: the title phrase, spelled throughout as "clap-a yo' hand!," repeated cries of "Halleluyah!," biblical references to "the Jubilee" and, most surprisingly, a lapse into dialect, with "the Debble." The spoken song cue dubs the tune "a Mammy song," effectively putting the entirety of "Clap Yo' Hands" under the sign of blackness. All the above numbers celebrate the power of music understood to be black in origin to cure the troubles or bring happiness to whomever sings or dances along – in this context, fashionable, white youth. Energetic, rousing songs designed to elevate the spirits are central to Broadway's historic emphasis on feel-good entertainment. Linking such sentiments to blackness was in no way required in the latter 1920s. Indeed, the Gershwins wrote other rhythm "hits" that make no reference to blackness as a necessary "tonic" and simply advise the listener to be optimistic about life – for example, "It's a Great Little World" (*Tip-Toes*) and "Heaven on Earth" (*Oh, Kay!*).

In the early 1920s, jazz was a controversial music, slowly moving toward general acceptance among white audiences. Bandleader Paul Whiteman's description of *Rhapsody in Blue* and its concert hall premiere as an attempt to "make a lady" out of jazz signaled these anxieties in February 1924. The important music magazine *The Etude* highlighted "The Jazz Problem" in its August and September issues that same year, with prominent white male musicians and cultural figures weighing in on the music, many with grave concerns about its dangers. But jazz was winning this debate – *Rhapsody in Blue* rapidly became a global hit – and *Lady, Be Good!*, opening in November, offered jazz made safe for Broadway whiteness in the breakout performances of Fred and Adele Astaire. The Astaires' personas as Jazz Age exemplars of youthful urban whiteness, unafraid of and glorying in the new syncopation, were reinforced several times over in the Gershwins' score. (The dancers Vernon and Irene Castle – models for the Astaires – did similar cultural work on behalf of ragtime music and dance on the Broadway stage in Irving Berlin's 1914 musical *Watch Your Step*.)

Like the rhythm tunes described above, "Fascinating Rhythm" was *Lady, Be Good!*'s Act I rouser and finisher. The number built from a solo for Cliff Edwards, into a duet for the Astaires, then, in the words of the script, into a "BIG ENSEMBLE DANCE NUMBER USING ALL THE GIRLS AND BOYS." (There were twenty-four women and twelve men in the chorus, typical numbers for a Gershwin show.) The lyric to "Fascinating Rhythm" speaks, in the first person, of the singer being obsessed with a syncopated pattern that "pit-a-pats" through his brain and that he fears will drive him to insanity. The chorus lyric, addressed to the "fascinating" rhythmic pattern itself, has the singers begging to be set free, longing to live their former lives, before the rhythm started "picking" on them. Ira's lyric neatly captures the dilemma some white listeners felt in the face of the new syncopated music, but it does so without dropping any load of moral opprobrium on jazz or without implying the music has any specific racial origins. All the rhythm does is get in the way of daily life. Crucially, any effective performance of "Fascinating Rhythm" ends up being a celebration of the new rhythmic world of jazz. Edwards, the Astaires, and the boys and girls of the *Lady, Be Good!* chorus helped secure such jazz "fascination" as something wholly part of the world experienced by fashionable, white elites – indeed, as an attractive and desirable feature of modern urban subjectivity. In short, the lyric protests too much: jazz is here to stay and, as Ira's later lyrics suggest, offers a positive development in white culture. (Later songs following the model of "Fascinating Rhythm" include "Fidgety Feet" from *Oh, Kay!* and "I Got Rhythm" from *Girl Crazy*.)

The return of "Fascinating Rhythm" at the close of Act I staged just how delightful life with that "pit-a-pat" in your brain could be. The Astaires' brother and sister characters, Dick and Suzie, are arguing loudly when Victor Arden and Phil Ohman, duo pianists onstage as specialty performers within the party scene, begin playing a reprise of the song. Verbal argument and jazzy musical specialty compete and the music – the rhythm – wins: Dick delivers the act's final line, "Why is it every time we are having a good fight, somebody has to play that tune?" Stage directions describe what happened next: "The tempo proves too infectious for Susie and Dick, and they start dancing together. Business, during dance, continuing quarrel. Susie licking [sic.] Dick – making faces at one another etc. Work dance up to big climax and CURTAIN." The word *infectious*, invoked here with no sense of societal danger, tracks a mid-1920s shift from jazz as cause for concern to jazz as a hallmark of youthful high spirits and vitality.

Fred Astaire powerfully embodied the new jazz-infused, white style on the Broadway stage that Gershwin introduced with such conviction in the concert hall. Indeed, the sensibilities of the two – both informed by black music – were understood to be remarkably similar. Kay Swift, Gershwin's confidante and musical assistant, recalled in 1973, "Astaire and Gershwin were particularly one in music and dance. The dance expressed the music so well." Astaire himself recalled, also in 1973, that he and Gershwin "had a good little game going with each other," where both suggested ideas in the other's domain: Gershwin in dance, Astaire in music.[24]

The title and lyric of Astaire's solo in *Lady, Be Good!*, "The Half of It, Dearie, Blues," explicitly and cheekily paired the racially specific musical indication "blues" with white 1920s slang of the sort Ira liked to mine for his lyrics. (A girl tosses off the line "You don't know the half of it, dearie" in F. Scott Fitzgerald's 1920 story "May Day." It was also the catch phrase of the white vaudeville female impersonator Bert Savoy, who died in 1923.) But the full lyric is positively old-fashioned: the singer longs to wed. Ira's pop culture reference and the song's traditional sentiment are wrapped in music that tapped the current understanding of "blues" and that welcomed jazz-oriented performance, as one African American musical authority recognized. W. C. Handy, composer of "The Saint Louis Blues" (1914, the first pop blues song hit) and known as the "Father of the Blues," included annotated sheet music for "The Half of It, Dearie, Blues" in his 1926 book *Blues: An Anthology*. Handy put the song beside excerpts from *Rhapsody in Blue* and Gershwin's Concerto in F as evidence for the composer's "place as a second pioneer in blues territory." The annotations involved sample "breaks ... fillers-in between the phrases of the old blues."[25] Astaire improvised his own breaks in tap dance onstage in *Lady, Be Good!* Astaire and Gershwin's 1926 recording of "The Half of It, Dearie, Blues," made during the show's London run, reveals similar investment by Gershwin and Astaire in musical styles being innovated in Harlem in the 1920s: jazz tap and stride piano, respectively. In their respective areas on this disc, Astaire and Gershwin display evidence they had journeyed "down" to the sort of cabarets described in "Sweet and Low-Down" and listened closely: for these white men, slumming was professional research. Their similar career breakthroughs in 1924 mark the mainstreaming within white establishment culture of black-infused syncopated musical performance by young white talents who enjoyed access to the concert hall and Broadway stage their black peers and models did not.

All the rhythm numbers described above were introduced by men. Women on the stage at the time, especially the "girls" in the chorus, might join in and dance, but the jazz "tonic" was first served by men. And while men like Gershwin and Astaire might be in a position to make jazz "a lady" in the concert hall or on Broadway, the relationship of leading ladies to jazz in the Gershwins' musical comedies proves more tentative. For example, Adele Astaire was less identified with jazz and more praised for her silly faces and "nutty" persona. The Astaires' specialty number late in *Lady Be Good!*, "Swiss Miss" (recorded by the duo in 1926), captures Adele's comfort zone as a performer (while also providing ample evidence for the Gershwins' ability to compose to order for established personalities). Other recordings, such as the Astaires' version of "Hang On to Me" with Gershwin at the piano, suggest Adele did not inflect her singing with the jazz-derived rhythmic style that was Fred's signature. On this disc, George and Fred shape their respective fills within a common feeling of swing: George slyly leans on a syncopated triplet figure; Fred falls right into this relaxed, stride-derived groove. Adele, in sharp contrast, phrases stiffly with square little fills set against George's swung triplets.

The London *Lady Be, Good!* included a new duet for the Astaires: "I'd Rather Charleston," with music by George and lyrics by Desmond Carter. This rhythm tune situated the Astaires in the popular dance craze of the mid-1920s, casting Adele as a young lady gone "dancing mad" and Fred as a frowning fuddy duddy of a brother. The song's conceit, however, gets the Astaire siblings precisely backwards: Fred was much more likely to Charleston than Adele. On their 1926 recording, Adele sings the syncopated rhythm of the Charleston in as square a manner as possible and gives no musical expression to the lyric about the dance making her feel "elastic." Adele, a major star of the 1920s, was surely too good of a dancer not to have felt the pulse of her times. Any performer with her credentials did not do things accidentally. The squareness in her style was a choice – just as rhythmic flexibility was for her brother. Gender holds a key to understanding why the brother gets to swing while the sister stays square. In her recording of "I'd Rather Charleston," Adele comes off as a girl who wants to Charleston but doesn't know how – a girl who is not especially experienced, who apparently has not gone slumming, who has only heard about the Charleston and is certainly no expert in the dance. She remains a suitably marriageable young white woman, an ingénue worthy of a wedding at show's close. And indeed, in 1932 Adele Astaire left the stage, married Lord Charles Cavendish, and moved into a castle in Ireland. Not putting her whole self into a dangerous new beat like the Charleston kept Adele to one side of a cultural line while also offering her Broadway and West End audiences a glimpse across that line, into the world of syncopated social dancing they had perhaps heard about but which was not necessarily onstage in all its glory. A similar moment was offered Gertrude Lawrence in the title song to *Oh, Kay!*, which had British stage star sing a slangy "Hey! Hey!," spiking her big number with just enough jazz to show she was up to date but not enough to compromise her credentials as an ingénue (a stage type defined by whiteness as much as conventional femininity).

The blues persona that was open to white women was that of the torch singer, "a specialized blue mood in which is sung (by a female) the burning pangs of unrequited love."[26] The Gershwin shows set among fashionable East Coast society opened no space for such low-down female characters. *Girl Crazy* and *Pardon My English*, however, did. In the former, Merman's Kate hails from San Francisco – a "down" location for finding "red hot" music, as suggested in the lyric for the song "Barbary Coast." Two of Merman's songs suggest a torch singer persona informed by "low-down" music: "Sam and Delilah" and "Boy! What Love Has Done to Me."

In analogous fashion, the Dresden cabaret singer Gita in *Pardon My English* sings two torchy songs, although her numbers are more analytical. "The Lorelei" spikes the German legend of a singing female river creature who lures sailors to their deaths with a jazzy idiom taken from the black bandleader Cab Calloway: Gita's German temptress sings in Harlem-ese – "hey ho dee ho hi dee hi" – that, by 1933, had been fully absorbed into the global white mainstream. Offering a more concrete geographical explanation, Gita's Act II solo "My Cousin in Milwaukee" spells out the source of her skills – an émigré relative, resident in an American city with a large German population, who sings "hot" and "blue" and "always gets the men," she explains, "taught me how." Lyda Roberti introduced the role of Gita. Born in Warsaw to a showbiz family, Roberti built a short American stage and film career on comically accented and fractured English and a sexy, giggling, bleached blonde, shimmying-shoulders persona (exemplified in her recording of "My Cousin from Milwaukee"). On the 1994 reconstruction recording of *Pardon My English*, the role of Gita is taken by African American performer Arnetia Walker, a performer with Broadway experience in black-cast shows like *The Wiz* (1975) and *Dreamgirls* (1981). Walker substitutes Roberti's now perhaps offensive (or just unfunny) bad English and oversexed persona with a forceful belted vocalism and a flexible rhythmic sensibility that stays just this side of the black diva persona familiar from many post-1970 Broadway scores. Walker sings her numbers straight, with no gospel-derived pyrotechnics.[27] Her approach delivers Gershwin's songs, with their textual links to jazz and blackness, in a style more appropriate for a 1990s listener: in the process, the original show's joking use of Roberti and equation of black style with ditsy sexual availability is lost.

Gershwin's scores for the Broadway stage, built to succeed under specific conditions, are period pieces in form and content. And while reconstruction recordings might restore each show's combination of "production" songs and "hits," the larger theatrical whole of these musicals in live performance in a Broadway theater is gone forever. Still, examining the shows George and Ira made for Broadway – a creative arena that defined their partnership – adds nuance to our understanding of Gershwin's achievement as a songwriter and expands to the realm of commercial musical theater his importance as a white concert hall composer known for incorporating jazz content into his music.

Notes

1. Isaac Goldberg, *George Gershwin: A Study in American Music* (New York: Simon & Schuster, 1931), 86.
2. Ibid., 115.
3. *George Gershwin: Of Thee I Sing and Let 'em Eat Cake* (1987), conducted by Michael Tilson Thomas, CBS Masterworks S2M 42522.
4. On the Elektra Nonesuch label: *George & Ira Gershwin, Girl Crazy* (1990), conducted by John Mauceri, 79250–2; *George & Ira Gershwin, Strike Up the Band*, 1927 version with select numbers from 1930 version (1991), John Mauceri, 79273–2; *George & Ira Gershwin, Lady, Be Good!* (1992), conducted by Eric Stern, 9 79304–2; *George & Ira Gershwin, Pardon My English* (1994), conducted by Eric Stern, 79338–2; *George & Ira Gershwin, Oh, Kay!* (1995), conducted by Eric Stern, 79361–2.
5. *Strike Up the Band* (1930) (2011), conducted by John Mauceri, PS Classics, B013H15YA4.

6. *George and Ira Gershwin: Tip-Toes/Tell Me* More (2001), conducted by Rob Fisher, New World Records 80598–2.
7. Liner notes to *Tip-Toes/Tell Me More*, New World Records.
8. *George Gershwin and B.G. DeSylva's Sweet Little Devil* (2011), conducted by Sam Davis, PS Classics B0084LRDDE.
9. Tommy Krasker, *Catalog of the American Musical: Musicals of Irving Berlin, George & Ira Gershwin, Cole Porter, Richard Rodgers & Lorenz Hart* (Washington, DC: National Institute for Opera and Musical Theater, 1988); *The Complete Lyrics of Ira Gershwin*, ed. Robert Kimball (New York: Alfred A. Knopf, 1993); and Richard Norton, A *Chronology of American Musical Theatre* (New York: Oxford University Press, 2002). Howard Pollock, *George Gershwin: His Life and Work* (Berkeley: University of California Press, 2006) offers detailed narratives of the making and content of each Gershwin show.
10. Goldberg, *George Gershwin*, 189.
11. Ibid., 188.
12. Ibid., 190.
13. *Lady, Be Good!* (1924), typescript, NCOF+ 1154/5, New York Public Library for the Performing Arts, Lincoln Center.
14. Richard Crawford, *The American Musical Landscape: The Business of Musicianship from Billings to Gershwin*, updated edn (Berkeley: University of California Press, 2000), chapter 7.
15. "Could You Use Me?" (*Girl Crazy*) stands out for the specificity of its lyrics, which peg the male singer as an "Easterner" and the female singer as from the West.
16. The published ballads in the five shows discussed here include "Hang on to Me," "So Am I," and "Oh, Lady Be Good" (*Lady, Be Good!*); "Tell Me More!" and "Three Times a Day" (*Tell Me More*); "Looking for a Boy," "That Certain Feeling," and "Nightie-Night" (*Tip-Toes*); "Maybe," "Do-Do-Do," and "Someone to Watch Over Me" (*Oh, Kay!*); and "Could You Use Me?," "Embraceable You," and "But Not for Me" (*Girl Crazy*).
17. Goldberg, *George Gershwin*, 179.
18. Also reused in the *Oh, Kay!* Act I finale are: "Clap'Yo Hands," "Dear Little Girl," "Do-Do-Do," and "Someone to Watch Over Me."
19. Jeffrey Magee, *Irving Berlin's American Musical Theater* (New York: Oxford University Press, 2012), 48–51.
20. Deena Rosenberg, *Fascinating Rhythm: The Collaboration of George and Ira Gershwin* (New York: Dutton, 1991), 83–84.
21. Pollock, *George Gershwin*, 404, 471.
22. *Lady, Be Good!* typescript.
23. Ira Gershwin, *Lyrics on Several Occasions* (New York: Alfred A. Knopf, 1959), 182.
24. Cf. Todd Decker, *Music Makes Me: Fred Astaire and Jazz* (Berkeley: University of California Press, 2011), 58.
25. W.C. Handy, *Blues: An Anthology* (New York: Albert and Charles Boni, 1926), 39.
26. Goldberg, *George Gershwin*, 189.
27. Todd Decker, "Race, Ethnicity, Performance," in Raymond Knapp, Mitchell Morris, and Stacy Wolf (eds.), *The Oxford Handbook of the American Musical* (New York: Oxford University Press, 2011), 207–08.

7 The Works for Piano and Orchestra

TIMOTHY FREEZE

Like his other concert music, Gershwin's four works for piano and orchestra – *Rhapsody in Blue* (1924), Concerto in F (1925), *Second Rhapsody* (1932), and *"I Got Rhythm" Variations* (1934) – showcase a composer who roamed freely across traditional musical boundaries and pioneered stylistic hybrids of lasting enjoyment and value. Taken as a group, they also contribute unique perspectives on the multifaceted artistry of his concert works. Only the concerti were conceived as vehicles for Gershwin the pianist, resulting in extant recordings featuring the composer as a central musical protagonist. These recordings, unlike those of him performing popular song, convey a less familiar image of Gershwin as a score-oriented composer-pianist in the European tradition, at once revealing a pianist assiduously attuned to the notated part while also yielding insights into the composer not accessible through his scores alone. And although Gershwin often related his music generally to the spirit of the modern American metropolis, the concerti comprise his most vivid and varied portraits of New York City in particular.

This chapter explores Gershwin's concerti with respect to his creative sensibilities as both a composer and a pianist. Building on an examination of the corpus of original manuscripts and extant recordings of Gershwin as soloist, it considers the works as Gershwin composed and performed them, as opposed to the modified editions and re-arrangements that tend to be heard today. Of particular interest are the varying ways that Gershwin managed to weigh the demands of popular appeal and artistic sophistication, striking a balance in each work between the occasional circumstances, a sense of musical place, and his increasing command of compositional craft, as apparent especially in the handling of form and motive.

Rhapsody in Blue

The genesis of *Rhapsody in Blue*, more than Gershwin's other concerti, mirrored the fundamentally collaborative milieu of 1920s popular music. Paul Whiteman, leader of New York's prominent dance orchestra, commissioned the work for his highly publicized "Experiment in Modern Music" in Aeolian Hall on February 12, 1924. Gershwin was by then already an established piano-roll artist and composer of popular song and Broadway musicals, genres of so-called performer's music in which composers supply the basic musical shape that performers, arrangers, and producers mold to their needs.[1] Such was the case with *Rhapsody in Blue*. In reportedly as little as ten days, Gershwin produced a sketch that closely resembled a two-piano score. Each day, he handed off fascicles of freshly notated manuscript to Ferde Grofé, the gifted arranger for Whiteman's ensemble of some two-dozen reeds, brass, percussion, and violins. Grofé orchestrated the work, tailoring it to the abilities of the ensemble's individual players, who in turn contributed distinctive touches of their own.

Even after the enduring popularity of *Rhapsody in Blue* became evident, Gershwin never made a performable score himself. As a result, the work's performance history consists entirely of arrangements.[2] Grofé's version for theater orchestra (1926) quickly became the most commonly performed, but it was eventually overtaken by his arrangement for full orchestra (1942). This latter score, like the published two-piano reduction (1924), suggests optional cuts. In modern concert settings, however, preference is given to the unabridged work, an inclination seemingly shared by the composer.

The stated aim of Whiteman's "Experiment" was to demonstrate, before an audience including luminaries of classical music, the viability of jazz as the basis for a new and distinctively American style of art music. It is important to bear in mind that, in the mid-1920s, jazz had still not acquired its strong identification with improvisation and swing. Instead, it encompassed any youth dance music with roots in syncopated styles and performing techniques of African American culture, from ragtime to the blues. It was this commercialized music, cultivated foremost by New York's pianists, dance bands, and society orchestras, that became the symbol for the fast-paced and rebellious spirit of the age and helped motivate Gershwin's claim that *Rhapsody in Blue* "is all New York, all America."[3]

The opening of *Rhapsody in Blue* brims with blues signifiers. Some of these, like the blue notes and modal inflections, are still strongly suggestive of the idiom today. But several traits are more specifically associated with urban blues of the 1920s. The solo clarinet timbre (an orchestration choice made by Gershwin) and its ascending sweep, for instance, invoke the texture and instrumental effects common to a band blues. Still other traits derive from specific gestures that Gershwin honed at the piano as a roll artist. A comparison of the sheet music and Gershwin's roll recording of C. Conrad and J.R. Robinson's "Singin' the Blues" reveals that Gershwin, as

Example 7.1 a) C. Conrad and J. R. Robinson, "Singin' the Blues"

b) Transcription of Gershwin's roll recording

early as 1920, associated the start of a blues number with a middle-register trill and ascending slides into the first melodic pitch (Example 7.1a and b). The grace notes were probably imitations of trombone glissandos like those performed in the introduction to Aileen Stanley's recording of "Singin' the Blues" (Victor 18703), which was issued a month earlier than Gershwin's version. Gershwin's decision to have the melody enter an octave higher (on the last beat of the example) also points to the heightened theatricality he encountered in Grofé's charts for the Whiteman band.

Even before European composers began to experiment with the rhythms and timbres of jazz, popular arrangers like Grofé were among the first to blur the art/jazz divide, endowing their dance band arrangements with more sophisticated introductions, modulations, textures, and dramatic contrasts suggestive of symphonic composition. Many aspects of *Rhapsody in Blue*'s design, as John Howland has documented, directly extend these techniques.[4] Grofé's introductions, for instance, typically subject a phrase of the main theme to sequences and striking contrasts. The introduction to *Rhapsody in Blue* does this too, but on a grander scale, with two theme fragments and a precipitous descent through the circle of fifths from B♭ to V/A. After the introduction, Grofé's arrangements typically feature a series of regularly phrased musical strains linked together, often with short interludes that provide the possibility to modulate. Some two-thirds of *Rhapsody in Blue* (R5^{-3}–R33) follows this approach to form, too, unfolding as a chain of strain statements of five themes, which are frequently identified in the literature by David Schiff's thematic labels: Ritornello (R5^{-3}), Train (R9), Stride (R12), Shuffle (R14), and Love (R28).[5] Similarly, the patterned repetition of catchy four-bar phrases underlying these themes are themselves extensions of the standardized, thirty-two-bar structures that Gershwin cultivated as a composer of popular song.

As much as *Rhapsody in Blue* builds on popular idioms and approaches to form, the work distinguishes itself by drawing on classical techniques and formal characteristics that would become recurring preoccupations in Gershwin's concert works. For one thing, the themes stand apart from his song melodies in their instrumental idiom, internal modulations, and irregular phrase lengths. In addition, their concluding cadences are systematically omitted, a feature that helps propel the music ever forward. On a formal level, the ordering and diversity of expression and tempos recall a one-movement sonata cycle. Gershwin was acquainted with such forms from the music of Liszt among others, but his use of it was idiosyncratic. Seemingly drawn foremost to the general aesthetic balance that its expressive contrasts secured, Gershwin always set the outline of a one-movement sonata cycle in dialogue with another form like the strain-based episodic structure discussed above. Liszt's influence is also palpable in the thematic transformation of the "love theme" in the toccata finale (R34), though the comic inflections of Gershwin's transformation channel the popular piano tradition of "ragging" the classics, too. Perhaps the most profound connections to the techniques of classical composition occur in the handling of theme and motive.[6] A number of recurring rhythmic and tonal traits create a sense of motivic unity among the themes that also extends to the connective tissue between the strain statements. These links were often held up by critics as evidence of the artlessness of Gershwin's handling of form, but this material is in fact strikingly thematic, assembled largely from manipulations of the famous "Man I Love" tag.[7] Such concern for motivic economy grows ever more evident throughout Gershwin's oeuvre.

In addition to extending the tradition of nationalist rhapsodies popularized by Liszt, *Rhapsody in Blue* set the course for symphonic jazz. A short-lived genre of the 1920s and 1930s, symphonic jazz epitomized the middlebrow aesthetic, mixing elements of high and low in amusing pieces that generally lacked higher artistic pretensions. The genre also bore strong cultural associations with New York City, home to its most visible practitioners and the distinctive jazz styles they employed. This connotative power only intensified with the advent of talking pictures and the onset of the Great Depression,[8] helping solidify the identification of *Rhapsody in Blue*, like Gershwin's other concerti, with the city. Although most symphonic jazz languishes in obscurity today, *Rhapsody in Blue* has stood the test of time, a testament not only to its immediate appeal, but also to the artful qualities of its materials and construction – qualities more strongly manifest in Gershwin's other concerti.

Concerto in F

In 1925, Gershwin stepped squarely into the domain of score-oriented composer's music for the first time. The occasion was provided by the conductor Walter Damrosch, who commissioned Gershwin to write a *New York Concerto* and perform it as soloist in a series of concerts with the New York Symphony Orchestra. Gershwin's approach to the composition, retitled Concerto in F just days before its Carnegie Hall premiere,[9] established the process that he would follow in his subsequent concert works. He first completed a sketch score sprinkled with instrumental cues, then produced a full orchestration, in this case his first. True to his pedigree in popular music, he often solicited feedback from friends and associates throughout the compositional process, and, in rehearsal, he continued to make revisions, mostly involving minor cuts and instrumental doublings. In addition, the notation of lengthy passages of the Concerto, unlike his later orchestral scores, lack the expressive and tempo markings necessary for performance. Providing this missing information was a primary task of Frank Campbell-Watson, editor of the posthumously published score (1942), who also modified many of Gershwin's expressive markings and orchestral doublings.

Gershwin cast Concerto in F as an extension of the nineteenth-century symphonic concerto. Its three movements, arranged fast–slow–fast, give far greater prominence and independence to the orchestra than had been the case in the piano-heavy *Rhapsody in Blue*, and the solo-orchestra interaction is often scripted according to generic conventions. Gershwin may also have had eighteenth-century models in mind, as suggested by the first two movements, which begin with the orchestral exposition of functional material followed by the entrance of the solo with a contrasting theme. Within this classical frame, Gershwin again drew on up-to-date fashions in jazz and popular music of New York. The main thrust for the first movement comes from the syncopated rhythm of "The Charleston," a dance tune that swept the country after being featured in James P. Johnson and Cecil Mack's all-black Broadway show *Runnin' Wild* (1923). Notably underrepresented among the Concerto's popular aspects, however, are the distinctive timbres of jazz. Aside from the derby mute used in the second movement's trumpet solos, Gershwin chose to suggest the sounds of popular ensembles using the colors of a standard orchestral palette.

Table 7.1 *George Gershwin, Concerto in F, Mvt. 1: formal overview*

a)	Exposition					Recapitulation					Coda	
b)	Exposition					Development					Recapitulation	
c)	1st-mvt. exposition					1st-mvt. development		Slow mvt.	Scherzo		Finale	Coda
	R1⁺¹ R2 R3 R4 R5 R11					R14		R20 R21	R22 R25⁺¹⁵		R29	R31 R34
d)	⌐P P⌐	⌐Tr Tr⌐	⌐S S S⌐			P	[P, Tr, S]	⌐D D⌐	[P] ⌐[P] [P]⌐		⌐S⌐	[P] P
	F		f (+A♭)			F → E	(modulations)	E	e	D♭	b♭	→ F

a) expanded type 1 sonata
b) tripartite sonata
c) one-movement sonata cycle
d) strain-based repetitions marked by square brackets

Boldface identifies formal features directly related to Rubinstein, Piano Concerto No. 4, mvt. 1.

Concerto in F also resembles a symphonic concerto in its invocation of sonata form in the first movement. This issue is worth examining in some detail, for the idiosyncratic structure reveals much about Gershwin's approach to form and synthesizing disparate traditions, and because recognition of its sophistication has been hampered by the composer's penchant for self-deprecation. In particular, Gershwin was fond of saying that, before he started to compose the Concerto, he purchased a book "on musical structure to find out what the concerto form actually was."[10] Indeed, the first movement makes blatant references to the typical features of a tripartite sonata often found in such books: an exposition with contrasting themes, an apparent development and a recapitulation launched by a *grandioso* return of expositional material. But just as Gershwin's anecdote ironically misrepresented his compositional abilities, the blunt rhetorical signposts convey an incomplete, and even misleading, sense of the underlying form. The following discussion teases apart three structural strands in the movement: those features Gershwin retained from *Rhapsody in Blue*, those that he borrowed from Anton Rubinstein, and those novel twists that he added to the mix (Table 7.1).

Like the similarly proportioned *Rhapsody in Blue*, the first movement of the Concerto contains both the vestiges of a strain-based, episodic structure and the range of tempos and expression of a one-movement sonata cycle. Another slow section in E major provides the expressive center of gravity and later serves as the basis for a thematic transformation, this time as a gliding foxtrot (R26). Yet underlying these commonalities are important differences that reflect Gershwin's growing compositional ambitions. Musical ideas continue to be organized in two-bar groups and four-bar phrases, but they are seldom assembled into units larger than a single period. As a result, the Concerto's strain-based repetitions are not generally premised on song structures. Rather, the primary theme group (P) consists of a collection of brief motives, and the transition (Tr) is based on an eleven-bar telescoping phrase. Closer to popular models are the secondary (S) and slow themes (D), each of which contains an eight-bar period.

Another formal strand seems to have been borrowed from a specific model: Anton Rubinstein's Fourth Piano Concerto (1864). Gershwin revered the composer as a youth, and during his formative years of study with Charles Hambitzer, he heard his teacher perform the first movement in concert. Its structure – unusual not only for a concerto, but also for an opening movement – illustrates what James Hepokoski and Warren Darcy call the "Expanded Type 1" sonata.[11] Unlike a tripartite sonata, such forms work through just two cycles, or "rotations," of the sonata's basic material. Their telltale feature is a statement of P in tonic immediately after the conclusion of the exposition. In addition, it is common for development-like material to delay the return of S. Many features of Gershwin's movement appear to be inspired by, if not directly modeled on, Rubinstein's. The lyrical second theme, led by piano, begins perched on a dominant chord in disorientating inversion and contains prominent melodic leaps of a seventh. The first rotation ends with piano filigree adorning back-to-back authentic cadences that descend by minor third to the tonic, a moment that almost rises to the level of quotation (Examples 7.2a and 7.2b). The second rotation begins with a version of P that starts in tonic but modulates before its cadence, and the eventual return of S is transposed a fifth lower, to the off-tonic key of B♭. A two-part, P-based coda then builds intensity and dramatizes the return to tonic. In light of these myriad similarities, it seems far more likely that Gershwin consulted a score of Rubinstein's work than a book on musical structure.

Although the Concerto's first movement conflates aspects of tripartite and bipartite forms, the resulting structure does not obviously function as a sonata. In fact, Gershwin's movement violates precisely the one essential trait both sonata formats hold in common: an expositional tonal polarity that is resolved in the recapitulation or coda. The Concerto seemingly reverses this trajectory, remaining moored to F in the exposition and moving to the subdominant in the recapitulation. Far from a sign of a deficient grasp of sonata procedures, such idiosyncrasies are coordinated with other tonal and thematic features – the movement's third formal strand – to suggest that Gershwin set out to compose a deliberate misreading of classical music's most venerated form.

Simply put, just as the *Rhapsody* could be understood as being "in Blue," the first movement of the Concerto is, in part, about being "in F." This idea plays out not only at the level of the "monotonal" exposition, but also in the themes themselves. The initial presentation of P is marked by modal equivocation. After the initial timpani motive outlines an ambiguous open fifth, the bluesy harmonies of the Charleston motive suggest F minor, but the cadence unexpectedly resolves in the major. Modal clarification comes in the strain-like repetition of P, which inflects the harmonies to the major, an orientation they retain in subsequent appearances.

It is in S, however, that the idea of being "in F" is most extensively explored. Although its key signature, dominant preparation, and melodic emphasis of the pitch C all point to F minor, this impression is undercut by such features as the unusual inversions, incomplete ninth chords, and sequential harmonic motion. At the end of the first period, it is not even clear what key is being tonicized: F minor (with a seventh), or A♭ major (with an added sixth)? The tonal orientation seems to be clarified in the theme's second half, which twice states a two-bar, ii–V–I–i progression in F. But a third repetition, sequenced up a step on G, leaves S tonally open-ended.

The f/A♭ duality of S is explored further in the remainder of the exposition. The subsequent statements of S re-adjudicate the relative emphases of the keys, but without dislodging F as the ultimate tonal center. Despite significant differences in length and detail, the three thematic extensions of S all entail a failed move to A♭. The first extension (R5^{-6}–R5) builds to a climactic G♭min7 chord that relaxes into a dominant of A♭, only to dissolve into a linear wedge figure that leads into the next statement of S. The second, and longest, extension (R7–R11), includes an expansive dominant preparation and cadence in F major, but this is immediately followed by a circle-of-fifths sequence that ends on the dominant of A♭ – its cadence once again thwarted by a linear wedge figure. The final extension, which culminates in the near-quotation of Rubinstein's concerto (Example 7.2b), does achieve a cadence in A♭, but this is undermined by the persistent presence of the pitch F, a jazzy added sixth emphasized in the treble voices, and the F-major cadence that immediately follows.

The idea of being "in F" is cleverly expressed in the coda. The return to the tonic key coincides with the culmination of a gradual process by which Gershwin synthesizes the movement's central thematic materials. With each structural return of P, the Charleston motive takes on more of the shape, length, and accompaniment of the first phrase of S (Example 7.3). Their complete synthesis, a notable thematic achievement in its own right, also marks one last development in the movement's idiosyncratic tonal plan. Previously, S had consisted of $\hat{5}$ repeated over an unstable dominant in F; here, it features $\hat{1}$ repeated over a stable F-major triad.[12] In other words, Gershwin manages to "recapitulate" S down a fifth while also remaining in tonic. With this self-conscious reference to the movement's

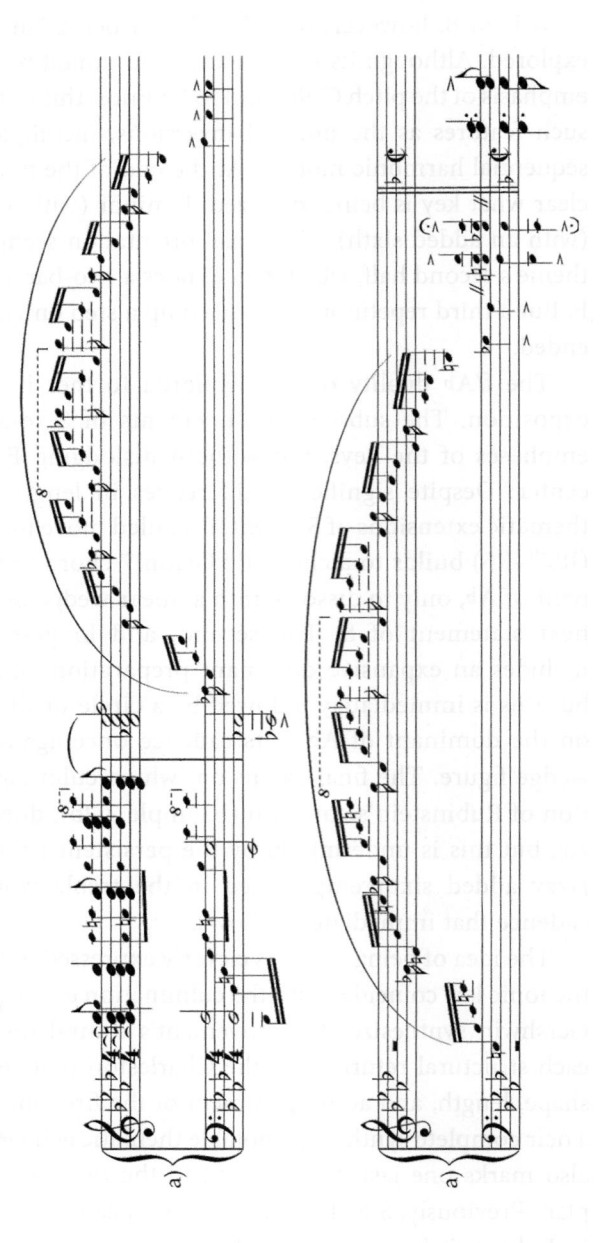

Example 7.2a) George Gershwin, Concerto in F, Mvt. 1, R13-1–R14

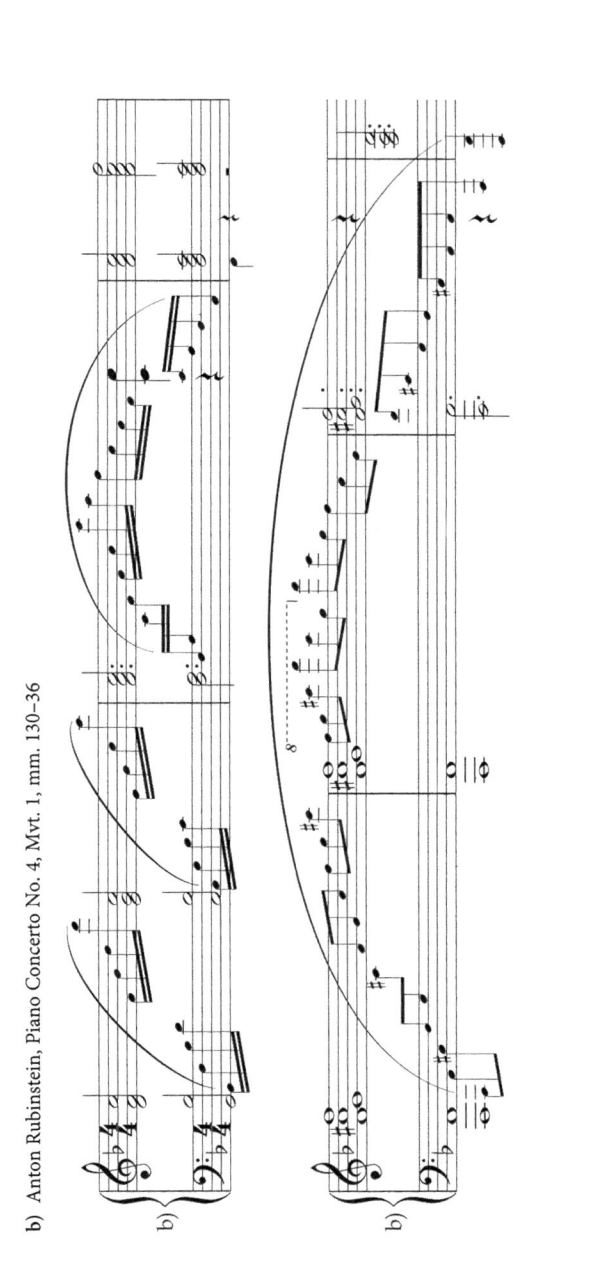

b) Anton Rubinstein, Piano Concerto No. 4, Mvt. 1, mm. 130–36

Example 7.3 George Gershwin, Concerto in F, Mvt. 1: Gradual Synthesis of P and S

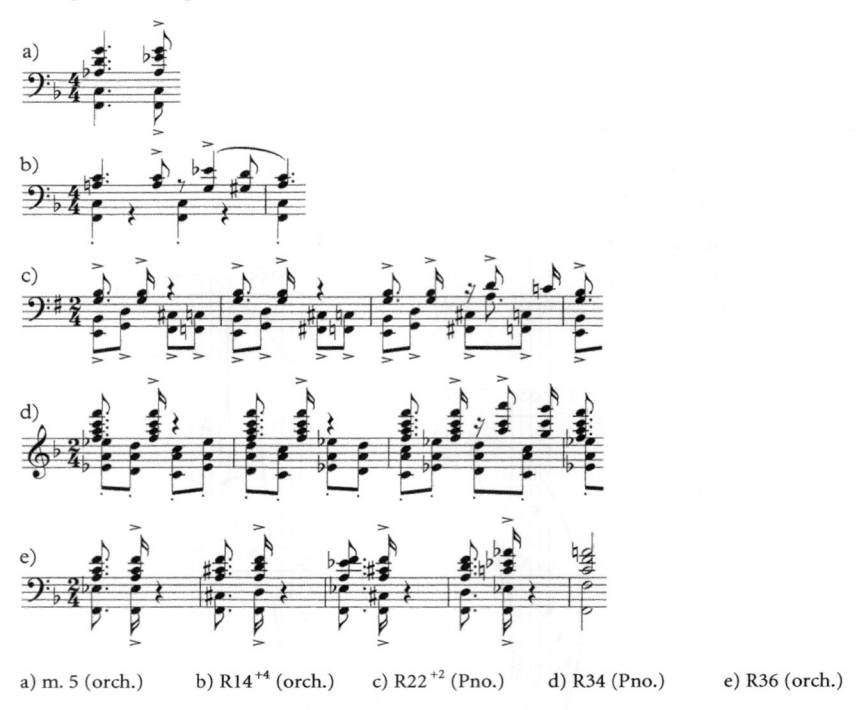

a) m. 5 (orch.)   b) R14^{+4} (orch.)   c) R22^{+2} (Pno.)   d) R34 (Pno.)   e) R36 (orch.)

flouting of sonata conventions, Gershwin has found one final way for S to be "in F."

In the second movement, Gershwin returned to formal strategies more akin to those in *Rhapsody in Blue*. The five-part rondo showcases the blues, drawing not only on its distinctive harmonic, rhythmic, and expressive dispositions, but also on its structure.[13] Like the urban blues, the movement is organized around strain repetitions of modified blues refrains. The sixteen-bar refrain of the opening section features a muted trumpet solo in one of Gershwin's most arresting utterances in the style. The entrance of the piano solo ushers in the first episode, a series of jaunty, eight-bar strains that, in place of turnarounds, end with quick modulations to unexpected keys. The movement's melodic center of gravity, however, comes in the second episode, based on a Gershwin trademark: the ravishing, blues-inflected melody in E major.

Rhythm is thrust to the fore in the third movement. The high-velocity refrain of this rondo form recalls both the toccata-like finale of *Rhapsody in Blue* and, more immediately, the first two bars of S in the first movement. The rondo's episodes consist mostly of thematic transformations of ideas from previous movements, their pert renditions again reminiscent of "ragging" the classics. In the same spirit, Gershwin includes a cheeky send-up of fugal procedures, a distant echo of his irreverent handling of sonata form.

As Gershwin's only multimovement concert work, the Concerto offers a unique perspective on his concern for organic unity. The parade of thematic transformations in the finale is only the most obvious strategy. A small set of tonal centers – F, B♭, E, and D♭ – also create a network of key relationships between the movements. But more sophisticated devices occur across movements and structural levels. The harmonic motion from supertonic to tonic chords, for instance, appears conspicuously throughout the Concerto. In the second half of S in the first movement, the two-bar groups trace an elaborated progression from G minor to F minor. As described above, S ends tonally open-ended when the two-bar group is sequenced up in G minor – itself a higher-order instantiation of the ii–i progression in reverse. This lack of resolution to tonic may be a motivating factor for an even higher-order appearance in the finale, which begins off-tonic with a statement of the S-derived refrain in G minor followed immediately by another in the tonic, F minor.[14] The blues-inspired IV–I cadence functions similarly. In the closing section of the first movement, B♭ constitutes the structural opposition to F, as it will again in the finale. At the climax of the second movement, a bombastic IV–iv–I progression is dramatically cut off before reaching tonic ($R17^{-1}$). This interrupted cadence is completed in the finale by the Concerto's final harmonic progression ($R23^{+20}$), whose IV–iv–I resolution initiates a cyclical return of the percussion motive with which the work began.

Such inter-movemental links in the Concerto point to a far deeper engagement with classical traditions than had been the case in *Rhapsody in Blue*. Although some of this difference may be attributable to the additional compositional craft that Gershwin developed in the intervening year, most of it surely results from the Concerto's longer genesis and from its fundamental conception as composer's music. Gershwin approached *Rhapsody in Blue* as an artistic take on traditions of performer's music, and the speed of its composition only reinforced his reliance on the musical materials and procedures most familiar to him. In Concerto in F, in contrast, he sought to make a direct contribution to concert-hall repertoire, more flexibly deploying elements of jazz and popular music within the basic framework and procedures of a nineteenth-century symphonic concerto.

Second Rhapsody for Orchestra with Piano

In the five years that separate the Concerto in F from *Second Rhapsody*, the stock market crash devastated the livelihoods of countless Americans.

Gershwin remained relatively unscathed by the economic disaster, but the broad cultural changes of the Great Depression influenced his choice of creative pursuits. The frothy musical comedies he favored in the 1920s gave way to projects – operetta, concert works, film, and opera – with more pointed socio-political themes. Something of these changes can be felt in *Second Rhapsody*. Gershwin began the work while in Hollywood to compose a handful of songs for the film *Delicious* (1931). Inspiration came in part from the picture's close-to-home scenario, which raises issues of immigration and assimilation that resonated with his own life and aspirations.[15] As Gershwin later explained: "in the picture a composer [Sascha] comes to the United States, and I decided to write some music which would express the composer's emotional reaction to New York."[16]

At some point after Gershwin began the sketch score, it was decided that room for his new composition would be made in the film, too. Given various names in the script – *Manhattan Rhapsody*, *Rhapsody in Rivets*, and *New York Rhapsody* – the music serves both as Sascha's latest composition and, in abridged form, as the underscore for an innovative sequence in which Sascha's love interest flees through the streets of New York before ultimately surrendering to immigration authorities. Gershwin completed the score to *Second Rhapsody* before the script was finalized or filming began, thus precluding anything but a general influence of the film on his music.

As with the Concerto, Gershwin sketched and orchestrated *Second Rhapsody* and organized a run-through of it all in a semi-private atmosphere amidst friends and colleagues whose feedback he sought.[17] He expressed pride in the work's technical advances and orchestration, a sentiment echoed by Serge Koussevitzky, conductor of the premiere with the Boston Symphony Orchestra in January 1932.[18] Since then, however, *Second Rhapsody* has rarely been performed as Gershwin wrote it. For the published full score, Campbell-Watson commissioned an arrangement by Robert McBride. The only orchestral version available, it lacks the lush, blended textures and even some of the rhythmic vitality of the composer's original.[19]

Second Rhapsody represents Gershwin's continued development of a compositional approach more heavily imbued with classical techniques and aesthetic concerns. As in *Rhapsody in Blue* and the Concerto's first movement, the broad outlines of a one-movement sonata cycle can be detected (Table 7.2), but here they are set into dialogue with a carefully wrought ternary form whose basic design – excited outer sections framing a slow, lyrical interior – may be linked to nineteenth-century keyboard rhapsodies. Gershwin's interest in thematic synthesis, evident in the Concerto and *An American in Paris*, gives shape to the final A section

Table 7.2 George Gershwin, Second Rhapsody: *formal overview*

A											
1st-mvt. exposition						1st-mvt. development		Scherzo		[Reprise]	
R1	R5	R6^{+5} R8		R9	R10^{+12}		R11^{+2}	R13 R15 R16^{+6}	R17	R19^{+2}	R20^{+3}
I	⌐P¬	⌐S¬ ⌐P¬	Tr	⌐S¬	cad. 1 (I, S)	+P		⌐P$_{Sch.}$ P$_{sch.}$¬ cad. 2	⌐P(+S)¬	[P$_{Sch.}$]	cad. 3
F		Bb	D	→ F	Eb		→	A Db →	F		→

B											
Slow											
R21	R22^{-2} R22		R23	R24^{-3} R24		R25^{+3} R27		R28	R29	R30	R31^{-1} R33^{+2}
⌐C1¬	C2	⌐C1¬	C2	[C1]	⌐C1¬	C2	⌐C1¬	C2	[C1]	C2	[C1] ⌐C1¬
A			Db		Bb	A	F			A	C

A									
Retransition				Finale			Coda		
R34	R36^{-4}	R36^{+5}	R37	R38	R40	R41	R43	R44	R46
⌐[P$_{Sch.}$] [P$_{Sch.}$]¬		P	Tr	P(+S) Tr.		P(+S)	C1	P(+S)	C1(+S)
C		G	D	→ F	→	Ab → F	F		

I = introduction P = "rivet theme"
S = secondary theme
PSch. = scherzo C1 = "Brahms theme"
C2 = corollary

Strain-like repetitions marked by square brackets.

and can be felt in the texture, too. *Second Rhapsody* begins in the vein of a concerto, with the individuality of the piano on full display, but increasingly positions the soloist as a prominent member of the orchestra.

A classical orientation is especially apparent in the motivic economy and self-imposed compositional constraints. From this perspective, *Second Rhapsody* can be seen as a study in generating musical interest from minimal and rhythmically monotonous materials. Nearly the entire composition derives from just three themes, each consisting predominantly of constant note values. The impetus for this likely came from Gershwin's professed starting point, a so-called "rivet theme" inspired by the noisy streets of New York.[20] The theme features an onomatopoetic stream of repeated eighth notes, prepared and underpinned by a plodding two-bar vamp. This rigid rhythmic frame is animated by shifting accent patterns and colorful layers of busy accompanimental flourishes. The first phrase of the "rivet theme" also serves additional roles in the work, both as a motto, bluntly hammered at the outset by solo piano, and as the basis for a lilting transformation that comprises the scherzo-like material. The relaxed groove of this section, together with the preparatory vamp in the introduction, betray Gershwin's growing interest in the rumba and other Latin American musical styles that became more prominent in tandem with changes in New York's demographics in the 1930s.[21]

In the lyrical secondary theme, a string of even beat-length values organizes both the melody and accompaniment. Lurking beneath the glassy surface is an undercurrent of disquiet, a product of the sustained metrical displacement and off-beat melody. It is as if the theme were conceived with an utterly square-cut design whose three layers were then systemically offset from the meter by their own number of eighth notes: -2 (Pno. LH), -3 (Pno. RH), -4 (orchestra). The effect is so prolonged as to cause a disorienting metrical hiccup when the melody suddenly snaps to the beat and the accompaniment to the off-beats. The secondary theme also possesses tonal characteristics that will become important later in the work, including the unprepared #$\hat{2}$ dissonances and parallel $^6_4$ triads in its first period and, in its close, a chromatically descending melody and atonal triads (R6^{-6}).

The secondary theme has a curious profile in the overall form. Initially presented as a sonata-like contrast, it quickly loses its independent formal role, becoming instead subsumed into the contrapuntal layers of the "rivet theme." The turning point occurs in the first cadenza (R11^{-5}), where repetitions of the secondary theme's three-note chromatic descent turn menacing and precipitate the first crisis moment. After this point, the theme is never restated intact or on its own. Rather, its salient melodic, harmonic, and rhythmic features are assimilated in the returns of the "rivet theme," distorting its expressive character each time. The procedure can be seen as a variation on the thematic reconciliation in the Concerto's first movement. But instead of drawing out similarities by transforming one theme into the other, the synthesis of themes in *Second Rhapsody* seems to point to a fundamental incommensurability.

The third theme that proceeds in constant note values is, in Gershwin's words, the "Brahms theme."[22] Cut from the cloth of the slow themes found in the earlier concerti, it conveys an earnest aspiration in the artful counterpoint between its melody, which balances stepwise ascents with large downward leaps, and bass, which rises chromatically. In length, emotional depth, and design, however, the lyrical section outstrips its predecessors, a consequence largely of its juxtaposition of the "Brahms theme" with a corollary, marked "fervently." Whereas the "Brahms theme" is treated to strain-like repetitions, the corollary is subjected to a process of growth unprecedented in Gershwin's concert works. Indeed, by ending with two pick-up notes that imply a diatonic resolution, its melodic line embodies the potential for growth and fulfillment. When the corollary is followed by the "Brahms theme," the melodic resolution is chromatic, a harsh reminder of the static status quo that the section seeks to transcend. The diatonic resolutions, in contrast, mark the moments in which the corollary grows longer and more impassioned, spurring the music to ever higher expressive peaks that ultimately culminate in the work's only bright, clear-skied climax.

That these peaks have something to do with the main themes of the outer sections is suggested by numerous motivic and gestural linkages. The "Brahms theme" emerges as an elision with the motto, recasting its final pitch as $\#\hat{2}$ of the new key (A major), and it closes with an allusion to the $\flat\hat{3}-\hat{2}-\hat{1}$ descent heard in the "rivet theme" (R2^{-3}). Likewise, the piano's entrance in the middle section is couched as an allusion to its dialogic appearance in the A section (R3). At the same time, the "Brahms theme" can be seen as an idealized projection of the secondary theme. Not only do its melody and accompaniment move together in constant note values, but also its initial $\#\hat{2}-\hat{3}-\hat{5}$ ascent resolves the lingering dissonance of the secondary theme's opening phrase, which rises $\#\hat{2}-\hat{3}-\hat{4}$ and then $\#\hat{2}-\hat{3}-\#\hat{4}$. As the "Brahms theme" modulates to B♭ major, the original key of the secondary theme, an intimate chamber texture highlights the pitch-specific connection.

Whatever aspirations and ideals the middle section seems to represent, they are obliterated in the final A section. It begins with a retransition-like passage based on material that had previously led to the F-major statement of the secondary theme. Yet in place of its original goal is a return of the "rivet theme" in tonic, its sturdy vamp and whirring woodwinds entirely replaced by a bevy of elements from the secondary theme. This frantic new conflation lasts but one phrase before yielding to discordant orchestral convulsions. Similarly, the climactic orchestral return of the "Brahms theme," gutted of its original harmonies and bass-line ascent, is shot through with searing dissonances verging on atonality. Finally, in the work's perorational statement of the "Brahms theme" (R46), the piano loses its way, spiraling downward as it becomes engulfed by the descending atonal triads. With these strident sonorities, Gershwin's darkest concerto, and most pessimistic portrait of New York City, comes to a close. *Second Rhapsody* punctures the myth, promoted by Depression-era film and symphonic jazz, of the city as glamorous dreamscape. Having thus pulled back the curtain on the grim realities of everyday life, however, Gershwin allowed it to close again for his final work for piano and orchestra.

"I Got Rhythm" Variations

In early 1934, Gershwin undertook a concert tour with the Leo Reisman Orchestra to celebrate the tenth anniversary of *Rhapsody in Blue*. The itinerary was grueling – twenty-eight concerts in as many days and cities – and the evening-length program kept an almost non-stop spotlight on Gershwin at the piano. Gershwin performed as soloist in *Rhapsody in Blue*, Concerto in F, and an orchestral potpourri of his tunes, and as accompanist for a set of his songs. These demands were no doubt on his mind as he composed yet another concerted work for the program. *"I Got Rhythm" Variations* is his shortest concert work, and its instrumentation is tailored to the idiosyncratic make-up of Reisman's touring ensemble, essentially a wind-heavy chamber orchestra with saxophones. Although *Variations* returns to the dance-band textures of *Rhapsody in Blue*, its composition takes a further step into the domain of composer's music. Gershwin added to the compositional process an additional stage of revision devoted to fine-tuning the notation of the piano part. For the published full score in 1953, Campbell-Watkins again commissioned a new orchestration. This time, his decision reflected not just the general lack of regard that dogged Gershwin's concert music, but also a legitimate concern about the commercial viability of the original instrumentation. William Schoenfeld's arrangement disrupts Gershwin's intentions less than McBride's version of *Second Rhapsody*, and it serves as the basis for nearly all modern recordings.

Gershwin presumably chose the refrain of "I Got Rhythm" as his variation theme because of its immense potential for elaboration. On its own, the song, which debuted in Gershwin's *Girl Crazy* (1930), enjoyed only mild success. But the economy of its rhythmic, harmonic, and melodic design made it an ideal basis for creative departures, as jazz musicians had already begun to discover. Gershwin's concert work, however, gives the tune a more classical treatment: a theme and six character variations framed by an introduction and brief close.

The musical topics in *Variations* collectively conjure the distinctive image of New York. Unlike *Second Rhapsody*'s gritty soundscape, though, *Variations* provides an escapist return to the carefree days captured by *Rhapsody in Blue*. The solo piano introduces the thirty-four-bar, AABA tune in a stripped-down *Song-Book* style that suggests the manner in which Gershwin might have begun an actual evening-party improvisation. Var. 1 shifts to the outdoors, its rhythms and tutti texture giving a general sense of the bustling streets and jagged skyline. A hint of nostalgia bubbles to the surface in the dreamy, pentatonic-flavored *valse triste* (Var. 2). Aspects of New York's ethnic and musical diversity are captured in the remaining variations, which include an imitation of out-of-tune Chinese flutes (Var. 3), the improvisatory style of a "hot" jazz band (Var. 4), and an up-tempo rendition of the theme akin to its performances as a jazz standard (Var. 5, 6).

The modest dimensions and descriptive qualities of *Variations* might lead one to think that the work is a retreat from the compositional ambitions evinced in previous concerti. But such is not the case. The accessible exterior belies a harmonic and motivic sophistication whose modernist stance surpasses that of the more overtly pungent *Second Rhapsody*. Already in the opening bars Gershwin signals that this piece will be as much a vehicle for his compositional ingenuity as his pianism. As if to highlight the expansion of his creative abilities since composing *Rhapsody in Blue*, he begins *Variations* with a solo clarinet that presents the theme's iconic head motive four times in mathematically expanding intervals that are then abruptly collapsed again by the piano. Over the course of the brief introduction, the motive is verticalized as a quartal harmony, given in rhythmic diminution, presented in interlocking chains, and contrapuntally combined with its retrograde. In like manner, the tonal language is at turns pentatonic, diatonic, quartal, pandiatonic, and chromatic. Such overt displays of compositional technique can be attributed in part to Gershwin's concurrent studies with the theorist Joseph Schillinger. The opening clarinet and piano passage, for example, exemplifies Schillinger's principle of geometric expansion. Though obscure today, Schillinger's methods were well known among popular composers of the time, and they exhibited a similar interest in systematic and mathematical manipulations that animated Bartók, Stravinsky, and the Second Viennese School.[23] But the Schillinger influence can be easily overstated, for all of these traits are anticipated in Gershwin's earlier works.

In spite of its brevity and the potential limitations of variations as a form, *Variations* illustrates Gershwin's ongoing concerns for structure and unity. Once again, the work exhibits aspects of a one-movement sonata cycle. The theme and first variation together create an exposition-like opening in tonic, F major, and then a lyrical variation in a different key constitutes the work's (relatively) slow section. The Chinese and "hot" jazz variations provide scherzo-like energy before the finale (Var. 5, 6), which includes a dramatized return to tonic. As a form, variations have a natural affinity with the episodic strain structures and linking passages that Gershwin inherited from popular music. But in *Variations* more than his previous works, Gershwin departs significantly from the theme's underlying AABA form. In addition, these moments of thematic departure are aligned with inter-variational linkages. Var. 2, for example, consists of two statements of the theme's last phrase. The first statement falls a note short of its cadence ($R9^{-5}$), releasing impressionistic ripples whose extended tertian harmonies and rhythmic layers forecast the explicit orientalisms of Var. 3 as much as they invoke Debussy's "Pagodes." Such linkages are especially prominent in the last two variations. Var. 5, in D♭ major, begins with the high violin pedal point from the introduction, then uses an "accelerating" complementary rhythm between piano and orchestra to build to a climax in the theme's b phrase. Here the variation breaks off with a remarkable chord that combines both the dominant and tritone substitution of F major (R26^{-1}), a sonority last heard at the corresponding moment in the piano's original statement of the theme. The start of Var. 6 brings about the return of tonic, and another complementary rhythm leads to a climax at the end of the b phrase. This time, however, it manages to cadence and proceed to the final a phrase, whose parallel 4ths and 2nds allude to the orientalisms of Var. 3.

In the monothematic *Variations*, Gershwin's long-standing concern for motivic connections between themes finds an outlet in the contrapuntal layering of the theme's head motive. Two extraordinary moments merit mention. First, in the brief transition between Var. 1 and Var. 2, the motive is presented simultaneously at multiple speeds and pitch levels, forwards and backwards, and verticalized as a quartal harmony (R3). The moment can be regarded as the apotheosis of Gershwin's thematic linking material, evident since *Rhapsody in Blue*. And second, after achieving the cadence at the end of the b phrase in Var. 6, the work reaches its climax with the head motive presented at three pitch levels in the pianist's right hand at the same time that it plays the inversion at three pitch levels in the left (Example 7.4). What is more, the texture is divided into three layers staggered by a sixteenth note, creating composite rhythm of running sixteenth notes. The moment provides a fitting end to a work designed to show off both the compositional and the pianistic aspects of Gershwin's creativity.

Gershwin as Pianist

Gershwin enthusiastically embraced technology to foster the dissemination of his music, and these efforts gave rise to a number of extant recordings of his performances of the concerti. Their variability in origin, sound, completeness, and performance quality reflects transformations in the economics and technology of sound recording and radio broadcast during his lifetime (Table 7.3). Of the concerti, only *Rhapsody in Blue* was released commercially. Its roll recording documents the work uncut and with the composer performing both the solo and the orchestral reduction. But for nuanced questions about Gershwin's style and touch, it is of limited value due to the editorial interventions typical of the medium and to the technological compromises necessary to accommodate such a long work on two rolls.[24] More informative in

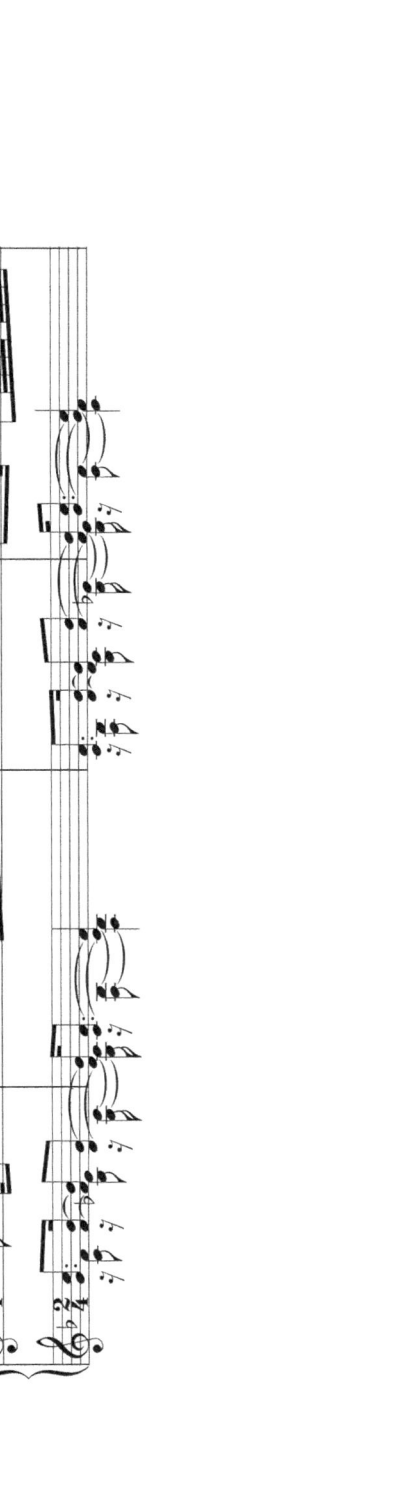

Example 7.4 George Gershwin, "*I Got Rhythm*" *Variations*, Piano Solo, R28^{+10}–R28^{+13}

Table 7.3 *Extant recordings of concerti with George Gershwin as soloist*

Work	Details
Rhapsody in Blue abridged	• rec. 1924: studio recording, acoustic (Victor 55225) • Paul Whiteman and the Paul Whiteman Orchestra
Rhapsody in Blue unabridged	• rec. 1925: piano-roll recording (Duo-Art 68787, Duo-Art 70947)
Rhapsody in Blue abridged	• rec. 1927: studio recording, electric (Victor 35822) • Nathanial Shillkret and the Paul Whiteman Orchestra
Rhapsody in Blue "Andante" (*sic.*) only	• rec. 1928: studio recording, electric (Columbia 50107-D)
Concerto in F, mvt. 2 m. 127 to end	• rec. 1935: radio broadcast • conductor, ensemble unknown
Concerto in F, mvt. 3 abridged; arr. Eliot Jacoby	• rec. 1933: radio broadcast • Rudy Vallée and the Rudy Vallée Orchestra
Concerto in F, mvt. 3 abridged	• rec. 1934: radio broadcast • Louis Katzman and the WJZ studio orchestra
Second Rhapsody unabridged; predates final version	• rec. 1931: private rehearsal recording
"I Got Rhythm" Variations slightly abridged	• rec. 1934: radio broadcast • Louis Katzman and the WJZ studio orchestra

this regard are the studio recordings, which unfortunately required draconian cuts to fit onto a single 78 rpm record. As the Depression hastened the demise of the player-piano industry and slowed the phonograph market, Gershwin took ever greater advantage of the more ephemeral and less costly medium of radio. The only documentation of Gershwin's performances of the Concerto and *Variations* consist of such broadcasts fortuitously captured on shellac discs. Anomalous among the recordings is the single take of *Second Rhapsody*, which preserves the private rehearsal that Gershwin organized before finalizing the score.

Taken together, the recordings offer ample support for both the effusive praise and the occasional critiques of Gershwin's pianism by his contemporaries.[25] The clear-cut voicing, rhythmic clarity, and sensitivity to the ebb and flow of dramatic tension possess an authority befitting the music's composer. Both versions of *Rhapsody in Blue* with the Whiteman Orchestra are consistently assured and often exude a strong sense of rhythmic vitality. Likewise, Gershwin's renditions of the *Second Rhapsody* and *Variations* remain at the top of their undeservedly meager discographies. Nonetheless, Gershwin's playing often falls surprisingly short. His execution can be sloppy and the expression dull, creating the impression, most common in lyrical passages, that he was just going through the motions. To be sure, concertizing was but one of Gershwin's varied professional activities. The careful preparation that informed the relatively polished studio performances of *Rhapsody in Blue* was not practical for each one-off broadcast or rehearsal. Lack of rehearsal may explain Gershwin's desire, especially apparent on the 1933 broadcast of the Concerto's finale, to lead from the piano by doubling the orchestra when the soloist otherwise has rests. But one also senses that performing with an ensemble from notated music was something of an artificial undertaking for a pianist who honed his skills through countless moments of spontaneous creation at brisk tempos and in intimate settings. As Jonathan Bellman memorably observed, Gershwin's performances of the concerti often sound as if he were imitating a concert pianist.[26] To be sure, Gershwin was a virtuoso by the standards of novelty and stride piano, possessing a supreme ability to maintain rhythmic élan through an improvised series of musical strains in characteristic textures and figurations. Many of his recorded song improvisations brilliantly model this ability, and it is only natural that high points in his performances of the concerti cluster in passages indebted to these styles.

Gershwin offered practical tips for rendering popular song at the piano in the introduction to his *Song-Book* (1932), a collection of eighteen songs for voice and piano followed by a transcription of his improvisation on the song's refrain. This advice has some relevance for his concerti, too. His caution against overuse of the sustaining pedal and romantic legato is reflected in his recordings, which feature the pedal less as a means for connection than as a timbral device that highlights important chords or moments of arrival. Yet Gershwin's concerto performances often fall short of his other recommendation, which calls for a staccato style with stark accents: "the more sharply the music is played, the more effective it sounds."[27] Although these shortcomings may betray the relative brevity of his formal study of the instrument (about eight years), other factors are in play. For one, subjective impressions of sharpness have likely shifted with time. After Virgil Thomson, who witnessed the premiere of *Rhapsody in Blue*, attended a recreation of Whiteman's "Experiment" in 1984, he was asked to compare the performance with the original. Reluctant to answer, he simply remarked: "But [in 1924] they all played *lighter* than we do now."[28] For another, the editors of the concerti's published scores often included more exaggerated articulations and dynamics than those in the manuscripts, making these scores a misleading basis of comparison for Gershwin's performances. And Gershwin himself seems to have understood that such generalized rules of performance practice can only be taken so far. Indeed, the "stenciled" style he describes is perhaps most consistently realized, by both the ensemble and the soloist, in the recordings of the Paul Whiteman Orchestra with Roy Bargy. The mannered quality of their renditions, however, confirms the superiority of Gershwin's subtle control of note length and articulation, which is especially evident in repetitive left-hand patterns and repeated quarter-note themes in the right hand.

Gershwin's recordings of the concerti, like those of his songs, are often marked by driving tempos. Time constraints of a 78 rpm record or radio segment may have influenced these choices, but their consistent presence in diverse performance settings suggests that they were his preference, too. Gershwin compounded their effect with targeted accelerations. Sometimes subtle but always sudden, they galvanize the music's energy both at potential moments of dramatic sag, including phrasal seams and repetitions and at the inherently exciting bursts of rhythmic activity that appear in fills, links, and runs to the cadence. In his recording of *Variations*, for example, Gershwin plays the first phrase of the theme at 108 bpm until the sixth bar (R2). Here the apex pitch gets an extra kick by arriving slightly early – the first sign of an increased tempo for the phrase's cadential descent. The same process, only more exaggerated, occurs in the second phrase, whose base tempo is also slightly elevated compared to the first.

The rhythmic vitality of Gershwin's performances also arose from his flexible division of the beat. The ten-year span of the concerti recordings extended from the relative strictness of ragtime rhythms to the coalescence of triplet-based swing in jazz. How strictly to play the dotted-eighth-and-sixteenth rhythms, especially prevalent in the Concerto's first movement, was already open to interpretation during the composer's lifetime. Gershwin clearly preferred a strict rendering of rhythms on his recordings, reserving asymmetrical eighths for occasional effects. The roll recording of *Rhapsody in Blue* nicely captures the spectrum of unevenness Gershwin employed, from slightly unequal eighths to a two-to-one relationship ($R21^{-1}$). His recordings of the Concerto's finale are useful for showing two different approaches to the same brief passage ($R20^{-16}$), which he rendered in a triplet-based swing in 1933 and a more idiosyncratic rushing of the beat in 1934.

Popular piano styles are but one stylistic influence in the concerti, and they are seldom presented with the stereotypical accompaniments of rag and stride intact. As if to compensate for the absence of metrically regular left-hand patterns, Gershwin's performances tend to emphasize strong beats, creating a metrical framework against which tempos can change and rhythms unfold with far greater freedom than on his recorded song improvisations. The effect is dependent on context, underpinning such diverse passages as the comically jerking rhythms in *Rhapsody in Blue* (R19), the exaggerated rubato in the bluesy recapitulation in the close of the Concerto's slow movement (R17), and the relentless forward momentum of the toccata theme of the Concerto's finale. Elsewhere, however, it seems more of a liability, as in lyrical passages like the love theme of *Rhapsody in Blue*, where the attention it draws to the bar lines disrupts the musical flow. It is one thing to avoid sentimentality, as Gershwin wished to do, and another to abandon musical sensitivity altogether.

Gershwin surely picked up some of this pliability of tempo and rhythm from his studies of classical music. He even seems to have absorbed from this repertoire a particular notational convention for indicating rubato. Since the early nineteenth century, expanding and contracting hairpins were often viewed, particularly in piano and chamber literature, as expressive markings calling for an intensification and relaxation through any means, but especially through rhythmic inflection.[29] The lyrical secondary theme of the Concerto's first movement is adorned with expressive hairpins of this kind.[30] No recording of the passage with Gershwin at the piano survives, but on both recordings of the theme's tutti return in the finale, Gershwin alters the piano's triplets to accommodate a pronounced rubato in the orchestra that corresponds with the expressive hairpins marked in the first movement.

Gershwin's apparent awareness of this notational convention may help explain one of the biggest puzzles for the performance practice of *Rhapsody in Blue*: how to handle the tempo in the unusually proportioned "love theme," which features two bars of quarter notes followed by a three-note ascent with eight beats per pitch. In both recordings with the Whiteman Orchestra, the theme is played as written, with no tempo modification, resulting in an utter loss of momentum in the second half of each phrase. (One wonders if Gershwin had this passage in mind when he complained about Whiteman's tempos.) Modern performance practice, which can be traced back to Gershwin's lifetime, addresses the problem by doubling the tempo for the bars with tied whole notes. An easy and compelling solution for an ensemble to implement, it is not the one chosen by Gershwin when he had sole control of the pacing. Instead, he preferred an approach to tempo reminiscent of the expressive hairpin tradition, surging ahead and relaxing again in each two-bar group of the three-note ascent. Indeed, this interpretation corresponds with actual hairpins entered into Gershwin's pencil sketch score. In light of this notation and Gershwin's recordings, it seems that he composed the "love theme" in terms of a romantic, pianistic idiom unfamiliar to many popular ensembles of the time but brought to life whenever he had unfettered control of the performance.

For all that the recordings tell us about Gershwin the pianist, they provide new insight about him as a composer, too. Mistakes and context-driven doublings of the orchestra notwithstanding, his performances

Example 7.5 *Rhapsody in Blue*, m. 302: voicing of final chord

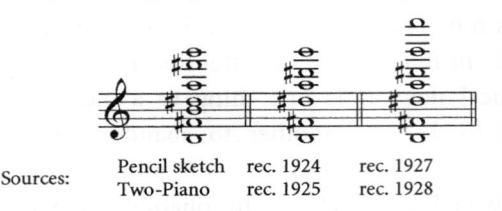

Sources: Pencil sketch / Two-Piano   rec. 1924 / rec. 1925   rec. 1927 / rec. 1928

of the concerti, unlike his songs, are all marked by a conspicuous fidelity to the notated parts. Not even the cadenzas give rise to extemporaneous flights of fancy. The only glimmers of improvisational intent come in small grace-note flourishes. Such a direct correlation between performance and part reflects Gershwin's conception of his concerti as composer's music, whose notation was intended to be realized within the restrictive interpretational limits of the concert repertoire. This view even extends to *Rhapsody in Blue*. In spite of the collaborative nature of its genesis and the domain of performer's music from which it sprang, Gershwin's recordings stick to the script.

A host of small discrepancies between Gershwin's performances and the notated parts take on considerable significance in the combined context of his overriding concern for fidelity and his penchant to tweak compositions after completing their scores. More than mere artifacts of a particular performance, these departures can be seen as revisions to the underlying musical work. They are extensions of the act of composition itself. This process of honing is most obvious in *Rhapsody in Blue* and Concerto in F, his earliest concerti and those with the greatest legacy of recorded performances. A slight but informative example involves the arpeggiated chord that prepares the entrance of *Rhapsody in Blue*'s "love theme" (Example 7.5). None of Gershwin's recorded performances follow his original notation, and for good reason. The chord fits awkwardly in the hands, and its overemphasized fifth makes for a hollow sonority ill suited to the moment. On all four recordings, Gershwin re-voiced the chord in the same way, making it fuller and more idiomatic. The new voicing also emphasizes the tritone, an interval that would takes on increasing prominence in his later works. And on the recordings from 1927 and 1928, he went a step further, adding the gleam of an additional upper octave. That Gershwin intended these changes as revisions is further suggested by a similar alteration that he made at an analogous moment in the 1935 broadcast of the Concerto's slow movement (R10).

The three recordings of the first tutti passage in *Rhapsody in Blue* illustrate other types of revisions that Gershwin made to the concerti in performance. He consistently added a lower octave to the grace notes at m. 21, supplying needed heft and linking the gesture registrally with preceding and subsequent material. The clumsiness of the intended ricochet effect between orchestra and piano (mm. 22–23) must have been quickly apparent, for the chords are brought into alignment on all the recordings and, unlike most other small revisions, in the published two-piano score, too. Subtler are the inner voices that Gershwin supplied to the final two chords of the descent, distinguishing the piano from the octaves of the orchestra.

Of course, it is not always possible to definitively separate revisions to the underlying work from artifacts of particular performances. At some point after *Rhapsody in Blue* had been arranged by Grofé, for instance, Gershwin entered a *luftpause* at the end of m. 23 of his sketch score. Despite its effectiveness, this gesture, unlike the other departures in these bars, is observed only on the roll recording. Perhaps this is because Gershwin did not control the pacing of this tutti passage on the recordings with the Whiteman Orchestra. Alternatively, he may have felt that only the roll recording required an extra pause because it lacked the timbral contrast that helped define the moment in performances with an ensemble. Whatever the case may be, it is among surprisingly few deviations that are ambiguous in this way. Rather, the recordings of the concerti reveal a composer who welcomed the chance to fine-tune details of his concert works, and a performer keen to adhere strictly to the given part.

Broadly speaking, three interpretative approaches can be identified in the modern discography of Gershwin's concerti. Each emphasizes an important aspect of the composer's distinctive synthesis of musical styles. The least common approach is the one taken by Gershwin himself. These recordings foreground the indebtedness to post-rag popular music of the 1920s, emphasizing tempo and rhythm at the expense of the range and intensity of expression, especially in lyrical passages. More common, especially for *Rhapsody in Blue* and Concerto in F, are recordings that connect the works back to romantic traditions, rendering the solo part with an interpretational sensibility appropriate to a concerto by Tchaikovsky or Grieg. A third approach connects them forward to later jazz music by modernizing the piano's harmonies, improvising cadenzas, and interjecting decorative flourishes and a pronounced swing.

Gershwin's early death robbed us of the opportunity to know what he would have thought of these developments. But one can easily imagine. In 1926, a year after his Carnegie Hall debut with Concerto in F – a stunning achievement for any composer's first orchestral opus, not to mention for a pianist with little classical training – Gershwin remarked that he was about to summit an even higher artistic peak: performing the same work with the same musicians, but on live radio for a million listeners.[31] As Gershwin flouted aesthetic boundaries and composed ever more sophisticated works for the concert hall, he never grew suspicious of the desire to entertain the public. What remained most important to him was that his music be part of a living tradition that brings pleasure to new and diverse audiences.

Acknowledgments

I would like to acknowledge the feedback and suggestions I received from Jonathan Guez, Peter Mowrey, Paul Sherrill, and Logan Skelton. I also thank Lindy Marie Smith of the Jerome Library at Bowling Green State University for making the sheet music to "Singin' in the Blues" available.

Notes

1. Richard Crawford, *America's Musical Life: A History* (New York: W.W. Norton, 2001), x.
2. Ryan Raul Bañagale, *Arranging Gershwin:* Rhapsody in Blue *and the Creation of an American Icon* (Oxford: Oxford University Press, 2011).
3. "Gershwin Plays His Rhapsody," *New York Sun* (7 May 1930); cf. Howard Pollack, *George Gershwin: His Life and Work* (Berkeley: University of California Press, 2006), 309.
4. John Louis Howland, "Between the Muses and the Masses: Symphonic Jazz, 'Glorified' Entertainment, and the Rise of the American Musical Middlebrow, 1920–1944," Ph.D. dissertation, Stanford University (2002), 1–25.
5. David Schiff, *Gershwin:* Rhapsody in Blue (Cambridge: Cambridge University Press, 1997), 13–14.
6. Arthur Maisel, "Talent and Technique: Gershwin's *Rhapsody in Blue*," in Allen Cadwallader (ed.), *Trends in Schenkerian Research* (New York: Schirmer, 1979), 51–70; Susan Neimoyer, "*Rhapsody in Blue*: A Culmination of George Gershwin's Early Musical Education," Ph.D. dssertation, University of Washington (2003), 157–68.
7. Schiff, *Gershwin*, 24–25.
8. Howland, "Between the Muses and the Masses," 1–3.
9. Gershwin still referred to the work as *New York Concerto* in late November. See Leon Lipsky, "George Gershwin: Jazz Glorifier," *American Hebrew* (November 27, 1925), 59.
10. The anecdote originally appeared in Isaac Goldberg's biography (*George Gershwin: A Study in American Music* [New York: Simon & Schuster, 1931], 178). Gershwin also retold a version on a broadcast of "Music with Gershwin" in 1934. Edward Jablonski wrongly attributes the statement's origin to a newspaper interview that preceded the Concerto's premiere (*Gershwin Remembered* [Portland, OR: Amadeus Press, 1992], 174).
11. James Hepokoski and Warren Darcy, *Elements of Sonata Theory: Norms, Types, and Deformations in the Late-Eighteenth-Century Sonata* (Oxford: Oxford University Press, 2006), 349–50. Gershwin called the music at R14 a "development," but this does not invalidate seeing the form in other ways.
12. The reorientation is made possible by replacing the original ninth, which had appeared in the bass, with a tonic pedal, and by the fact that the most prominent blues notes, $\hat{7}$ and $\hat{3}$, are separated by a fifth.
13. Charles Hamm, "A Blues for the Ages," in *Putting Popular Music in Its Place* (Cambridge: Cambridge University Press, 1995), 330–31.
14. Steven Gilbert, *The Music of Gershwin* (New Haven: Yale University Press, 1995), 106–08, suggests that the finale's off-tonic opening creates a tonal bridge from the end of the second movement, whose final sonority, a second-inversion tonic triad, emphasizes A♭.
15. Larry Starr, *George Gershwin* (New Haven and London: Yale University Press, 2011), 3–4.

16. Edward Jablonski and Lawrence D. Stewart, *The Gershwin Years* (Garden City, NY: Doubleday, 1958), 212.
17. James Wierzbicki, "The Hollywood Career of Gershwin's *Second Rhapsody*," *Journal of the American Musicological Society* 60/1 (2007), 141–46 and others have cast doubt on the reliability of Hugo Friedhofer's and Edward Kilenyi's claims to have made substantive contributions to the work's composition.
18. Pollack, *George Gershwin*, 496.
19. Recordings featuring Gershwin's orchestration and piano part include: Michael Tilson Thomas, conductor and pianist, with the Los Angeles Philharmonic (Sony MK39699); and Roberto Minczuk and the Calgary Philharmonic with pianist Stewart Goodyear (*Rhapsody in Blue: The Best of George Gershwin*). Oscar Levant's recording with Morton Gould and His Orchestra, which appeared before the publication of McBride's score, makes substantive interventions in the orchestration (Sony MK42514).
20. Gershwin to Isaac Goldberg, cf. Jablonski and Stewart, *Gershwin Years*, 212.
21. Pollack, *George Gershwin*, 491.
22. Oscar Levant, *A Smattering of Ignorance* (New York: Doubleday, Doran, 1940), 191.
23. Paul Nauert, "Theory and Practice in *Porgy and Bess*: The Gershwin-Schillinger Connection," *Musical Quarterly* 78/1 (spring 1994), 9–33; Noel Brooks, "A Schillingerian and Schenkerian Approach to George Gershwin's '*I Got Rhythm*' *Variations*," M.M. thesis, University of Western Ontario (1998).
24. Artis Wodehouse, "Tracing Gershwin's Piano Rolls," in Wayne Schneider (ed.), *The Gershwin Style: New Looks at the Music of George Gershwin* (Oxford: Oxford University Press, 1999), 221.
25. See Pollack, *George Gershwin*, 61–80.
26. Jonathan Bellman, "Performance Practice Methodology and Its Limits: The Case of George Gershwin," paper read at the 78th annual meeting of the American Musicological Society, New Orleans, 2012.
27. George Gershwin, introduction to *George Gershwin's Song-book* (New York: Simon & Schuster, 1932), x.
28. Maurice Peress, *Dvořák to Duke Ellington: A Conductor Explores America's Music and Its African American Roots* (Oxford: Oxford University Press, 2004), 96.
29. David Hyun-Su Kim, "The Brahmsian Hairpin," *19th-Century Music* 36/1 (2012), 48.
30. I am indebted to Logan Skelton for bringing to my attention the expressive hairpins in the context of the Concerto.
31. George Gershwin, "Jazz Is the Voice of the American Soul," *Theatre Magazine* 45/3 (March 1927), 14.

8 Harmonizing Music and Money: Gershwin's Economic Strategies from "Swanee" to *An American in Paris*

MARK CLAGUE

George Gershwin has been both celebrated and reviled as a hybridizer of musics popular and classical. The tale that he was turned down as a pupil by Stravinsky is a case in point. In this frequently reprinted anecdote, the young American met Stravinsky (or Ravel in some tellings) and asked for lessons. The European master replied by asking Gershwin how much money he made and, after Gershwin named an astronomical sum, quipped: "Then I should take lessons from you!" Whether the story is true or not is irrelevant to the argument here. It is the persistence of the tale and its humor that highlight an ideological fault line between Old World and New, classical and popular, artistic accomplishment and economic success.

Scholars have long recognized Gershwin's concomitant financial success, but the interrelationship of his artistic and economic accomplishments only rarely receive sustained attention. This chapter argues that Gershwin's economic and artistic fortunes were deeply intertwined. Documents in entertainment trade magazines and the composer's personal legal/financial records deposited at the Library of Congress reveal that Gershwin brought the economic experience of popular music to the concert hall, applying for-profit strategies from Tin Pan Alley and Broadway to the tradition of classical music. Raised in a musical world defined by hits, Gershwin sought "hits" in the concert hall as well. He was as ambitious in his artistic dreams as he was in his quest for financial reward.

Gershwin's pursuit of profit was in harmony with his pursuit of compositional craft, musical innovation, and emotional expression. For Gershwin, writing original music that delivered a message, whether as a freestanding song, as part of a Broadway spectacle, or as a piece of concert music, was what led to hits that would be successful both musically and financially. Gershwin's strategies for wealth, fame, and artistic achievement were all part of the same ambition to write great music that would reach large audiences. He saw musical excellence as a market opportunity; melody propelled by original, sophisticated music would triumph as art and product. He would write great music, and great music would sell.

Gershwin's *An American in Paris* offers a signal example. This orchestral tone poem was not commissioned, but a project of Gershwin's own. He received no fee to compose it, yet the resulting high-profile premiere in December 1928 established the reputation of Gershwin's first work for orchestra alone. The composer then leveraged this success not only for subsequent concert performances, but also for a series of radio, recording, publishing, and stage projects that within one year reached larger audiences and returned significantly more financial reward than would be realized even today through a traditional orchestral commission. While *An American in Paris* continues to thrive as a concert hall staple (not only in pops programming but now also as a subscription concert feature that sells tickets), during its first year of existence it was heard more often outside the concert hall than within it. Gershwin's approach to *An American in Paris* is as indebted to the patterns established by his first Tin Pan Alley hit "Swanee" as his experience with Concerto in F.

Gershwin's creative and business practices are best described as a symbiosis. His success in popular music, as well as *Rhapsody in Blue*, subsidized the creation of *An American in Paris*, allowing him to compose without a commission or promise of performance. The payoff came later, when radio, recording, and Broadway performances carried the music to an increasingly broad audience, propelling its success both financially and critically. Such additional revenue streams led to financial freedoms that furthered Gershwin's focus on creating music and his increasing independence in terms of how he composed, what he composed and for whom. Economic stability enabled artistic risk taking. Gershwin's artistic achievements thus were often nurtured and amplified by commercial success. In turn, such success provided a financial base to support further artistic exploration. Money and music were harmonized.

George Gershwin's first published song was the 1916 title "When You Want 'Em, You Can't Get 'Em, When You've Got 'Em, You Don't Want 'Em," with lyrics by Murray Roth. Although in 1914 Gershwin dropped out of school to work for Remick & Co. for a weekly salary of $15 as a staff pianist (also known as a "song plugger"), the firm at first refused to publish his songs.[1] On the recommendation of Sophie Tucker, Gershwin's first title was published by the rival house of Harry Von Tilzer. Together Roth and Gershwin were paid $1 for the song with the promise of a half cent royalty on every printed copy sold in the United States and Canada, plus 25 percent of any recording fees received by the publisher.[2] Gershwin reportedly made a grand total of only five dollars on the song.[3] But sheet music sales were not his only source of income from this tune. In September of the same year, Gershwin recorded a piano roll of "When You Want 'Em" as a "fox trot" instrumental for Universal.[4] Thus, from even this first song publication, Gershwin leveraged connections with a star performer to create opportunity and then used multiple product streams to increase the economic reach of a single creative work.

After leaving Remick on March 17, 1917, Gershwin worked as an accompanist, landing a job for the Broadway show *Miss 1917*, produced by Charles Dillingham and Florenz Ziegfeld and directed by Ned Wayburn.[5] The music was by Jerome Kern, a composer and partner in the Harms publishing firm. Gershwin described the resulting career breakthrough in an interview with *The Billboard* magazine in 1920:

> After I got to know the music of the show, I started to put little frills and furbelows into it. This made a hit with the chorus girls and Ned Wayburn found they worked better when I played for them. Jerome Kern had written the music for the show and both he and Harry Askins, the manager, took an interest in me. I had written a song called "The Making of a Girl," which was in *The Passing Show of 1917* and made quite a hit. On the strength of this, Mr. Askins offered to introduce me to Max Dreyfus, the head of T.B. Harms and Francis, Day & Hunter, the publishers.
>
> I accepted gladly and the following day we went to see Mr. Dreyfus. He asked me to play for him and I played four of my songs. When I finished, he said "Come and see me next Monday." At this I laughed inwardly, for it had a familiar sound by that time [of polite refusal]. It so happened that I had been engaged to play the piano for Louise Dresser's vaudeville act and I didn't consider Mr. Dreyfus' invitation to call again very seriously. You can judge of my surprise then, when on going to see him the next Monday, he said, "Gershwin, I believe you've got the stuff in you. I'm willing to back my judgment by putting you on the salary list. You may make good the first year, but if you don't, you will in the second or third or fourth or perhaps the fifth. Go to it."[6]

Gershwin signed with Dreyfus on February 21, 1918.[7] His was a remarkable contract for a young songwriter with more promise than hits to his credit.

Founded in 1881 as the Thomas B. Harms Music Publishing Company and known as Harms, Inc. from 1921, the house would remain Gershwin's publisher under one imprint or another throughout his creative life, publishing both his songs and his concert music. Dreyfus had purchased the firm in 1904 from Thomas Harms, gradually turning it into the most prestigious publisher of New York's Tin Pan Alley. By 1918 when Gershwin signed, it was known as T. B. Harms, Francis, Day, & Hunter and was fast becoming a Broadway powerhouse. Dreyfus discovered and promoted Jerome Kern, Vincent Youmans, Richard Rodgers, Oscar Hammerstein, Kurt Weill, Alan Jay Lerner, and Cole Porter as well as Gershwin.[8] In 1920 Harms, Inc. was named as one of the defendants to a US Justice Department lawsuit under the 1890 Sherman Antitrust Act.

Together the seven defendants allegedly controlled some 80 percent of the US music publishing business.[9] In time, Harms would combine with the English firm of Chappell, Inc. to publish some 90 percent of Broadway's songs.[10]

Gershwin's contract with Harms granted the publisher exclusive and comprehensive ownership of Gershwin's music and the "sole, exclusive, absolute and unlimited right, license, privilege and authority to publish, copyright, re-copyright, print, reprint, copy and vend, throughout the civilized world, all the music and all the ensembles, concerted numbers, solo numbers and all other numbers composed and written" by the composer.[11] Any lyricist collaborating with Gershwin would be bound by the same stipulation, and the company retained the right to change title or lyrics to any work. Harms negotiated agreements with his lyricists separately, but they were required to sign, or they could not work with Gershwin.

The composer was at liberty to compose for any Broadway production company, as long as the music would be published exclusively by Harms. Gershwin could not publish with anyone else, even as a collaborator, nor allow his name to be used by another publisher. There was only one exception – three works already under contract to Remick: "There's More to a Kiss," "Loving Makes Living So Sweet," and "A Corner of Heaven with You."

In exchange Gershwin received the promise that Harms would publish any and all of the works created by the composer. If the company chose not to publish a work within a year, ownership of that work would revert to its author. Gershwin received an initial royalty of three cents per copy for each piece of sheet music sold (publicity and professional copies exempted). And he was given a weekly salary of $35, payable on Saturday, for the rights to whatever he might compose. In 2018 dollars, this salary would have amounted to approximately $30,000 a year. The contract includes no requirement that any composition be delivered, but Gershwin negotiated a handwritten addition to the contract – he would receive an additional advance of $15 each week against future royalties. The composer thus increased his living allowance, but incurred a debt to the company that would necessitate publication success to offset. The advance can be seen as a sign of his confidence and determination. It also allowed and required a greater focus on composition; by signing, Gershwin committed to being a full-time songwriter. Any other income earned by the company off of Gershwin's music, say in licensing the music for foreign publication or for a recording or for use in a stage show, would net Gershwin 25 percent of the publisher's receipts. The parties paid each other $1 to seal the deal.[12]

Dreyfus's offer represented an investment in Gershwin's all-but-unproven talent and economic potential. It also amplified and propelled this potential. With the Harms' marketing machine leveraging Gershwin's music, both composer and company sought to benefit. An important clause in the contract at once flattered and disciplined the composer:

> It is further agreed upon between the parties hereto that the said Composer is well, favorably and extensively known as one of the leading composers of music, and that his services as such are peculiar, exceptional, unique and extraordinary, and that his compositions have been uniformly distinctive; that his compositions cannot be duplicated, and that in the event of a breach of this agreement by the said Composer, the Company will sustain irreparable damage and inestimable loss, due to the fact, among other things, that immediately upon the execution of this contract the Company will incur considerable expense in advertising and popularizing the compositions of the said Composer, and it is agreed that in the event of any such breach upon the part of said Composer, the Company shall thereafter be wholly and absolutely released from any and every obligation hereunder.[13]

If Gershwin were to renege on the deal, he would lose everything. Everything included the rights in perpetuity to all of the music published under the terms of the deal. The compositions would become the sole property of the publisher. In addition, the company would no longer need to pay any royalty due on this music now or in the future.

The terms and conditions applied indefinitely to Gershwin's musical works "in full force and effect forever." The contract would be valid for just a year, but Harms had the option to renew on the same terms for an additional year at its own discretion. Such a renewal would presumably include a similar one-year renewal clause, so Gershwin was, in effect, signed for life.

In 1945, eight years after Gershwin's death, his music industry friends created the reverential biopic film *Rhapsody in Blue*.[14] While Robert Alda appeared as Gershwin, many of the industry figures who played a role in the composer's success appeared in cameos as themselves, and maybe not surprisingly with a bit of self-aggrandizement as to their personal impact on Gershwin's career. Oscar Levant and Al Jolson appeared as themselves. Both figure prominently in the scenes addressing Gershwin's initial song hit, "Swanee" (1919), a major episode in both the composer's life and the biopic. About twenty minutes into the film, Levant encounters Gershwin in the waiting room of Harms, Inc., where the young George is hoping to meet Dreyfus for the first time and introduce him to his music. Levant looks over the song Gershwin has brought to pitch to the publisher and remarks wryly: "Hmm, diminished ninth; if I had your talent, I'd be a pretty obnoxious fella." Dreyfus (played by Charles Coburn) soon meets privately with Gershwin. Reviewing the manuscript to "Swanee," Dreyfus similarly identifies a "diminished ninth" chord and remarks that it is "unusual for popular music." The filmic George points out that in popular music "we gotta have something different." Certainly, a diminished ninth chord would be innovative and a signal of the influence of jazz, but it is not precisely clear what this non-standard musical term might indicate in the script. It could be a joke, a reference to jazz-sounding chord extensions, or literal description.

The film then compresses two events into one: Dreyfus's negotiation of Gershwin's Harms contract and the introduction of Gershwin's soon-to-be hit to star Al Jolson, who would make "Swanee" famous in his musical revue *Sinbad*. In the film, Dreyfus immediately offers Gershwin a two-year contract at $30 a week. When Gershwin expresses surprise, Dreyfus raises his salary to $35. The incredulous composer remarks: "You mean you'd *pay* me to write my own songs." Dreyfus quickly realizes his error, smiling as he recognizes Gershwin's noble naiveté. Next, George sits at the piano and plays an ornamented accompaniment to "Swanee." Without another word, Dreyfus walks to his desk and phones the Winter Garden Theatre, where *Sinbad* is running. Jolson answers backstage and hears Gershwin playing in the background. He asks: "Who's that guy plunkin' the piano?" Dreyfus replies "Gershwin," and Jolson responds: "Gershwin! Never heard of him." Yet after listening a bit more, Jolson remarks "Say, that ain't a bad ditty" and wants to know "Who wrote it?" After being introduced to the composer, Jolson remarks to Dreyfus: "Max, look, send that song over to me, and I guarantee I'll make 'em beat a path to it a mile long."

While exaggerating Gershwin's passive role in this business opportunity and thus amplifying the role of Dreyfus and Jolson in launching the young composer's career, the scene communicates two ideas. First, that George was either too pure of musical heart or simply too naïve to be aware of the art's business side. Second, it depicts Dreyfus as Gershwin's career mastermind, immediately making a connection to Jolson that would guarantee the composer's success. Neither of these claims ring precisely true to history.

In reality, Gershwin had worked his way up from song plugger to vaudeville accompanist to Broadway rehearsal pianist with grit, determination, and savvy, all the while writing songs and gaining musical skills, artistic insights, and a network of professional connections. Gershwin first met Jolson at the Atlantic City tryouts for his show *La-La-Lucille!* in April of 1919, likely through the show's lyricist Buddy DeSylva, a Gershwin collaborator and Jolson friend.[15] DeSylva, in fact, co-wrote one of the songs originally featured in *Sinbad*, "I'll Tell the World," as well as two song hits later interpolated into the revue: "I'll Say She Does" and "Chloe," both co-authored with Jolson.[16] It was some eight months later, in December 1918, with Jolson no doubt searching for new songs to add to *Sinbad*, that Gershwin – not Dreyfus – pitched "Swanee." In the company of DeSylva and "Swanee" lyricist Irving Caesar, Gershwin performed the song for Jolson. Dreyfus was not present, although the fact that the composer had signed with Harms the previous year would have been both a significant professional endorsement and a signal to Jolson that pushing the young composer's song offered an economic opportunity for him as well.

Jolson soon incorporated "Swanee" into his ongoing revue *Sinbad* during a December 22 to January 3 run at the Crescent Theatre in Brooklyn. The song was featured subsequently in the show's run at Poli's Theater in Washington, DC beginning on January 11.[17] A review in *The Washington Post* described "Swanee" as "the biggest hit of last evening."[18] Sheet music for the song sold concurrently for 35 cents a copy at a local store.[19] Dreyfus certainly shares credit for the song's success, rushing a new sheet music edition into stores. Jolson's portrait nearly fills the cover page of this Harm's imprint, leveraging the singer's celebrity to sell the song. Using the endorsement of a star performer to spur sales was a time-tested technique, and given Jolson's unparalleled celebrity and popularity as an entertainer and recording artist at this time, the singer's bold "guarantee" as voiced in the 1945 film was a realistic boast. Likely more influential than Jolson's stage performance, however, was the recording he made for Columbia on January 8, 1920, immediately after its original New York run in *Sinbad*.[20] The recording featured the singer's characteristic birdsong whistling and helped sell the sheet music. Again, Harms marketing machine capitalized.

When Jolson's recording was released around February 20, Harms placed a two-page advertisement in the music industry magazine *Variety*, touting "Swanee" as a "sensational song success."[21] By April, Columbia Records was placing illustrated advertisements coast to coast.[22] These make no mention of Gershwin, who did not yet have a national following, and who was not a Columbia artist. Nonetheless, the composer benefited. Jolson's recording sold an estimated two million copies, twice that of the music, and in doing so secured Gershwin's first triumph. In May, Jolson's recording hit number one on the Billboard chart. It remained on the charts for eighteen weeks, holding the top position for nine. Gershwin himself released two recordings of "Swanee" seemingly timed to take advantage of the Jolson boost. The first was a solo piano roll recorded in February 1920.[23] For the second, released the next month, Gershwin performed as pianist with banjoist Fred Van Eps and his quartet.[24]

It is important to note that while the success of "Swanee" was certainly propelled by Jolson, it did not begin with Jolson. "Swanee" was originally featured as the music for a production number in the *Demi-Tasse Revue* – a twelve-scene spectacle created by *Ziegfeld Follies* choreographer Ned Wayburn for the October 1919 grand opening of New York's luxurious Capitol Theatre at Broadway and 51st Street.[25] With 5,300 seats, the Capitol was touted as "the largest theater in the world" and targeted an upscale, but necessarily broad, popular audience. Although located in the theater district, the Capitol was first and foremost a "silent" movie house whose musicians provided accompaniment to the film. The *Demi-Tasse Revue* stage show was performed twice daily to entertain an audience anticipating the rotating cinema feature.[26]

Gershwin contributed two songs to the revue: "Swanee" as well as the final production number, "Come to the Moon." "Swanee" appeared in Scene V as one of two "Shadowland" dance numbers. While the up-tempo syncopation of "Swanee" spoke to post-war optimism, the lyric's nostalgic references to the antebellum South inspired the costuming. Its eight dancers are listed as four "Old Fashioned Belles" and four "Old Fashioned Beaux."[27]

To make money on music in Tin Pan Alley in 1919 was to sell sheet music. The first edition of "Swanee" was published by Harms for the Capitol Theatre show, and it appeared months before Jolson had even heard the song. Printed in two colors (black and olive green), the sheet music's cover features a line drawing of a dapper couple, the man wearing a top hat and the woman wearing a white hat, reflecting both the pairs of dancers in the revue, and no doubt aimed at couples attending the show who might want a souvenir from their romantic evening. With economic efficiency, this identical design was used – the title and lyricist's name changed – for "Come to the Moon."

The *Demi-Tasse Revue* continued through November and December 1919, and Gershwin's song gained prominence. The November 15 issue of *The Billboard* touted "Swanee" as a hit and its future success is predicted: "The big song hit of the Ned Wayburn Revue at the Capitol Theater is 'Swanee.' This is a new number by George Gershwin, the composer of 'La La Lucille.' I. Caeser [sic.] is responsible for the lyric 'Swanee' is sung in the revue by Muriel De Forrest and has scored strongly at all performances. It is a different sort of a Southern song and will probably be classed among the hits of the day ere long."[28]

The December 27 issue of the same trade journal notes that "Swanee" has been moved to the top of the show as the "first number" and "should be a big hit for dances."[29] Received wisdom in the Gershwin literature explains the triumph of "Swanee" as a result of Jolson's star power.

Certainly, Jolson propelled the music to nationwide fame and made this first hit the biggest seller of Gershwin's career, but it was the Capitol Theatre Revue that first launched "Swanee" toward success. Jolson thus adopted a regional hit, transforming it into a national one. That Jolson came to play this role, however, may have been part of the songwriters' creative inspiration, if not a savvy and bold business plan.

The tale of Gershwin's "Swanee" typically depicts the writing of the tune as a bit of good fortune. Caesar claimed it was written in about fifteen minutes, while Gershwin gave it "about an hour."[30] Apparently the pair began composing the song on a bus ride to the Gershwin family apartment, having just visited the Harms offices. The rapid timeline of its creation mythologizes Gershwin's genius but fails to recognize how the song's themes and style may have been intentionally calculated to meet the needs of popular success. Tin Pan Alley cared about hits and little else. As aspiring songwriters, Gershwin and Caesar would undoubtedly have had the same goal, and their publisher would no doubt have offered advice on what and how to write.

"Swanee" is a parody of songwriter Stephen Foster's pre-Civil War tune "Old Folks at Home." A parlor minstrel tune in dialect, Foster's song opens with the line: "Way down upon the Swanee Ribber," thus giving Gershwin's "Swanee" its name. "The word ["Swanee"] fascinated me," Gershwin later explained.[31] Gershwin's music as well as Caesar's words – particularly the concluding reference to the "old folks at home" – make the connection to Foster's song immediate and clear. Likewise, Gershwin's melody for the chorus paraphrases Foster's opening melody.[32] In "Swanee," minstrelsy, nostalgia, exoticism, and ragtime are wrapped into one, lyrically and musically.

Although written in 1851, Foster's song was alive and well in Gershwin's sound world more than six decades later. It had been reborn in the midst of World War I through the community singing movement as an expression of homesickness and patriotic nostalgia. Jolson himself had struck this vein of gold with his 1916 hit recording of "Down Where the Swanee River Flows," written by Charles S. Alberts and Charles K. McCarron with music by Albert Von Tilzer. It reached number three on the Billboard chart in August.[33] Its lyrical themes – love and longing for "home," "Dixieland," "the Swanee River," "the banjo," "my dear old mother," and singing birds – all prefigure Caesar's lyric three years later. Yet another Swanee song triumphed just the month before Gershwin's own premiered, Harry Hamilton's "My Swanee Home." This sentimental ballad, which likewise made both melodic and lyrical reference to Foster's original, peaked at number five on October 18.[34] Thus Gershwin's fascination with the word may well have been genuine, but it was seeded by fashion and economic opportunity. A standard Tin Pan Alley songwriting strategy was to mimic the themes and styles of a current hit to create a new one.

Gershwin's "Swanee" seems all but calculated to the commercial needs of Tin Pan Alley generally and a Jolson hit song in particular. The blackface performer specialized in mammy songs and up-tempo ragtime numbers. "Swanee" met both needs with its syncopated rhythms and references to the Deep South, "Dixie," and the singer's "Mammy, waiting for me." Jolson's show *Sinbad* traded upon a fascination with exotica, specifically the Arabian nights, so Gershwin's use of an exotic sonic model, the 1918 hit "Hindustan" by composer Harold Weeks, made a song about the past, stylistically current.[35] Further, a long-running show such as *Sinbad* demanded new material. Revues had to be updated with new songs to keep audiences coming back for more. This continual revitalization of repertoire provided economic opportunities to launch a sequence of hit songs, sell sheet music, and sell recordings.

Gershwin's "Swanee" seems almost custom built for Jolson's revue. In this regard, it is possible that the 1945 *Rhapsody in Blue* biopic may hint at the truth. If Caesar and Gershwin wrote "Swanee" on the way home after a meeting at Harms, maybe Dreyfus or another Harms's employee had suggested that the pair create a song for Jolson. In any event, the extraordinary success of the *Sinbad*/"Swanee" combination inspired future efforts of undeniable economic calculation. Gershwin, with both DeSylva and Caesar, continued to write songs for Jolson's show, including "Tomalé (I'm Hot for You)" and "Swanee Rose" (also known as "Dixie Rose").[36] The latter was a direct attempt at a follow-up hit. As a Harms advertising notice put it, "Swanee Rose" "looks like another 'Swanee.'"[37]

Yet Gershwin's "Swanee" was much more than a vapid commercial product. In an interview for *Edison Musical Magazine*, Gershwin expressed pride in the economic and artistic synthesis of the song:

> I am happy to be told that the romance of that land [the South] is felt in it ["Swanee"], and that at the same time the spirit and energy of our United States is present. We are not all business or all romance, but a combination of the two, and really American music should represent these two characteristics which I tried to unite in "Swanee" and make represent the soul of this country.[38]

Gershwin's artistic ambition is embedded in the harmonies of "Swanee." His "diminished ninth" (in the form of the song's unusual augmented chords in the insistent chorus) broke the mold of the typical Tin Pan Alley song structure. Gershwin did, in fact, do something "different" musically with "Swanee" to make it stand out from its competitors as something special. For Gershwin, artistic innovation was a feature of value, a feature that would appeal to the public and help create a hit.

In many ways, Gershwin's alloy of romance and drive, passion and profit, inaugurates the Roaring Twenties, a time when the ragged rhythms of African American culture catalyzed the peace-time prosperity of the industrial age in the United States. Gershwin's art seems to resolve at once the tension between Old World and New, between the ambition for artistic expression and the drive for business success. Passion and profit seem, if not harmonized, then at least placed in a constructive partnership that brings the Ziegfeld Theatre and Carnegie Hall – Tin Pan Alley song and orchestral composition – into conversation.

In early 1925, conductor Walter Damrosch of the New York Symphony Society asked the society's president, Harry Harkness Flagler, to commission a piano concerto from George Gershwin. Flagler phoned Gershwin with the proposal. "This showed great confidence on his [Damrosch's] part," Gershwin noted, "as I had never written anything for symphony before."[39] Gershwin stopped by the symphony offices in Steinway Hall on April 17, 1925 to sign the contract with manager George Engles. The composer agreed to deliver score and parts to a work for piano and orchestra, tentatively titled "New York Concerto," a week before rehearsals for a premiere on December 3. The contract anticipated seven performances: two in New York, for which Gershwin would receive $500; and five additional performances compensated at a rate of $300 each. The December 3 date at Carnegie Hall was specified to be "the first performance of the work in New York."[40] Gershwin was thus set to earn $2,000 total.[41] That the fee was tied to performances – which were likely to be highly anticipated and sold out – adroitly served the needs of the Symphony Society, which was in significant financial trouble.[42] Gershwin only performed Concerto in F with the society six times, and he seems to have received no advance financial support or fee for composing the piece.

Certainly, the motivations of both composer and commissioner were more than financial. A composer himself, Damrosch was a regular supporter of contemporary music. He gave the American premiere of Mahler's Fourth Symphony and performed new works by Elgar, Debussy, Strauss, Stravinsky, and Milhaud. He supported American composers as well, conducting music by John Alden Carpenter, George Chadwick, Aaron Copland, Charles Martin Loeffler, Daniel Gregory Mason, and Deems Taylor, as well as Gershwin. Damrosch not only knew Gershwin through the composer's friendship with his daughter Alice, but he had also attended both a rehearsal and the 1924 premiere of *Rhapsody in Blue*. Talking about the composer in the press, Damrosch echoed Paul Whiteman's rhetoric that Gershwin's classical efforts made jazz respectable as art. According to

Damrosch, Gershwin was a musical "prince who has taken Cinderella by the hand and openly proclaimed her a princess to the astonished world."[43]

For Gershwin the concerto was a claim to artistic respectability. He sought to prove that the 1924 success of *Rhapsody* was not a fluke. "Many persons had thought that the Rhapsody was only a happy accident. Well, I went out, for one thing, to show them that there was plenty more where that had come from. I made up my mind to do a piece of absolute music. That Rhapsody, as its title implied, was a blues impression. The Concerto would be unrelated to any program."[44] That Gershwin changed the title from *New York Concerto* to the more prosaic, standardized classical moniker, Concerto in F, signaled his attempt to cleave to the traditions of absolute music. Three years later, his orchestral tone poem would embrace these same ideals of symphonic concert music to please the critics, but with the addition of a narrative program to please the public.

An American in Paris was premiered by the same conductor and ensemble, and represents another step in Gershwin's quest to earn both a living and critical respect. Gershwin's interest in composing the tone poem seems to have been ignited not by a call from an orchestra manager, but by a one-week visit to the European cultural capital in 1926. He had visited with friends Mabel and Bob Schirmer in Paris during a break from the London launch of his hit musical *Lady, Be Good!* An inscribed photograph dated April 11 thanking the Schirmers for their hospitality includes notation for two musical themes: the opening "Andantino" from *Rhapsody in Blue* and a new melodic motif labeled "Very Parisienne" and prophetically titled "An American in Paris." The four-bar fragment would find its way into Gershwin's "Orchestral Tone Poem" two years later as its opening "walking theme."

Gershwin started composing *An American in Paris* in January of 1928. Unlike Concerto in F or *Rhapsody in Blue*, he wrote without the promise of performance. He had no particular deadline in mind, yet continued work on the score from March to June, during a three-month tour of England, France, Austria, and Germany, and completed a draft on August 1 back in New York. Described variously in the press as a "symphony," a "ballet for symphony orchestra" and a "jazz symphony," the ultimate title of the work had been announced even before Gershwin had set sail for London.[45] A May 29 Parisian premiere at an all-Gershwin concert had been contemplated if Gershwin could finish the score in time.[46] Instead, it appears that a meeting between Gershwin and Damrosch in Europe led to the plan for a Carnegie Hall debut.[47] On June 5, the New York Philharmonic-Symphony (the now combined forces of the New York Symphony and New York Philharmonic Society), announced it would perform Gershwin's "orchestral rhapsody" that fall.[48] When Gershwin got word on November 5 that Damrosch would lead the premiere in December, he retreated to Bydale, the Connecticut home of Kay Swift and James Warburg, where he sequestered himself in a private cottage to work. A little more than two weeks later, on November 22, Gershwin was pictured in the *New York Sun*, sitting next to the conductor at the piano, the pair reportedly reviewing the new score.[49]

It is perhaps an indication of his characteristic confidence that Gershwin composed *An American in Paris* without a commission. Yet the score also contains a shadow of the composer's professional anxiety. The cover page proudly proclaims that its contents were "Composed and Orchestrated by George Gershwin." Such a declaration suggests that the work was meant as an answer to critics who had branded him an incapable orchestrator. Each page of sketch, draft, and full score are written entirely in the composer's own hand. Gershwin was proud of this work, and, not coincidentally, it seems intended as a kind of artistic manifesto, simultaneously accessible to a broad swath of listeners due to its sonic narrative while also demonstrating polished compositional skills, especially in the integrated development of its themes. The melodies and mottos of *An American in Paris* are derived primarily from the original "Very Parisienne" theme inscribed to the Schirmers. Each theme in the work's A section (bars 1–383) is developed from this single two-eighths and quarter-note motif and presents a remarkable example of motivic cohesion. *An American in Paris* is thus a proclamation of compositional authority on a symphonic scale.

Gershwin was certainly paid for the New York premiere of *An American in Paris*. He received a rental fee for the "orchestration" of $25 and an additional $25 for each performance. In December 1928, the orchestra performed the work four times: the December 13 premiere plus performances on December 14, 21, and 22. There appears to have been no extra fee assessed for the rights to the world premiere. A Philharmonic receipt reports a payment of $125 to "New World Music Corp.," a Harms subsidiary that handled only the Gershwin catalog.[50] Considering that Gershwin spent approximately six months on the composition, this fee is far from a just wage and is far below the sum he might earn in the popular music realm. However, Gershwin was financially successful enough to afford a three-month European tour. He could effectively subsidize his own time through previous earnings. Further, he was about to earn significantly more money from his new orchestral work by licensing it to popular outlets outside the concert hall.

Gershwin's largest single payday for *An American in Paris* came in January 1929 when he sold the rights for its radio broadcast premiere to the Godfrey Wetterlow Company representing the W.S. Quinby Company.[51]

Quinby was a tea and coffee importer, roaster, and wholesaler located in Boston and Chicago.[52] Like many companies in the first decades of radio, it sponsored a radio show to reach customers across a wide geography. In Quinby's case, this show was the La Touraine Coffee Concerts on NBC, which was broadcast through WCAE in Pittsburgh. Gershwin's radio contract was pathbreaking. According to the *Pittsburgh Press*, the agreement marked "the first time in the history of radio that sponsors of commercial features have contracted for the rights to the first performances of such a work." The composer and Deems Taylor seem to have helped narrate the show on January 30, 1929 beginning at 7:30 p.m. Nathaniel Shilkret conducted the La Touraine Orchestra. The program also included "excerpts from the famous Gershwin 'Rhapsody in Blue,' and a medley of his musical comedy, revue and dance hits."[53]

Gershwin was paid the astonishing fee of $5,000 for this broadcast premiere, a fee not much different from what an A-list composer might receive for an orchestral commission today.[54] Adjusted for inflation, $5,000 in 1929 is roughly equivalent to $73,000 in 2018 and would thus equate to around $4,000 per minute for the 18-minute musical work.

The radio premiere secured, Gershwin then released a recording. Victor Recording Company logs report that conductor Nathaniel Shilkret, fifty-three instrumentalists, and Gershwin himself gathered in New York City's Liederkranz Hall on February 4, 1929 to record *An American in Paris*. According to Shilkret's autobiography, the composer had asked him personally to conduct the recording. Gershwin himself played celeste, and Shilkret reported that the composer was so deeply invested in offering suggestions to the orchestra, that he had to request that Gershwin leave the soundstage for an hour so that the musicians could rehearse uninterrupted.[55] The resulting two-disc 78 rpm set was nominally part of Victor's May 1929 releases, but newspaper reviews and store advertisements appear as early as April 19, less than three months after the recording session. Each premium 12 inch disc sold for $1.25.[56] Four years later, a second "recording" was released. In June 1933, master piano-roll maker Frank Milne arranged *An American in Paris* for player piano. It was published by the Aeolian American Corporation on both the Duo-Art and the Ampico series.[57] "Milne and Leith" are credited as pianists to give the impression of a full four-hands arrangement, but Milne made the rolls alone, using the added pseudonym "Ernest Leith." The rolls were coded with unusual dynamic detail and required a reproducing piano in excellent condition. Such rolls were considered of special artistic value.

A review of the performance history of *An American in Paris* tells a story of artistic success and financial innovation (see Table 8.1). In the first year after its premiere, *An American in Paris* was performed in some

Table 8.1 *Performances of* An American in Paris *1928–1929*

Dates	Orchestra/Conductor	Location	Perfs.
Dec 13–14, 1928	New York Philharmonic-Symphony/Damrosch[b]	Carnegie	2
Dec 20–21, 1928	New York Philharmonic-Symphony/Damrosch	Carnegie	2
Jan 30, 1929	La Touraine Orchestra/Nathaniel Shilkret[ab]	Pittsburgh (NBC)	1
March 1–2, 1929	Cincinnati Symphony Orchestra/Reiner[b]	Music Hall	2
April 8, 1929	Cincinnati/Reiner (on tour in Indianapolis)	Murat	1
April 9, 1929	Cincinnati/Reiner (on tour in Lafayette)	Memorial Gymnasium, Purdue University	1
April 14, 1929	Cincinnati/Reiner (on tour in Dayton)	Victory Theater	1
June 25, 1929	Off-Broadway Opening of *Show Girl*[b]	Colonial Theatre (Boston)	7[58]
June 27, 1929	Boston Symphony Orchestra/Alfredo Casella[59, b]	Symphony Hall	1
July 8, 1929	NY Philharmonic-Symphony/Willem van Hoogstraten[ab]	Lewisohn Stadium	1
July 2–Oct 5, 1929	*Show Girl* on Broadway[b]	Ziegfeld Theatre	111
Aug 22–24, 1929	Garden Theatre Orchestra/Adolphe Kornspan	St. Louis	3
Aug 26, 1929	NY Philharmonic-Symphony/George Gershwin[b]	Lewisohn Stadium	1
Sept 3, 1929	Milwaukee Philharmonic Orchestra/Frank Laird Waller	Pabst Theatre	1
Nov 10, 1929	Manhattan Symphony Orchestra/George Gershwin	Mecca Temple	1
Dec 8, 1929	Arnold Johnson Orchestra/George Gershwin[ab]	CBS Radio	1
Dec 27, 1929	Minneapolis Symphony Orchestra/Henri Verbrugghen	Lyceum Theater	1

[a] radio broadcast;
[b] Gershwin attended at least one performance

twenty instrumental concerts – a remarkable level of interest in a new work, then as now. The New York Philharmonic-Symphony performed the work six times, while the Cincinnati Symphony Orchestra under the baton of Fritz Reiner undertook five renditions. Other performances were done by the Boston, Milwaukee, Manhattan, and Minneapolis symphonies, while a St. Louis theater orchestra presented the work three times. Three other performances were broadcast via radio, including a coast-to-coast performance for CBS.

Gershwin was present for most of these performances. His participation would have facilitated the delivery of the four pitched taxi horns that he had composed into the work. Initially, Gershwin's participation typically involved attending a performance and acknowledging the enthusiastic appreciation of the audience, but for the Lewisohn Stadium concert on

August 26 Gershwin appeared in the triple role as composer, soloist, and conductor. This drew a standing-room audience of some 12,000 to the New York University sports stadium. After playing Weber's *Der Freischutz* overture, Willem van Hoogstraten conducted the New York Philharmonic-Symphony, with Gershwin at the keyboard, for *Rhapsody in Blue*. *Three Hungarian Dances* by Brahms followed and gave Gershwin a few minutes' break before he returned to the stage to close the first half of the program by conducting *An American in Paris* himself. One reviewer described the dramatic scene and less-than-stellar conducting:

> In due time Mr. Gershwin reappears to conduct his newest opus, "An American in Paris." So tensely quiet are these 15,000 listeners that voices in the street two blocks away can be plainly heard. The young maestro is nervous. He stands rigid, merely beating time and marking the attacks of the violins on the one side and of the horns on the other.[60]

After the performance Gershwin was "hardly able to contain his enthusiasm," the *New York Times* explained. "Never," the paper quoted Gershwin as saying, "had he conducted before an orchestra or even a jazz band." While observing that the composer would not claim to be a "virtuoso conductor," the *Times* review describes the rookie effort more generously as displaying "a clear and admirable sense of rhythm" and notes that "he watched his score closely . . . giving these musicians the clean beat and the occasional cue."[61]

Conducting the Manhattan Symphony three months later, Gershwin as maestro got an even stronger review from critic Edward Cushing: "The composer himself conducted, and with a competence that enlarged our opinion of his versatility."[62] Gershwin's enthusiasm led to other conducting engagements with his tone poem, including a national broadcast on CBS on December 8 and a return to Lewisohn the next summer as both soloist and conductor.[63] By adding conductor to his musical repertory, Gershwin opened up a new professional pathway. Rather than sit among the audience and acknowledge their appreciation after a performance of *An American in Paris*, the composer could now conduct onstage, earning an additional fee plus additional press that augmented his artistic reputation, celebrity, and income.

By far the largest audience reached by Gershwin's new work was on Broadway as *An American in Paris* was incorporated as the Act II ballet of *Show Girl* – a theatrical narrative by Florenz Ziegfeld. While not a financial success, the lavish production dominated Broadway in the summer and early fall of 1929 and offered 118 performances from its Boston previews through its New York run. The Ziegfeld Theatre where it was produced had a capacity of 1,638 and thus the music of *An American in Paris* was heard by upwards of 100,000 ticket-buying patrons. Plans for a national tour and film version never came to fruition.

Based on a best-selling 1928 novel by J.P. McEvoy initially serialized in *Liberty Magazine*, *Show Girl* was already hugely popular before Ziegfeld took on the subject. Described in one review as "not overburdened with plot,"[64] the backstage musical featured a spunky, aspiring Broadway showgirl named Dixie Dugan pursued by four suitors: saccharine salesman Denny Kerrigan; fiery tango dancer Alvarez Romano; Wall Street sugar daddy John Milton; and the ultimately successful suitor, writer Jimmy Doyle. In this rags-to-riches tale, Dixie finds not only love but also Broadway stardom.

The music was to be entirely by George Gershwin with lyrics by Ira Gershwin and Gus Kahn. Although facing what the composer called "the greatest rush job I've ever had on a score" after the hit *Show Boat* closed earlier than anticipated and the producer was faced with the prospect of a dark house, Gershwin still wrote some twenty-five new songs for the show.[65] The most famous was and remains "Liza," which brings the Act II show-within-a-show to a close. In several performances, including the Boston opening, Al Jolson rose from the audience to sing this song to his actual bride Ruby Keeler, who played the lead role of Dixie. The composer and lyricist's brother Arthur Gershwin remembered that Jolson substituted "Ruby" for the title lyric.[66] The stunt inspired considerable publicity.

As was typical of Ziegfeld's lavish productions, *Show Girl* included a large and expensive cast: some fourteen principals, an oversized orchestra (to handle the instrumentation of Gershwin's tone poem), three comedians including Jimmy Durante, and an all-female chorus of some seventy dancers. To this the impresario added Duke Ellington and his ten-piece Cotton Club jazz orchestra, which performed onstage for the Act I finale as well as the Act II floor show that culminated in "Liza." The band then hustled off to play its regular sets at Harlem's Cotton Club at midnight and 2 a.m.[67]

An American in Paris appeared in a fifteen-minute arrangement (slightly shortened by the composer) as the opening of a "new" Ziegfeld Follies show for which the heroine was competing for a featured role. The orchestra was conducted by Gershwin's friend William Daly and may even have involved members of the Ellington band. The tone poem's adaptation was likely inspired, if not made necessary, by *Show Girl*'s accelerated production timeline. By contract Gershwin had just four weeks to deliver the music.[68] When Gershwin complained that he could not write an entire score in just a few weeks, Ziegfeld responded: "Why sure you can, just dig down in the trunk and pull out a couple of hits."[69] Gershwin ignored Ziegfeld's suggestion when it came to the songs, but adapting *An American in Paris* as the instrumental dance number for the Follies show-within-a-show certainly saved the composer time and leveraged the new tone poem's own popularity to boost Ziegfeld's production. Reusing songs was anathema on Broadway, as it wasted the economic opportunity to feature a potential hit. Each new song was a new chance to sell more sheet music. Incidental music, however, was not typically sold in sheet music form and thus recycling previously composed work did not squander the chance to make more money.

Albertina Rasch, a frequent Ziegfeld collaborator, choreographed the *An American in Paris* ballet, featuring premier dancer Harriet Hoctor. The choreography was divided into three named scenes – "La Rue St. Lazare," "Le Bar Americain," and "Le Reve de l'Amerique" – that traced the orchestral work's A (Paris)–B (New York)–A (back to Paris) form. The ballet focused on "half a dozen vividly colorful tableaux" and was generally praised as the "outstanding feature of the evening's entertainment"[70] and the "most magnificent number in the show."[71] The central homesick blues theme of Gershwin's tone poem, intoned by a jazzy solo trumpet in the orchestral work, is reimagined in *Show Girl* as a song sung by Dixie's Latin suitor Alvarez Romano. He is described as the son of the president of "Costaragua" and is presumably far from home.[72] New lyrics created for *Show Girl* extend the melody's theme of homesickness, already central to the orchestral work's original narrative program, to Broadway:

> Home ... that's where the sunshine learned to shine,
> Home ... a place that love has made divine.
> So my eyes are turning to where I left this yearning heart of mine.
>
> Blues ... I get the blues when I'm away
> Blues ... I hear them calling night and day
> Going back forever, I'll never, never, never more to roam.

It is unclear if the Gershwins made much money from *Show Girl*. Ziegfeld liked to have his songwriters on retainer even after a show opened in order to revise and respond to changes, but George, at least, did not report for this duty. By July 25, only a bit more than three weeks after the show's Broadway debut, the impresario's lawyer put the composer on notice that "although repeated demands have been made upon you to be present at rehearsals and fix the music of *Show Girl*, which you have agreed to do, you have failed to do the same, making it necessary for Mr. Ziegfeld to call in others to do your work."[73] Dated April 1929, Gershwin's contract with Ziegfeld required that the music of *Show Girl* be made up exclusively of Gershwin compositions. The lawyer's notice thus amounted to a breach of contract claim, releasing Ziegfeld from these original terms and allowing him to hire composer Vincent Youmans to revise the score.

The financial terms of the Ziegfeld contract were generous for Gershwin. The composer was due a royalty of 3 percent of *Show Girl*'s gross weekly box office receipts (i.e. of all ticket sales income before accounting for expenses), which should have amounted to a generous sum. In addition, Gershwin would receive 25 percent of any subsidiary monies – from radio licenses, other performances, foreign adaptations, etc. – received by Ziegfeld. If a film was made including Gershwin's music, he would receive one-third of Ziegfeld's royalty. Rights to the music itself, however, remained the sole property of the composer through New World Music Corporation. Ziegfeld was not entitled to any publication or mechanical rights to the music.

It may be that Ziegfeld stopped paying royalties once his lawyer got involved. In whatever event, the Gershwins ended up suing Ziegfeld for royalties due, but these appear never to have been paid. *Show Girl* closed on October 5, and on October 10 Gershwin wrote to a relative: "Ziegfeld (the rat) sent for me. On arriving in his office, he immediately threw both arms around me & only my great strength kept him from kissing me. He informed me he was so sorry we had a disagreement & was anxious to make up – send me a check for back royalties – & be friends. I consented but as yet no check has arrived."[74] The US stock market crashed just a few weeks later. Gershwin and Ziegfeld never again worked together.

The final strategy Gershwin used to earn revenue from *An American in Paris* was publishing. In 1927, Dreyfus formed New World Music Corporation as a Harms subsidiary to hold the works of George and Ira Gershwin. In early 1929, a photostatic copy of much of Gershwin's handwritten score was made, bound, and sent to the Library of Congress for the purpose of copyright registration. It remains in the library's collection and was stamped as received on February 15, 1929.[75] Later that year, New World Music published a "solo piano" version of the score transcribed by William Daly. The piano edition is more accurately described as a proxy conducting score that contains indications of orchestration and muting as well as additional lines of music that go beyond the typical pair of piano staves. In 1930, *An American in Paris* was published as a full orchestral score – a largely unedited, but careful transcription of the manuscript – although without Gershwin's handwritten changes to the score.

The economic strategies used by Gershwin to earn a living from *An American in Paris* run the gamut of the techniques he learned from his experience in Tin Pan Alley and Broadway as exemplified by "Swanee." He wrote without a commission, confident of finding collaborators to propel the work and create a hit. Instead of Jolson as his outside celebrity sponsor, however, Gershwin leveraged the cultural authority of the New York Philharmonic-Symphony, the nation's oldest and most prestigious orchestra, conducted by famed conductor Walter Damrosch. The attendant publicity led to subsequent orchestral performances, even in the first year of the work's existence. Gershwin then sold non-exclusive licenses to others, initially for a radio premiere, earning money from the score while retaining the right to license subsequent uses. Recording created further avenues for both royalties and to reach new audiences, leveraging and reinforcing the work's popularity and reputation. Soon the tone poem became the centerpiece of a Broadway show, at least theoretically helping to earn 3 percent of receipts while bringing Carnegie Hall respectability to Ziegfeld's theater. Orchestral performances cross-promoted the new musical, most directly in Boston.

In turn, Ziegfeld's show may have increased interest in summer orchestral performances for thousands at New York University's Lewisohn Stadium. There Gershwin made his conducting debut, serving not only as composer of *An American in Paris* but also becoming one of its performers. Gershwin had long expanded his income as a composer by writing orchestral music that included piano solos for himself, as he did with *Rhapsody in Blue* and Concerto in F. Now he could appear in gala concerts, enhancing his celebrity, as a triple threat: composer, pianist, and conductor. Finally, Gershwin published *An American in Paris* as both a solo piano work and a full orchestral score, generating sales and a royalty through his publisher's Gershwin subsidiary, New World Music Corporation. As with "Swanee," one musical composition led to multiple streams of revenue. Gershwin thus saw *An American in Paris* not as a sacred and immutable object of classical veneration, but rather as a mutable artistic product that could and should be repackaged and adapted to a series of economic opportunities, each one increasing the value of the others.

This linkage between economic and artistic success was part of Gershwin's creative identity from the very beginning. Responding to a 1920 interviewer in *The Billboard* on the heels of his success with "Swanee," he optimistically charted a course for future success, both for himself and for American music in general:

> I believe we are getting a better grade of music all the time. A composer doesn't have to be afraid of writing a musicianly score nowadays, if he will only provide melody ... I have used whole tone harmonies a la Debussy in one piece and it was very effective. One can write dissonances where a few years ago they would have been torn out of the score instantly ... Creative effort is what is needed. Melodies must be treated in a novel way ... and they must have a new

twist if they are to get into the hit class. If you will analyze the songs which have made the biggest hits lately, you will find that some part of them, if only a bar or two, is a passage which strikes the ear as something new and pleasant ... There is a lot of money waiting for the fellow who can write original scores.[76]

George Gershwin's success was twofold. Increasingly asserting his creative talents, he was a savvy entrepreneur. Gershwin's artistic ideology not only resolved the stylistic tension inherent in a distinctive US musical voice poised between classical and popular, but it also addressed the battle between music and money. As Gershwin's sonic inspiration could come from any source – Tin Pan Alley, vaudeville, Broadway, the jazz club, the concert hall, and the opera house – so too could his financial tactics. He earned money from publications and performances, but also from recordings, broadcast rights, and licensing. While classical music's economic anxiety is to avoid the dishonor of "selling out" one's creative independence to the marketplace, Gershwin discovered that by selling his art effectively, he could achieve independence and enable his artistry. In addition to lucrative profits, his contracts gave him full creative authority. Earnings from hit songs made it feasible for Gershwin to take time off to compose. *Rhapsody in Blue*, Concerto in F, and *An American in Paris*, not to mention *Porgy and Bess*, would never have come into existence without Gershwin's combination of artistic ambition and economic independence.

Notes

1. Howard Pollack, *George Gershwin: His Life and Work* (Berkeley, CA: University of California Press, 2007), 61–64; Remick eventually published three songs as well as Gershwin's ragtime instrumental *Rialto Ripples* in 1917 (contract signed February 27, 1917 held in Washington, DC: Library of Congress, Gershwin Collection (GC), box 126, folder 14). $15 per week in 1914 would be the equivalent of approximately $370 in 2018.
2. Agreement between Harry von Tilzer, Murray Roth, and George Gershwin, March 1, 1916. "Legal Documents" in GC, box 126, folder 34.
3. Pollack, George Gershwin, 221–22.
4. Universal 202864, recorded September 1916. See liner notes of *Gershwin Plays Gershwin* Elektra Nonesuch 9 79287-2; and Pollack, *George Gershwin*, 67–68.
5. Pollack, *George Gershwin*, 87–88.
6. Gordon Whyte, "Melody the Thing Young Composer Declares: George Gershwin, Writer of Musical Comedy Hits, Says Better Music Is in Demand," *The Billboard* (March 13, 1920), 26, 33.
7. Agreement between George Gershwin and T.B. Harms & Francis, Day & Hunter, February 21, 1918. "Legal Documents" in GC, box 126, folder 26.
8. "Max Dreyfus, Music Publisher Who Headed Chappell, 90, Dies," *New York Times* (May 16, 1964), 25.
9. "Music Publishers Sued Here as Trust," *New York Times* (August. 4, 1920), 19.
10. David A. Jasen, *Tin Pan Alley: An Encyclopedia of the Golden Age of American Song* (New York and London: Routledge, 2004), 53.
11. Agreement between George Gershwin and T.B. Harms & Francis, Day & Hunter (February 21, 1918).
12. Gershwin's February 8, 1923 Harms contract allowed for an advance of $100 per week. Rather than a salary, he received a higher royalty rate up to 15 cents per copy of theatrical piano

arrangements and 50 percent of the company's proceeds from foreign sales. The term was again renewable, but now lasted for two years (GC; box 122, folder 24).
13. Agreement between George Gershwin and T.B. Harms & Francis, Day & Hunter (February 21, 1918), 3.
14. *Rhapsody in Blue* (film), Warner Bros., 1945.
15. Pollack, *George Gershwin*, 240.
16. "I'll Say She Does" was added to *Sinbad* during its initial run. By July 1919 a recording of the song (A-2746) was being featured in advertisements by Columbia Records. See "Columbia Records: Al Jolson Sings 'I'll Say She Does,'" *Evansville Press* (July 29, 1919), 6.
17. "Sunday Theater Openings," *Washington Herald* (January 12, 1920), 6.
18. "Theaters Inaugurate the Current Week with Music," *Washington Post* (January 12, 1920), 5.
19. "Sheet Music," Washington, DC *Evening Star* (January 15, 1920), 23.
20. Columbia A2876 (also A 2895). The 10-inch 78 rpm recording sold for $0.85, see Munster, Indiana *The Times* (April 15, 1920), 7.
21. Pollack, *George Gershwin*, 241.
22. See "Columbia Records Jolson's 'Swanee' Whistling Song," which appeared in *Evening World* (New York), *Vicksburg Evening Post* (Mississippi), *Green Bay Press-Gazette* (Minnesota), *Ogden Standard-Examiner* (Utah), *The Courier* (Waterloo, Iowa), *Pensacola News Journal* (Florida), *Arizona Republic*, and *Los Angeles Times*. The author has located seventy-five additional advertisements that all ran April 8–10, 1920.
23. Duo-Art 1649, 1920; featured as track 6 on *Gershwin Plays Gershwin: The Piano Rolls*, realized by Artis Wodehouse, Elektra Nonesuch, 79287, pub. 1993.
24. Pollack, *George Gershwin*, 238.
25. Ibid., 237.
26. Arthur Pryor, a veteran of both Patrick Gilmore's and John Philip Sousa's bands, led a seventy-piece band in ensemble numbers and composed "The Capitol March" for the occasion.
27. "Program" in *Capitol Theatre* program book (1919), n.p.
28. Frank G. Baker, "The Song World: Capitol Theater Revue," *The Billboard* (November 15, 1919), 28.
29. Gordon Whyte, "Hits and Otherwise: Ned Wayburn's Demi Tasse Revue," *The Billboard* (December 27, 1919), 30.
30. Pollack, *George Gershwin*, 237, 748.
31. Ibid., 237.
32. Stephen Gilbert, *The Music of Gershwin* (New Haven, CT: Yale University Press, 1995), 52–54.
33. "Down Where the Swanee River Flows," Columbia 46460, recorded February 28, 1916.
34. Victor 18566, recorded June 3, 1919.
35. Pollack, *George Gershwin*, 237–38.
36. Ibid., 254.
37. "Swanee Rose," *The Billboard* (May 28, 1921), 39.
38. "Tales of Tin Pan Alley: 'Swanee' and Its Author," *Edison Musical Magazine* (October 1920), 9. Cf. Pollack, *George Gershwin*, 239.
39. George Gershwin, *New York Tribune* (November 29, 1925). Cf. Edward Jablonski, *Gershwin Remembered* (New York: Hal Leonard, 1992), 174.
40. Edward Jablonski, *Gershwin* (New York: Doubleday, 1987), 97–98; Pollack, *George Gershwin*, 344–45.
41. $2,000 in 1925 would be equivalent to about $29,000 in 2018.
42. Pollack, *George Gershwin*, 345.
43. Ibid., 345–46.
44. Ibid., 346.
45. "Gershwins Sail," *Brooklyn Daily Eagle* (March 10, 1928), 12.
46. "Opera to Honor Jazz Composer," *Asheville Citizen-Times* (May 13, 1928), 27.
47. "A Damrosch Quotation?," *Hartford Courant* (July 29, 1928), 45.
48. "Will Play Gershwin Piece," *New York Times* (June 6, 1928), 23.
49. "Damrosch to Conduct a Gershwin Symphony," *New York Sun* (November 22, 1928); Cf. Richard Crawford, *Summertime: George Gershwin's Life in Music* (New York: W.W. Norton, forthcoming in 2019).
50. $125 in 1929 is equivalent to about $1,800 in 2018. New York Symphony Society 1928–1929 rental fee cost sheet, New York Philharmonic Archives. While the New York Symphony, not the

Philharmonic, premiered the piece, the two orchestras soon merged, and their histories are both preserved by the current Philharmonic Archive.

51. "Gershwin Sells Rights," Wilmington, DE *Evening Journal* (January 12, 1929), 9; *Tampa Bay Times* (January 30, 1929), 6.
52. W.S. Quinby, *How to Make Perfect Coffee* (Boston and Chicago: W.S. Quinby Company, 1922).
53. "If You Tune In: A Forecast of Ether Attractions," *Pittsburgh Press* (January 30, 1929), 27.
54. "New Record: Sponsor Pays $5000 for Gershwin Number," *Pittsburgh Press* (January 13, 1929), 57.
55. Nathaniel Shilkret, "An American in Paris," in *Nathaniel Shilkret: Sixty Years in the Music Business* (Lanham, MD: Scarecrow Press), 99.
56. John K. Sherman, "Recorded Music," *Minneapolis Star* (April 19, 1929), 24; "May VICTOR Records," Connellsville, PA *Daily Courier* (April 26, 1929), 8. The Victor discs were numbers 35963 and 35964 and the entire work took up four sides, labeled Parts 1–4.
57. Duo-Art #7467(8) and #7468(8), Ampico and a jumbo Ampico B roll; musical details – mainly an early eight-bar cut – suggest that the Milne arrangement was made directly from the composer's autograph full score.
58. "Colonial Theatre," *Boston Globe* (June 8, 1929), B44.
59. "New Gershwin Suite at Pop Concert," *Boston Globe* (June 28, 1929), 12.
60. Morris Davidson, "A Night at the Stadium," Baltimore *Evening Sun* (September 13, 1929), 29.
61. "Gershwin Conducts Own Music at Stadium," *New York Times* (August 27, 1929), 36.
62. Edward Cushing, "Music of the Day," *Brooklyn Daily Eagle* (November 11, 1929), 20.
63. On August 28, 1930 Gershwin performed as soloist in Concerto in F before intermission, then back-to-back as conductor of *An American in Paris* and soloist in *Rhapsody in Blue*. Hoogstraten led the orchestra. Program held at the New York Philharmonic Archives.
64. "'Show Girl' Ziegfeld's Latest," *Daily Boston Globe* (June 26, 1929), 4.
65. Pollack, *George Gershwin*, 453.
66. Ibid., 458.
67. John Edward Hasse, *Beyond Category: The Life and Genius of Duke Ellington* (New York: Simon & Schuster, 1993), 122–23; the band was reportedly paid $1,500 per week by Ziegfeld.
68. Contract held in GC, box 126, folder 19.
69. Pollack, *George Gershwin*, 453.
70. "'Show Girl' Ziegfeld's Latest," 4.
71. "Broadway Banter," *Atlanta Constitution* (July 21, 1929), 67.
72. Pollack, *George Gershwin*, 454.
73. Ibid., 460.
74. Ibid., 460.
75. GC (ML31.G38, bound).
76. Whyte, "Melody the Thing Young Composer Declares," 26, 33.

9 Exploring New Worlds: *An American in Paris, Cuban Overture*, and *Porgy and Bess*

ANNA HARWELL CELENZA

George Gershwin was an avid traveler, and for most of his adult life he was on the move. There were work retreats in upstate New York, golf excursions and beach trips south (e.g. Florida, Cuba), premieres up and down the East Coast, a trip to Mexico, film projects in California and five trips to Europe. Gershwin's relationships with his cousins, the poet and folklorist B. A. (Ben) Botkin and his older brother, the painter Henry (Harry) Botkin, deserve to be foregrounded in any discussion of Gershwin's travels.[1] Through his relationships with them, Gershwin acquired a deep interest in, and knowledge of, folklore and modernist art – topics that increasingly influenced his approach to composition during the last decade of his life, when he went from being a mere traveler to a cultural tourist.

Gershwin's music is most often associated with the hustle and bustle of Manhattan, but three of his finest works are specifically linked to other cities, namely *An American in Paris* (Paris), *Cuban Overture* (Havana), and *Porgy and Bess* (Charleston, SC). In them, Gershwin was composing for the concert hall and opera house, and in doing so he adapted traditional compositional forms from the nineteenth century – namely the tone poem, concert overture and grand opera – and excerpts/characteristics of popular/folk music in an effort to capture the atmospheric spirit of foreign locales. Gershwin experienced Paris, Havana, and Charleston in markedly different, yet connected, ways. His preparations and goals for each trip varied, as did his choice of companions and daily activities. He visited each city either before or while working on the composition associated with it, and his impressions of his environs, both real and imagined, informed his compositional approach.

Paris

Gershwin made four trips to Paris, all of which contributed to his writing of *An American in Paris*. Few details are known about the first trip, in April 1923, with friends Jules Glaenzer and Buddy DeSylva, other than the brevity of the stay (just a few days), Gershwin's airsickness on the flight from London, and his reported visit to a high-end, Parisian brothel.[2] Gershwin's second trip, in June 1925, was a special treat he gave himself after the successful premiere of his musical comedy, *Tell Me More*, at the Winter Garden Theatre in London. Like countless Americans before him, Gershwin was drawn to the idea of Paris as the cultural capital of Europe. He and his cousin Harry Botkin had dreamed of visiting the City of Lights ever since they were teenagers. For them, the capital represented a necessary stop for up-and-coming artists in search of modernist inspiration. *Fin-de-siècle* Paris had produced an array of avant-garde painters and musicians, from Paul Cezanne, Henri Matisse, and George Roualt to Claude Debussy, Maurice Ravel, and Erik Satie. And in the 1920s, an alluring array of expatriate artists, from James Joyce and Ezra Pound to Pablo Picasso, Marc Chagall, Igor Stravinsky, and Sergei Diaghilev called the city home.

Gershwin met no such luminaries during his second brief excursion. Instead, his days were filled with typical tourist activities: visits to the Eiffel Tower and Louvre, sampling French wines (a special treat for an American traveling during the Prohibition era) and walks along the Champs-Élysées.[3] He traveled alone, and when homesickness set in he met up with friends from New York who were also in Paris, among them Lou and Emily Paley, Vincent Youmans, the ex-pats Robert and Mabel Schirmer, and Jules Glaenzer (who was now there on his honeymoon).

Gershwin's third trip to Paris took place the following spring. He arrived on April 1, 1926, this time as a guest of the Schirmers. They had invited him to Paris for a week-long break before the London launch of his hit musical *Lady, Be Good!* Robert Schirmer described the visit in a letter to Emily and Lou Paley:

> We've had no particularly thrilling news till the famous George arrived ... We met him at the station and escorted him home in triumph. He promptly got comfortably installed in our guest room and we began to talk – well, you can imagine the excitement, the joy of having him all to ourselves.[4]

Gershwin appears to have had little interest in seeing the sites. As Schirmer explained, Gershwin preferred to relax with them at home and socialize with other Americans during the evening.

> Our days consisted of breakfast together ... then lying around the house, playing the piano, the Victor, and our vocal chords till about 2 or 3 pm ... The evenings were usually spent with other people ... George saw a lot of Eddie Knopf, Irving Berlin, Michael Arlen and many other acquaintances.[5]

The Schirmers managed to drag him to the theater on at least one occasion to see the newest Maurice Yvain operetta, but Gershwin was reportedly unimpressed:

> We went to a French musical show, *Pas sur la Bouche*, which gave George some ideas about the Paris musical comedy stage – such ideas that he walked out in the middle of the 2nd Act because his bed at our house was more comfortable to sleep in than the theatre seat.[6]

The fact that Gershwin spoke no French likely contributed to his lukewarm reception of the operetta. This also helps explain why, according to Schirmer, Gershwin's preferred activity during his stay with them involved attending various sporting events, including "an evening at the Prize Fights" and "an afternoon at the Steeplechase racing in the Bois de Boulogne."[7]

Apparently, the only influential music-related event that occurred during Gershwin's stay with the Schirmers was a dinner they hosted in their home:

> One evening we had quite a lot of fun by inviting George Antheil and his wife to dinner ... Antheil is that young super-radical composer Mabel has written you about. He tried to give George an idea of his stuff [the soon-to-be-premiered *Ballet mécanique*] but since most of it is scored for 16 grand-player-pianos, with an obbligato by a boiler-factory, why I suppose it wasn't a very fair test. Then our George played excerpts from different things – show numbers, *Rhapsody* and *Concerto*.[8]

Schirmer claimed that "a pleasant evening was had by all," but one wonders. Antheil had a habit of name dropping, and he took great pride in his position as an up-and-coming American composer. For example, in an earlier letter to Mary Curtis Bok (founder of the Curtis Institute in 1924), Antheil described a concert in the "beautiful Champ Elysees [sic.] Theatre," where he "played to a brilliant audience," which included:

> Man Ray, Picasso, Jean Cocteau, Picabia and Heaven knows who else. In one box alone sat James Joyce, the author of *Ulysses* ... In another box sat Léger,
> the second greatest painter after Picasso. With him sat Ezra Pound, the world's greatest modern critic ... he has just yesterday sent in a thirty-page article to the "Criterian" [sic.] ... upon ME – in which he thoroughly analyzes my music, and says that I am the only artist who has revolutionized any one of the arts during the last three years – and "the only thing that America has ever given us."[9]

If Antheil's conversation with Gershwin was even half as inflated, it would have made for a tiresome evening. Neither composer appears to have taken much interest in the work of the other. In a letter written shortly after their meeting, Antheil bemoaned the fact that "a very mediocre piece 'Rhapsodie in Blue' [sic.] by Gershwin" had recently created "a great deal of excitement."[10] Gershwin was equally unimpressed by Antheil's *Ballet mécanique*, which he categorized as "one of those compositions of the Dada school, which employ the instrumentation of electric fans or couple fifty synchronized pianos in a riot of noisy cacophony."[11] Still, the competitive encounter appears to have motivated both men to commence new compositions. For Antheil, this friendly rivalry resulted in his *Jazz Symphony*, originally composed for Paul Whiteman but eventually premiered by W.C. Handy and his Orchestra.[12] For Gershwin, it was *An American in Paris*.

Gershwin left Paris for London on April 7 with the Schirmers in tow. Four days later they attended the premiere of *Lady, Be Good!* To mark the occasion, Gershwin presented his friends with a photo of himself seated at the piano. He inscribed the back: "For Mabel and Bob – Many thanks for a wonderful week in Paris. Love, George." The inscription included two musical themes: the opening "Andantino" from *Rhapsody in Blue*; and a new, four-bar motif labeled "An American in Paris" with the description "Very Parisienne."[13] Although nearly two years would pass before this Parisian musical seed grew into an orchestral tone poem, Gershwin's fascination with the city had taken root. His desire to visit again was strong.

Returning to New York, Gershwin continued to reflect on his time abroad. He sketched passages incorporating a popular dance tune he had heard in French cafés (Charles Borel-Clerc's "La Mattchiche") and devised a plan to incorporate the honking of Parisian taxi horns – perhaps a response to Antheil's "boiler-factory" obbligato. But as Gershwin explained to a reporter, he struggled at first to translate his experiences into music: "As I was not a Frenchman, I knew that I had gotten about as far as I could get with it," focusing only on the sounds of Paris.[14] He wanted to include himself – his *American* self – in the music, and as he later explained, his travels abroad helped him see his local surroundings on the Upper West Side in a new light:

> I live up on 103rd Street near Riverside Drive, and from the windows of my room I can get a pretty good view of the Hudson. I was walking up and down wondering how to develop this theme into a piece when I glanced out and saw the river. I love that river, and I thought how often I had been homesick for the sight of it, and then the idea struck me – An American in Paris, homesickness, the blues.[15]

As Gershwin explained it, the memory of the melancholy he experienced in Paris when thinking about home served as a turning point in his approach to the composition. He now had a general concept of how he could expand his "little French theme" into "another serious piece."[16]

According to this new scheme, the blues played a crucial role, not simply as a foil to the jocular opening theme, but as a sonic symbol of the United States – a counterweight to the original "Very Parisienne" idea. Gershwin's continued interest in the blues as material for "another serious piece" (the earlier ones being *Rhapsody in Blue* and Concerto in F) is not surprising, considering that shortly after his return to New York, he received a new book, W.C. Handy's *Blues: An Anthology*. Gershwin had known it was in production; before traveling abroad he had given permission to the publisher to include three of his works: "The Half of It, Dearie, Blues" from *Lady, Be Good!*, and excerpts from both *Rhapsody in Blue* and the second movement of Concerto in F. Much to Gershwin's delight, these works received special attention in the introductory essay penned by music critic Abbe Niles.

Adopting the literary language of an academic, Niles describes *Blues: An Anthology* as a scholarly collection of American folk culture.[17] The quantity and breadth of music included in the collection, "all drawn from the memory of W.C. Handy," was extraordinary for the time. In addition to traditional spirituals and work-songs, the volume included a wide array of vaudeville songs, contemporary commercial blues and excerpts of works commonly referred to as symphonic jazz.[18] Niles's essay covered a range of topics, from the folk-blues as verse and music and its pioneers to the modern blues and the adoption and influence of the blues on jazz, musical theater and extended works for the concert hall. It is in this last category that Gershwin's work is discussed, along with that of John Alden Carpenter. Niles identifies Carpenter as "the first 'serious' American white composer to flirt with Handy's idea" of modern blues. But he reserves for Gershwin the honor of being "the only insistent experimenter along this line whose work is unquestionably worth watching." According to Niles, Gershwin should be singled out, for he alone "has made a serious study of the question 'wherein blue,'" and "not content with abject imitation, he has thought out the philosophy for himself, making the old tricks his own where he uses them, and making his own point of view the flavor of his work."[19] The essay concludes with a description of Gershwin as the avant-garde representative of this distinctively American folk genre: "We find in this music [Gershwin's *Rhapsody* and Concerto in F] the blues exerting, in a new field, an influence still of undiminished vitality and suggestiveness."[20]

Around the same time Gershwin read Handy's anthology, he received another book that occupied his creative imagination for the next decade: DuBose Heyward's best-selling novel, *Porgy* (1925) – the tale of a disabled African American beggar in turn-of-the-century Charleston and his unlikely lover Bess. Emily Paley loaned Gershwin her copy of the book, and legend has it that he read it in a single sitting, after coming home late from a rehearsal of *Oh, Kay!*[21] Gershwin's interest in the novel is unsurprising. Since the failed performances of *Blue Monday* (later titled *135th Street*) – a blackface production labeled as "opera à la Afro-American" – in 1922 and

1925, he had been wanting to try his hand once again at writing an opera involving black characters.

One can see what drew Gershwin to Porgy's tragic narrative. Music is evoked from the beginning, with a prologue that imitates the metered invocations of ancient bards. Here the lives of the novel's primary characters – "Porgy, Maria, and Bess; Robbins, and Peter and Crown" – are described with musical metaphors. The "marvelous tunes" of their youth have become "demanding strange songs" played on "an instrument, terrible, new."[22] This affecting beginning is soon followed by the narrative itself, which opens, evocatively, in the manner of a folktale:

> Porgy lived in a Golden Age. Not the Golden Age of a remote and legendary past; nor yet the chimerical era treasured by every man past middle life, that never existed except in the heart of youth; but an age when men, not yet old, were boys in an ancient, beautiful city that time had forgotten before it destroyed.[23]

Gershwin was not the only one in the family taken with Heyward's novel. His cousin Ben Botkin, who in 1926 had just secured a position teaching literature at the University of Oklahoma, had also read the novel, and countless other works connected to African American culture.[24]

Ben was a poet and an intellectual, and in his letters to Ira and George he described his experiences as one of the first Jewish students admitted to Harvard University, where he earned a B.A. in English literature in 1920. After graduation, he moved to New York, where he enrolled as a graduate student at Columbia. As a friend and colleague of Botkin's later explained: "It was no mere coincidence that [Ben] shifted his studies from Harvard to Columbia, conscious as he was of the rising fortunes in new music of cousins Ira and George."[25] Ben became enamored of what he called George's "epoch-making experiments" with jazz. He compared *Rhapsody in Blue* to Carl Sandburg's poetry and predicted that it would "revolutionize the art" of "native music."[26] After attending a rehearsal for *Rhapsody in Blue* on February 5 (a week before the premiere) he described his impressions in a letter to a friend:

> The *Rhapsody*, as I heard it for the first time with Paul Whiteman's twenty-two piece band, was a "wow," and will simply kill the audience and critics (to use the Tin Pan Alley slang). It is marvelous and stands out ... George's music is at once native and bizarre. Remember, jazz is folk-music, only it has been disparaged because it is the product of the city instead of the country ... The "blue" theme itself is most unusual ... It may seem silly to you that I should go jazz-mad at this advanced age, but George's music is super-jazz, and having assisted at the birth and growth of the composition, I feel a paternal interest in it.[27]

This last comment is especially important. It was Ben who encouraged George to see the blues, and by extension jazz, as products of contemporary urban folk culture. As a graduate student at Columbia, Ben studied under the guidance of Franz Boas, who was receiving national attention at the time for his groundbreaking work in anthropology. Boas rejected evolutionary approaches to the study of culture. He argued that culture develops historically, rather than from biological traits. It was intersection that mattered, the interactions of groups of people and ideas across diverse geographies. Boas promoted the concept of cultural relativism, arguing that there was no such thing as an objectively superior race or culture. He proposed that humans see the world through the lens of their own culture, and judge it according to their own culturally acquired norms.[28] Botkin took these ideas to heart, and in the mid-1920s, while working in settlement houses and teaching English to newly arrived immigrants in New York, he began applying them to American literature, most notably the folklore of various regions and ethnic groups. By 1926, he had begun to develop and publish his own ideas about the intersections of folklore and popular culture.[29] Not surprisingly, some of his earliest essays touched on the blues and their place in American literature. As a colleague later noted, it was Ben, who "tutor[ed] George Gershwin in the black lore which would be reflected in Gershwin's *Porgy and Bess*."[30] And it was Ben who encouraged Gershwin to see the cultural isolationism promoted by many intellectuals as detrimental to the growth of American art. To grow as an artist, Ben often noted, one had to embrace the pluralistic culture of modern society.

With these thoughts in mind, Gershwin was eager to return to Paris, and he regularly mentioned these plans to reporters, describing his next trip as an educational experience, a requisite step in his development as a composer.[31] He solidified these plans in a letter to Mabel Schirmer in late February 1928:

> I expect that we will stay in Paris for about two weeks and then go someplace where the climate is right, and where I can do some work. If, however, I find somebody to study with in Paris, I may take a place on the outskirts of Paris and stay there most of the time ... Also, I'd like to find, when I get to Paris, a valet who speaks several languages, and possibly drives a car.[32]

This last detail was important. On this trip, Gershwin hoped to widen his interactions beyond the Anglo-American community. His ultimate goal was to find a composition teacher and make progress on his latest concert work. The "we" in his letter referred to his brother Ira, sister-in-law Leonore (Lee), and sister Frances (Frankie). While Gershwin worked, they would "travel around ... and see some of the sights."[33] For Gershwin's siblings, this trip was their first trans-Atlantic excursion. Ira kept a rather detailed diary during their travels, making note not only of the sites and the various people (celebrities and friends) they encountered, but also of George's activities.

When the Gershwin clan arrived at the Gare St. Lazare in Paris on March 25, Mabel and Robert Schirmer were waiting for them. Over the next few weeks, Robert took the lead in showing Ira, Lee, and Frankie the sites while Mabel accompanied George on various errands. "The most fun of all came when he went shopping for taxi horns," she later explained. "We walked all along the Avenue of the Grand Armée, where all the automobile shops used to be. We went to every shop we could find to look for taxi horns for *An American in Paris*. He wanted horns that could sound certain notes."[34]

Mabel also accompanied George when he went to visit Nadia Boulanger at her apartment in Montmartre. He arrived with a formal letter of introduction from Maurice Ravel, whom he had befriended a few weeks earlier in New York.[35] In his letter, Ravel describes Gershwin as "a musician ... endowed with the most brilliant, most enchanting, and perhaps the most profound talent," whose "worldwide success no longer satisfies him, for he is aiming higher." He explains that Gershwin "knows that he lacks the technical means to achieve his goal" but "[i]n teaching him those means, one might ruin his talent." Admitting that he doesn't have "the courage ... to undertake this awesome responsibility," Ravel hopes that she might. He concludes by saying: "I expect to return home [to Paris] in early May and will come to see you in order to discuss this matter. In the meantime, I send you my most cordial regards. Maurice Ravel."[36]

Boulanger did not wait for Ravel's return to make her decision, declining Gershwin's request. As she explained years later: "I had nothing to offer him. He was already quite well known when he came to my house, and I suggested that he was doing alright and should continue. I told him what I could teach him wouldn't help much ... and he agreed."[37] Gershwin's search for a teacher continued. In addition to querying Stravinsky – who is rumored to have dismissed the notion when he learned the immensity of Gershwin's annual income – he approached Jacques Ibert.[38] As Ibert explained, although he was "dazzled by [Gershwin's] prodigious technique and amazed at his melodic sense, at the boldness of his modulations, and by his audacious and often unexpected harmonic inventions," he didn't believe he could teach the American much in just a few weeks.[39]

If this stream of rejections dismayed Gershwin, he did not show it. His gifts as a pianist and his fame as the composer of *Rhapsody in Blue* brought countless professional opportunities in Paris, and musicians and artists, both famous and aspiring, sought him out on a daily basis. Ira recorded in his travel diary his brother's many visitors; they included Georges Auric,

Sergei Diaghilev, Arthur Honegger, Vladimir Horowitz, Fritz Kreisler, Darius Milhaud, Sergei Prokofiev, Man Ray, Rhené-Baton, and Dimitri Tiomkin.[40] Musicians were eager to perform for him. For example, the violinist Rudolf Kolish and the other members of his quartet offered a private performance of works by Schubert and Schoenberg on March 27. And on June 2, Gershwin joined Ravel, Alfred Cortot, and Edgard Varèse at a private recital given by the Cuban composer Ernesto Lecuona at the Salle Gaveau.[41] Gershwin also encountered countless admirers, among them Mario Braggiotti, an eighteen-year-old student at the Paris Conservatory, and his friend Jacques Fray, who arrived unannounced at Gershwin's hotel room:

> We walked in and there was his Steinway piano, right in the middle of his room. And I noticed on the piano, a collection of taxi horns, those old-fashioned ones they used on the Battaille de la Marne [sic.] which you pressed, you know, you squeezed. There were about twenty of them, just laying there. I hadn't been to New York for a few years and I thought maybe this is a new eccentricity, or fad. I didn't know what to make of it.[42]

By the time Gershwin left for Paris, he had already begun two drafts of what would become *An American in Paris*. He continued work on the composition during his travels, and, according to Ira, wrote "the entire 'blues' section" in his room "at the Hotel Majestic in Paris."[43]

When Gershwin's plan to find a teacher fell through, he traveled to Berlin and Vienna, where he came in contact with more composers. In Berlin, he spent most of his time with Franz Lehar. He also interacted with Kurt Weill and attended a performance of *Die Reise Benjamins des Dritten*, a Yiddish "folk musical" with music by Ernst Toch.[44] During an interview with a reporter in Berlin, Gershwin commented on the positive reception of jazz by local audiences: "Jazz is taken much more seriously here in Germany than it is in the United States and thanks to the phonograph, jazz and other American music is much better known here than one would expect."[45]

On April 27, Gershwin traveled to Vienna, where he met with Emmerich Kálmán, Albert Szirmai, and the writers Felix Salten and Ferenc Molnár. Both George and Ira were "astonished" by Kálmán's "knowledge of the New York stage."[46] Although the European had never traveled to the United States, he read the Broadway trade magazine, *Variety*, every week, from cover to cover. These American influences surfaced in the musical productions the Gershwins attended during their stay. At the Theater an der Wien they saw Kálmán's *Die Herzogin von Chicago*, a two-act operetta that addresses the impact of America and its social revolution on European culture. George and Ira also went to a performance of Ernst Krenek's *Jonny spielt auf*, which places American jazz in the realm of European modernism. "It was certainly worth seeing if only for its novelty," Ira explained: "It was put on like a revue – prodigious and picturesque. The last scene represented New York on the top of the World. I suffered from nostalgia when I saw the familiar signs of Broadway shooting from all directions on the stage."[47]

When George was later asked about his impressions of Vienna, he responded: "One of the high spots of my visit was my meeting with Alban Berg, an Austrian ultramodernist composer almost unknown in this country."[48] The pair met twice, on May 3 and 5. The second meeting was at the home of Rudolf Kolish and featured a performance of Berg's *Lyric Suite* for string quartet. As a friendly memento of the afternoon, Berg gave Gershwin an inscribed copy of the score and an autographed photo. Gershwin treasured both and later described the *Lyric Suite* as "dissonant to the extent of proving disagreeable to the average music-lover's consonant trained ear," even though "its conception and treatment are thoroughly modern in the best sense of the word."[49] After some encouragement from Berg, Gershwin performed *Rhapsody in Blue*. Later that evening, Ira noted in his diary: "George big hit with Berg."[50]

When Gershwin returned to Paris, he reconnected with his cousin, Harry, who was now living in the city. Harry had last seen Gershwin the year before, during a vacation in Ossining, New York, where he had introduced George to the art of painting. By that time, Harry had completed his studies at the Massachusetts School of Art in Boston and the Art Students League in New York and was working as an illustrator for the *Saturday Evening Post* and *Harper's*.[51] But like Gershwin, Harry was drawn to Paris, and with his cousin's financial help he moved to the capital in 1927, shortly before his first European exhibition at the Billiet Gallery.

Harry lived in a studio residence in the Montparnasse neighborhood, where his neighbors included André Derain, Georges Braque, Jean Lurçat, and Marcel Gromaire.[52] During his 1928 visit, Gershwin took a keen interest in contemporary art, and under Harry's guidance began collecting in earnest in 1931.[53] Over the next few years, Gershwin purchased nearly 200 works with Harry as his agent, many by world-famous artists, including Degas, Derain, Matisse, Modigliani, Picasso, and Roualt.[54] Gershwin found an affinity between the works of these artists and what he was trying to do with music. As he once explained: "The new music and the new art are similar in rhythm; they share a somber power and fine sentiment."[55] In addition to "paintings in oil by the [Modernist] masters," Gershwin collected works by American regionalist artists like Thomas Hart Benton and Maurice Stern. Harry encouraged Gershwin's interest in folk art. As he later explained, Gershwin "gathered a most varied group of important examples of Negro [African] sculpture, together with drawings, rare watercolors and lithographs. He never confined himself to the paintings of any one group or country, but was always interested in the various movements and schools of art."[56] Gershwin was especially drawn to the folk-like imagery of Chagall and Roualt, and he spent his last few weeks in Paris exploring the city's galleries. Although he had told various reporters he would finish *An American in Paris* in time for a Parisian premiere in May, this deadline came and went without a completed composition. Gershwin was still working on the piece when he returned to New York. The draft for solo piano remained incomplete until August 1, 1928 – roughly six weeks after arriving home.

On November 18, Gershwin finished the orchestration for *An American in Paris*, which was premiered on December 13 at Carnegie Hall, with Walter Damrosch conducting the New York Philharmonic Orchestra. To celebrate, Harry gave his cousin a large, sectional screen for his bedroom (George had recently moved into a spacious penthouse apartment at 33 Riverside Drive), on which he had painted scenes as imagined from *An American in Paris*.[57] The imagery on the screen evoked the narrative program, penned by Deems Taylor, distributed to audience members at the premiere. Although most commentators found the program helpful when writing their reviews of *An American in Paris*, Abbe Niles, the critic who had previously praised Gershwin's use of the blues, found the inclusion of such a program distracting:

> It is questionable whether the brilliant concert-notes supplied by Mr. Deems Taylor were as much a blessing as a curse at the christening ... *An American in Paris* represents an advance in Gershwin's ability both to get what he wants out of a symphony orchestra (no mean problem), and so to transform and combine his themes as to make a living organism of the sum total. [But] scarcely anywhere was it pointed out that Gershwin had gained considerably in his knowledge of how to write long compositions for large orchestras.[58]

Niles praised Gershwin's music for its "immense gusto for life," which he predicted would "not quickly fade" and which would "continue to arouse pleased surprise in the minds of intelligent hearers, including serious if not solemn musicians."[59]

This assessment likely appealed to Gershwin. He had recently noted how his time abroad had not only exposed him to the work of European avant-garde composers, but also instilled in him a newfound appreciation for his own distinctive approach to composition:

> It was quite a paradox to me to find that, although I went abroad largely to benefit my technic as much as possible from a study of European orchestral methods, much more attention is paid there to the *originality of musical material* than to the excellence of its technical development.[60]

For Gershwin, this "originality of musical material" was a reference to the "American" sound, created in his own works and in the works of others (namely Kálmán and Krenek) through the implementation of jazz and blues characteristics. For Gershwin's cousin Ben, the increasing popularity for such displays of "originality" served as confirmation of his developing theories concerning the "unifying and enlarging voice" folklore could provide contemporary artists. In a series of book reviews penned by Ben Botkin in 1927 and 1928, he encouraged readers to look more closely at the plurality of cultures surrounding them.[61] He was especially taken with the contributions of African American writers, as displayed in his review of Countee Cullen's *Color* and his article, "Self-Portraiture and Social Criticism in Negro Folk Song," which appeared in *Opportunity: A Journal of Negro Life*.[62]

In 1928 Ben Botkin was elected president of the Oklahoma Folklore Society, and it was around this time that he began to pay more attention to folksong, which he said was linked to his interest in "restoring the oral popular tradition to poetry."[63] Between 1929 and 1932, he published a series of four anthologies titled *Folk-Say: A Regional Miscellany*. "Folk-Say" was a term he had coined the year before, and as he explained, it "was not a substitute or synonym for folklore ... but an extension of the older term to include literature *about* the folk as well as *of* the folk and to center attention on the oral, story-telling phases of living lore conceived as literary material."[64] This conceptual move paralleled the newfound focus on the blues in contemporary concert music. As Ben Botkin explained, his fascination with the concept of folk was tied to a "profound interest in culture in the broader sense" and "folk culture in particular." Regarding the relationship between lore and art, he presented two guiding theories. First, in every age art moves on two levels: that of the folk and that of "culture." Second, in America "there is not one folk but many folk groups – as many folk groups as there are regional cultures or racial or occupational groups within a region."[65] Botkin's interest lay in folklore's contemporaneity. In his *Folk-Say* anthologies, he included works he described as "lore in the making" that demonstrated "the interplay between folk and popular influences."[66]

The inaugural volume of *Folk-Say* was published in June 1929. Ben sent copies of the book to friends and family, including his brother Harry and his cousins Ira and George.[67] Included in the volume was a scholarly essay by Botkin presenting his theories about regional cultures in the United States and their influence on contemporary society. According to Botkin, the role of contemporary artists was to create works that strengthen understanding of the country's diverse populations, an enterprise that would link the disparate parts of a fragmented society.[68] He was committed to bringing together the past, present and future under the capacious umbrella of folk culture. The customs and creative practices of America's many disparate cultures deserved the attention.

In the first volume of *Folk-Say*, George no doubt found many items of interest. For example, in his introductory essay Ben Botkin acknowledged the distinction between "folk literature" and "culture literature,"[69] but insisted that the distinction reflected "a difference in form, not in content."[70] An essay titled "Songs of Yesterday and To-day" brings together songs from "the oil fields . . . harvest fields . . . and a factory outside Chicago" that "illustrate a certain speeding or 'jazzing' up in the tempo" of American folk song.[71] Among the poems were some identified as "Blues." Included in a series of "folk-motifs" were "three sketches" for an "Oklahoma opera" concerning the prejudice faced by African Americans. The final sketch, titled "Holy Roller Elders," describes the services of a group of "shouting Methodists" and "jumping Baptists" who cause dismay in the community when they establish a local meeting-house in a well-to-do section of town.[72]

The second volume of *Folk-Say* appeared in December 1930. Larger and more ornate in appearance, this volume included scholarly articles discussing the current state of folklore. "There is a point where collection and classification . . . break down and creative interpretation must begin," argued Botkin. The crucial question is "not what is the folk and what is folklore but what can they do for our culture."[73] One of the artist's primary tasks, he noted, was to serve as an interpreter among disparate cultures. Consequently, he included black authors and poems and short stories about black life. Botkin was particularly interested in the relationship between folklore and modern technology. Accordingly, he included works highlighting the relationship between contemporary black folklore and the phonograph and film. Botkin did not see technology as a destructive force when it came to folklore. Instead, he embraced technology as an effective means for the creation and dissemination of folklore. Since a goal of the second volume was to flesh out, as Botkin put it, "the dangers, limitations and problems besetting the artist who tries . . . to convert folk materials into art," Botkin's publisher, the University of Oklahoma Press, engaged George Gershwin in its marketing campaign.[74] Consequently, the volume sold well and received numerous reviews in newspapers, magazines and scholarly journals.

Volumes Three and Four, published respectively in 1931 and 1932, dropped the scholarly essays and opened instead with poetic inscriptions. "The emphasis," as Botkin later explained, "was on cultural, racial and class conflicts" in contemporary society. "The forms were experimental rather than traditional."[75] By 1932, Ben Botkin was fully engaged in discovering new talent and promoting free expression. He called for a new generation of artists and intellectuals who refused to accept a culture that promoted "economic or cultural bondage." The question regarding folklore, was no longer "Where did we come from?" but rather "Where do we go from here?"[76]

It was ideas such as these that Gershwin recalled when he first encountered Havana's Afro-Cuban music culture during a two-week holiday in February 1932.

Havana

Gershwin once described his first trip to Cuba as "two hysterical weeks in Havana, where no sleep was to be had, but the quality and quantity of fun made up for that."[77] He went with a group of wealthy golfing friends: Everett Jacobs, Bennett Cerf, Daniel Silberberg, and Emil Mosbacher.[78] Their stay in Havana coincided with Carnival season. Although Gershwin did not go to Cuba looking for musical inspiration, once there, he witnessed firsthand the realization of his cousin Ben's theories concerning folk culture in modern society.

Gershwin and his friends rented two adjoining suites at the elegant Almendares Hotel and Golf Club, where the resident musical ensemble was the Palau Brothers Hollywood Orchestra. The most famous dance band in Cuba, the Palau Brothers had made their mark in Los Angeles with Ernesto Lecuona playing Moisés Simons's "The Peanut Vendor" (El manisero) in the film *Cuban Love Song* (1931). The *Havana Post*, an English-language newspaper for tourists, reported that "Mr. Gershwin was much interested in the Cuban music" they played.[79] In Havana, the Palau Brothers performed a wide range of music, from American jazz to Afro-Cuban dance tunes, serving, like other ensembles, as a bridge between Cuban and American popular music traditions. The Castro Brothers Orchestra, another such bridge, had the honor of being hired by Gershwin to play at a party he hosted at his hotel. On this occasion "the Cuban *son* and American jazz vied for popularity" as the Castro Brothers "demonstrated their unique interpretation of the Cuban native music, incidentally giving their visiting musician lessons in the use of the maracas."[80]

A gala at the Gran Casino Nacional, celebrating Cuba's national holiday, known as Grito de Baire, offered another encounter with Cuban music played by a large dance band.[81] Once again, the highlight was Moisés Simons's "El manisero." "Peanut Vendor" marionettes were handed out to a lucky few. Additional souvenirs included "maracas, guiros, claves and bongos," and lessons in the proper way to play them.[82] Gershwin collected a full set of these instruments, which he took home with him to New York. Each of these bands combined Cuban and American elements. The ensembles were relatively large – American jazz bands with Afro-Cuban percussion instruments added. As Gershwin discovered, there was more to Havana's music scene than the large dance orchestras employed by the hotels. Smaller ensembles, playing to locals in waterside nightclubs, called *fritas*, offered another style of Cuban "folk" culture, one that showed fewer signs of American influences. According to the *Havana Post*, Gershwin encountered such an ensemble his third night in Cuba, when he was unexpectedly serenaded outside his hotel room by "a group of itinerant musicians from Havana's popular 'fritas.'"[83] The next evening, Gershwin was treated to more music of this sort at a gathering in Miramar. According to the *Havana Post*, the party was a "typically Cuban gala" that included "various interpretations of the rumba by professional dancers, and instrumental music by the Habanero Sextet, the orchestra which first introduced the *son* several years ago."[84] The Habanero Sextet was a well-established group, formed in 1920. The instrumentation consisted of two singers playing maracas and claves, a bongo player, and three string players on guitar, bass and *tres* (a guitar-like instrument with three double strings).

Another traditional Afro-Cuban group Gershwin encountered during his stay was the Septeto Nacional, formed by Ignacio Piñeiro in 1927. Piñeiro lived in Pueblo Nuevo, the black quarter of the city. As a child, Piñeiro had sung in choirs and played drums with the Afro-Cuban cabildos. His group had the same instrumentation as the Habanero Sextet, but with a trumpet added to the mix. They performed regularly on Cuban radio during Gershwin's visit. He reportedly made a special trip to Havana's CMCJ radio station to meet the musicians and witness one of their performances in person.[85]

During Gershwin's stay in Havana, he discovered that the term "rumba" (or rhumba) could refer to a variety of things: a musical genre, a dance, or even the event where the music and dancing take place. Rumba was linked to both traditional folk music and cross-cultural tunes like "The Peanut Vendor." Associated in Cuba "with manual laborers, particularly dockworkers" its register – when it came to class – resembled that of the blues in the United States.[86] Gershwin discovered all of these things during his visits to Havana's *fritas*, and by the time he returned to New York, he envisioned the "Rhumba" as a symbol of Cuban folk culture, past and present.

Shortly after his trip to Havana, Gershwin reflected on his experiences in a letter to George Pallay: "Cuba was most interesting to me, especially for its small dance orchestras, who play [the] most intricate rhythms most naturally."[87] These rhythms, and the concept of the rumba as he experienced it in Havana's local *fritas*, served as the inspiration for a new work. Around this time, Gershwin began composition lessons with Joseph Schillinger, under whose guidance Gershwin composed his Cuban piece.[88] Gershwin returned to Havana briefly in June (this time with Ira and Lee) and in July finished the piano score and began work on the orchestration. The completed composition was premiered, under the title *Rhumba*, on August 16, 1932, at an all-Gershwin concert at Lewisohn Stadium in New York. To accentuate the importance of the Afro-Cuban percussion instruments in the overall character of the composition, Gershwin noted (in the score) that the musicians playing the maracas, bongos, claves, and guiro should stand at the front of the stage, right next to the conductor's podium.

Rhumba was greeted favorably by critics. Still, Gershwin seemed dismayed by their tendency to view the work as another narrative tone poem, a sequel to *An American in Paris*. Consequently, when Gershwin conducted a performance of the piece three months later, at a benefit concert at the Metropolitan Opera, he renamed it *Cuban Overture*. This new title provided "a more just idea of the character and intent of the music."[89] American audiences, whose familiarity with Cuban music was filtered through the lens of Hollywood, did not fully understand the context of Gershwin's original title. So, to distance his music from the Latin-tinged jazz of Hollywood and the novelty songs he had composed in his youth, Gershwin wrote his own program note for the second concert, wherein he highlighted the "Cuban Rhythms" he had encountered in Havana and his interest in "combining them" with his "own thematic material."[90] The result was a formal symphonic overture influenced by his recent studies with Schillinger.

While in Cuba, Gershwin had witnessed, firsthand, the transformational experience of encountering a rich folk culture drastically different from his own. As an artist, he followed his cousin Ben's advice and created a new work that interpreted Cuba's Afro-Cuban traditions through the lens of his own culture. Gershwin recognized in the rumba a distinctive folk characteristic that influenced a wide array of popular Cuban music and dance, just as the blues had done in the United States. More importantly, in Cuba Gershwin witnessed the collision of different regional styles, absorbing the way that sort of encounter could transform a culture. In the years that followed, the influence of Ben Botkin's theories on Gershwin's approach to composition grew increasingly stronger, as revealed in *Porgy and Bess*.

Charleston

Gershwin first experienced Charleston through DuBose Heyward's novel *Porgy*, wherein music plays a decisive role in describing the city's soundscape. Take, for example, this description of an African American band parading through the streets of Charleston:

> First came an infinitesimal negro boy, scarlet-coated, and aglitter with brass buttons. Upon his head was balanced an enormous shako; and while he marched with left hand on hip and shoulders back, his right hand twirled a heavy gold-headed baton. Then the band, two score boys attired in several variations of the band master's costume, strode by. Bare, splay feet padded upon the cobbles; heads were thrown back, with lips to instruments that glittered in the sunshine, launching daring and independent excursions into the realm of sound. Yet these improvisations returned always to the eternal boom, boom, boom of an underlying rhythm, and met with others in the sudden weaving and ravelling of amazing chords. An ecstasy of wild, young bodies beat living into the blasts that shook the windows of the solemn houses . . . Exotic as the Congo, and still able to abandon themselves utterly to the wild joy of fantastic play, they had taken the reticent, old Anglo-Saxon town and stamped their mood swiftly and indelibly into its heart.[91]

When *Porgy* was transformed into a play in 1927, this memorable scene was brought to life by the Jenkins' Orphanage Band, a black youth ensemble from Charleston known for their rag-infused marches. Spirituals were incorporated as well, promoted as "authentic" expressions of Charleston's "Gullah" culture. These performances, which Gershwin heard when he attended the play, added a soundtrack to his early conception of Charleston.

Scholars have noted the contrast between the ending of *Porgy* the play (and consequently the opera) and the conclusion of Heyward's original novel. There is a restlessness to the Porgy found in DuBose and Dorothy Heyward's play that is absent from the novel. Ben Botkin once reflected on this particular type of restlessness, which he found in the works of Countee Cullen and other African American writers, describing it as "akin to that of another 'man without a country,' the Jew."[92] Botkin linked this connection to musical sources. One cannot help but wonder if, while watching the play, Gershwin was reminded of his cousin's theory:

> It might be asked if the dominant note of all Negro song is not the homesickness of an alien, homeless folk, "po' boy long way from home,"
> a nostalgia born of a racial, traditional and ancestral longing for a home that no longer exists like the Promised Land which the Jews have codified in Zion, and like the heaven of the Christians to which the Negro has transferred his unsatisfied earthly longing.[93]

Both the novel and the play were doubtless in Gershwin's mind as he planned his first trip to Charleston in 1933. Gershwin visited in December, en route to a golf vacation in Florida. In preparation for the trip, he wrote to Heyward about what he hoped to accomplish: "I would like to see the town and hear some spirituals and perhaps go to a colored café or two if there are any."[94]

Gershwin stayed in Charleston for three days on his way down to Florida, and an additional day on his way back to New York. As his letters to friends and interviews with reporters reveal, he was generally impressed with the city he encountered during these brief, early visits. But as his host, DuBose Heyward, quickly realized, Gershwin's first impressions of Charleston may have been misleading. The image of the city presented to him had been carefully crafted, over the course of two decades, for tourists.

Around World War I, Charleston began to experience a cultural Renaissance. This effort was formalized in 1924, when Charleston's mayor, Thomas P. Stoney, noted in the *Yearbook of the City of Charleston*: "We have to sell the City of Charleston to the outside world."[95] Cultural leaders promoted the city through a range of creative endeavors, including the Society for the Preservation of Old Spirituals, the Charleston Etchers Club, the Jenkins' Orphanage Band, the Poetry Society of South Carolina, various artist renditions of the city and most notably James P. Johnson's "The Charleston," penned in 1923 for the Broadway show *Runnin' Wild*.[96] Descriptions of the city's gradual transformation, from a rundown, economically distraught, provincial town to a gem of high Southern culture, appeared in newspapers across the country. These reports drew artists and writers in search of unmarred, seemingly pure Americana. For example, in 1928, a reporter for the *Chicago Evening Post* noted: "Everywhere one turns there appears the inexhaustible picturesqueness of Charleston, and on every side an artist has set up an easel in his devotion."[97] Among the many visual artists who ventured to Charleston before Gershwin arrived were Edward Hopper, Childe Hassam, George Biddle, Palmer Schoppe, and the photographer Walker Evans.

The images these men created, along with Heyward's novel *Porgy*, influenced Gershwin's perceptions of the city before he arrived and continued to color his image of Charleston during his first visit. One of the highlights of his first encounter with the city was his witnessing of an "experience service" at the Macedonia Church and hearing performances by the Society for the Preservation of Old Spirituals (an organization in which Heyward's mother participated). As Gershwin explained to a reporter shortly after his return to New York, these encounters had turned him into "an eager student of Negro music."[98] Gershwin claimed to be equally charmed by the city's overall character. "The artistry of the architecture, the warmth of the coloring on the stones of the old buildings ... Everything [in Charleston] combines to give the place a beauty only found perhaps in some Old World city such as Paris."[99]

Such a description concerned Heyward. After many years of planning and negotiating, work was finally beginning on the *Porgy* opera. The endeavor would be doomed if Gershwin envisioned the action taking place in a quaint, European-inspired setting. Gershwin's comments made it abundantly clear to Heyward that his friend from up North had little understanding of the regional culture that had originally inspired *Porgy*. The "Negro culture" of Harlem and Paris was a far cry from the black "Gullah" traditions of the Southern Low Country. As Heyward wrote to Gershwin on February 6, 1934: "You really haven't scratched the surface of the native material yet."[100] Another trip was necessary.

Gershwin agreed, and on June 16, 1934 he boarded a train at New York's Penn Station bound for Charleston. Accompanying him was his cousin Harry, who had recently returned to New York after seven years in Paris. Upon arrival, the pair was met by Gershwin's valet, Paul Mueller, who had driven down in Gershwin's Buick with the luggage, art supplies, and George's music. From Charleston, they drove ten miles out to a ferry, which took them to Folly Island, a rustic beach resort where the Heywards owned a summer house called "Follywood." Gershwin and his companions spent the next five weeks in a four-room, clapboard cottage thirty feet from the shore. True, there was no electricity nor running water. But there was an upright piano, rented from Siegling's Music Store in Charleston, and a pair of domestic servants to haul water and take care of the cooking and cleaning. In a letter to his mother a few days after his arrival, Gershwin gave a vivid description of his new abode. Paris was long forgotten:

> The place down here looks like a battered old South Sea Island. There was a storm two weeks ago which tore down a few houses ... and the place is so primitive they may just let them stay that way. Imagine, there's not one telephone on the whole island – public or private. Our first three days have been cool, the place being swept by an ocean breeze. Yesterday was the first hot day and it brought out the flies and gnats and mosquitoes. There are so many swamps in the district that when the breeze comes in from the land there's nothing to do but scratch.[101]

In a letter to Ben, Harry offered a similar description:

> It is very lovely here – 12 miles from Charleston – on real South Sea island – covered with palms & very primitive. Sharks & porpoises & giant turtles a few yards ahead of us – negroes & cabins & plantations, alligators & all just back of us.[102]

Gershwin found it difficult, at first, to work on Folly Island. "I have never lived in such a back to nature place," he admitted to a local reporter named Frank Gilbreth Jr., who interviewed Gershwin a few days after his arrival. In his article, Gilbreth recalled the moment he first laid eyes on the composer: "Seated at his piano, Mr. Gershwin, tanned, muscular, dark, wearing a light palm beach coat and an orange tie, was playing jazz as it had never been played at Folly before."[103] Two weeks later, when Gilbreth returned, he discovered a composer more acclimated to his surroundings:

> Bare and black above the waist, an inch of hair bristling from his face and with a pair of tattered knickers furnishing a sole connecting link with civilization, George Gershwin ... has gone native ... Naturally brown, he is now black. Naturally sturdy, he is now sturdier.[104]

Abe Dumas, a local teenager Gershwin befriended during his stay, corroborated this description of Gershwin's transformation: "His trousers had been cut down to short pants and it looked as though he had done the job himself – with a pair of scissors."[105] Dumas also noted a few "Northern" habits that Gershwin had maintained: he reportedly enjoyed hitting golf balls into the waves and driving his Buick convertible on the beach at low tide.

Gershwin did not isolate himself completely during his stay. Local papers reported regularly on his outings to Charleston, where he visited the homes of the city's elite and played golf at the country club. He even served as judge at a local beauty contest. Heyward functioned as Gershwin's guide, steering the composer away from the city whenever possible and out to the barrier islands, where the region's African American inhabitants lived in partial isolation. According to Heyward, "James Island, with its large population of primitive Gullah Negroes lay adjacent [to Folly Island], and furnished us with a laboratory in which to test our theories, as well as an inexhaustible source of folk material."[106] During one of these visits, Gershwin encountered the musical practice called "shouting" that he had read about in Ben's first *Folk-Say* volume. As Heyward explained it, this practice involved "a complicated rhythmic pattern beaten out by feet and hands, as an accompaniment to the spirituals." Heyward was startled by Gershwin's reaction to the music:

> I shall never forget the night when at a Negro meeting on a remote sea-island George started "shouting" with them. And eventually to their huge delight stole the show from their champion "shouter." I think he is probably the only white man in America who could have done it.[107]

Gershwin remembered this evening. He later told Anne Brown (the first Bess) that an elderly member of the congregation had told him: "By God, you sure can beat out them rhythms, boy. I'm over seventy years old, and

I ain't never seen no po' little white man take off and fly like you. You could be my own son."[108]

Gershwin was not the first white outsider to visit the Gullah community – such excursions had become popular with adventurous tourists in the 1930s. But Gershwin undoubtedly was one of the first – if not the first – to transition consciously from an observer of Gullah performance to an active participant. Like his cousin Ben, Gershwin did not see the Gullah culture as a remnant of the past. Instead, it served as an example of America's multicultural present. His actions on James Island revealed his shared belief with his cousin that, to come to a deeper understanding of an unfamiliar folk practice, one had to embrace it, and at least for one evening, become a part of it.

Toward the end of his stay, Gershwin penned a letter to Emily Paley – the close friend who had first introduced him to *Porgy* – and reflected on his time in Charleston:

> The trip down here was a very good thing in many ways . . . the place itself is very different from anything I've ever seen or lived in before & appeals to the primitive man in me. We go around with practically nothing on, shave only every other day (we do have some visitors, you know), eat out on our porch, not more than 30 feet from the ocean at high tide, sit out at night gazing at the stars, smoking our pipes (I've begun on a pipe), the three of us, Harry, Paul & myself discuss our two favorite subjects, Hitler's Germany & God's women. We are in truth, Yankees from the North, always suspected a little by the southerner as being a bit slick. Lonesomeness has crept in and bit me quite a few times, but that is to be expected. Paul & Harry have also been bitten, so I suppose that should be a bit consoling.
>
>   I've finished one scene of the opera & am now working on the second. It's been very tough for me to work here as the wild waves, playing the role of a siren, beckon to me, every time I get stuck, which is often, and I like a weak sailor turn to them causing many hours to be knocked into a thousand tiny bits.
>
>   I've seen and heard some grand Negro sermons & when I see you I shall tell you all about them.[109]

Gershwin embraced the culture he encountered in South Carolina but never fully felt a part of it. His summer on Folly Island changed him, but not completely. A sense of restlessness pervaded his visit – a loneliness and longing that eventually found their way into *Porgy and Bess*.

On their way home from Charleston, Gershwin and Harry visited Heyward at his permanent home in Henderson, NC. Continuing their exploration of African American culture, they accompanied Heyward to a local meeting house known for its "Holy Roller" services. Henderson was not a tourist destination. Gershwin quickly discovered that visiting a black church in Henderson differed markedly from what he had experienced in

Charleston. As Heyward later explained, Gershwin stopped suddenly as they entered the building, grabbing tightly onto Heyward's arm:

> The sound that had arrested him was one to which, through long familiarity, I attached no special importance. But now, listening to it with him, and noticing his excitement, I began to catch its extraordinary quality. It consisted of perhaps a dozen voices raised in loud rhythmic prayer ... while each had started at a different time, upon a different theme, they formed a clearly defined rhythmic pattern, and ... this, with the actual words lost, and the inevitable pounding of the rhythm, produced an effect almost terrifying in its primitive intensity.[110]

Dorothy Heyward also remembered this encounter. She later described it in an unpublished memoir. She suggested that Gershwin became alarmed by the attendees' "frenzied movements and speaking in tongues" and soon left the church, "afraid for his safety."[111] Disconcerting as this encounter might have been for Gershwin, it nonetheless left its mark on *Porgy and Bess*. Gershwin evoked the "voices" he had heard "raised in loud rhythmic prayer" when composing the terrifying invocation to God at the beginning of the Hurricane scene. But it should be noted that the music Gershwin composed was not a transcription of what he heard when visiting black communities, but rather an evocation of the cultural encounter. Gershwin's approach to composing *Porgy and Bess* did not involve the creation of precise transcriptions. He did not directly incorporate the specific music he heard in Charleston and Henderson into *Porgy and Bess*. Instead, Gershwin inserted into his score what he interpreted as the most distinctive characteristics of the African American music he heard. This process of interpreting the music through the filter of his own tastes and experiences led to the creation of what his cousin Ben would have described as contemporary folk music; that is, original music drawing on an encounter with a culture or "folk" other than one's own.

There is a famous promotional photograph of Gershwin from 1934 that serves as a visual example of this process (Figure. 9.1). Gershwin is shown in his New York apartment, sitting at the piano supposedly working on *Porgy and Bess*. On the wall behind him is a portrait of a young African American girl he painted in the early 1930s. Note that the image of American black culture that is supposedly inspiring him is not a photograph depicting the girl as she actually is, but a painting by Gershwin reflecting how he envisions her. It shows *his* interpretation of who she is, painted in response to *his* encounter with her. This cross-cultural imperative similarly inflects all the music in *Porgy and Bess*. Even the Jenkins' Orphanage Band, who performed in the opera as they had in the play, were asked to refrain from playing their regular repertoire in

175 *Exploring New Worlds*

Figure 9.1 George Gershwin works on a score at the piano in his 72nd Street apartment, New York, New York, 1934. Photo by PhotoQuest/Getty Images

Porgy and Bess, performing instead new music composed by Gershwin specifically for the opera.

Ben Botkin's theories played a decisive role in the development of Gershwin's concept of folk culture, especially with regards to the effects, both positive and negative, that folklore could have on contemporary society. As Ben later explained in his forward to *A Treasury of American Folklore*:

> It is necessary to distinguish between folklore as we find it and folklore as we believe it ought to be. Folklore as we find it perpetuates human ignorance,

perversity, and depravity along with human wisdom and goodness. Historically we cannot deny or condone this baser side of folklore – and yet we may understand and condemn it as we condemn other manifestations of human error.[112]

"Folklore, like life itself," Botkin wrote, "is animal in its origins and spiritual in its possible fruit." Even lore reflecting prejudice must be acknowledged: "Such stories stick because they have the tang of life and are historical comment." The purpose of their retelling, however, is "not to perpetuate but to reveal and correct the errors and evil they narrate. With this perspective the whole of folklore may become an instrument for understanding and good will."[113] According to Botkin, the job of artists, like Gershwin, was to create the good in culture.

Gershwin's approach to depicting African Americans in *Porgy and Bess* emerges with more clarity when viewed through the lens of Ben Botkin's theories. Botkin's hitherto hidden contribution also helps explain why Gershwin defined his work as a "folk opera" when describing it to reporters:

> *Porgy and Bess* is a folk tale. Its people naturally would sing folk music. When I first began to work on the music I decided against the use of original folk material because I wanted the music to be all of one piece. Therefore I wrote my own spirituals and folk songs. But they are still folk music – and therefore, being an operatic form, *Porgy and Bess* becomes folk opera.[114]

Gershwin didn't define *Porgy and Bess* as a specifically African American opera. To him it represented more than the experiences of a single race. "It's an American opera," he explained to a reporter, "striving to depict an American scene in a purely American way." Asked to clarify this statement, Gershwin continued:

> I've taken advantage of the spiritual quality of colored singing and the blues quality and combined the two with what I know about American song writing. The result . . . has struck people as being something in opera that could not have been written in any country but here.[115]

Asked if he had "any other themes in mind" for an opera, Gershwin offered a response that echoed his cousin Ben's theories about regional folklore:

> America is so vast that it has many component parts . . . [Other composers] have tried the Indian dozens of times but unfortunately with very little success . . . Other American themes . . . that might be used are the Puritanical New England, the Northwest woodsman, and the cosmopolitan life of New York or Chicago.[116]

Travel enabled Gershwin to explore new worlds as a composer, and his experiences as an "outsider" in Paris, Havana, and Charleston loomed large in his imagination. As a cultural tourist, Gershwin's exploration of "foreign" locales during the height of his career pushed him in new

177 Exploring New Worlds

directions artistically. His cousin Harry said it best: "Art is a collision of new truths and awakened sensibilities; it is a serious understanding of the untried and unexpected."[117]

When *Porgy and Bess* premiered in New York on October 10, 1935 at the Alvin Theatre, reviews were numerous and mixed in their opinions. But of all the commentators, Brooks Atkinson came closest to the truth: "Although Mr. Heyward is the author of the libretto and shares with Ira Gershwin the credit for the lyrics ... the evening is unmistakably George Gershwin's personal holiday."[118]

Notes

1. Gershwin's grandmother on his mother's side was Mary Dechinik (1858–1940). Mary Dechinik was the older sister of Annie Dechinik (1873–1922), who married Aaron B. Botkin (1871–1942) in 1891 and was the mother of the painter Henry Albert Botkin (1896–1983) and the folklorist Benjamin Albert Botkin (1901–1975).
2. Edward Jablonski, *Gershwin: A Biography* (New York: Da Capo Press, 1998), 56.
3. We know from a letter written by Ira Gershwin to Emily and Lou Paley on June 8, 1925 that George was staying at the Hotel Chambord, located at 123 Avenue de Champs-Élysées. Cf. Robert Kimbal and Alfred Simon *The Gershwins* (New York: Atheneum, 1973), 49–50.
4. Robert Schirmer to Emily and Lou Paley, April 1926. Cf. Kimball and Simon, *The Gershwins*, 63.
5. Ibid.
6. Ibid.
7. Ibid.
8. Ibid.
9. George Antheil to Mary Curtis Bok, October 1923. Cf. Wayne D. Shirley, "Another American in Paris: George Antheil's Correspondence with Mary Curtis Bok," *The Quarterly Journal of the Library of Congress* 34/1 (January 1977), 7–8.
10. George Antheil to Mary Louise Bok, October 19, 1925. Cf. Shirley, "Another American in Paris," 13.
11. George Gershwin, "Does Jazz Belong to Art?" *Singing* (July 1926); Cf. Gregory R. Suriano, ed., *Gershwin in His Time: A Biographical Scrapbook, 1919–1937* (New York: Gramercy Books, 1998), 37.
12. Shirley, "Another American in Paris," 14.
13. Photograph of George Gershwin, inscribed on back to Mabel and Bob Schirmer, dated April 11, 1926. Reproductions of both sides of the inscribed photograph appear in Kimball and Simon, *The Gershwins*, 63.
14. C.J. Woolf, "Finding Jazz in the Spirit of His Age: George Gershwin, A Product of New York's East Side, Holds Art Music Must Always Express the Contemporary," *New York Times* (January 20, 1929), SM82.
15. Ibid.
16. Ibid.
17. Abbe Niles, "Introduction," in W.C. Handy (ed.), *Blues: An Anthology* (New York: Albert & Charles Boni, 1926), 1.
18. Elliott S. Hurwitt, "Abbe Niles, Blues Advocate," in David Evans (ed.), *Ramblin' on My Mind: New Perspectives on the Blues* (Champagne-Urbana, IL: University of Illinois Press, 2008), 110.
19. Niles, "Introduction," 21.
20. Ibid., 39.
21. Wayne D. Shirley, liner notes to *Oh, Kay!* (Washington, DC: Smithsonian American Musical Theater Series, ROII-RCA, 1978).
22. DuBose Heyward, *Porgy* (New York: Grosset & Dunlap, 1925), 7.
23. Ibid., 11.

24. Among a list of authors whom B.A. Botkin believed had broadened America's understanding of African American culture were Sterling Brown, Countee Cullen, Langston Hughes, DuBose Heyward, and Carl Van Vechten.
25. Louis Filler, "Ben Botkin: Much More Than Folklore," *New York History* 77/1 (January 1996), 35.
26. Benjamin A. Botkin to Mary Ritchey, February 3, 1924. Washington, DC. Archives of American Art, Henry Botkin Papers.
27. Benjamin A. Botkin to Mary Ritchey, February 5, 1924. Washington, DC. Archives of American Art, Henry Botkin Papers.
28. For a general overview of the Boas theories that influenced Botkin, see Franz Boas, *Race Language and Culture* (New York: Macmillan Company, 1940); Susan Hegeman, *Patterns for America: Modernism and the Concept of Culture* (Princeton, NJ: Princeton University Press, 1999), 32–49; Benjamin Filene, *Romancing the Folk: Public Memory & American Roots Music* (Chapel Hill, NC: University of North Carolina Press, 2000), 64; and Richard Handler, "Boasian Anthropology and the Critique of American Culture," *American Quarterly* 42 (1990), 252–73.
29. For a complete list, see "Bibliography of the Writings of Benjamin A. Botkin," in *Folklore and Society: Essays in Honor of Benj. A Botkin* (Hatsboro, PA: Folklore Associates, 1966), 169–92.
30. Louis Filler, "Ben Botkin: Much More Than Folklore," 38.
31. Jablonski, *Gershwin*, 152.
32. Kimball and Simon, *The Gershwins*, 91.
33. Ibid.
34. Cf. ibid., 90. For a thorough discussion of Gershwin's search for specifically pitched horns, see Mark Clague, "An American in Paris: A Gershwin Manifesto," in Mark Clague (ed.), *George Gershwin, An American in Paris: A Tone Poem for Orchestra*, The George and Ira Gershwin Critical Edition (Mainz and New York: Schott International/European American Music, 2019).
35. As Jablonsky, *Gershwin*, 154, explains, Gershwin first met Ravel on March 7, 1928 at the home of Eva Gauthier. The occasion was Ravel's 53rd birthday.
36. Cf. Arbie Orenstein, ed., *A Ravel Reader: Correspondence, Articles, Interviews* (New York: Columbia University Press, 1990), 289.
37. "Music," *Time* (February 28, 1938). Cf. Pollack, *George Gershwin*, 120.
38. Gershwin met with Ibert on April 3. Cf. Kimball and Simon, *The Gershwins*, 94.
39. Cf. Pollack, *George Gershwin*, 121.
40. Vernon Duke, "Gershwin, Schillinger, and Dukelsky," *The Musical Quarterly* 75 (Winter 1991), 119–24.
41. Carmela de León, *Ernesto Lecuona: El Maestro* (Havana: Música Mundana, 1995), 78.
42. Cf. Pollack, *George Gershwin*, 432.
43. Cf. Jablonski, *Gershwin*, 155.
44. Based on the novel by S.Y. Abramovitsh (Mendele Moykher Sforim), this production was produced by Alexis Granowsky and performed by the State Jewish Theatre from Moscow. As Ira noted to a reporter in Paris, he was surprised to discover that not all Yiddish music was the same: "The music [performed by the Moscow artists], while Yiddish, was absolutely different from the Yiddish music of Rumshinsky on Second Avenue in New York, who obviously emulates the style of the Broadway tin-pan alley scriveners." Cf. Alan Hutchinson, "A Song-Writer Listens to Some Foreign Melodies," *Paris Comet* (July 1928), 55.
45. "Germany Taking Jazz Seriously, Gershwin Finds," *New York Herald – Paris* (April 28, 1928). Clipping preserved in George Gershwin Scrapbook 3 (1927–29), Library of Congress, George and Ira Gershwin Collection, Box 74.
46. Hutchinson, "A Song-Writer Listens to Some Foreign Melodies," 55.
47. Ibid.
48. Hyman Sandow, "Gershwin 'Pariscopes': An American Abroad," *Musical America* (August 18, 1928), 12.
49. Ibid.
50. Cf. Pollack, *George Gershwin*, 145.
51. In his letters home, Harry often described his daily interactions with George. For example, in a letter dated October [1917] he wrote: "George is home. Invested $110 on a saxophone. He is learning to play the instrument so that he can get in the band if drafted." Henry Botkin to

Aaron B. Botkin, Annie Botkin, and Benjamin Botkin dated October [1917]. Washington, DC. Archives of American Art, Henry Botkin Papers.
52. "Gershwin's Compositions in Paint," *American Art* 7/3 (Summer 1993), 92.
53. Henry Botkin to George Gershwin dated March 27, 1931. Washington, DC. Archives of American Art, Henry Botkin Papers.
54. A series of twenty-three letters between George Gershwin and Henry Botkin dated March through August 1931 offer a detailed view of Gershwin's early collecting activity. Washington, DC. Archives of American Art, Henry Botkin Papers.
55. "Gershwin's Compositions in Paint," 94.
56. Cf. Merle Armitage, ed. *George Gershwin* (New York: Longmans, Green, 1938), 138.
57. Ben Botkin to Harry Botkin, March 22, 1931 (University of Nebraska, Special Collections, Benjamin Botkin Collection) mentions the appearance of Harry's "An American in Paris" screen in the February issue of *Ladies Home Journal*.
58. Abbe Niles, "A Note on Gershwin," *The Nation* (February 13, 1929), 194.
59. Ibid.
60. Sandow, "Gershwin 'Pariscopes': An American Abroad," 12, emphasis added.
61. See, for example, the following reviews in the *Daily Oklahoman* by B.A. Botkin: "*Poems*, by T.S. Elliott" (March 6, 1927); "*Fandango*, by Stanley Vestal" (April 24, 1927); "*Destinations, American Caravan*, and *Cities and Men*, by Ludwig Lewisohn" (May 20, 1928). The finest article to date outlining the development of Botkin's theories concerning folk culture is Jerold Hirsh, "T.S. Eliot, B.A. Botkin, and the Politics of Cultural Representation: Folklore, Modernity and Pluralism," in Jeffrey Melnick (ed.), *Race and the Modern Artist* (Oxford: Oxford University Press, 2003), 16–41.
62. B.A. Botkin, "Review of *Color* by Countee Cullen," *Daily Oklahoman* (March 14, 1926); "Self-Portraiture and Social Criticism in Negro Folk Song," *Opportunity: A Journal of Negro Life* V (February 1927), 38–42.
63. B.A. Botkin, "*Folk-Say* and *Space*: Their Genesis and Exodus," *Southwest Review* 20 (July 1935), 323.
64. Ibid., 324
65. B.A. Botkin, "The Folk in Literature: An Introduction to New Regionalism," in B.A. Botkin (ed.), *Folk-Say: A Regional Miscellany*, vol. I (Norman, OK: Oklahoma Folk-Lore Society, 1929), 9.
66. Ibid.
67. Harry Botkin to Ben Botkin, January 13, 1931. University of Nebraska Library, Special Collections, Benjamin Botkin Collection. Ira and George's copy of the book is in the private collection of Anna Celenza.
68. B.A. Botkin, "The Folk in Literature: An Introduction to New Regionalism," 17.
69. Ibid., 9.
70. Jerrold Hirsh, "Folklore in the Making: B.A. Botkin," *The Journal of American Folklore* 100/395 (January–March 1987), 12.
71. Acel Garland, "Songs of Yesterday and To-day," in B.A. Botkin (ed.), *Folk-Say: A Regional Miscellany, vol. I*, 95–107.
72. George Milburn, "Oklahoma Opera: Three Sketches from a Book of Tales," in B.A. Botkin (ed.), *Folk-Say: A Regional Miscellany*, vol. I, 115–19.
73. B.A. Botkin, "Introduction," Folk-Say: A Regional Miscellany, vol. II, in B.A. Botkin (ed.), (Norman, OK: University of Oklahoma Press, 1930), 17.
74. Ben Botkin to Harry Botkin, March 22, 1931. University of Nebraska Library, Special Collections, Benjamin Botkin Collection.
75. B.A. Botkin, "Introduction to the *Folk-Say* Series," 320.
76. Hirsh, "Folklore in the Making," 17.
77. Cf. Pollock, *George Gershwin*, 534.
78. According to the *Havana Post* (February 18, 1932), 6, Gershwin, Cerf, Jacobs, and Silberberg arrived from New York on the S.S. *Veendam* on February 16. Mosbacher arrived four days later. An unpublished article by Andrew Lamb titled "Gershwin's Cuban Vacation" serves as the source for all the quotes taken from the *Havana Post*. www.academia.edu/10986708/Gershwins_Cuban_Vacation_written_pre-2006_
79. Ibid. (February 19, 1932), 9.
80. Ibid. (February 22, 1932), 2.

81. Ibid. (February 25, 1932), 6. Grito de Baire commemorated the beginning of Cuba's war for independence against Spain in 1895. Gershwin and his friends attended the gala as the guests of Howard Hughes.
82. Ibid. (February 27, 1932), 6.
83. Ibid. (February 20, 1932), 3.
84. Ibid. (February 20, 1932), 2.
85. Helio Orvio, *Diccionario de la Música Cubana* (Havana: Letras Cubanas, 1981), 356. Cf. Lamb "Gershwin's Cuban Vacation."
86. Ned Sublette, *Cuba and Its Music: From the First Drums to the Mambo* (Chicago: Chicago Review Press, 2004), Chapter 17, Rumba.
87. George Gershwin to George Pallay, March 8, 1932. Cf. Pollock, *George Gershwin*, 534.
88. Schillinger's methods involved systematic and mathematical manipulations of harmony and melody. As Warren Brodsky, "Joseph Schillinger (1895–1943), Music Science Promethean," *American Music* 21/1 (Spring 2003), 45, notes, "Schillinger was a music scientist receptive to new technologies and experimentation related to the arts."
89. Cf. Pollock, *George Gershwin*, 536.
90. Cf. Douglas Lee, *Masterworks of 20th-Century Music: The Modern Repertory of the Symphony Orchestra* (New York: Routledge, 2002), 167–68.
91. Ibid., 113–15.
92. B.A. Botkin, "Self-Portraiture and Social Criticism in Negro Folk Song," *Opportunity: A Journal of Negro Life* 5 (February 1927), 42.
93. Ibid.
94. Cf. Pollock, *George Gershwin*, 577.
95. Cf. Martha R. Severens, "The Charleston Renaissance," *The Resource Library* (July 3, 2007) http://tfaoi.org/aa/7aa/7aa788.htm
96. The most thorough description of this cultural transformation is Stephanie E. Yuhl's *A Golden Haze of Memory: The Making of Historic Charleston* (Chapel Hill, NC: University of North Carolina Press, 2005).
97. "Renaissance of the South," *Chicago Evening Post* (April 17, 1928).
98. *New York Herald Tribune* (January 5, 1934).
99. Cf. Pollock, *George Gershwin*, 577.
100. Ibid.
101. Cf. James M. Hutchisson, *DuBose Heyward: A Charleston Gentleman and the World of Porgy and Bess* (Jackson: University of Mississippi Press, 2000), 151.
102. Harry Botkin to Ben and Gertrude Botkin, July 3, 1934. Library of Congress, George and Ira Gershwin Collection, Box 63, folder 45.
103. Frank B. Gilbreth, "Gershwin, Prince of Jazz, Pounds Out Rhythm at Folly," *News and Courier* (June 19, 1934), 12.
104. Frank B. Gilbreth, "Gershwin, Gone Native, Finds It 'Shame to Work' at Folly," *News and Courier* (June 29, 1934), 9-A.
105. Abe Dumas interview conducted by Michael Samuel Grossman on December 14, 1996. College of Charleston, Jewish Heritage Project.
106. DuBose Heyward, "Porgy and Bess Return on Wings of Song," in James M. Hutchinson (ed.), *A DuBose Heyward Reader* (Athens, GA: University of Georgia Press, 2003), 49.
107. Ibid., 50.
108. Cf. David Zax, "Summertime for George Gershwin," *Smithsonian Magazine* (August 8, 2010). www.smithsonianmag.com/arts-culture/summertime-for-george-gershwin-2170485/
109. George Gershwin to Emily Paley, July 11, 1934. Library of Congress, George and Ira Gershwin Collection, Box 64, folder 51.
110. Cf. James M. Hutchisson, *DuBose Heyward: A Charleston Gentleman and the World of Porgy and Bess* (Jackson: University of Mississippi Press, 2000), 152.
111. Cf. Ellen Noonan, *The Strange Career of Porgy and Bess: Race, Culture and America's Most Famous Opera* (Chapel Hill: University of North Carolina Press, 2012), 177.
112. B.A. Botkin, "Preface," in *A Treasury of American Folklore: Stories, Ballads, and Traditions of the People* (New York: Crown Publisher, 1944).
113. Ibid.
114. George Gershwin, "Rhapsody in Catfish Row," *New York Times* (October 20, 1935), 1.
115. "'Porgy' Finished, Opens Sept. 30," *Charleston Evening Post* (September 20, 1935), 12-A.

181 *Exploring New Worlds*

116. Ibid.
117. Henry Botkin, *Henry Botkin: 10 Years of Painting*, Exhibition Catalogue, Lowe Art Gallery, Syracuse University, October 10–November 9, 1971 (Syracuse, NY: School of Art, Syracuse University, 1971), 2.
118. Brooks Atkinson, "*Porgy and Bess*, Native Opera, Opens at the Alvin; Gershwin Work Based on DuBose Heyward's Play; Dramatic Values of Community Legend Gloriously Transposed in New Form with Fine Regard for Its Verities," *New York Times* (October 11, 1935), 30.

10 Complexities in Gershwin's *Porgy and Bess*: Historical and Performing Contexts

NAOMI ANDRÉ

There are many things to love about Gershwin's 1935 opera, *Porgy and Bess*. Most of the tunes are already familiar through jazz standards ("Summertime," "I Got Plenty o' Nuttin'," "Bess, You is My Woman Now"), and Gershwin's music has that perfect combination of an undulating Puccini-esque lyricism and catchy syncopations that capture the rhythms of the English language. Gershwin's music achieves many things at once: it involves full-out operatic singing, yet still has moments that feel like a spontaneous outpouring of emotion. Serena's "My Man's Gone Now" at the funeral of her husband in Act I showcases operatic virtuosity and brings on the chills of a new widow's wail. The "Six Simultaneous Prayers" chorus during the Act II hurricane makes you feel like you have walked into a black church vigil. The creators' insistence on a black cast makes going to *Porgy and Bess* a unique experience, and one especially exciting for black audiences, for nowhere else in the repertory do we have the chance to see so many black people on the opera stage – and in the audience (Figure 10.1).

Yet *Porgy and Bess* is also deeply troubling. The most disheartening part of the opera is the hopelessness of the characters' fates. It is distressing to see the drinking, gambling, murder, and sexual assault that take place. Even more devastating is that the characters we cheer for – the loving young family of Clara and Jake, the rehabilitated Bess – end up dead or broken by the end. In the finale, when Porgy sings "Oh Lawd, I'm On My Way," we know that he – a poor, crippled black man – will never make it to New York. Although the residents of Catfish Row sing about the "Heav'nly Lan'" of promise and opportunity, we know they will most likely never see it in their lifetimes.

Telling the Stories of Porgy: Characterization across the Novel, Play, and Opera

The opera *Porgy and Bess* was first performed in Boston at the Colonial Theatre on September 30, 1935 and then officially opened

183 Complexities in Gershwin's Porgy and Bess

Figure 10.1 The cast of George Gershwin's *Porgy and Bess* performing on stage, 1935. Photo by Pictorial Parade/Archive Photos/Getty Images

at the Alvin Theatre in New York October 10, 1935. But the genesis of the story goes back to the novel *Porgy*, written by DuBose Heyward in 1925, and the play *Porgy*, adapted from the novel by Dorothy (DuBose's wife) and DuBose Heyward.

The play was premiered by the Theatre Guild at the Republic Theatre on 42nd Street, west of Broadway, in New York on October 10, 1927. George Gershwin's first interaction with the story was through the novel; from that exposure, he contacted DuBose Heyward about the possibility of adapting the work into an opera.

Most of the discussions about the opera do not focus on the *Porgy* novel or play, probably because the opera's history is already complicated with its own compositional story, the structure of the work, and its later reception. Briefly here, I will spend a little time on these earlier sources, with a few excerpts from the novel and play that differ from the opera.[1] The relationships among these works deserves further attention, given the widespread popularity of Heyward's novel and play, and the close proximity of the New York venues for *Porgy* the play and *Porgy and Bess* the opera, which were within ten blocks of each other. Additionally, all three (novel, play, and opera) appeared within the same decade, 1925–1935.

Porgy, the 1925 novel, is organized in six parts (they can be thought of as chapters, but are labeled as "Parts") and outlines the characters who later appear in the opera as well as many of the same narrative elements and situations. The novel presents expanded characterizations and deepens certain themes given the breadth a prose novel can contain. One example that links this story to other tellings of black life is the emphasis on superstition and the supernatural; the novel has several points when superstition is woven into the story. In Part Three, Maria gives Mingo money to pay the conjurer woman to help Bess get out of her delirium (though Mingo does not get to the conjurer woman, Bess does revive). Clara's concern for Jake during the hurricane in Part Five is heightened from a conjurer woman having told her that Jake will die by drowning.

Putting the *Porgy* story in a larger context, a common trope in early twentieth-century operas on black subjects is the reference to Voodoo/Vodoun, which is presented as a practice in the United States that has connections to customs in Africa, the Caribbean, and the wider black diaspora.[2] Frederick Delius's *Koanga* (1897) gets inspiration from his father's orange plantation in Florida and from West African practices. Clarence Cameron White's *Ouanga!* (1932) was composed after his trip to Haiti and dramatizes the story of Jean-Jacques Dessalines, who continued Toussaint L'Ouverture's revolution from the French into Haitian independence at the end of the eighteenth century. Two operas with stories set during Reconstruction also feature the association of black life and the supernatural. Harry Lawrence Freeman's *Voodoo* (1914, first performed in 1928) sets the story in Creole Louisiana, and Scott Joplin's *Treemonisha* (1911) is set in Arkansas and promoted the idea that valuing education over superstition would move the race forward.[3] While Heyward's novel invokes conjuring and the supernatural at several points, Gershwin's opera limits these references. The bad-luck Buzzard from Part Six of the novel is the most concentrated mark of superstition in the opera with Porgy's "Buzzard Song," when it is performed, in Act II, Scene 1.

Porgy, the 1927 play, streamlines the action of the novel and focuses the dramatic narrative into an evening's performance of four acts. The opera libretto by DuBose Heyward and Ira Gershwin is closely based on the 1927 play with a little more tightening, since singing an opera takes longer than speaking a play. However, many of the lines in the opera's libretto are drawn directly from the play. The play calls for a few musical numbers, but these are limited in scope, mostly traditional spirituals. The opera, however, is nearly entirely sung, with all the music newly composed by Gershwin. The main exception to the sung-throughout texture of the opera are the lines spoken by the white characters, who are distinguished from the African American characters in that they do not sing. The opera is in three acts that have multiple scenes (Act I has two scenes, Act II has four scenes, and Act III has three scenes). Unlike the play, which keeps the full action in Catfish Row, the opera adds the scene on Kittawah Island (Act II, Scene 2).

From the novel, we learn how Porgy got his goat cart. Before Peter is taken to jail as a witness to Crown killing Robbins, he gives rides into town on his horse-drawn carriage. After Peter has been gone ten days, the horse he was leasing is taken away (since Peter has missed two weekly payments), and we witness the resourceful side of Porgy as he fashions a means for his own transportation:

> Two days later, Porgy drove his chariot out through the wide entrance into a land of romance and adventure. He was seated with the utmost gravity in an inverted packing-case that proclaimed with unconscious irony the virtues of a well-known toilet soap. Beneath the box two solid lop-sided wheels, turned heavily. Before him, between a pair of improvised shafts, a patriarchal goat tugged with the dogged persistence of age which has been placed upon its mettle, and flaunted an intolerable stench in the face of the complaisant and virtuous soap box.[4]

The florid, vivid prose well illustrates DuBose Heyward's writing in the narrative portions of the novel. Here we have the determination and triumph of Porgy in his goat cart, coupled with the satirical image of our novel's disabled title character perched in his make-shift throne being pulled by a pathetic, elderly, and odiferous goat. Porgy's ability to use such transportation is referred to several times in the novel as an "emancipation," and while it gives Porgy some mobility, his heroism is undermined by the pity and laughter that follow him.

DuBose Heyward wrote that a real-life incident involving Samuel Smalls, a crippled beggar who had a goat cart, served as inspiration for the Porgy of the novel, and this feature of his character made it into the play and opera.[5] The disabled aspect of Porgy's character resonates with the origin story of minstrelsy back in the 1830s, when theatrical Irishman Thomas Dartmouth Rice (T.D. Rice) saw a crippled black man begging on the side of a road and decided that it would enhance his comedy act onstage if he blackened his face and impersonated the beggar.[6] But the portrayal of Porgy undergoes great transformation from the novel to the opera. The novel presents different sides of Porgy from the first time he is introduced with "something Eastern and mystic about the introspection of his look." As the omniscient narrator explains: Porgy "never smiled, and he acknowledged gifts only by a slow lifting of the eyes that had odd shadows in them. He was black with the almost purple blackness of unadulterated Congo blood."[7] There is an exoticism about Porgy in the novel; he is not just a poor black beggar in Charleston, but has a mysterious, foreign quality about him with supposed links to Africa. These "Eastern" and

African characteristics work to separate Porgy from fully belonging in his geographical surroundings. He is both a part of the Catfish Row community in South Carolina and foreign to it. Porgy is presented as an outsider who embodies difference both in his physical appearance as well as his demeanor. What would normally be seen as potentially dangerous and threatening are minimized by Porgy's physically broken body. Within the Catfish community of the novel, Porgy is an outsider not just for the obvious marker of his physical disability, but also for these additional differences about the particular blackness of his skin and his detachment from fully interacting with his surroundings.

The image of Porgy embodying a remoteness at the beginning of the novel returns at the conclusion. By contrast, in the opera, Porgy is an outsider only based on his physical disability. These dynamics are set up soon after Porgy's first entrance in Act I of the opera when he states: "When Gawd make cripple, he mean him to be lonely. Night time, day time, he got to trabble dat lonesome road." This line does not appear in the novel, and it is sung in the opera when the men tease Porgy, telling him that he is "soft on Crown's Bess." Porgy, indeed, is attracted to Bess, and we see this in his attempt to defend her reputation from what he calls the "Gawd fearin' ladies and the Gawd dammin' men." His comments about being lonely are made because he really does not want to be lonely, but he also wants to protect Bess from slander and does not want to be seen as one of her many suitors.

In the opera, whose title has been changed to *Porgy and Bess*, the stories of the two title characters have become more intertwined as Gershwin worked within the conventions of opera to highlight a primary romantic couple, struggling against vast obstacles to their relationship. A major difference between the opera and the novel is that, at the end of the opera, a rousing crowd-pleasing number turns Porgy into the predictable mock-heroic minstrel character. Most stagings of the finale, "Oh Lawd, I'm On My Way," present Porgy as rising up victoriously, despite insurmountable circumstances, and setting off on a quest to find Bess in New York City. While the text of the number (with Porgy and chorus) is exultant, a skillful director could present the Catfish Row community on stage singing in the chorus as having doubts as to whether Porgy should even make this trip. Given the drastic odds against him, and the pathos of the scene where Bess has become re-addicted to "happy dust" and leaves with Sportin' Life, a triumphant finale only distracts the audience from true emotion in an attempt to mask the tragic ending.[8]

The novel presents a different outcome for both Bess and Porgy. When Porgy comes back to Catfish Row looking for Bess (after he was imprisoned for contempt of court when trying to escape instead of identifying

Crown's body), Maria tells him what has happened in his absence. In the novel, Bess did not choose to accompany Sportin' Life to New York City. The original Bess took another journey, against her will. Maria narrates:

> "De mens all carry she away on de ribber boat," she sobbed. "Dey leabe word fuh me dat dey goin' tek she all de way tuh Sawannah, an' keep she dey. Den Serena, she tek de chile, an' say she is goin' gib um er Christian raisin."[9]

> ["The men all carried her away on the river boat," she sobbed. "They left word for me that they were going to take her all the way to Savannah and keep her there. Then Serena took the child and said she is going to give him a Christian upbringing."][10]

As we hear the conclusion of the novel narrated from Maria's vantage point, we get a very different Porgy from the celebratory false optimism of the opera's protagonist. In the opera, Porgy is determined to rescue Bess. In the novel, he has become a broken man:

> The keen autumn sun flooded boldly through the entrance and bathed the drooping form of the goat, the ridiculous wagon, and the bent figure of the man in hard, satirical radiance. In its revealing light, Maria saw that Porgy was an old man. The early tension that had characterized him, the mellow mood that he had known for one eventful summer, both had gone; and in their place she saw a face that sagged wearily, and the eyes of age lit only by a faint reminiscent glow from suns and moons that had looked into them, and had already dropped down the west.
>   She looked until she could bear the sight no longer; then she stumbled into her shop and closed the door, leaving Porgy and the goat alone in an irony of morning sunlight.[11]

Here in the novel, we are given a final view of the defeated, aged Porgy in the harsh daylight of morning. It is a sobering image of a man in isolation – an alienated outsider, who verges on the heroic, but reverts to being unknowable to his community. This imagery, defined by the nostalgia of plantation fiction, differs markedly from the three-dimensional heroic figure in the opera, who undergoes change and is positively shaped by new experiences. Reading the one leads to a desire for the other.

By looking at how these Porgy stories work together – with an emphasis on the novel and opera – we can expand our view of how this narrative had meaning in its own time. Many of the people who were in the opera's first audience likely had some earlier experience with the novel and/or play and were able to see the nuances of how black life was represented through these different media. My point is not to argue that any of the Porgy stories present an "authentic" experience of black life during the antebellum period, Reconstruction, or the Harlem Renaissance. Instead, I propose that the different versions of the Porgy story reveal gradations of variation in the representation of black existence during the first decades of the twentieth century. These gradations are valuable, for their blending gives a depth to multiple black male and female characters in the same narrative and simultaneously references older and contemporaneous stereotypes about blackness that came out of the minstrel tradition.[12] The novel, play, and opera are products of these currents at the beginning of the twentieth century, and they reflect both the biases of the past and new desires for the future. Furthermore, through it all, an important "bigger picture" emerges. The people who first gave the novel, play and opera life – the Southern white Heywards, first-generation Jewish Gershwins, and black actors and singers who performed *Porgy* the play and *Porgy and Bess* the opera – were creating a new history by working together in an evolving America with the first generations of people born free after slavery.

Porgy and Bess: Historical Context, Language, and Performance

The opera *Porgy and Bess* was written in a historical moment that saw great hope as well as deep racial conflict. During Reconstruction, post-Reconstruction, and beyond, Jim Crow practices developed into laws, and lynching became a regular threat. With the Great Migration of poor black Southerns moving north and west for jobs and better opportunities, Harlem emerged as a place for great optimism and accomplishments. The Harlem Renaissance was fueled by the coming of age of the first generation born after slavery. Publications such as W. E. B. DuBois's *The Souls of Black Folk* (1903) and Alain Locke's *The New Negro* (1925) outlined a new construction of black identity in the United States and showed how a post-slavery society could thrive with members from all races. There was an energy and excitement for black achievement in the arts – literature, music, dance, and theater all had a place in the racial uplift movement.

Outside of Harlem, themes around blackness were also moving through artistic circles – the art of Picasso, the dances of Diaghilev, the jazz-inspired scores of Stravinsky, Milhaud and others – as the vogue of Primitivism and the "noble savage" continued to re-shape representations of black people. Though 1920 saw the triumph of the suffrage movement giving women the right to vote, the legal status of black people was challenged through the backlash to emancipation and the proliferation of Jim Crow laws. With the older history of minstrelsy, slavery, the Civil War, and Reconstruction still relevant, newer developments of jazz, cultural motifs around the idealized "primitive," and the energy of the Harlem Renaissance created new images of blackness.

Gershwin wrote an opera in his own style, on his own terms. He called *Porgy and Bess* an American "folk opera," a designation open to possibility and one that has caused much speculation. In using these words, Gershwin brought together the connection to the people, in this case black people, and the elevated genre of opera. The term "Folk" had varied meanings in the beginning of the twentieth century as the development of Folklore Societies in Europe and the United States were founded to preserve oral traditions not written down. This energy was bolstered during the Depression in the 1930s when the US government sponsored several folk-related projects (such as the Federal Music Project).[13] "Folk" also had a special resonance in the black community. In *The Souls of Black Folk*, DuBois began each chapter with a few bars of a spiritual in music notation, thus linking the uplift of the race with the music of the people. Though Gershwin did not use authentic spirituals in his opera, he and DuBose Heyward spent a month on Folly Island, off the coast of South Carolina, to be with Gullah and African American people and learn about their culture.

One of the most complex issues around the novel, play, and opera is the representation of the characters' speech and the use of a language meant to express the dialogue and thoughts of the residents of Catfish Row. Coming out of a time when minstrelsy, radio shows such as *Amos'n'Andy*, and other media where white actors, singers, and novelists relied on negative stereotypes of black people, *Porgy and Bess* sounds awkward and dated, at best, to many people today. With recent controversies around the use and importance of what is variously called Black English Vernacular, Ebonics, African American Language, and African American Vernacular English, the quest for representing black culture in ways other than through the use of Standard English has resonance.[14] The principle of linguistic subordination, where language variabilities associated with socio-economically oppressed groups are viewed as linguistic deficits rather than neutral linguistic variations, helps explain how attitudes about such language differences come about.

Successful precedents of presenting a Black English Vernacular in the beginning of the twentieth century go back to the poetry of Paul Laurence Dunbar as well as art songs, spirituals, and choral arrangements by John Wesley Work, Jr. (as well as his son John Wesley Work, III), Nathaniel Dett, Hall Johnson, Undine Smith Moore, and Eva Jessye – who was a composer as well as being the choral director for the first production of *Porgy and Bess*. What becomes tricky in terms of representation and performance is when someone outside of the subordinated group approximates the structure and syntax of the non-standard version of the language and the result sounds and feels uncomfortable to those who know the true tradition. While *Porgy and Bess* was written in a type of African

American Vernacular English, the style of the language was not directly replicating a specific variant of the language. In 1990, Gullah speaker and long-time preservationist Virginia Mixson Geraty published a Gullah version of the *Porgy* play, an effort to present the play in the language DuBose and Dorothy Heyward were trying to represent in their original version. The Gullah languages (also known as Sea Island Creole English and Geechee) developed along the coasts of South Carolina and Georgia and their Sea Islands and follow their own grammar and syntax. It is a combination of English with various West African languages. The African languages influence the Gullah's pronunciation, the grammar and syntax, and there are many words in Gullah borrowed from African languages. As a primarily oral language, the presentation of Gullah on the page was not an established or straightforward venture in the 1920s and 1930s, and its representation visually and aurally have been complicated issues that have followed the opera and have been perceived as insensitive and demeaning to many.

Such themes present a microcosm of how representation is fraught in *Porgy and Bess*. George and Ira Gershwin and DuBose and Dorothy Heyward gave us a compelling picture of black Southern life that by contract, and in an uncommon practice for the time, was required to be portrayed by black performers in true-to-color casting (not blackface) when staged in the United States. This provided black artists, from a wide spectrum of opera singers (Howard Voice Professor Todd Duncan as Porgy and Julliard-trained Anne Brown as Bess) to Broadway dancers (John William "Bubbles" Sublett as the original Sportin' Life), the opportunity to perform on stage. Black artists and composers from the early part of the twentieth century did not have the economic and social capital of the Gershwin family to pull off a venture in writing and producing a work such as *Porgy and Bess* that would eventually have such staying power.

Recent scholarship is helping reveal a new historiography of blackness in opera by uncovering the narratives of black opera impresarios, such as the Theodore Drury Grand Opera Company that produced a few operas in the first decades of the twentieth century and Mary Cardwell Dawson's music school and National Negro Opera Company that mounted a few productions in the 1940s to early 1960s.[15] Composers such as Scott Joplin, Clarence Cameron White, Harry Lawrence Freeman, James P. Johnson, and William Grant Still, all of whom wrote operas that are beginning to resurface now, were accomplished in the Western European tradition and wrote in a musical style that expands our understanding of how black culture was represented in American opera during the first decades of the twentieth century. As new scholarship uncovers the operas written by black composers contemporaneous with *Porgy and Bess*, there is also a shadow culture lineage of operas by interracial teams (black and non-black composers, librettists, and producers) that continues into the present day. When Marian Anderson sang Ulrica from Verdi's *Un ballo in Maschera* at the Metropolitan Opera on January 7, 1955 she broke a barrier that had kept black singers from performing on the major opera stages of the world. Since then, we continue to see singers of all races, albeit still in small numbers, singing on stages in the United States and across the world.

The performance history of *Porgy and Bess* has been fraught with several issues, primarily: (1) the questions around the full, complete version of the opera, (2) a bias that felt it was more of a musical theater piece than an opera, and (3) questions around racial representation. Regarding the first point, a critical edition of the opera is complete, and the full score that Gershwin wrote is finally available. The second issue has also become less pressing, as American opera occupies a wider terrain than it had in the beginning of the twentieth century, when newly composed English-language opera (as opposed to the translations into English from another language) was still relatively new for the United States. Since the premiere of *Porgy and Bess* in 1935, there have been adaptations of the work that include spoken dialogue and were performed as a musical theater piece.[16] The historic performance by the Houston Grand Opera in 1976, one of the early full-opera productions in the United States after the premiere, helped pave the path for the work to find its place in opera, which it finally did – albeit slowly. An important production was by the Metropolitan Opera, which first performed the opera in 1985 – the fiftieth anniversary of its first performance. *Porgy and Bess* is now regularly performed on opera stages in the United States and abroad.

The third question, around racial representation, is still a complicated and relevant issue in the first decades of the twenty-first century. The Gershwin estate requires true-to-color casting with staged productions in the United States (concert versions of the opera may be sung in a color-blind casting). While this makes a lot of sense visually and socio-politically for the difficult racial climate in the United States, there are two unfortunate consequences. First is that the roles occupy a type of ghettoized position in that non-black performers are kept from singing this powerful music in staged productions. Second, there has been the dilemma of black opera singers getting stuck on Catfish Row; many black singers have found that they are no longer cast for traditional mainstream roles (e.g. Tosca, Figaro, Sieglinde, Faust) after they are known to sing *Porgy and Bess*.[17]

In January 2018 the Hungarian State Opera performed *Porgy and Bess* with a predominantly white cast in a setting that took the opera out of

Catfish Row and put it in the present time focused around European migration issues. This practice was contrary to the wishes of the Gershwin estate, that required the opera company "to add a sentence to all printed materials stating that the production is taking place without authorization and 'is contrary to the requirements for the presentation of the work.'"[18] Many people support the Gershwin estate's stance and feel that this opera is situated in a specific time and place that is relevant to the original context that still has meaning today. A member of the audience for the Hungarian State Opera performance admitted to not knowing the opera's historical context and said, "I just love the music. I saw the 1983 production of *Porgy* [*and Bess*] here. The singers blackened their faces, but I didn't know what that meant in the US. The music is what I remember."[19] A standard convention in opera production is that an opera may be set in various adaptations, following the director's vision. This situation opens up provocative questions for *Porgy and Bess*. Does keeping *Porgy and Bess* rooted in Catfish Row of the 1920s/1930s limit the scope of the opera's future?

Over time, people have thought of *Porgy and Bess* as the Great American Opera, as well as a frustrating collection of stereotypes that emphasize a vision of black people who speak in dialect-ridden English, drink and gamble too much, and have a loose moral code. And to some extent, both of these assessments are true. The opera touches on intensely human emotions that lead to both great passion and heart-wrenching devastation. It is the music that touches us and gets under our skin in such a way that it feels like a part of us. And this is what makes Gershwin's opera so easy to love and so difficult to stay mad at. Yet no matter how *Porgy and Bess* is performed today, it is going to raise many complicated and tender issues around the representation of African Americans.

Singing on Catfish Row

On February 17, 2018, I had the opportunity to sing in the chorus of *Porgy and Bess* for the debut of the new critical edition of the score, edited by Wayne Shirley. The performance was in Hill Auditorium in Ann Arbor, Michigan. This score will be published by the Gershwin Initiative that is housed at the University of Michigan, with Mark Clague as the Executive Director.

The production was a joint venture between the University of Michigan's School of Music, Theatre, and Dance who supplied the orchestra and chorus and the University Musical Society. UMS (a major production company) provided the soloists, who were all professional singers who had performed these roles before. The Metropolitan Opera in New York has included a production with this score in its 2019–20 season, and the Michigan performance was, in large part, to make sure the soloists, chorus, and orchestral parts all coordinated.

In addition to the university student choirs, Willis Patterson's Ann Arbor-based Our Own Thing Chorale was asked to join the chorus. Dr. Willis Patterson, a classically trained opera singer and a renowned bass-baritone, is Emeritus Professor of Voice at the UM School of Music, Theatre, and Dance. Patterson's Chorale is a community choir, primarily African American, that specializes in singing African American art songs and spirituals. That is where I come in – a member of the Patterson Chorale. The Chorale is a heterogeneous group of singers who include a few professional musicians and a lot of church musicians and amateurs. Some of us have had extensive musical training; others do not read music and learn the notes by ear. There were a few challenges in bringing together the university students in the School of Music and this adult choir, but overall the experience ended up being very positive and one we were proud to be in.

There are published and filmed interviews of black singers who have sung *Porgy and Bess* that talk about the conflicts between singing gorgeous music which has become wrapped into American culture (through the covers/adaptations of the music and its extreme popularity) and the grim story of violence, addiction, and hopelessness. Being a choir that regularly sings works by John Rosamond Johnson, William Dawson, Florence Price, Adolphus Hailstork, and other black composers who use African American Vernacular English, it was odd to have the "black dialect" written by DuBose and Dorothy Heyward and Ira Gershwin in our mouths; it felt different from what we were used to singing.

Black opera singers have had a fraught relationship with the opera. As previously mentioned, it had been a truism that if you sang *Porgy and Bess*, your career singing other opera was compromised; you should not be surprised if you do not get calls to sing *Lucia di Lammermoor*, *Rigoletto*, or other mainstream roles. In the past there had been an understanding that if you sang *Porgy and Bess* you would be ghettoized on Catfish Row. Yet a new practice seems to be emerging. At the symposium that accompanied the Ann Arbor performance, I had the pleasure of moderating a panel with all of the singers from the production (and a few others from earlier productions), who talked about what singing *Porgy and Bess* meant to them professionally and personally.[20] The narrative began to shift, as all the singers noted that they were singing mainstream roles in addition to *Porgy and Bess*. Talise Trevigne (Bess) talked about trying to get on Catfish Row because she wanted to sing Bess. Morris Robinson (Porgy) spoke about being coached for the role by other Porgys and the nurturing mentoring that went on. The most common point, first mentioned by Chauncey Packer (Sportin' Life), and then agreed upon by everyone, was how wonderful it was to be in an opera and not be the only "chocolate drop" (Packer's term) on stage. The community element during the run of the production – both on and off stage – was something these singers talked about with great appreciation and fondness.

I actually had a deeper understanding of this communal concept as a singer in the chorus. For a week, I spent three to four hours each night in rehearsal. Though it was a "concert performance" and not staged (the chorus stood along the back of the stage on bleachers, behind the soloists and orchestra), the soloists would turn to us when their lines addressed Catfish Row. The creation of a neighborhood is a big part of *Porgy and Bess*, and the choir sings a lot, compared to most operas. Somehow, we all became a part of Catfish Row. As a black singer – really a musicologist who sings in a local choir – I suddenly felt like I was part of something bigger. I felt as though I was allowed to keep my identity as a musicologist who has a complicated relationship loving and being frustrated by the opera. I also felt that I had been given entrance into a special, welcoming community of black operatic singing.

I close with a few notes to opera companies and production agencies as I encourage them to perform this opera. Having recently participated in a performance myself, I can say what an incredible experience it can be for performers and audiences alike. That said, entering into a performance of *Porgy and Bess* will likely be met with resistance from some with concerns about the issue of race, which is completely understandable (and this was our experience in Ann Arbor). A strong way to address these concerns is to provide sensitive program notes and programming (e.g. pre-concert talks, community forums) that treat these themes directly and allow for a wider discussion. Knowledgeable facilitators who know the history of *Porgy and Bess* and who have good mediation skills around complicated issues related to race will bring success to such an event. Program notes are critical, because it is a way to help audiences process the experience of the opera after the performance, when they get home. Another way to combat negative repercussions is to hire the *Porgy and Bess* singers in other productions that year and in the future. Additionally, make sure that *Porgy and Bess* is not the only representation of blackness in your repertoire. Do not let *Porgy and Bess* stand alone as the only opera on your roster that is on a black subject or includes black singers. Consider operas by black and interracial compositional teams.[21] A way to learn about these operas and singers of color is to ask your production team, administrative group, and board of directors – and please be encouraged to have more people of color in these slots in your company. There are many things to love about Gershwin's *Porgy and Bess*. Informed and thoughtful performances highlight what is best in the opera.

Notes

1. The three works (*Porgy* novel, *Porgy* play, *Porgy and Bess* opera) are taken up by Ellen Noonan, *The Strange Career of Porgy and Bess* (Chapel Hill, NC: University of North Carolina Press, 2012), where most of the discussion looks at the sources independently, rather than a progression from one to the next. The Gershwin Initiative is publishing the critical edition of *Porgy and Bess*, edited by Wayne Shirley. I have not had access to the critical notes and commentary, but I did sing in the chorus for a concert performance of the complete score on February 17, 2018 at Hill Auditorium in Ann Arbor, Michigan.
2. The topic of Voodoo is broad and complex with different religions, beliefs, and practices that come from West Africa and circulate among the diaspora in the United States (especially around Louisiana), the Caribbean (especially in Haiti), and Latin America (especially in Brazil). The spelling can be varied and mean diverse things in different contexts: Voodoo, Vodou, Vodoun, Vodú, and other terms.
3. For in-depth discussions of these operas by Delius (*Koanga*), White (*Ouanga!*), and Joplin (*Treemonisha*), see the essays by Eric Saylor, Karen Bryan, and Ann Sears in Naomi André, Karen M. Bryan, and Eric Saylor (eds), *Blackness in Opera* (Urbana, IL: University of Illinois Press, 2012).
4. DuBose Heyward, *Porgy* (New York: Grosset & Dunlap, 1925), 45–46.
5. For a discussion on Samuel Smalls as a model for Heyward's Porgy, see Kendra Hamilton "Goat Cart Sam a.k.a. Porgy, an icon of the Sanitized South," *Southern Cultures* 5/3 (Fall 1999), 31–53.
6. Naomi André, *Black Opera: History, Power, and Engagement* (Urbana, IL: University of Illinois Press, 2018), 105–06.
7. Heyward, *Porgy*, 12–13.
8. Naomi André, "From Otello to Porgy: Blackness, Masculinity, and Morality in Opera," in André, Bryan, and Saylor (eds.), *Blackness in Opera*, 11–31.
9. Heyward, *Porgy*, 195.
10. Author's transliteration. The use of an African Vernacular Language for the characters on Catfish Row is in the novel, the play, and the opera. This will be further discussed below.
11. Heyward, *Porgy*, 195–96.
12. For a deeper discussion of minstrel stereotypes in *Porgy and Bess*, see André, *Black Opera*, 85–119.
13. Richard Crawford, "Where Did *Porgy and Bess* Come From?" *The Journal of Interdisciplinary History* 36/4 (Spring, 2006), 706–08. See also, Ray Allen, "An American Folk Opera? Triangulating Folkness, Blackness, and Americaness in Gershwin and Heyward's *Porgy and Bess*, *Journal of American Folklore* 117 (June 2004), 243–61.
14. Geneva Smitherman, "African American Language and Education: History and Controversy in the Twentieth Century" in Jennifer Bloomquist, Lisa J. Green and Sonja Lanehart (eds.), *The Oxford Handbook of African American Language* (New York: Oxford University Press, 2015), 547–65.
15. For work on Theodore Drury, see Kristen M. Turner "Class, Race, and Uplift in the Opera House: Theodore Drury and His Company Cross the Color Line," *Journal of Musicological Research* 34 (2015), 320–51. For work on Mary Cardwell Dawson, see Karen Bryan, "Radiating a Hope: Mary Cardwell Dawson as Educator and Activist," *Journal of Historical Research in Music Education* 25/1 (October 2003), 20–35.
16. A successful recent production opened in 2012 on Broadway was directed by Diane Paulus, adapted by Suzan-Lori Parks and Diedre L. Murray and had Audra McDonald and Norm Lewis as Bess and Porgy, respectively.
17. Wallace Cheatham, ed., *Dialogues on Opera and the African-American Experience* (Lanham, MD: Scarecrow Press, 1997); Alison Kinney, "Conversations with Black Otellos," *Van* Magazine

(June 9, 2016) https://van-us.atavist.com/black-otellos; and James Sandifer, *Porgy and Bess: An American Voice* (Princeton, NJ: Films for the Humanities & Sciences, 1999).
18. Alexandra Ivanoff, "*Porgy and Bess* with a White Cast Stirs Controversy," *New York Times* (February 3, 2018), C6.
19. Ibid. The person quoted is identified as a sixty-nine-year-old academic.
20. Roundtable Discussion: "Singing Porgy & Bess." February 16, 2018 at 3:45 in The Gallery, Hatcher Graduate Library, University of Michigan. Participants: Janai Brugger, Norman Garrett, Chauncey Packer, Willis Patterson, Morris Robinson, Karen Slack, Reginald Smith, Jr., Rehanna Thelwell, Talise Trevigne, Daniel Washington (moderated by Naomi André). Broadcast on Livestream video: https://livestream.com/accounts/13187677/events/8014706/videos/170317169.
21. A few operas to consider are: Scott Joplin's *Treemonisha* (1911); William Grant Still's *Troubled Island* (1939); Harry Lawrence Freeman, *Voodoo* (1928); Anthony Davis, *X, The Life and Times of Malcom X* (1985); Dorothy Rudd Moore, *Frederick Douglass* (1985); Richard Danielpour and Toni Morrison, *Margaret Garner* (2005); Bongani Ndodana-Breen, *Winnie The Opera* (2011); Nkeiru Okoye, *Harriet Tubman* (2014); Douglas Tappin, *I Dream* (2010); Daniel Bernard Roumain, *We Shall Not Be Moved* (2017).

11 Writing for the Big Screen: *Shall We Dance* and *A Damsel in Distress*

NATHAN PLATTE

When George and Ira Gershwin returned to Hollywood in 1936, the town had changed. New songwriters, stars, and sound technologies had made the Hollywood musical a much more appealing medium for the Gershwins; their first effort, *Delicious* (1931), had fallen short of George's hopes for the form.[1] Among those in the vanguard of the film musical were Fred Astaire and Ginger Rogers, both of whom had worked with the Gershwins on Broadway and now enjoyed star duo status at RKO. Gershwin's reputation had changed too. His most ambitious composition, the "folk opera" *Porgy and Bess*, had opened in 1935. Some in Hollywood wondered whether the new opera composer would deign to write catchy tunes. "They are afraid you will only do highbrow songs," explained a California-based associate. Gershwin's wired response was unequivocal: "Rumors about highbrow music ridiculous. Stop. Am out to write hits."[2]

As biographer Howard Pollack notes, the two films that Gershwin worked on next at RKO treat stories preoccupied with highbrow/lowbrow, serious/popular distinctions that Gershwin's music repeatedly undermined. In *Shall We Dance* (1937), a Russian ballet dancer is not who he seems. "The great Petrov" (Astaire) is really "Peter P. Peters of Philadelphia, PA," an aspiring tap dancer who has fallen for American musical theater star Linda Keene (Rogers). In *Damsel in Distress* (1937), Jerry Halliday (Astaire) is an American hoofer performing in England. His reputation as a tap-dancing Don Juan makes him *persona non grata* at Totleigh Castle, the home of his romantic interest, Lady Alyce. There, Jerry must navigate a gauntlet of madrigal singers and an operatic butler to win his beloved.

Despite these broad similarities, the films differ in significant ways. For *Shall We Dance*, George and Ira had to slot their contributions within the familiar template of Astaire–Rogers musicals. This meant fashioning songs for specific nodes in reliably bumpy relationships that always unfolded between Astaire's character and Rogers's. For this, Gershwin and scriptwriters alternately tweaked and overturned examples of his predecessors. In contrast, *Damsel in Distress* was a more novel project: the first RKO film in which Astaire would be "Gingerless."[3] The production – an adaptation of a 1919 P. G. Wodehouse novel selected by the Gershwins – allowed the composer more creative flexibility. But Gershwin only lived to compose the film's songs. He passed away before the film entered production. Directed by George Stevens, *Damsel* offered a markedly different cinematic setting of Gershwin's music. Whereas director Mark Sandrich had exercised comparative restraint in *Shall We Dance*, filming numbers in stage-like settings, Stevens set Gershwin's music to a more cinematically flamboyant style. The stories and songs from these two films are already surveyed in multiple Gershwin biographies and studies of Astaire and Rogers, so this chapter will examine more closely select numbers from the two films to consider how the mechanisms of film production, especially visual editing and music department practices, constructed complementary views of Gershwin's legacy and music.

First Impressions of Hollywood and *Shall We Dance*

Initially Gershwin had high hopes for music in Hollywood. In 1928, when sound films were rapidly gaining ground among filmgoers and filmmakers, Gershwin informed a reporter that he had "decided that [sound film] constituted a good vehicle for jazz and other forms of modern music."[4] Two years later, Gershwin had the opportunity to see firsthand just what sort of vehicle sound film might be. Although the price was right – Fox Studios lured him west with a contract for $100,000 – Gershwin found Hollywood living exhausting. Every conversation, it seemed, revolved around movies.[5] The film on which George and his brother Ira worked, *Delicious* (1931), showcased Gershwin's name below the title and introduced several new songs and an instrumental work (ultimately revised and retitled the *Second Rhapsody*).[6] Although a commercial success, critics were not ecstatic. The *New York Times* found the dialogue "scarcely inspired," while allowing that "here and there David Butler's direction is effective" and "Mr. Gershwin's melodies are a help."[7] More recent assessments are less charitable. "About thirteen minutes of *Delicious* lived up to the promise movie musicals had intimated from the beginning," writes Richard Barrios. "Unfortunately, there remained about an hour and a half of film."[8] Dispirited by his experiences on and off the studio lot, Gershwin left the production early, mailing in his final contributions from New York. After the film's release, Gershwin confided privately: "I was very disappointed in the picture ... it could have been so swell but imagination in producing it and cutting it was lacking."[9]

The shortcomings of *Delicious* notwithstanding, two points merit emphasis, as they return in Gershwin's subsequent work for Hollywood. First, Gershwin remained ambivalent toward studio filmmaking:

compartmentalized production practices meant Gershwin had less control over the project and his contributions to it. Second, *Delicious* introduced a narrative pattern that recurred in Gershwin's later productions. In *Delicious*, a Scottish immigrant woman, having illegally entered New York, must choose between a wealthy, American bachelor and a poor, Russian songwriter, both of whom seek to ensure her citizenship through marriage. The film's story, then, hinges on the divisive distinctions of class, nationality, and ethnicity, with music and romance providing opportunities to transcend and reconcile these differences. This narrative trope paired well with the broad outlines of Gershwin's biography (New York born, son of Russian immigrants) and boundary-defying compositional career, which now spanned popular song, musical theater, concert pieces, and opera.

When George and Ira Gershwin returned to Hollywood in the summer of 1936 to begin work on *Shall We Dance*, they found a more satisfying social scene. With Eddie Cantor, Jerome Kern, Harold Arlen, and Yip Harburg all living near George and Ira's Beverly Hills home, "it was more a reunion than a move into a strange new land."[10] Concert pianist, composer, and longtime friend Oscar Levant describes a lively environment at the Gershwins' house, with Arnold Schoenberg stopping by to play tennis and bringing "an entourage consisting of string-quartet players, conductors and disciples."[11] It was easy to be sociable, as RKO's script department was still struggling with the story. George and Ira had arrived in Hollywood with some songs at the ready; others would be written once more narrative details were fleshed out.

At RKO, Gershwin found himself once again among familiar company. Fred Astaire and George had met when both were in their teens, when Gershwin was a song plugger at the publisher Jerome H. Remick & Co. and Astaire was in vaudeville with his sister.[12] In the 1920s, the Gershwins' first big Broadway success, *Lady Be Good!* (1924), also helped establish the Astaires as a reckonable duo. The dual pair of siblings teamed up again for *Funny Face* in 1927. Ginger Rogers encountered the Gershwins when she starred in *Girl Crazy* (1930) and sang "But Not For Me" and "Embraceable You."[13] Nat Shilkret, the RKO music director, had worked with George since the mid-1920s, when he had assisted Paul Whiteman in the recordings of *Rhapsody in Blue* that had featured George as soloist.[14] Later, Shilkret worked with Gershwin on an early recording and broadcast of *An American in Paris* in 1928.[15] Orchestrator Robert Russell Bennett also had worked with George since *Lady Be Good!*, serving among the team of orchestrators that tackled the songs for the Gershwins' shows. The RKO team was uncommonly prepared for working with the Gershwins, although their past experience was based in George Gershwin's 1920s work, and his shows in particular. This history – and the studios' practice of dividing musical labor among specialists – caused some frustration for George when he found limited interest in his skills beyond songwriting.

Shall We Dance begins in London. Linda Keene (Rogers) is an American musical theater star who, irritated by romantically harassing co-stars, intends to return to New York. Peter P. Peters (Astaire) is an American too, but his stage identity as Petrov compels him to behave like an aloof Russian ballet dancer. Offstage, he practices tap instead of ballet. Peter has seen a flipbook of Linda dancing and wishes to partner with her. She, exhausted by unwanted advances, is uninterested. A shared ride on an ocean liner brings them closer together, but false rumors of a secret marriage between the two splinters the tentative romance. Resolution arrives later, through a New York stage show.

As a story, *Shall We Dance* is both derivative and reflexive: much of the story's fun depends upon an almost virtuosic array of correspondences. Arlene Croce notes that the film's ocean-liner escapade is modeled after the Bing Crosby vehicle, *Anything Goes* (1936).[16] The Marx Brothers' *A Night at the Opera* (1935) is another source. Like *Shall We Dance*, *A Night at the Opera* features an eventful transatlantic crossing and ends with a pretentious performance in New York (opera for the Marx Brothers, ballet for *Shall We Dance*). In each, the culminating entertainment is punctured with irreverent humor (much to the annoyance of stuffy patrons) and rescued through musical resolution provided by the stars. As the seventh Astaire–Rogers film (and the third directed by Mark Sandrich), *Shall We Dance* alternately plays to and against expectations established in their earlier films. Both stars are introduced through still images that they immediately undermine. Astaire is first shown in a painting; his balletic pose and dress run counter to audience expectations, but the "real" Astaire character appears moments later, practicing tap in a private room. Similarly, Rogers first appears as a picture on a flipbook that Petrov studies admiringly. The animated pages of the book pivot to Linda's actual performance, which concludes – after the curtain has fallen – with her angrily pushing an amorous costar into an onstage pool of water. By introducing Linda through this behind-the-curtain fiasco, the film creates a premise that is particularly apropos for the Gershwins: a musical comedy has gone awry, and it will be up to Astaire, Rogers, and the songwriters to concoct a more satisfying conclusion that bridges the disparate worlds of serious ballet and popular musical theater.

The Gershwins were familiar with the Astaire–Rogers formula and composed several songs before a story was even in place.[17] Their "Let's Call the Whole Thing Off" mimics the spirit of "A Fine Romance" from *Swing Time* (1936), with both pointing amiably to incompatibilities in the relationship. (In its staging, "Let's Call the Whole Thing Off" also resembles "Pick Yourself Up, Dust Yourself Off" from *Swing Time*, with both featuring comedic tumbles for the duo.) Once the film's script was finalized and production began, George Gershwin watched with fascination from the sidelines, noting to a friend: "I have never really seen a picture made before. It fascinates me to see the amazing things they do with sound recording, for instance."[18] Although Gershwin relished this new proximity to filmmaking, he learned that in studio hierarchy, no amount of external recognition could protect one from a producer's disinterest. The film's culminating ballet suffered just this fate, with Gershwin's concluding song and ballet music summarily rejected by both director Sandrich and Astaire. In efforts to rectify the circumstance, the studio music department worked frantically at cross-purposes. Miscommunications led to frustration, more rejected music, and conflicting accounts of who-did-what-wrong. The debacle merited mention in the respective memoirs of Shilkret and orchestrator Bennett, who handled much of the film's instrumental scoring. Shilkret and Bennett describe an all-night musical triage working with Gershwin's melodies while the composer himself was absent. Gershwin's biographers assert that Gershwin was also there, helping Bennett and Shilkret finish the job.[19]

If the Gershwins had composed their songs to slip smoothly into the Astaire–Rogers relationship, the setting of musical numbers resisted established patterns. The film's first number, "Slap That Bass," is a case in point. On board the ocean liner, the ballet troupe rehearses on deck. Petrov is absent, and an inquiry to his whereabouts initiates a cut to the ship's engine room. The room is a gleaming white, art-deco confabulation staffed by African American men, who sing a syncopated bass line and move in rhythm as they tend the space. As other singers enter the frame, they add textless-lines above the bass line; several others join in with conveniently available instruments. (Although many of the singers heard on the soundtrack are those shown onscreen, the sounds of the instrumentalists were provided by members of the Jimmy Dorsey band.[20]) Petrov watches and listens as one man (Dudley Dickerson) sings the verse of "Slap That Bass." Petrov then takes the chorus and dances for the crew in a man-vs.-machine routine, his combustive taps playing against the rhythmicized squeaks and clangs of the engine. As Todd Decker notes in an illuminating analysis of the scene, the sequence is exceptional in many ways, beginning with Sandrich's elaborate, introductory crane shot, which gradually reveals the scene's African American cast before cutting to Astaire, watching.[21] The scene upholds Morris Dickstein's observation that *Shall We Dance* "works hard, usually successfully, to find offbeat settings for the songs and dances."[22]

But if the scene stands conspicuously apart from other Astaire–Rogers routines, it connects to the Gershwins' earlier work. For one, the decision to build a near-autonomous scene for an all-black cast (with Astaire as interloper) invokes the Gershwins' most recent major work, the black-cast *Porgy and Bess*. The mingling of rhythmic engine noise and scat from the men resonates with that opera's "Occupational Humoresque," which sets synchronized onstage noises – pounding, sweeping – to a groove before Gershwin's orchestral music enters. (Joseph Horowitz tracks this scenario to director Rouben Mamoulian, who debuted a "symphony of noises" in the play *Porgy*, reprised it under different circumstances in his film, *Love Me Tonight* (1932), and incorporated it yet again in the premiere production of *Porgy and Bess*.[23])

The setting for "Slap That Bass" teases at cultural hierarchies by having Petrov play hooky from a boring, on-deck ballet rehearsal to spend time below with the swinging, singing workers whose toil moves the boat to America. This use of space to emphasize racial and musical hierarchies had precedent in the Gershwins' oeuvre. As noted previously, *Delicious* opens on a New York-bound liner and juxtaposes shots of poor, ethnic immigrants making music as wealthy, white, passengers literally look down on them. One man on an upper deck admits "they look awfully happy," to which his companion responds: "The poor things don't know any better." This sets the stage for *Delicious*'s romantic triangle, which places a Scotch immigrant woman between the affections of a rich, polo-playing American and a poor, Russian composer. Not incidentally, the Russian's compatriots are introduced singing "Ochi Chyornye," the very song Petrov playfully references when he meets Linda. Thus, while "Slap That Bass" is dropped as a surprise variable within the more familiar Astaire–Rogers equation, its ties to Gershwin's earlier efforts as a builder of musical bridges between races and ethnicities gives this scene a distinct cachet.

The scene also reflects racist constrictions placed on black culture and performers. Like *Porgy and Bess* and Hollywood's black-cast musicals of the era,[24] the scene provides a limited number of black performers an opportunity to work while simultaneously reinforcing racial difference and separation: their contributions are tightly circumscribed by setting, narrative, and musical style. Nonetheless, several factors that Decker notes give this scene special value, including the presence of Petrov, whose participation lends the number an interracial dimension. Similarly, the filmmakers' lavishing of resources – special camera work, expensive set, extra chorus, complicated rehearsal period – show an eager effort to mark the Gershwins' first song for the Astaire–Rogers cycle as a unique experience grounded firmly in the Gershwins' broader legacy. To drive that point home, the Gershwins drop a playful self-reference at the end of the song, quoting a lyric and melodic fragment from "I Got Rhythm": "Today, you can see that the happiest men/All got rhythm!"[25]

The film's next musical number continues in this mischievous vein. Instead of a song or a dance, George Gershwin provides walking music for Linda and her dog, who are soon joined by Petrov. Gershwin composed whimsical clarinet and piano solos (perhaps an orchestral allusion to *Rhapsody in Blue*?) backed by muted brass, saxophones, violins, bass, and drums. Oscar Levant's remark on the instrumentation is often quoted: "George deliberately, and with superb effect, scored [the scene] for only eight instruments as a private commentary on the plushy, overstuffed scoring favored by most Hollywood orchestrators."[26] But Levant's jibe misrepresents both parties (Gershwin's ensemble is not *that* small) and directs attention away from the sequence's more obvious flaunting of cinematic norms. For one, the scene unfolds like a silent film with instrumental accompaniment. Although the setting is a dog-walking area populated with animals and people, there are no sounds or even footfalls. Petrov and a deck officer engage in pantomime so as not to speak over the "background" music that is clearly enjoying foreground exposure. Only at the very end of the sequence does Petrov begin to speak with Linda, signaling the music's imminent closure. Here the filmmakers are once again emphasizing the Gershwin brand – namely George's fame as a composer of instrumental music, not just songs – while simultaneously playing against Astaire–Rogers expectations. At thirty minutes into the film, they still are not quite dancing together. Instead, they will each walk in time to Gershwin's walking bass, a bit of choreographed Mickey-Mousing tucked slyly beneath the clarinet's impish solo. "Walking the Dog" even enjoys an encore. After an intervening scene set elsewhere on the ship, the music returns for a second dog-walking outing. Gershwin injects extra energy by having the walking bass move in double-time while the clarinet continues to lope amiably about at its original pace. Once again, the soundtrack is kept almost entirely clean of other sounds – only a few off-screen barks are inserted to make a comical point about Petrov's growing interest in ... dogs. And yet this not-dancing number does the same work as Astaire and Rogers's dances in earlier films. Somehow the music magically draws them together, so that by the end they are shown happily walking arm-in-arm and chatting. Oddly, we do not hear their words, which are muted out on the soundtrack. Gershwin's music plays over, not under, their dialogue.

One of the film's most important songs is "They Can't Take That Away from Me," one of the film's final numbers. Linda and Petrov-now-Peter have just married in New Jersey and are on a ferry returning to Manhattan. An establishing shot of the boat as it makes its way to New York draws a downhearted parallel to their happier partnership on another boat – the ocean liner, when they had enjoyed friendship before rumors of marriage prompted Linda to flee the vessel on a mail plane. Now, having finally succumbed to the pressures of the press, they have reluctantly married in private so that they may dissolve their union in public. In a clever twist on the formula, Rogers has once again rushed into marriage, but instead of attempting to marry Astaire's romantic rival, as in *Top Hat* and *Swing Time*, she and Astaire's character have collaborated on an even graver error: marrying the right person for the wrong reason. Their decision weighs on them. Peter sings "They Can't Take That Away from Me" to reassure his bride that whatever the state of their relationship, memories of what they had will remain. In terms of narrative placement, the song's closest corollary may be "Never Gonna Dance," another exquisitely melancholy number performed at the nadir of the duo's relationship in *Swing Time*. But in that number, they had danced, gliding across a jet-black set. "They Can't Take That Away from Me" offers no such opportunity. After Astaire completes his song, a brief instrumental coda plays as the scene fades to black.

As Pollack notes, the song embodies "bittersweet poignancy," and it is worth considering how visuals – in lieu of a choreographed dance – further serve this theme.[27] Following the establishing shot of a nighttime ferry making its way to Manhattan, a crane shot allows the camera to float over the ferry's deck toward the parked car where Peter and Linda sit. A woman selling flowers on deck calls "Gardenias!" The sound of quietly lapping water mingles with strings playing "They Can't Take That Away from Me." After purchasing a flower for Linda, Peter leads her away from the car, where they come to stand at the boat's edge – a position they had occupied when he sang "I've Got Beginner's Luck" to her on their earlier voyage.[28] The camera closely frames the two from the waist up – low-key lighting allows shadows to shroud them. The lights of the city skyline are only dimly perceptible in the distance. The underscore – which exclusively "plugs" the impending song – is unobtrusive but responsive. As Peter leans toward Linda and tells her "tomorrow you'll be on your way, and I'll [pause] be on my way," the music cadences, then rests. In the musical silence, Linda asks "Where?" Peter responds: "I have to get back to being a bachelor again," a light remark that reignites the musical accompaniment, now with solo winds and more scherzo-like strings. Despite the momentary levity, a shift from the melody of the chorus's A section to its B section anticipates lyrics appropriate to the moment: "We may never, never meet again." As Linda sighs and turns away from Peter, he begins to sing. Unlike other instances, where an instrumental introduction might signal the start of a song, here Peter's shift from speaking to singing feels unprepared, nearly spontaneous. The underscore has been present for the entire scene; he has only now decided to join it. During the verse, Linda's body faces the camera directly, her gaze shifts from looking down at her gardenia to up at Peter's face. As Peter commences with the chorus – "The way you wear your hat" – she turns away from her partner. From this semi-profile position directed away from Peter, her eyes roam more easily, visualizing the images the lyrics evoke – "The way your smile just beams." For a minute and half, the camera is motionless. The song's repeating rhythmic kernel – three eighth notes followed by a quarter note, all on the same pitch – ebb and flow, from accompaniment to melody, weaving a murmuring spell. Not until Peter has sung the verse and the first three-quarters of the chorus is there a cut to a close-up of the two. The tighter frame compels Peter, rocking gently in time with the music, to move still closer to Linda as she continues to gaze away from him. Timed to align with the return of the A section, this closer shot shows Linda's eyes are moist. When Peter's melody crests on the final "No, no, they can't take that away from me – no . . . " a cut to an extreme close-up of Linda's stock-still face shows her transported. With so little motion from the characters and camera, every movement matters. Sandrich's direction here achieves a remarkable feat: by favoring Roger's face and culminating in a boldly disruptive close-up, he makes her act of listening as integral to the performance of the song as Astaire's singing.[29] Performed in shadows, the song's *mise en scène* is so plain as to be drab, but the restraint marks a meaningful departure from the Astaire–Rogers formula. This unusual scenario – Astaire and Rogers, *unhappily* married – unfolds as unadorned, unforgettable intimacy.

Gershwin famously complained that the film let the song be "thrown away" without sufficient plugging.[30] But this widely quoted objection about the melody's scarcity is at odds with the film, which revisits Gershwin's melody in two significant scenes. The first is when Peter and Linda have each returned to their adjacent suites following their marriage. A shot through the exterior windows of the hotel shows Peter and Linda in their respective rooms, each regarding the lone door separating their spaces. Through this sequence, there is no dialogue, only an instrumental arrangement of "They Can't Take That Away from Me," laced with quavering vibraphone sonorities and meandering counterlines in the strings. No dialogue or sound effects compete with the melody, but the circumstances are suspenseful. Linda finally moves toward the door, tries the handle, and jumps back when the lock rattles – the sudden sound elicits a reciprocating jump forward from Peter in the other room. Despite the colorful writing and exposed melody, narrative tensions draw attention away from the music.

The melody returns in the film's extended ballet finale, in which Petrov dances to "They Can't Take That Away from Me" with the willowy Harriet Hoctor. In this part of the ballet, Hoctor is choreographed to represent Linda, who has severed her relationship with Petrov over a misunderstanding. The ballet between Petrov and another blond dancer to the familiar melody adds yet another layer of bittersweet sentiment. By dancing with another woman who eventually disappears into the stage wings, Petrov reenacts through ballet his romantic loss. But once again unusual circumstances create tension, diminishing enjoyment of the melody for its own charms. The scene is clearly "wrong" in the Astaire–Rogers sense, in that Astaire does not otherwise dance with anyone but Rogers in the earlier films. This mismatch is emphasized when Rogers enters the theater just after Hoctor leaves the stage, raising the possibility of a happier reunion, but closing the door on any opportunity for Astaire and Rogers to dance to the song – at least in this film. Twelve years later *The Barkleys of Broadway* (1949) brought Astaire and Rogers together to reprise the song with dancing. Critic Arlene Croce concedes that the later film at least "rights the wrong committed by *Shall We Dance*, but neither the choreography nor the performance is what it might have been in 1937."[31] But it is precisely this "what might have been" that makes the delayed gratification of the *Barkleys* performance one of the most satisfying scenes from the film and a fitting finale to their partnership, set to Gershwin's song.

Damsel in Distress

For their next project, the Gershwins convinced studio producer Pandro Berman to purchase the P.G. Wodehouse novel *Damsel in Distress*. The Gershwins had worked with Wodehouse, whom they met during their London sojourn in the 1920s, and Wodehouse's book (although published in 1919) seems to match uncannily Gershwin's own circumstances: the novel concerns an American composer of musical comedies named George Bevan, who finds himself romantically involved during a stay in England. Wodehouse biographer Robert McCrum asserts that Gershwin's attraction to the project was in part his self-identification with the protagonist (whose name is changed to Jerry in the film), and it is not difficult to see why.[32] One passage from the novel could almost describe Gershwin's experiences of late, as an observer of his own work from the margins of the *Shall We Dance* set:

> George ... looked down upon the brilliant throng with impatience. It seemed to him that he had been doing this all his life. The novelty of the experience had long since ceased to divert him. It was all just like the second act of an old-fashioned musical comedy ... a resemblance which was heightened for him by the fact that the band had more than once played dead and buried melodies of his own composition, of which he had wearied a full eighteen months back.[33]

When it comes to the setting of Gershwin's music to film, the most significant contrast between *Shall We Dance* and *Damsel in Distress* is that Sandrich privileges a theatrical unity of space and George Stevens, director of *Damsel*, does not. Many of the numbers in *Shall We Dance* could easily be set on a stage; the camera frame frequently serves as proscenium. Outdoor spaces are tightly, even comically, defined. Astaire and Rogers fall on their roller skates when they fail to abide by the skating circle in "Let's Call the Whole Thing Off." Linda and Peter's back-and-forth pacing in the confined dog-walking area of the ocean liner offers another source of humor. Their other dance numbers – "They All Laughed" and "Shall We Dance" – are set on literal stages before onscreen audiences. In *Damsel in Distress*, director Stevens chaffed against such restrictions. In "I Can't Be Bothered Now," Astaire's dance floor is a busy street, a setting that practically requires director and sound team to flaunt the film's unrealistic audio mixing. Astaire's taps easily drown out the steady traffic passing by him. Toward the end of the song, the orchestration incorporates car horns – a device lifted from Gershwin's *An American in Paris* – just before Astaire leaps onto a double-decker bus and is carried out of the frame. Did Stevens perhaps have the opening paragraph of Wodehouse's novel in mind when he introduced this clever exit? The novel begins: "Unfortunately, in these days of rush and hurry, a novelist works at a disadvantage. He must leap into the middle of his tale with as little delay as he would employ in boarding a moving tramcar ... Otherwise, people throw him aside and go out to picture palaces."[34]

Stevens and the film's writers – one of whom included Wodehouse – took the sentiment to heart. Action and interest are heightened through the presence of Gracie Allen and George Burns, who serve as Astaire's American sidekicks. Their onscreen characters' names are, helpfully, Gracie and George. In the film they do double duty by accompanying Astaire in two rollicking dance numbers and focusing comic energies in a film nearly overrun with them. Although the film is nominally about whether Jerry (Astaire), an American stage star performing in London, will succeed in wooing the emotionally erratic Lady Alyce (Joan Fontaine) of Totleigh Castle, this narrative thread delivers relatively little narrative satisfaction. Rather, it is Jerry's routines with Gracie and George and

Stevens's dynamic camera work during Gershwin's songs that inject the film with peculiar mirth and beauty.

When Jerry sings "Things Are Looking Up" to Lady Alyce on the grounds of Totleigh Castle, Stevens rapidly deconstructs the proscenium-like frames that dominate *Shall We Dance*. At the start, Jerry and Alyce are in the center of the frame, medium distance, as though the spectator were enjoying a good seat at the theater. But as Astaire continues singing, he begins to wander the garden paths, compelling Alyce and camera to follow. As they meander, Stevens uses long trucking shots to have the camera glide alongside them. The spectator's view is repeatedly interrupted, however, by trees along the path that interrupt the sightline between moving camera and principals. The point of this curious gimmick becomes clear when Jerry and Alyce begin to dance. Fontaine lacked training as a dancer and was "terrified" by the prospect of being Astaire's partner.[35] The filmmakers worked overtime to downplay this reality. The previously inconvenient trees now have a critical part to play: by interrupting the choreography, they force viewers' imaginations to fill in the gaps. Stevens also uses high angle shots of the couple dancing up steps and down a hill – Astaire is always closer to the camera and dominates the frame. But these various devices cannot be attributed solely to a desire to conceal Fontaine's dancing. By having the camera move almost continuously throughout the sequence, Stevens suggests not just that the onscreen characters are moved to dance by the Gershwins' song, but also that the lyricism of the melody merits a sympathetic motion that only cinema can deliver. The effortless glide of the camera merges particularly well with the smooth, sure contours of Gershwin's refrain, which uses scalar motion with repeated pitches, parallel harmony, and seamless, rhythmic easing from eighth notes, to triplet quarter notes, to quarter notes, to a half note: "I've been looking the landscape over / and it's covered with four-leaf clover."

"A Foggy Day" follows mere minutes after "Things Are Looking Up," but a plot twist now threatens their affair. Having seen an unflattering news item, Alyce now believes Jerry to be an incorrigible womanizer. Jerry is unaware of her change in attitude. As he whistles and sings outside the castle, waiting for the evening's ball to commence, Alyce looks down on him from a window. The spatial separation (their distance precludes even showing both in the same shot) reflects the new status of their relationship and allows Stevens to move even further from the manners of staged theater. Jerry whistles, then sings "A Foggy Day" as obligatory mists pile past him. As he continues singing, Jerry walks the fog-filled grounds – traversing much of the same terrain as he had with Alyce minutes earlier. Although Astaire walks during the song, John Mueller notes that through this sequence "the simplest walk is a dance, and the shifts of momentum, the slight hesitations, the quiet gestures combine with Stevens's evocative photography to make this stroll down a foggy country lane one of the most visually arresting dance moments in his career."[36] Once again, Stevens's camera is nearly always in motion, a dance partner for Jerry. The blocking for the sequence is also unusual: Astaire often faces away from the camera while singing. With his face concealed and his figure at a distance, the close miking of his voice gives the performance an ethereal sheen. The song nearly becomes a voiceover, wafting over silent, dreamlike visuals.

Stevens also opts for more distance from his subject, and that distance only grows over the course of the song, allowing for an especially striking effect in the song's final shot. For the chorus's final lines ("For, suddenly, I saw you there – and through foggy London Town / The sun was shining ev'rywhere"), Stevens's visuals mimic the song's sentiment. A choreographed fog bank moves steadily toward the camera through beams of light as Jerry emerges at a great distance from the camera. As Deena Rosenberg notes, Gershwin's music here deploys harmonic complexity and bluesiness to characterize the song's "fog" and hymn-like chordal simplicity to represent the cloud-dispelling sun: "as the sun comes out, the song switches clearly into major for the first time. The shining sun with which the song concludes comes as both a rhythmic release and a melodic breakthrough into an apparently simple sing-song chant."[37] But this readily perceived musical contrast is complicated by Stevens's visuals, as the commixture of sun and fog over Astaire's distant body renders his presence almost ghostly. In the film's world, sunshine does not dispel fog; their coexistence renders an effect eerie but beautiful. Would the swathing of a Gershwin ballad in this otherworldly aura have carried special meaning so shortly after Gershwin's death? How many might have recalled that Jerry's character in Wodehouse's novel is a composer named George? Although the point of Stevens's haunting depiction of "A Foggy Day" is to elude single readings, the scene shows cinema to be an accommodating space for contemplating loss and presence through one of Gershwin's final songs.

If Stevens's direction of "Things Are Looking Up" and "A Foggy Day" wrap Gershwin's songs in visually cinematic reveries, the film's other songs are beset with comical hijinks. Stevens already had used comedy as a reliable frame around songs in Astaire and Rogers's *Swing Time*. Physical incompatibility and pratfalls serve as introduction to that film's "Pick Yourself Up." When Astaire croons "The Way You Look Tonight," Rogers's character becomes an absorbed listener, not realizing until the end that she has left shampoo lather in her hair. Such humor is relatively restrained, however, when compared with *Damsel*, where few musical performances go unthwarted. The film's first song, "I Can't Be Bothered Now," cleverly mocks its own title: a street performer impersonating Jerry

Halliday is interrupted by Jerry himself. Although neither was anticipating being "bothered now" they embrace the moment, with Jerry gratifying delighted onlookers with an impromptu song (that is itself interrupted by the aforementioned car horns). Later, when Jerry is denied entry to Totleigh Castle, he sneaks in the back entrance with a group of madrigal singers. When the singers strike up their song, "A Jolly Tar and the Milk Maid," Jerry is obliged to follow along, ducking among the ranks of singers like Harpo and Chico Marx's infiltration of an opera chorus in *A Night at The Opera*. Standing among women and reading from their scores, Jerry delivers solo lines intended for a female singer: "I happen to be / a mother of three." Some look momentarily surprised, but the castle's mistress, monitoring the performance closely, is appalled. The group's selection was one of two pieces that the Gershwins had composed for choral performance. (The other, "Sing of Spring" serves as a musical backdrop for another comical romp, with the singers only occasionally onscreen.)

After *Shall We Dance*, George had expressed some impatience with Astaire and Rogers's vocal performances, explaining that "the amount of singing one can stand of these two is quite limited."[38] *Damsel*'s choral numbers, Gershwin hoped, would give the audience "a chance to hear some singing besides the crooning of the stars."[39] Gershwin's deliberate effort to sideline Astaire, then, is foiled by the song's integration into the story, which requires Astaire's comical intervention. The ploy is repeated again in the film's last song, "Nice Work If You Can Get It." Jerry has again made a surreptitious entrance into the castle and must hide among the ubiquitous singers and participate in their performance. Whereas "Jolly Tar's" irrepressibly bouncy melody and formal-yet-funny lyrics emulate Gilbert and Sullivan operetta, "Nice Work" features a trio of women singing in close, bluesy harmonies akin to the Andrews Sisters, with Astaire punctuating the performance with smartly syncopated entrances. The ending of a phrase with "who could ask for anything more?" was a canny reference back to "I've Got Rhythm," from *Girl Crazy* (1930).[40]

The notion of interruption – with Jerry repeatedly barging in on others' performances – extends beyond Gershwin's songs. Reggie, a character played by band leader Ray Noble, exists primarily to provide musical disturbances. He announces his entrance into the film with a trumpet call from atop the castle that suddenly breaks into a swinging, hot riff – much to the annoyance of Lady Alyce's father. His wholly unexplained indoor performance on bagpipes is brought to a wheezing halt by a scorching glare from the master of the castle, Lord Marshmoreton. Ray Noble's band also enjoys an onscreen cameo. When they accompany the madrigal singers in "Nice Work If You Can Get It," their hot rhythms offend Marshmoreton's sister. Even Keggs, the opera-loving butler, runs afoul of the mistress, who considers nineteenth-century arias just as vulgar as American swing. When Keggs grows unable to manage his singing urges, he must bolt from the castle. Once outdoors, he is free to bellow "Ah! Che a voi perdoni iddio" from Flotow's *Martha*. The peculiar outburst – which receives sympathetic orchestral support – gives even Jerry pause.[41] In all cases, these recurring bouts of musical comedy do little to serve character or narrative. Like the comic episodes from the Marx Brothers films, they serve more to characterize the register of the film, clearly delineating it from the more emotionally earnest Astaire–Rogers formula executed in *Shall We Dance*.

The film's *raison d'être* for humor and cinematic fantasy is "Stiff Upper Lip," a simple patter song in which Ira collated various British expressions. Colloquialisms are pitched for playfulness rather than accuracy. Exhortations of "stout fella" and "old bean" coexist with "old man trouble" (a "Fascinating Rhythm" quote). George considered it no more than "a little English comedy song."[42] That it was then chosen for the film's most elaborate musical number reflects, in part, the absence of Rogers. As music, romance, and dance could not produce catharsis in the Gingerless world of *Damsel*, cinematic energies had to be released elsewhere. In this case, the alternative spectacle came from choreographer, Hermes Pan. After visiting the carnival with his children, Pan pitched a funhouse dance number to Astaire. After Astaire's dance with machinery in "Slap That Bass," having Astaire maneuver on and around swirling parts was a fitting next step. "But there's no reason," Astaire responded, not unreasonably. Pan replied, "Let them find a reason."[43] If plausibility was not a concern for Pan, neither was it for the scriptwriters. Jerry, Gracie, and George visit a fair on the pretext of interrupting an ill-advised proposal. During their stay, they wander into a prank elevator that dumps them down a slide into a fun house. With no exit in sight, they gamely sing and dance for eight and a half minutes.

After instructing art director Van Nest Polglase to "give me everything you can think of," Pan crafted a routine around the funhouse's mechanized movements, which included turntables, rhythmically shifting floors, and rotating tunnels. This "everything but the kitchen sink" aesthetic extended to musical arranging, with orchestrator Robert Russell Bennett arranging his most complicated cue. After breaking the sequence into nine sections, Bennett gave each distinct instrumentation.[44] Although the ensemble changes are not so drastic as to distract, they allow Bennett to shift coloration like a twisting kaleidoscope. The early segment featuring Gracie's performance of Ira's lyric is the closest Bennett comes to a standard theater orchestra: flute, oboe, four clarinets (one bass), trumpets and trombones, rhythm section, and four violin parts. For the section labeled "Fun House Dance," Bennett removed the violins, rebalancing the wind section for three clarinets and three flutes. By giving the upper winds a rhythmically square setting of the melody, Bennett makes the band sound bright and brittle as the trio of dancers take their first tentative steps on moving floor boards. As the dancers loosen up and tackle two rapidly moving treadmills, two flutes switch to clarinets, and the band begins to swing. "Turn Table I" has the trio of dancers working on a carousel-sized turntable. Bennett returns to square rhythms and layers in carnivalesque instrumentation: calliope and mallet percussion.[45] When Gracie and Jerry briefly partner, Bennett adds three horns, baritone, and tuba before shifting to a jaunty march drawn from "Swiss Miss" in the Gershwins' *Lady Be Good*. Astaire and his sister had danced to this "Oompah Trot" in their first show with the Gershwins; here, Astaire reprises the steps with Gracie in the last show he and George worked on together.[46]

When a dance chorus crowds onto the turntable – curiously, there are no children in this funhouse[47] – Bennett shifts to a more typical big band sound, with heavily swung rhythms and exuberant falls tossed among a clarinet, four saxophones, three trumpets, three trombones, and rhythm section ("Turn Table II" and "Table Dance"). At "Fun House Part II," two inebriated gentlemen attempt to navigate the same gauntlet threaded by Jerry. For this, Bennett sets "Stiff Upper Lip" as a galumphing 6/8 march. Big band becomes marching wind band, with baritone and horns reinstated alongside piccolo and E♭ clarinet. For the routine's final and lengthiest segment, the trio dance in front of a series of flexed mirrors. With cameras emphasizing their distorted reflections, the fun house – and, by extension, the cinematic apparatus – comes closest to stretching the film's stars beyond recognition. But, of course, Astaire, Allen, and Burns are too familiar to be hidden that easily, and Gershwin's "Stiff Upper Lip" melody – given its own funhouse mirror treatment – is the same. To match the three dancers, Bennett selects three soloists to play the melody, but in different keys. Solo trumpet plays through a stuffy harmon mute in G major; tenor sax, in E♭major; and piccolo, in B major. If the unflattering mix of tone colors does not unsettle, hearing Gershwin's melody in parallel, augmented triads will. (The rhythm section plays along in E♭, as if nothing here were unusual, but interjections from the full band are less tonally secure). As the dance trio moves on to other mirrors, Bennett reprises earlier melodies from the routine. The tune played by calliope is swung by the most robust trumpet section yet (now at four, up from three). The "Swiss Miss" march is plied by jaunty saxophones as piccolo, clarinet, and xylophone tear through a rapid descant above them. As the dancing chorus returns for the big finish (also viewed through bent mirrors), Bennett unleashes the full big band, with trombones gleefully smearing their glissandi and trumpets ripping up toward their highest notes. It is a jubilant finish that every member of the effort – from dancer to arranger to set designers to piccolo player – has earned.

The sequence is an affront to critical assessment. "Stiff Upper Lip" is not the Gershwins' finest work, nor was it intended to be. Astaire's contribution is modest: in choreography and execution he makes no attempt to elevate his role above that of Allen and Burns. And although the concept of the routine came from choreographer Hermes Pan, the funhouse distracts from choreography per se, subsuming it to novel machines and mirrors. Stevens's camerawork is similarly engaging – he even mounts one camera to a turntable for dizzying effect – but is also constrained by the unusual set. Bennett, in comparison, enjoyed relative freedom with his shape-shifting ensemble. However one chooses to parse it, the routine remains a collaborative marvel, eschewing greatness and, for that matter, authorial control. In some respects, it is a fitting analogy for Gershwin's Hollywood experience, which required entrusting so much to a studio machine whose musical transformations could depart wildly from original expectations. Whatever its shortcomings, the routine remains irrepressibly memorable. It garnered Pan an Academy Award for Best Dance Direction. "Astaire, Burns, and Allen become *plus surréalistique que les surréalistes*" wrote Basil Wright in *World Film News*. "This sequence is pure Jabberwocky."[48]

After *Damsel in Distress*

Damsel in Distress was not the last production for which George Gershwin wrote songs. Before his death, he and his brother Ira also contributed material to the *Goldwyn Follies*, although the writing of the songs long predated the start of the production. Once again, the question of whether social and cultural divisions may be transcended is central to the plot. A Hollywood producer realizes his films fail because they no longer appeal to everyday Americans. To address this, the producer hires a young woman from outside Hollywood as his consultant. "Miss Humanity" informs the producer when Hollywood artifice strains credulity. This conceit allowed the filmmakers to pad the production with absurd scenarios and musical numbers that justify Miss Humanity's corrective presence. The Gershwin numbers – "Love Walked In" and "Love Is Here to Stay" – enjoy more normal exposure. The first song is sung by a cook (Kenny Baker) as he slings burgers at a diner. Miss Humanity enters his establishment and is immediately entranced. She requests that he sing the song again, so he does – resetting the needle on his phonograph to restart the orchestral accompaniment. If Gershwin had been bothered by the insufficient plugging of his songs in *Shall We Dance*, he could not have objected to this indulgent encore, although the cook continues to flip meat while he sings. (The song is sung a third and fourth time later in the film.) But ultimately these Gershwin songs required rescuing from the dismal plot and performances that *Follies* offers. One does not watch the film so much as wince at it. Producer Samuel Goldwyn, whose credits include such distinctive work as *Dodsworth* (1936), *Wuthering Heights* (1939), and *The Best Years of Our Lives* (1946), had intended the film to be the first of a series of *Follies* films. Although it is tempting to wonder if the film might have fared better if George had lived to assist with its production, the best that can be said of Goldwyn's cinematic experiment is that he chose not to repeat it.

On June 10, 1937, Gershwin mentioned in a letter to his mother that he had "had quite enough of Hollywood and can't wait until the Goldwyn picture is finished, so that I can go to New York and possibly to Europe." In the next sentence he wrote: "Of late I haven't been feeling particularly well." One month later, on July 11, 1937, George Gershwin died from a brain tumor. Gershwin's death came as a terrible surprise, but his interest in filmmaking had been fading for months. After *Shall We Dance*, he admitted that he no longer minded leaving background music in his films to the "hacks," a remark that biographer Walter Rimler registers as "strangely vituperative," as it applied to longtime colleagues Shilkret and Bennett.[49] And yet it is in step with Gershwin's frustrations with the studio machine and his limited capacity to shape his own work. Before coming to Hollywood, Gershwin had promised that his only desire for film was "writing hits." Gershwin was perhaps hurt that Hollywood's powerbrokers and music staff seemed intent on holding him to that statement. And yet, if Gershwin was done with Hollywood, Hollywood was nowhere near done with him.

After Gershwin's passing, the teams assigned to *Damsel* and *Follies* had to finish their respective scripts, complete filming, and proceed through postproduction. This included Bennett's composition of colorful and boisterous incidental music for *Damsel* based on Gershwin's song melodies. Bennett's contribution – as with the song arrangements described earlier – are a distinguishing facet of the film. In the years that followed, Gershwin's music and legacy continued to enjoy prime placement in works like Warner Bros.' *Rhapsody in Blue* (1945, a biopic of the composer), the aforementioned *Barkleys of Broadway*, and MGM's *An American in Paris* (1951), a jukebox musical built around Gershwin songs and concert music. Gershwin's friend, Oscar Levant, starred in all three, playing himself in the first and changing in name only for the latter two.

But Gershwin's impact spanned far beyond the reuse of his music in Hollywood studio films. Film composers, orchestrators, and writers of the studio era took careful note of Gershwin's jazz-infused symphonic style and deployed it frequently. In the months following Gershwin's death, lightly veiled tributes found their way to Hollywood screens. After performing Gershwin's Concerto in F at the Gershwin Memorial Concert at the Hollywood Bowl, Oscar Levant tucked references to *An American in Paris* and "Bess, You Is My Woman Now," in the score for *Nothing Sacred* (1937), a screwball comedy set in Gershwin's hometown of New York. Writers and musicians at Warner Bros. quietly drew on Gershwin's memory when they set about imagining a composer and orchestrator who battle for the affections of a young woman in *Four Daughters* (1938). The script by Julius Epstein and Lenore Coffee describes the composer's music as "of the Gershwin type," a resemblance further encouraged by the composer's collaboration with an orchestrator.[50] (In a bit of dialogue cut from the film, the fictional composer even defends Gershwin's music to another musician of conservative tastes.) Heinz Roemheld, the staff musician tasked with providing a fictional composition by the fictional composer, modeled his melody on the so-called "Love Theme" from *Rhapsody in Blue*. In 1941, Warner Bros. redeployed a plot point from *Delicious*, in which a Russian composer writes a "New York Rhapsody," for *City for Conquest*, where an aspiring, working-class composer finally succeeds in premiering his "Magic Isle Symphony," a tribute to New York that – although composed by Max Steiner – features several Gershwin-inspired flourishes. Steiner, who had served as music director for a shaky RKO adaptation of *Girl Crazy* (1932), would later explicitly invoke Gershwin's style for *They Made Me a Criminal* (1939), when, alongside a blue-note love theme, he wrote "Gershwinesque." Months later, Steiner would return to this theme, remove its blue notes and swung rhythms, and repurpose the melody as the Tara theme for *Gone with the Wind* (1939).[51]

Alongside these explicit and more oblique tributes are the memoirs of people working in Hollywood who relished Gershwin's brief time with them there. Oscar Levant writes in adoring terms of George's contributions to the social scene in Southern California in a chapter of *A Smattering of Ignorance* titled: "My Life: Or the Story of George Gershwin." Harpo Marx, whose dinner date with Schoenberg and Gershwin was covered by the *Los Angeles Times*, described George's basement as "my regular nighttime hideout ... There was a ping-pong table there, two pianos, and built-in kibitzer – Oscar Levant. It was the best clubhouse in town."[52] Dimitri Tiomkin offers a particularly touching tribute. After having championed Gershwin's work during his earlier career as a piano soloist – Tiomkin gave the European premiere of

Gershwin's Concerto in F – Tiomkin and Gershwin crossed paths again in Hollywood, where Tiomkin had found work as a composer. Frank Capra had given Tiomkin a tremendous opportunity to write for large orchestra and chorus in *Lost Horizon* (1937). In his autobiography, *Please Don't Hate Me*, Tiomkin wrote:

> At the Hollywood premiere of the picture, I met George Gershwin going into the theater. "They tell me, Dimi, you have something special here," he said. He spoke with his usual smiling courtesy, but I thought I detected an amused skepticism – the Russian pianist who played Gershwin jazz at the Paris Opera now a composer for Hollywood films.
>
> During the picture I sat just behind him, and soon he turned, nodded, and gave the Broadway-Hollywood sign of excellence – thumb and forefinger making a circle. That, I felt, was tops in criticism.[53]

One of the crowning paradoxes of George Gershwin's silver screen legacy is the disconnect between Gershwin's versatile skills as a composer and the studios' narrow interest in Gershwin as a songwriter. Although Gershwin's onscreen doppelganger, Astaire, managed to breach cultural, social, and stylistic barriers in order to find romance and terpsichorean satisfaction, Gershwin, the multifaceted and stylistically pluralistic composer, only rarely managed to do more in Hollywood than write hits. But as the recurring narrative tropes from Gershwin's films show, the studios' fascination with Gershwin's music had much to do with the cinematic realization of it through particular stories, characters, and visual frames. For this, the studios did not need all of George Gershwin: what they needed was what he had already accomplished in concert halls and on Broadway stages. The main title music of *Shall We Dance* – another Bennett arrangement – conveys this succinctly. When George Gershwin's name appears on the screen, the orchestra halts on a sustained chord, and a quote from *Rhapsody in Blue* issues forth. The calling card is unsubtle, and it offers an insight into how we might approach Gershwin's Hollywood films. The value of these films resides not only in the new music they elicited from Gershwin in his final year, but also the opportunity they presented for construing Gershwin's life, music, and iconic status, a task that required considerable coordination among scriptwriters, stars, directors, choreographers, and orchestrators – many of whom had enjoyed relationships with the man extending as far back as the *Rhapsody* (and sometimes further). Although it is ironic that these individuals at times crowded out Gershwin himself, films like *Shall We Dance* and *Damsel in Distress* remain compelling frames through which to experience Gershwin's legacy as it was built by those who had worked so closely with him.

Notes

1. Howard Pollack, *George Gershwin: His Life and Work* (Berkeley: University of California Press, 2006), 489.
2. Edward Jablonski, *Gershwin: A Biography* (New York: Da Capo Press, 1987, 1998), 297.
3. Astaire uses this whimsical descriptor in his memoir, *Steps in Time* (New York: Harper & Brothers, 1959), 218.
4. Pollack, *George Gershwin*, 482.
5. Ibid., 484.
6. James Wierzbicki, "The Hollywood Career of Gershwin's *Second Rhapsody*," *Journal of the American Musicological Society* 60/1 (Spring 2007), 133–86.
7. Mordaunt Hall, "The Screen," *New York Times* (December 26, 1931), 15.
8. Richard Barrios, *A Song in the Dark: The Birth of the Musical Film*, 2nd edn (New York: Oxford University Press, 2010), 340.
9. Cf. Pollack, *George Gershwin*, 489.
10. Jablonski, *Gershwin*, 300.
11. Oscar Levant, *A Smattering of Ignorance* (New York: Doubleday, Doran & Co., 1940), 187.
12. Kathleen Riley, *The Astaires: Fred & Adele* (New York: Oxford University Press, 2012), 45.
13. Ginger Rogers, *Ginger: My Story* (New York: Harper Collins, 1991), 75.
14. Nathaniel Shilkret, *Nathaniel Shilkret: Sixty Years in the Music Business*, ed. Niel Shell and Barbara Shilkret (Lanham, MD: Scarecrow Press, 2005), 58.
15. Ibid., 99.
16. Arlene Croce, *The Fred Astaire & Ginger Rogers Book* (New York: Outerbridge & Lazard, 1972).
17. Other songs written before the script was in place included "They All Laughed" and "Hi-Ho!" The latter went unused – perhaps due to the proximity of "Heigh-Ho" in *Snow White and the Seven Dwarfs*, which was in production and set to be distributed by RKO. The Gershwin's song is included in *The Songs of George & Ira Gershwin: A Centennial Celebration*, vol. 2 (Miami: Warn Bros., 1998).
18. Jablonski, *Gershwin*, 306.
19. Shilkret, *Nathaniel Shilkret*, 173–74; Robert Russell Bennett, *The Broadway Sound: The Autobiography and Selected Essays of Robert Russell Bennett*, ed. George Ferencz (Rochester, NY: University of Rochester Press, 1999), 155–56; Jablonski, *Gershwin*, 304; Pollack, *George Gershwin*, 675; and Edith Garson's supplement in Isaac Goldberg's *George Gershwin: A Study in American Music* (New York: Frederick Ungar, 1958), 343.
20. Todd Decker, *Music Makes Me: Fred Astaire and Jazz* (Berkeley, CA: University of California Press, 2011), 283.
21. Ibid., 277–86.
22. Morris Dickstein, *Dancing in the Dark: A Cultural History of the Great Depression* (New York: W.W. Norton, 2009), 392.
23. Joseph Horowitz, *"On My Way": The Untold Story of Rouben Mamoulian, George Gershwin, and Porgy and Bess* (New York: W.W. Norton, 2013), 118.
24. Arthur Knight, *Disintegrating the Musical: Black Performance and American Musical Film* (Durham, NC: Duke University Press, 2002), 128.
25. Steven Gilbert, *The Music of Gershwin* (New Haven, CT: Yale University Press, 1995), 219.
26. Levant, *A Smattering of Ignorance*, 208.
27. Pollack, *George Gershwin*, 672.
28. The two scenes are visually complementary. In "I've Got Beginner's Luck," Astaire is positioned on the left; Rogers, the right. The placement is reversed in "They Can't Take That Away from Me." In the earlier song, Rogers's body is angled toward Astaire, whom she gazes at during the song, looking away to smile after punchlines. She is turned away from Astaire for most of "They Can't Take That Away from Me," forcing him to address her over her shoulder. In "I've Got Beginner's Luck," Astaire has a white flower pinned to his lapel; in the later song, Rogers holds a white flower and regards it during Astaire's singing. For the earlier song, the entire performance is shot in one take; in the "They Can't Take That Away from Me," Sandrich moves the camera increasingly closer to Rogers's face.
29. Edward Gallafent, *Astaire and Rogers* (New York: Columbia University Press, 2004), 71.
30. Jablonski, *Gershwin*, 302; Pollack, *George Gershwin*, 675.
31. Croce, *The Fred Astaire & Ginger Rogers Book*, 176.

32. Robert McCrum, *Wodehouse: A Life* (New York: W.W. Norton, 2004), 245.
33. P.G. Wodehouse, *Damsel in Distress* (London: Herbert Jenkins, 1919, 1956), 94.
34. Ibid., 1.
35. Cf. John Mueller, *Astaire Dancing: The Musical Films* (New York: Alfred A. Knopf, 1985), 135.
36. Ibid., 136.
37. Deena Rosenberg, *Fascinating Rhythm: The Collaboration of George and Ira Gershwin* (Ann Arbor, MI: University of Michigan Press, 1991), 362.
38. Cf. Pollack, *George Gershwin*, 675.
39. Cf. Jablonski, *Gershwin*, 311.
40. Gilbert, *The Music of Gershwin*, 219.
41. Tenor Mario Berini's performance was dubbed in for the occasion. Mueller, *Astaire Dancing*, 136.
42. George Gershwin to Henry Botkin, May 17, 1937, in Robert Wyatt and John Andrew Johnson (eds.), *The Gershwin Reader* (New York: Oxford University Press, 2004), 261.
43. John Franceschina, *Hermes Pan: The Man Who Danced with Fred Astaire* (New York: Oxford University Press, 2012), 94.
44. Bennett's orchestration is held in RKO Studio Records Collection at UCLA Special Collections, Boxes 68 M, 69 M, and 1006 M. Special thanks to Todd Decker, for sharing his research notes on the *Damsel in Distress* files, and to David Lim, who helped arrange and transcribe my digital images of this arrangement.
45. The RKO rehearsal pianist Hal Borne also contributed a few pages during the calliope-sounding passage.
46. Riley, *The Astaires*, 65, 81.
47. Thanks to my daughter, Anna Platte, for noticing this peculiar detail.
48. Basil Wright, "Fred Astaire at Blandings Castle," *World Film News* 3/2 (May–June 1938), 83.
49. Walter Rimler, *George Gershwin: An Intimate Portrait* (Urbana, IL: University of Illinois Press, 2009), 137–38.
50. Julius Epstein and Lenore Coffee, "Four Sisters, Rev. Temp. Script" (February 12, 1938) Robert Blees Papers, The University of Iowa Libraries, Iowa City, Iowa, 29.
51. Nathan Platte, "The Epic and Intimately Human: Contemplating Tara's Theme in *Gone with the Wind*," in Stephen C. Meyer (ed.), *Music in Epic Film: Listening to Spectacle* (New York: Routledge, 2017), 149–69.
52. Isabel Morse Jones, "Music and Musicians," *Los Angeles Times* (January 3, 1937), C9.
53. Dimitri Tiomkin and Prosper Buranelli, *Please Don't Hate Me* (Garden City, NJ: Doubleday, 1959), 186–87.

PART III

Influence and Reception

12 The Coverage of Gershwin in Music History Texts

HOWARD POLLACK

George Gershwin has long been a challenging figure to categorize and evaluate within mainstream music historiography. Few have gone as far as the Russian composer Alexander Glazunov, who, after attending a performance of *Rhapsody in Blue*, deemed him "half human and half animal."[1] But music historians and chroniclers have reacted variably to the composer's rather anomalous achievement and place in the history of Western music.

To explore and gauge such differing perspectives on Gershwin, in particular his more serious compositions, I have examined his coverage – or lack thereof – among a fairly broad range of mainly American texts on Western and in particular American and twentieth-century concert music. For the most part, I have excluded from this survey music appreciation texts (to the extent that these can be distinguished from general histories) as well as more specialized studies, such as surveys of opera, popular musical theater, popular song, and jazz, along with essayistic monographs more obviously subjective in nature, such as Paul Rosenfeld's *An Hour with American Music* (1929), Daniel Gregory Mason's *Tune In, America* (1931), Lazare Saminsky's *Living Music of the Americas* (1949), Vernon Duke's *Listen Here!* (1963), Nicholas E. Tawa's *Serenading the Reluctant Eagle* (1984), and Richard Crawford's *The American Musical Landscape* (1993). Nor was every edition of some popular texts consulted, as revealing as such a project might be. Indeed, this study, limited to sources in English, makes no claim for systematic comprehensiveness on any level, but more simply considers a large sampling of some of the more prominent music histories from Gershwin's time to our own.

Gershwin made an early entry into music textbooks with his 1929 appearance in the first edition of music critic John Tasker Howard's *Our American Music*, a book that enjoyed four editions and numerous printings, making it the predominant chronicle of American music in the first half of the twentieth century.[2] A composer of light music who also penned landmark biographies of Stephen Foster (1934) and Ethelbert Nevin (1935), Howard (1890–1964) held Gershwin's Broadway shows and *Rhapsody in Blue* – which he first heard at the famous February 5, 1924 run-through of the work that preceded its February 12 premiere – in the highest regard. He thought, however, that the Concerto in F (1925) and *An American in Paris* (1928), two works also written early enough to be discussed in the book's first edition, came at a sacrifice of the composer's "natural charm."[3] The use of the *Rhapsody* as a benchmark by which to assess the composer's later compositions, already a fixture of journalistic criticism, would surface in subsequent history texts as well, although no consensus emerged, with some arguing for the superiority of *Rhapsody*, others favoring one or another later piece.

Initially, Howard discussed Gershwin in a section devoted to popular music and theater entitled, "Our Lighter Musical Moments," as opposed to his voluminous chapter on "Our Contemporary Composers." But by the time of the book's third edition in 1946, he thought that it behooved him to "change the emphasis on Gershwin's twofold output, and to present him in the gallery of serious composers."[4] Nonetheless, Howard remained committed to the idea of surveying Gershwin's "twofold output," that is, essentially, his concert pieces and his musical comedies, in tandem as he had done prior, arguing: "Gershwin's lighter works are so much the germ and source of his larger compositions, that they cannot be considered separately" – a sensible and helpful tactic, but one not necessarily taken in later histories.[5]

As its subtitle might indicate, Aaron Copland's *Our New Music: Leading Composers in Europe and America* (1941), which originated as a series of lectures, did not aim for anything like Howard's sort of comprehensiveness, but nevertheless deserves attention here because of the author's importance and authority. Like the monograph on contemporary music by composer-critic Marion Bauer (1882–1955) that preceded his own, Copland (1900–90) placed Gershwin alongside those composers associated with jazz – for many years a broad context that over time largely dwindled to a consideration of just three works from the mid-1920s: Milhaud's *The Creation of the World*, Gershwin's *Rhapsody in Blue*, and Copland's own Piano Concerto. Otherwise, Copland had little to say about Gershwin but that his works "made up in originality and individuality what they lacked in technical finish."[6] Copland's short shrift of Gershwin, expressed both here and elsewhere, for years attracted the attention of commentators, especially given the fact that from the beginnings of their careers, these two composers for various reasons – including their closeness of age, their Russian-Jewish backgrounds, and their relation to jazz – were often compared and contrasted. Accordingly, some ascribed Copland's offhand treatment of Gershwin in *Our New Music* to some sort of psychological or professional need to distance himself from his more popular colleague, although few of Copland's contemporaries, whether or not encumbered by any such rivalry, would have considered Gershwin a "leading composer" either, especially during this time period. Copland appreciated Gershwin enough to perform Three Preludes (published 1927) on early lecture recitals, and to conduct some of the famous orchestral pieces in his later years, but his reservations about the composer seem genuine enough – revealingly the flip side of his similarly cool 1936 appraisal of Samuel Barber as someone who "writes in a somewhat outmoded fashion, making up in technical finish what he lacks in musical substance" (an opinion later revised in light of Barber's mature work).[7] Indeed, among American composers, *Our New Music* singled out for detailed consideration only Charles Ives, Roger Sessions, Walter Piston, Roy Harris, Virgil Thomson, Marc Blitzstein, and the author himself. If Copland sidelined Gershwin, the latter found himself in good company.

First published in 1955, and revised in 1966 and 1987, Gilbert Chase's *America's Music, From the Pilgrims to the Present*, a notable successor to John Tasker Howard's *Our American Music*, took issue (in its first and second editions) with the latter's discussion of Gershwin, arguing that the Concerto in F constituted "a better work of art than the *Rhapsody in Blue*."[8] An expert on Latin American as well as American music, Chase (1906–92) gave ample space to Gershwin, including *Porgy and Bess*, although with no acknowledgment of that opera's checkered textual history, one marked by dramatic cuts and rewrites – a problematic lapse common to discussions of the piece. Calling Gershwin "a composer of the people and for the people," at least in the book's first edition,[9] Chase also underestimated Gershwin's connections with both jazz and serious music as opposed to popular music, an oversight encountered in many other accounts as well, and one attributed in part to a narrowing sense of what constituted jazz. Chase's significantly revised second edition (1966) lavished rare praise on the "brilliant" *Variations on "I Got Rhythm"* for piano and orchestra (1934), and eliminated the erroneous claim that Arnold Schoenberg had orchestrated Gershwin's Three Preludes, a blunder that in the interim had made its way into William Austin's text discussed below.[10] The similarly overhauled and expanded third edition (1987) showed the influence of Charles Schwartz's 1973 Gershwin biography,[11] especially in its emphasis on the composer's Jewish background and his connection with Yiddish theater, to the point that Chase now grouped Gershwin with Copland and Leonard Bernstein as one of several prominent Jewish-American composers, whereas he previously had not so much as mentioned Gershwin's Jewish background. This third edition also made welcome reference to the highly neglected *George Gershwin's Song-Book* (1932), and observed, again thanks to evolving scholarship on the composer, Gershwin's relation to some of the stride and jazzy popular pianists of the day, such as Luckey Roberts and Zez Confrey.[12]

As already seen in the publications by Bauer and Copland, Gershwin naturally commanded less attention in more general music histories than those devoted to American music, at least during this earlier era. *Exploring Twentieth-Century Music* (1968) by the Hungarian-American cellist and writer Otto Deri (1911–69), for instance, gave Gershwin no more than a passing glance.[13] In due time, however, Gershwin gained increasing prominence even among such general surveys, as suggested by the many editions of musicologist Donald Jay Grout's ubiquitous *History of Western Music*, initially published in 1960. In the book's debut edition, Grout (1902–87) devoted a short paragraph to Gershwin, but couched so subjunctively – the composer "hoped to bridge the gulf between popular music and the concert hall audience," his *Rhapsody in Blue* consisting of "an attempt to combine the language of jazz and Lisztian Romanticism" – as to suggest merely quixotic aspirations on Gershwin's part.[14] This discussion remained in place after Claude Palisca (1921–2001) began to co-author the text in the late 1980s.[15] But with the appointment of J. Peter Burkholder (b. 1954) as the book's third author in the late 1990s, coverage of Gershwin expanded, reflecting not only the growing presence of popular music in academia but also Burkholder's background as an American music specialist. By the time of the volume's ninth edition (2014), Gershwin received two full pages of text, one for his popular theater works (with the book's ancillary anthologies including the music for "I Got Rhythm" and a recording of that number by Ethel Merman), and another page, placed elsewhere, for his concert works and *Porgy and Bess*, with the composer credited for having created "a distinctively American modernist style."[16]

Meanwhile, a few histories from the 1960s – *Introduction to Contemporary Music* (1961) by the Latvian-born Queens College professor Joseph Machlis (1906–98), *Music in a New Found Land: Themes and Developments in the History of American Music* (1964) by the British composer-critic Wilfrid Mellers (1914–2008), and *Music in the 20th Century, from Debussy through Stravinsky* (1966) by Cornell musicologist William W. Austin (1920–2000) – demonstrated Gershwin's growing stock among music historians, even though the authors differed somewhat in their conclusions. Surprisingly unusual in its recognition of Ira Gershwin, George's principal collaborator on his musical comedies and songs, Machlis deemed the composer "one of the most gifted musicians this country has produced," and showed even greater esteem in the book's 1979 second edition, which privileged Gershwin, along with Ives, Varèse, Ruggles, Copland, and Sessions, as one of only a few Americans with a chapter of his own. However, this same second edition made the grievous mistake of maintaining the false though widely circulated claim (found in other histories as well) that Duke Ellington thought *Porgy and Bess* diminished by its alleged "lampblack Negroism" (whereas that phrase had originated with Ellington's white interlocutor, Edward Murrow).[17]

Typical of European response in taking the composer more seriously than many comparably sophisticated American commentators, Wilfrid Mellers went even further than Machlis, deeming Gershwin "certainly among the three or four finest composers ever produced by America," the adjective "finest" in some distinction to the more familiar American description of the composer as "gifted." Although lavish in his praise of Gershwin's popular theater songs, which showed him "an adult and unexpectedly deep composer," Mellers focused primarily on *Porgy and Bess*, taking the opera's use of African American lore somewhat for granted, and, by sensing the composer's identification with Porgy, honing in rather on the work's autobiographical resonance. Mellers also proved unique in comparing the opera not only to the work of Menotti, Blitzstein, and Bernstein, but also to that of Mozart, Donizetti, and Verdi, concluding: "There are greater twentieth-century operas: but not one which offers more of the qualities that opera used to have in its heyday, and must have again if it is to survive."[18]

William Austin, although more circumspect than either Machlis or Mellers, likewise acknowledged Gershwin's importance by devoting two paragraphs to the composer in a book astonishingly encyclopedic in breadth. Moreover, Austin brought unprecedented attention to the composer's development, writing: "In later works Gershwin's Lisztian exuberance was restrained by a growing respectful awareness of Stravinsky, Schoenberg, and Berg, a growing appreciation of Beethoven, and an effort to emulate these masters with the help of Joseph Schillinger's methods" (even if, as mentioned, Chase misled him with regard to Schoenberg's alleged orchestration of the Three Preludes, whose date of composition Austin also got wrong). Austin's wide-ranging knowledge and concerns allowed him not only to make the common references to Copland and Liszt, but in the course of the text, to draw connections with, in addition to Beethoven, Berg, Stravinsky, and Schoenberg as seen above, Debussy, Delius, Puccini, Ravel, Anton Rubinstein, Irving Berlin, John Alden Carpenter, Vernon Duke, Jerome Kern, William Grant Still, several leading jazz musicians, and by implication, Kurt Weill, Isaak Dunayevsky, and many others, stating: "A synthesis of popular and prestigious elements was achieved without any theory of 'gestic music' or 'realism' by the American George Gershwin."[19] At the same time, Austin's carefully calibrated rankings prompted distinctions not always to Gershwin's advantage. He claimed that Prokofiev "was not rightly to be classified with that of

Glazunov or Khachaturian, much less with Lehár or Gershwin"; that Gershwin did not, like Copland, share those "international standards" exemplified by Walter Piston, Roger Sessions, and Elliott Carter; and that Poulenc's *Les Biches* "could never provide comfort or thrills to the naive audience of Gershwin, nor could it command the respect of all admirers of Stravinsky's *Pulcinella*." Austin imagined nonetheless that the "usefulness and influence [of Gershwin's music] might well outlast the later hit shows of Frederick Loewe."[20]

Two other texts from the 1960s, part of a classroom-friendly series published by Prentice-Hall – *Twentieth-Century Music: An Introduction* (1967) by composer Eric Salzman (1933–2017), and *Music in the United States: A Historical Introduction* (1969) by musicologist H. Wiley Hitchcock (1923–2007) – added little to the conversation. In referring to *Porgy and Bess* as "in spite of its ambitions, a masterpiece of musical comedy," Salzman perpetuated a misnomer encountered endlessly in studies especially of the Broadway musical, and one the author corrected in his 1988 third edition of the text by calling the work "actually a full-scale grand opera."[21] Hitchcock's cavalier treatment of Gershwin, which differed markedly from the roughly contemporary assessments by Machlis, Mellers, and Austin discussed above, represented a low point with regard to the academic reception of Gershwin, beginning with the fact that the author, in odd disregard to both genre and chronology, situated the composer, including his concert music and *Porgy and Bess*, in the "Popular Music and Musical Comedy" section of a chapter entitled, "The 1920s." Nor did Hitchcock show much enthusiasm for Gershwin's work itself, relying on fellow historian Richard Crawford to say something mildly approving about *Porgy and Bess* – a discussion hardly modified in the text's three successive editions.[22]

Although the eminent composer-critic Virgil Thomson (1896–1989) achieved some notoriety for his condescending review of *Porgy and Bess* at the time of its premiere (when the work represented a rival to his own opera, *Four Saints in Three Acts*),[23] he showed greater forbearance in his overview of *American Music Since 1910* (1970), which regarded the "sweet-singing" *Porgy and Bess* as a milestone in the history of American music, and which summarized Gershwin as possessing "[l]ively rhythm, graceful harmony, and a fine melodic gift."[24] Another composer, Edith Borroff (b. 1925), in her sprawling *Music in Europe and the United States* (1971), took respectful note of Gershwin as well, while painting, like many others, an exaggeratedly bleak picture with regard to Gershwin's reception among his contemporaries.[25]

Even prior to its landmark 1976 revivals, the growing prestige of *Porgy and Bess*, as evidenced in Mellers, Borroff, and others, could be discerned in the chapter contributions of music librarian Wayne Shirley (b. 1936) in

Music in the Modern Age (1973) and conductor-composer Richard Franko Goldman (1910–80) in the *New Oxford History of Music* (1974), although the latter also included a sizeable excerpt from *Rhapsody in Blue*. Shirley, meanwhile, demonstrated the influence of both Stravinsky's "Petrushka chord" and Southern black folk music on *Porgy and Bess* by way of two musical examples, thereby neatly illustrating the incorporation of modernist and vernacular styles in the composer's work. *Porgy and Bess* also emerged as a prominent focus in *American Music: A Panorama* (1979) by composer Daniel Kingman (1924–2003), although the book's 1990 second edition, aware of shifts in the cultural climate, acknowledged some recent "rejection" of the work as "racially exploitative and demeaning."[26]

Gershwin made at least a cursory appearance as well in some monographs from the 1980s (all written by an emerging generation of "baby boomers") that, no doubt stimulated by current trends, addressed questions of American musical "identity," including *A History of Musical Americanism* (1980) by musicologist Barbara A. Zuck (b. 1946), and three books by historians: *Musical Nationalism: American Composers' Search for Identity* (1983) by Alan Howard Levy (b. 1951); *Yankee Blues: Musical Culture and American Identity* (1985) by MacDonald Smith Moore (b. 1945); and *An American Music: The Search for an American Musical Identity* (1986) by Barbara L. Tischler (b. 1949).[27] Surprisingly, Gershwin figured only peripherally in these studies, which largely viewed American musical identity in terms of such composers as Copland and Roy Harris, thereby maintaining Gershwin's long-established segregation from other serious composers, although Moore took the novel approach of placing Gershwin in the context of the Jewish Swiss American composer Ernst Bloch, and Tischler offered a corrective by noting similarities in the critical reception of Gershwin and Copland.[28] Such publications as these found precedent in, among other titles, *Composer and Nation: The Folk Heritage in Music* (1960) by the Marxist arts critic Sidney Finkelstein (1909–74), who applauded Gershwin's concert works and musicals, if not the "patronizing" and "melodramatic" *Porgy and Bess*.[29]

In 1983, musicologist Charles Hamm (1925–2011) brought forth a large history, *Music in the New World*, notable for its emphasis on vernacular American musics, the author's principal field of scholarship. Hamm duly presented Gershwin – in the tradition of Isaac Goldberg's seminal 1931 biography – as a sort of folk hero, an untrained and unequipped composer incapable of growth, who succeeded nevertheless in achieving "what no 'serious' American composer of the 1920s was able to achieve – a sense of being truly American in character."[30] Such an assessment, easily challenged by the facts, managed both to obscure Gershwin's real skills and capacity for development and to minimize the accomplishments of such contemporaries as Thomson, Harris, and Copland. None of this prevented Hamm from declaring *Porgy and Bess* "the greatest nationalistic opera of the century, not only of America but of the world."[31]

Two music appreciation texts from 1990 – *America's Musical Landscape* (now in its seventh 2013 edition) by Jean Ferris (b. 1936) and *The Musical Art: An Introduction to Western Music* by R. Larry Todd (b. 1952) – revealed not only Gershwin's solidifying academic reputation, but in particular, the increasing centrality of *Porgy and Bess* as compared to *Rhapsody in Blue*. Ferris aptly selected the opera's love duet, "Bess, You Is My Woman Now," as an accompanying listening example.[32] And Todd, although he somewhat misleadingly represented the composer's achievement by discussing his serious work under the subheading, "Other Developments in Jazz and Popular Music" and included a misstatement about an alleged consultation with Ravel in Paris, recognized *Porgy and Bess* as Gershwin's "masterpiece."[33]

In contrast, two notable books from the same time period with more of a focus on style analysis, as evidenced by their titles – *Music of the Twentieth Century: Style and Structure* (1986) by Bryan R. Simms (b. 1944), and *Twentieth-Century Music: A History of Musical Style in Modern Europe and America* (1991) by Robert P. Morgan (b. 1934) – had nominal use for Gershwin. Simms's one sentence on Gershwin appeared in a section, "Interactions with Rock," in which the author contended that Gershwin's "attempts to synthesize the realms of popular and serious composition" anticipated the likes of Peter Nero and Emerson, Lake, and Palmer.[34] Morgan, who spotlighted Copland, Sessions, Cowell, Partch, and Varèse among American composers of Gershwin's generation, similarly took only parenthetical notice of the composer; apparently unaware of such works as *Lullaby* (1919) and *Blue Monday Blues* (1922), this scant mention tapped the familiar but erroneous notion that "before the *Rhapsody* Gershwin had been exclusively a composer of popular songs."[35]

Five texts from the later 1990s – *Modern Times: From World War I to the Present* (1993), edited by the same Robert Morgan; *Soundings: Music in the Twentieth Century* (1995) by musicologist Glenn Watkins (b. 1927); *The History of American Classical Music: MacDowell Through Minimalism* (1995) by composer-pianist John Warthen Struble (b. 1952); *American Music in the Twentieth Century* (1997) by composer and music critic Kyle Gann (b. 1955); and the *Cambridge History of American Music* (1998), edited by British composer and musicologist David Nicholls – offered a variety of perspectives.[36] Carol Oja (b. 1953), in her chapter on American music for the Morgan book, for example, knowingly alluded to Gershwin's impact on the new-music community and his association with African American artists and intellectuals. Glenn Watkins's interest centered rather on Gershwin's influence on especially European composers of distinction, to the point of discussing him in a chapter entitled, "The New Simplicities: Germany." Even so, Watkins seems to have underestimated Gershwin's importance to George Antheil and John Alden Carpenter (perhaps because, with respect to the latter, he cited *Skyscrapers* as dating from 1921 as opposed to 1924).[37] John Struble favored Gershwin with unusually expansive coverage, devoting single chapters only to him and Ives; but his appraisal proved highly mixed, stressing formal deficiencies and somewhat slighting the composer's seriousness as a student of music even as he expressed admiration for Gershwin's "holistic" welding of melody, harmony, and orchestration, and his capacity for growth, as exemplified by the *Second Rhapsody* (1931).[38] Kyle Gann, whose preoccupation with America's more avant-garde traditions pushed Gershwin somewhat to the side, also seems to have underappreciated the composer's early formal training, although he recognized connections with both Alban Berg and the Schillinger method with regard to *Porgy and Bess*. (Like many others, Gann mistakenly ascribed the famous anecdotal exchange between Gershwin and Stravinsky – with the latter saying, after hearing about the former's earnings, "perhaps it is I who ought to study under you!" – to Gershwin and Ravel.[39])

The *Cambridge History of American Music* dramatically bifurcated Gershwin's achievement by discussing his popular theater work in the chapter "Popular Song and Popular Music on Stage and Film" by British musicologist Stephen Banfield (b. 1951), and his more serious compositions in "Tonal Traditions in Art Music from 1920 to 1960" by American musicologist Larry Starr (b. 1946).[40] The latter essay, mostly devoted to Gershwin and Copland, constituted a fresh approach to Gershwin in a number of ways: it underlined the composer's evolution as he matured, highlighted the limits of *Porgy and Bess* criticism based on abridged texts, and shed new light on Gershwin's formal finesse, including the observation that "beginning with the *Rhapsody*, Gershwin wrote instrumentally conceived, often asymmetrical themes with complex harmonic implications – frequently involving blue notes – for his concert works, and spun his distinctive forms out of their unusual potential."[41]

Such reassessment continued with musicologist Richard Crawford's generous consideration of Gershwin in his *America's Musical Life: A History* (2001), a successor to those copious texts by John Tasker Howard, Gilbert Chase, and Charles Hamm. Crawford (b. 1935) noted Gershwin's abilities as a pianist, and offered sensitive analyses of both "The Man I Love" and *Rhapsody in Blue*, even if he appeared to underrate the organic tightness of the latter as had been recently detailed by Steven

Gilbert (1943–99) in his landmark treatise, *The Music of Gershwin* (1995), as well as by composer David Schiff (b. 1945) in *Gershwin: Rhapsody in Blue* (1997).[42] Crawford's discussion of *Porgy and Bess*, imprecisely included in a chapter entitled "The Golden Age of the American Musical," further seemed problematic in its willingness to raise challenges to the work's operatic pedigree and "authenticity" without countervailing facts and opinions, including any discussion of Gershwin's travels south to research Southern black music.[43]

In their somewhat revisionist discussions of Gershwin, both cultural historian Joseph Horowitz (b. 1948) in *Classical Music in America: A History of its Rise and Fall* (2005) and musicologist Richard Taruskin (b. 1945) in *Music in the Early Twentieth Century* (2005) showed a heightened interest in the comparative reception histories of Gershwin and Copland.[44] Such discourse drew on the writings of musicologist Carol Oja, including *Making Music Modern: New York in the 1920s* (2000), which stated, "Copland was elevated at Gershwin's expense," although the author herself considered such matters only in the context of Copland, with her report on Gershwin centering rather on an analysis of the Concerto in F.[45] For Horowitz, who declared Gershwin, along with Ives, one of his "heroes," preferences for Copland over Gershwin signaled the country's immature subservience to "the 'white' Eurocentricity of American classical music and the masterpiece obsession of its culture of performance," but his broad claim that "American classical music closed ranks against Gershwin" conflicted not only with the historical record, but also with observations made elsewhere in the book.[46]

Music in the Early Twentieth Century, the penultimate text in Richard Taruskin's epic five-volume *Oxford History of Western Music*, devoted more space to Gershwin than any other American composer aside from Ives and Copland, further evidence of Gershwin's growing stature. Taruskin committed a few faux pas in his treatment of Gershwin, including failing to recognize that the composer pursued a formal musical education in his teens even while working as a popular song plugger and pianist; again confusing Ravel with Stravinsky in the aforementioned anecdote (a misstep only partially emended in the history's abbreviated college edition prepared with Christopher H. Gibbs); and crediting the libretto of *Porgy and Bess* to Ira Gershwin (who only wrote a few of the lyrics) rather than DuBose and Dorothy Heyward (the latter name, incidentally, commonly and unfairly omitted in discussions of the opera, both in textbooks and elsewhere).[47] Moreover, heading his discussion of Copland "Transgression" and Gershwin "Redemption," Taruskin took to extremes stock notions regarding the early reception of these two contemporaries as antithetical.[48]

In his popular survey of "twentieth-century classical composition," *The Rest Is Noise: Listening to the Twentieth Century* (2007), the longtime *New Yorker* music critic Alex Ross (b. 1968), representing a still younger generation, offered a refreshingly appreciative account of Gershwin, even opening his book with some thoughts on the relation between *Porgy and Bess* and Berg's *Wozzeck*, a topic considered in greater detail later in the book.[49] Ross proved not only deft in circumventing some of misconceived lore surrounding Gershwin, but also particularly eloquent in his depiction of the music, whether describing the "graceful merry-go-round of major, minor, dominant-seventh, and diminished-seventh chords" in "'S Wonderful," or "the tunes [that] undergo kaleidoscopic development and are stacked up in wickedly dissonant polytonal combinations" in *An American in Paris*.[50]

Admittedly, Gershwin remained a marginal figure in texts that continued to privilege high modernist art, such as *A Concise History of Western Music* (2006) by music critic and writer Paul Griffiths (b. 1947), and *Music in the Twentieth and Twenty-First Centuries* (2013) by musicologist Joseph Auner (b. 1959).[51] But despite such continued disengagement, especially among music theorists, academic texts increasingly came to regard Gershwin as one of the most important American composers of the twentieth century. Thanks to a new era of Gershwin scholarship ushered in by Edward Jablonski's 1987 biography and the aforementioned monograph by Steven Gilbert, as well as by *The Gershwin Style: New Looks at the Music of George Gershwin* (1999), edited by musicologist Wayne Schneider, with its important contributions by, among others, Wayne Shirley and Larry Starr, historians also proved more accurate in their reportage.[52]

Some false claims and dubious views naggingly persisted, nonetheless. Moreover, certain aspects of Gershwin's life and work still warranted greater attention, including his involvement with modernist musics, friendship with black musicians and artists, activities as a painter and art collector, contribution to the development of the Broadway musical, and musical growth as seen in his underrepresented work from the 1930s. But given the current flourishing of Gershwin studies – including new biographies by William Hyland (2003), the current author (2006), and Walter Rimler (2009); specialized monographs by Larry Starr (2010), Ellen Noonan (2012), Joseph Horowitz (2013), and Ryan Raul Bañagale (2014); various scholarly articles, including those by Ray Allen (2004), Christopher Reynolds (2007), Andrew Davis with the current author (2007), Susan Neimoyer (2011), Naomi André (2012) and Gwynne Kuhner Brown (2012); and the recent initiation of critical editions of the composer's work (under the auspices of the University of Michigan and the supervision of editor-in-chief Mark Clague)[53] – there seems little reason to doubt that future texts will provide students of music history with ever more nuanced and judicious accounts of the composer and his work.

Notes

1. Howard Pollack, *George Gershwin: His Life and Work* (Berkeley: University of California Press, 2006), 123.
2. John Tasker Howard, *Our American Music: Three Hundred Years of It* (New York: Thomas Y. Crowell, 1st edn, 1929; 2nd edn, 1939; 3rd edn, 1946; 3rd edn with supplementary chapters by James Lyons, 1954; 4th edn with supplementary chapters by James Lyons, 1965).
3. Howard, *Our American Music* (1929), 449–50.
4. Howard, *Our American Music* (1946), 447.
5. Ibid., 446.
6. Marion Bauer, *Twentieth Century Music: How It Developed, How to Listen to It* (New York: G.P. Putnam's, 1933); Aaron Copland, *Our New Music: Leading Composers in Europe and America* (New York: McGraw-Hill, 1941), 99; *The New Music 1900–1960*, revised and enlarged edn (New York: W.W. Norton, 1968), 70.
7. Aaron Copland, *Copland on Music* (New York: W.W. Norton, 1960), 162.
8. Gilbert Chase, *America's Music, From the Pilgrims to the Present* (Urbana: University of Illinois Press, 1st edn, 1955; 2nd edn, 1966; 3rd edn, 1987), 492 (1955), 494 (1966).
9. Chase, *America's Music* (1955), 493.
10. Ibid., 493; William W. Austin, *Music in the 20th Century, from Debussy through Stravinsky* (New York: W.W. Norton, 1966), 385.
11. Charles Schwartz, *Gershwin: His Life and Music* (New York: Bobbs-Merrill, 1973).
12. Chase, *America's Music* (1987), 473, 475, 477.
13. Otto Deri, *Exploring Twentieth-Century Music* (New York: Holt, Rinehart and Winston, 1968).
14. Donald Jay Grout, *A History of Western Music* (New York: W.W. Norton, 1960), 623.
15. Donald Jay Grout and Claude V. Palisca, *A History of Western Music*, 4th edn (New York: W.W. Norton, 1988).
16. J. Peter Burkholder, Donald Jay Grout, and Claude V. Palisca, *A History of Western Music*, 9th edn (New York: W.W. Norton, 2014), 861–62, 897–98.
17. Joseph Machlis, *Introduction to Contemporary Music* (New York: W.W. Norton, 1st edn, 1961; 2nd edn, 1979), 562 (1961), 383 (1979); Pollack, *George Gershwin*, 166–67.
18. Wilfrid Mellers, *Music in a New Found Land: Themes and Developments in the History of American Music* (London: Barrie and Rockliff, 1964), xiii–iv, 392–413.
19. Austin, *Music in the 20th Century*, 6, 62, 89, 384–85, 471, 502–03, 518.
20. Ibid., 503.
21. Eric Salzman, *Twentieth-Century Music: An Introduction* (Englewood Cliffs, NJ: Prentice-Hall, 1st edn, 1967; 2nd edn, 1974; 3rd edn, 1988; 4th edn, 2002), 103 (1967), 95 (1988).
22. H. Wiley Hitchcock, *Music in the United States: A Historical Introduction* (Englewood Cliffs, NJ: Prentice-Hall, 1st edn, 1969; 2nd edn, 1974; 3rd edn, 1988; 4th edn, 2000), 206 (1969).
23. Virgil Thomson, "George Gershwin," *Modern Music* 13 (November–December 1935), 13–19.
24. Virgil Thomson, *American Music Since 1910* (New York: Holt, Rinehart and Winston, 1970, 1971), 84, 146.
25. Edith Borroff, *Music in Europe and the United States: A History* (Englewood Cliffs, NJ: Prentice-Hall; 1st edn, 1971; 2nd edn, New York: Ardsley House, 1990).
26. W.D. Shirley, "North America," in F.W. Sternfeld (ed.), *Music in the Modern Age* (New York: Praeger, 1973), 363–406; Richard Franko Goldman, "Music in the United States," in Martin Cooper (ed.), *New Oxford History of Music*, vol. 10, *The Modern Age* (New York: Oxford University Press, 1974), 569–634; Daniel Kingman, *American Music: A Panorama* (New York: Schirmer, 1st edn, 1979; 2nd edn, 1990; concise edn, 1998; 2nd concise edn, 2003), 474 (1990).
27. Barbara A. Zuck, *A History of Musical Americanism* (Ann Arbor, MI: UMI Research Press, 1978, 1980); Alan Howard Levy, *Musical Nationalism: American Composers' Search for Identity* (Westport, CT: Greenwood Press, 1983); MacDonald Smith Moore, *Yankee Blues: Musical*

Culture and American Identity (Bloomington: Indiana University Press, 1985); Barbara L. Tischler, *An American Music: The Search for an American Musical Identity* (New York: Oxford, 1986).

28. Moore, *Yankee Blues*, 164; Tischler, *An American Music*, 103.
29. Sidney Finkelstein, *Composer and Nation: The Folk Heritage in Music* (New York: International Publishers, 1st edn, 1960; 2nd edn, 1989), 316 (1960).
30. Charles Hamm, *Music in the New World* (New York: W.W. Norton, 1983), 424; Isaac Goldberg, *George Gershwin: A Study in American Music* (New York: Simon & Schuster, 1931).
31. Hamm, *Music in the New World*, 450.
32. Jean Ferris, *America's Musical Landscape* (Madison, WI: WCB Brown & Benchmark, 1990).
33. R. Larry Todd, *The Musical Art: An Introduction to Western Music* (Belmont, CA: Wadsworth, 1990), 475–76.
34. Bryan R. Simms, *Music of the Twentieth Century: Style and Structure* (New York: Schirmer, 1st edn, 1986; 2nd edn, 1996), 435 (1986), 420 (1996).
35. Robert P. Morgan, *Twentieth-Century Music: A History of Musical Style in Modern Europe and America* (New York: W.W. Norton, 1991), 285.
36. Robert P. Morgan, ed., *Modern Times: From World War I to the Present* (New York: Macmillan, 1993); Glenn Watkins, *Soundings: Music in the Twentieth Century* (Belmont, CA: Schirmer/Thomson Learning, 1995); John Warthen Struble, *The History of American Classical Music: MacDowell through Minimalism* (New York: Facts on File, 1995); Kyle Gann, *American Music in the Twentieth Century* (New York: Schirmer, 1997); David Nicholls, ed., *The Cambridge History of American Music* (New York: Cambridge University Press, 1998).
37. Watkins, *Soundings*, 305 (that the author thought "I Got Rhythm" and "Who Could Ask for Anything More?" were two separate songs suggested some unfamiliarity with Gershwin's more popular work).
38. Struble, *The History of American Classical Music*, 108–10, 115–18.
39. Gann, *American Music in the Twentieth Century*, 67–68; Pollack, *George Gershwin*, 121.
40. Stephen Banfield, "Popular Song and Popular Music on Stage and Film" (309–44), and Larry Starr, "Tonal Traditions in Art Music from 1920 to 1960" (471–95) in Nicholls, ed., *The Cambridge History of American Music*.
41. Starr, "Tonal Traditions in Art Music from 1920 to 1960," 474–75.
42. Steven E. Gilbert, *The Music of Gershwin* (New Haven, CT: Yale University Press, 1995); David Schiff, *Gershwin: Rhapsody in Blue* (New York: Cambridge University Press, 1997).
43. Richard Crawford, *America's Musical Life: A History* (New York: W.W. Norton, 2001), 677.
44. Joseph Horowitz, *Classical Music in America: A History of Its Rise and Fall* (New York: W.W. Norton, 2005); Richard Taruskin, *Music in the Early Twentieth Century* (New York: Oxford University Press, 2005, 2010).
45. Carol Oja, *Making Music Modern: New York in the 1920s* (New York: Oxford University Press, 2000), 356.
46. Horowitz, *Classical Music in America*, xvi, 470, 472.
47. Taruskin, *Music in the Early Twentieth Century*, 623, 628; Richard Taruskin and Christopher H. Gibbs, *The Oxford History of Western Music: College Edition* (New York: Oxford University Press, 2013), 931.
48. Schiff, *Gershwin: Rhapsody in Blue*, 91–92; Howard Pollack, *Aaron Copland: The Life and Work of an Uncommon Man* (New York: Henry Holt, 1999), 519.
49. Alex Ross, *The Rest Is Noise: Listening to the Twentieth Century* (New York: Farrar, Straus and Giroux, 2007), xi–xii, 148–49.
50. Ibid., 144, 147.
51. Paul Griffiths, *A Concise History of Western Music* (New York: Cambridge University Press, 2006); Joseph Auner, *Music in the Twentieth and Twenty-First Centuries* (New York: Norton, 2013).
52. Edward Jablonski, *George Gershwin: A Biography* (New York: Doubleday, 1987); Gilbert, *The Music of Gershwin*; Wayne Schneider, ed., *The Gershwin Style: New Looks at the Music of George Gershwin* (New York: Oxford University Press, 1999).
53. William G. Hyland, *George Gershwin: A New Biography* (Westport, CT: Praeger, 2003); Pollack, *George Gershwin*; Walter Rimler, *George Gershwin: An Intimate Portrait* (Urbana: University of Illinois Press, 2009); Larry Starr, *George Gershwin* (New Haven, CT: Yale University Press, 2010); Ellen Noonan, *The Strange Career of* Porgy and Bess: *Race, Culture, and America's Most*

Famous Opera (Chapel Hill: University of North Carolina Press, 2012); Joseph Horowitz, *"On My Way": The Untold Story of Rouben Mamoulian, George Gershwin, and* Porgy and Bess (New York: W.W. Norton, 2013); Ryan Raul Bañagale, *Arranging Gershwin: Rhapsody in Blue and the Creation of an American Icon* (New York: Oxford University Press, 2014); Ray Allen, "An American Folk Opera? Triangulating Folkness, Blackness, and Americaness in Gershwin and Heyward's *Porgy and Bess*," *Journal of American Folklore* 118 (Summer 2004), 243–61; Christopher Reynolds, "*Porgy and Bess*: An American *Wozzeck*," *Journal of the Society for American Music* 1 (February 2007), 1–28; Andrew Davis and Howard Pollack, "Rotational Form in the Opening Scene of *Porgy and Bess*," *Journal of the American Musicological Society* 60/2 (2007), 373–414; Susan Neimoyer, "George Gershwin and Edward Kilenyi, Sr.: A Reevaluation of Gershwin's Early Musical Education," *Musical Quarterly* 94 (Spring–Summer 2011), 9–62; articles by Naomi André and Gwynne Kuhner Brown, in Naomi André, Karen M. Bryan, and Eric Saylor (eds.), *Blackness in Opera* (Urbana: University of Illinois Press, 2012), 11–32, 164–86.

13 When Ella Fitzgerald Sang Gershwin
A Chapter from the Great American Songbook

WILL FRIEDWALD

> You know, a couple of weeks ago, when somebody told me that there was a record album coming out that was going to sell for $100, I figured he was a real ding-a-ling. When I learned that it was really five albums, I felt, "Well, that's closer to reality. Twenty clams apiece, that's not bad." And then when I found out that it was recorded by Ella Fitzgerald, with Nelson Riddle's arrangements, and that it was an autographed set of all Gershwin songs, well, I ran right out and grabbed me a few.[1] FRANK SINATRA (1959)

Ella Fitzgerald launched her career in a highly inauspicious way, with the humblest of songs, "A-Tisket, A-Tasket." This swinging adaptation of a traditional nursery rhyme – it really was about a little yellow basket – was such a hit that it led to other novelty-type songs that made even her "Tisket" look positively erudite by comparison: "Melinda the Mousie," "Gotta Pebble in My Shoe," and even the inevitable sequel, "I Found My Yellow Basket." Yet within twenty years, Fitzgerald had moved from such ephemeral material all the way up to the top of the food chain, to the most sophisticated and highly regarded songs ever written, most notably those by George and Ira Gershwin. By the late 1950s, she had reinvented herself as a key player in the process of defining what would come to be known as "The Great American Songbook."

Norman Granz, Fitzgerald's producer and manager for what might be described as the glory years of her career, occasionally gets credit for inventing the idea of the songbook album. Granz was not a humble man, but even he would have hesitated to take a bow for this particular innovation. "Songbook" albums dedicated to the canon of a single composer, lyricist, or team, go back at least as far as 1939, when the jazz and torch singer Lee Wiley launched a series of songbook projects that ultimately extended to six different albums. The songbook's growing popularity as a format appears to have gone hand-in-hand with the introduction of the long-playing record in 1948: Margaret Whiting did a Rodgers and Hart collection for Capitol Records in 1947 (released as a 10 inch LP in 1950), and even more notably, Fitzgerald herself recorded her first songbook, *Ella Sings Gershwin*, in 1950.

That premiere Fitzgerald songbook was produced by Milt Gabler, an under-appreciated figure in the arc of Ella's career and in jazz in general. Yet Norman Granz deserves credit for something else, something closely related. Although Gabler produced Fitzgerald's breakthrough album in 1950 (as well as the masterpiece *Lullabies of Birdland* in 1955), his goal for the most part was to provide new songs for the great singer that could potentially be hit singles. While Fitzgerald topped the charts only rarely (her biggest hits, after "Tisket," were two rather unlikely numbers, "My Happiness" and "Stone Cold Dead in the Market," the latter a duet with Louis Jordan), she nonetheless sold a ton of product in these years and overall was the most significant female singer on Decca Records.

Granz's masterstroke, however, was to take Ella out of the singles market. This became possible with the new long-playing technology, first the 10 inch LP, beginning in 1948, and then the 12 inch, which became the dominant long-playing format around 1955. In that same year, Granz, who had been producing jazz for Mercury Records, founded Verve Records. Building on what Gabler had already accomplished with *Ella Sings Gershwin* and *Lullabies of Birdland*, Granz further established that the long-playing format complemented Ella's evolving artistry. Granz had the vision to take her out of the singles format dominated by singers like Jo Stafford and Patti Page, and put her in a whole new arena, one where she set the standards for those who followed. Granz and George Avakian (of Columbia Records) were among the visionaries – another was Frank Sinatra – who realized that the traditional songs were ideally suited to the new media, like long-playing albums and television, while the so-called new music, the baby-boomer centric pop that was being dubbed rock 'n' roll, was a perfect fit for the old media, like single records and radio.

More than anyone else, it was the dual impact of Fitzgerald and Sinatra that solidified the album as the vehicle for what Alan Livingston, then president of Capitol Records, described as "standard product." Yet their approaches could not have been more different. Sinatra's concept was to construct albums of works by multiple composers but arranged to fit into a common mood, unified by tempo and orchestra. Fitzgerald became most famous for the songbook albums, which were unified by focusing on songs by a single composer. Each album also tended to have only one arranger (there was considerable consistency in that). Consequently, on a Fitzgerald album, a slow ballad might be followed by a fast swinger, a phenomenon that almost never occurred on one of Sinatra's classic "concept" albums.

For Granz, the songbook albums were a win–win on multiple levels. He was not only a major jazz buff, who, as an impresario a few years earlier, had done much to make the music acceptable in the concert halls with his Jazz at the Philharmonic tours, but also an equally tireless advocate for the better class of American song. Granz is part of the reason why what we now call the Great American Songbook is so closely tied to the films of Fred Astaire. (The overwhelming majority of writers in the Ella songbook series wrote specifically for the great song-and-dance man.) Granz seems to have been well aware that there had been songbook albums before him, but only he approached the idea with such ambition and scope that his intention seems to have been to make everybody forget the idea had been done previously: all of the songbooks thus far were double disc sets containing at least thirty-two songs, and he made a point to keep up the schedule of at least one songbook per year:

> *Ella Fitzgerald Sings the Cole Porter Song Book* (1956)
> *Ella Fitzgerald Sings the Rodgers & Hart Song Book* (1956)
> *Ella Fitzgerald Sings the Duke Ellington Song Book* (1957)
> *Ella Fitzgerald Sings the Irving Berlin Song Book* (1958)

The Ellington album was the most ambitious of them all, originally released as a four-LP set. Granz clearly knew what he was doing: it was the quality of Fitzgerald's voice and the charm of her personality that made us want to listen to her longer than any other vocalist. When one listens to Anita O'Day on Verve, for instance, as great as she is, her single disc songbooks of *Cole Porter* and *Rodgers & Hart*, done for Verve with Billy May, are all that one needs to hear.

With Porter, Rodgers and Hart, Ellington, and Berlin under their belts, it was clear that the Ella/Verve songbook series was going to have to address George Gershwin. In fact, in the wake of the Ella/Verve songbooks, two of Fitzgerald's "rival" female vocalists recording for other labels, Sarah Vaughan (on Mercury) and Chris Connor (on Atlantic), had already done double-length Gershwin collections that were clearly modeled on Granz and Ella. Yet Fitzgerald had already done a Gershwin songbook – the aforementioned *Ella Sings Gershwin* in 1950 – how to deal with that?

One thing was clear, the 1950 album was not a pushover. In fact, near the end of Fitzgerald's life, singer-scholar Michael Feinstein met Fitzgerald in person and told her that he actually preferred the more modest 1950 effort to the 1959 masterpiece. "I know what you mean," Ella answered, "it's more intimate." She was right of course: *Ella Sings Gershwin* consists of eight exquisitely-sung tracks with equally jewel-like piano settings provided by one of the all-time giants of vocal accompaniment, the brilliant and understated Ellis Larkins. It is a particularly far-sighted venture; the recordings were done on tape, which gives them a very modern sound. Indeed, the whole project, in terms of conception and audio quality, is much more like a product of the LP era than the 78 rpm era. In tempo and mood as well: Fitzgerald began most of the eight songs with the verses – something rarely, if ever, heard during the big band era. Supported by Larkins's brilliant accompaniment, Fitzgerald offers some of the most poignant lyric interpretations she had done to date. She is vulnerable on

"Someone to Watch Over Me," pouty and diffident on "My One and Only," inquisitive and introspective on "How Long Has This Been Going On?" and coy and playful on "I've Got a Crush on You." To many observers in 1959, it must have seemed like the better idea for Ella and Granz to simply skip Gershwin altogether.

Yet Granz was nothing if not supremely competitive; besting the 1950 album was a matter of scope and ambition. The 1950 album had been a mere eight songs on a humble 10 inch disc; the 1959 package would include about fifty-five songs (give or take a few bonuses and extras) in a lavish five-LP set. The 1950 album had used the intimate, knowing piano accompaniment of Ellis Larkins; the 1959 would employ a large symphonic orchestra helmed by Sinatra's principle lieutenant, and the man regarded as the number one ace arranger of great songs for great singers, Nelson Riddle.

Getting Riddle for the project was not a foregone conclusion, even after Granz realized that utilizing a musical director of his caliber was crucial. As Peter Levinson relates in his 2001 biography of Riddle, the singer Anita O'Day tried to push Granz to hire Riddle as early as 1956. Riddle scored one single for Fitzgerald ("Beale Street Blues") in 1958, but when Granz hesitated to offer him more work, Riddle then signed an exclusive contract with Capitol Records, where he continued to craft beautiful charts, most famously for Sinatra and Nat King Cole. For Granz to use him in 1959, he had to get a special release from Capitol.

But the Gershwin project was worth the additional effort. Even twenty-two years after his death, George Gershwin seemed more relevant than ever: there were probably more songbook albums dedicated to his music than any other composer, in 1956 there was a major 90-minute TV special titled *The Music of Gershwin* featuring not only Broadway stars Alfred Drake and Ethel Merman (as well as pop singer Tony Bennett), but also classical pianists and ballet dancers – clearly no other songwriter was getting that kind of treatment. In 1957, *Funny Face*, the best of the posthumous Gershwin movie musicals, was released, and in 1958, the best biography up until that point, *The Gershwin Years*, by Edward Jablonski and Lawrence D. Stewart, was published. Stewart would be a key player in the Fitzgerald/Granz Gershwin project; it was the affable academic, who spent most of his career as a professor of English at the University of California, Northridge, who supplied Granz with a list of Gershwin songs to consider.

With the exception of George Gershwin and, later, Jerome Kern, all the songwriters in the Fitzgerald songbook series were still alive and highly supportive when the albums were produced. When Granz sent test pressings of the first set to Cole Porter, he responded enthusiastically. Richard

Rodgers, who was widely perceived as not liking jazz (and who had little use for the songs from his first partnership, with Lorenz Hart) also gave Fitzgerald and Granz the thumbs up. In 1958, Irving Berlin even tried to initiate a *Songbook* volume of his own with Verve Records by offering to cut his usual royalty rate in half. But thanks to Stewart, Ira Gershwin became a more active participant. After Stewart sent Granz a list of suggestions and a pile of sheet music, Ira Gershwin added his own, and decorated one of Stewart's typed song lists with a signature doodle. (In other instances, the elder Gershwin also offered to help adapt certain lyrics for Fitzgerald.)

Granz was so impressed that the veteran lyricist had taken an interest in the project that he changed the focus of the project halfway through production. When the project began, its tentative title was *Ella Fitzgerald Sings the George Gershwin Songbook*. But in January 1959, after the first batch of sessions were done (nineteen usable masters taped over three days), Granz retitled the project *Ella Fitzgerald Sings the George and Ira Gershwin Songbook*, in deference to Ira's participation, and from that point on, all the lyrics were Ira's.[2]

Overall, the basic fifty-three songs included in the original five-LP set are a vital survey of the conjoined careers of the Gershwin brothers, from their first notable song together, "The Real American Folk Song (is a Rag)" (and also Ira's first song in a show, from the 1918 *Ladies First*) to "Love Is Here to Stay" (from *The Goldwyn Follies*, 1938), which Ira identified as his brother's final song. The bulk of the songs were somewhat familiar from show and film scores, including the majority of the standards that the brothers wrote for Fred Astaire on stage and screen, for the productions *Lady, Be Good!*, *Funny Face*, *A Damsel in Distress*, and *Shall We Dance*. The Astaire–Gershwin relationship was regarded as still very much alive at this point, thanks to the 1957 release of the film version of *Funny Face*.

With room for fifty-three songs, the team went beyond well-known classics like "The Man I Love," "Someone to Watch Over Me," and "But Not for Me." Stewart suggested a few Gershwin oddities that Granz did not approve, such as "In the Mandarin's Orchid Garden," written in 1930 for the unproduced *East is West*, and "The Jolly Tar and the Milkmaid," a parody of a traditional English madrigal from *A Damsel in Distress*, which is one of the few songs that I cannot imagine Fitzgerald actually singing. But the producer did green light a few oddities that counterbalanced the familiar standards, and it is worth noting that these – starting with "The Real American Folk Song (Is a Rag)" – all draw on Fitzgerald's highly developed senses of rhythm and humor.

"Just Another Rhumba" had been written for, but not used in, *Goldwyn Follies*. When Fitzgerald recorded it, the song was pretty much unknown. Lyrically, it is a Caribbean update of "Fascinating Rhythm" in which the singing protagonist is colorfully complaining about a piece of music that is driving him crazy – he dismisses it as "just another rhumba," but it has a strange power over him that he cannot resist. Musically, the song gives Riddle a chance to use all sorts of Pan-American effects, reminiscent of Gershwin's concert work, *Cuban Overture*. (The song is also a cousin of "Island in the West Indies," which Ira Gershwin wrote with Vernon Duke.) "By Strauss" is a comedy waltz that owes its existence to Vincente Minnelli, who insisted on using it in his 1936 Broadway revue *The Show Is On* and more famously in the classic 1951 *An American in Paris*.

After the three dates in January, work continued on the epic project for another eight months; there were two dates in March, and a sprint of four consecutive days of recording sessions in mid-July. As a special bone to throw longtime Fitzgerald fans, Granz had Riddle prepare a new arrangement of the 1924 jam session perennial "Oh, Lady Be Good." For a long time this was the most frequently heard Gershwin number in the Fitzgerald repertoire, in the customary form of an extended scat improvisation. However, instead of doing it as a wild uptempo improv, as she usually sang it (as on the 1955 album *Lullabies of Birdland* and on thousands of live concerts), this performance features a slow ballad arrangement that begins with the verse, which automatically differentiates it from the many other Fitzgerald performances of this Gershwin classic. But because Fitzgerald usually included at least one extended scat solo in every concert set and most of her albums (i.e. "Blue Skies" on *The Irving Berlin Songbook*), this time the honor went to Gershwin's most iconic jazz standard, "I Got Rhythm."

Every jazz singer in the world had already done "I Got Rhythm" (Nat King Cole, as pianist and singer, had recorded roughly a dozen variations on those familiar chord changes), thus Riddle and Fitzgerald were inspired to come up with a completely different approach: Riddle opens with the rubato, minor key verse in a contemporary classical setting, with modish, polytonal chords that suggest Aaron Copland; then, for the chorus, while keeping the whole thing swinging, they take a Broadway-like approach, with several tempo changes and a beat that stops and starts, much more like concert music than big band dance music.

Overall, the Gershwin Songbook is also the best example of two major features of Ella Fitzgerald's music, especially at this moment, which might be considered the midpoint of her career: for one thing, she had come a long way since the days of "A-Tisket, A-Tasket," which was hardly the worst song she ever sang during the Chick

Webb period. Not only is there a feeling that she is now singing the greatest songs ever written in all of the twentieth-century American experience, but that the songs themselves could have no better interpreter. Ella doing this music, in this songbook, is a case of what her friend Joe Williams referred to as "water seeking its own level." The Gershwin package even puts the previous Verve *Songbooks* to shame, particularly the first two, *Cole Porter* and *Rodgers and Hart*, where Bregman's arrangements sound like hack work compared to Riddle.

The other point best illuminated by the Gershwin project is in Fitzgerald's singing itself, which represents a case of what I call "Garbo's foot syndrome": in the 1930s, at the height of the Hollywood studio system, Greta Garbo was the most beautiful woman in the world, but the caricaturists and other wisenheimers who wanted to make fun of her decided to harp on this idea that she had unusually large feet. They had to find something wrong with her! Fitzgerald was the greatest singer in the world, and those negative Nellies and moaning minnies who are determined to find fault with everything started promoting the false notion that Fitzgerald was only "about" the music, never about the words. One of the more satisfying aspects of the *Gershwin* album is that it represents some of Fitzgerald's best singing of lyrics as well as melodies. Even the naysayers knew to expect that Fitzgerald's uptempos were going to be awesome, like "Strike Up the Band," with its march-time intro and college football fanfare.

But there was no denying that this album would contain some of the greatest and most moving ballad singing Fitzgerald would ever do, in track after track. We have already mentioned "Oh, Lady, Be Good," and that is a key track that must have really caught listeners off guard – Ella is so effusive, so forthcoming with all of her emotions, so overwhelmingly warm and full of heart, that the word "disarming" barely begins to describe it.

For this particular project, Riddle and Fitzgerald came up with a whole new way to use time: few of the tracks are very fast or very slow. Instead, nearly all of them have elements of both. Fitzgerald does not need the crutch of a super slow tempo to be effective: she can break our hearts even while the beat is still going, as on "Somebody from Somewhere." "I Was Doing All Right" is one of the faster pieces on the package, but still it is barely fast at all, compared to one of Fitzgerald's horse-race tempo bebop excursions, like many of those found on her epic scat collection, *Lullabies of Birdland* (including the original, mostly scatted 1947 version of "Oh, Lady Be Good" – now *that is* fast!) Keeping the tracks both fast and slow, and, with exceptions (like the new "Lady, Be Good"), both happy and sad helped enhance the album as a whole: it is one occasion when you can listen to almost sixty songs by one composing team, one vocalist, and one arranger and never feel the monotony. Like so much of the best Fitzgerald, when you get through all five albums, you only want to listen to more Ella Fitzgerald.

In August, Granz asked Riddle to work up arrangements on two special bonus tracks – unusual material that would be issued in an unusual format. These would be Gershwin's Three Preludes (his most famous instrumental compositions after *Rhapsody in Blue* and *An American in Paris*) and three other instrumental pieces that all pertained to the act of walking, "Promenade (Walking the Dog)," "March of the Swiss Soldiers," and "Fidgety Feet," which Riddle joined together and christened as *The Ambulatory Suite*. The two extraordinary sets, which timed at six and a half and seven minutes, respectively, were issued in the finished set as a bonus disc, in the unusual format of a 7 inch 33⅓ rpm extended play single.

Granz was a fervent art buff, and it shows. He was also a maven for packaging. The *Gershwin Songbook* package was issued in various formats, the most notable of which was the deluxe $100 edition – at a time when the average price of a new album was about $3. The deluxe edition was housed in a box with a cover illustration by the contemporary French artist Bernard Buffet; in addition to the cover, a set of lithographs by the artist was included in the edition. These were used as the covers of the individual volumes when the set was eventually issued as five separate LPs. Also included was a substantial hardcover booklet by Lawrence D. Stewart, which made a proper companion volume to *The Gershwin Years*. Then, there was the 7 inch EP, containing the two Riddle/Gershwin instrumental suites. And, of course, there were the five 12 inch LPs containing the fifty-three Gershwin songs.

Frank Sinatra helped launch the album on his November 25, 1959 ABC-TV special (with the introductory line included at the top of this chapter). In a case of *noblesse oblige* that was especially magnanimous, Sinatra devoted eight full minutes, the finale of his special, to the *Gershwin Songbook* with Nelson Riddle himself conducting the studio orchestra. Fitzgerald opened with "He Loves and She Loves," the Hi-Los vocal group sang "Love Walked Right In," then Sinatra did his solo, "Love Is Here to Stay" (the classic Riddle arrangement from *Songs for Swingin' Lovers*, 1956), and, for a climax, "Love Is Sweeping the Country" was performed by the entire cast: Fitzgerald, Sinatra, the HiLos, plus Peter Lawford, Hermione Gingold, and dancer Juliet Prowse. It was probably the best prime time exposure that any new album ever received in that period.

You might say Sinatra had a vested interested in promoting *Ella Fitzgerald Sings the George and Ira Gershwin Songbook*, and I do not mean because he was, at the time, attempting to purchase the entire operation outright from Granz. Rather, he had always known that he and Fitzgerald and Granz were going for the same thing: to achieve a new level of respect for jazz, popular singing, and the Great American Songbook. When Fitzgerald and Sinatra were young band vocalists, dancing to big bands was just something that teenagers did, and that no one else took seriously; places where jazz was heard were considered dives where no respectable person would ever bring his wife or his mother (his mistress, maybe); and there was no "Great American Songbook," there was only the *Lucky Strike Hit Parade*, where forgettable novelties like "Mairzy Doats" usually took top place. The gatekeepers of high culture looked down their noses (and through their lorgnettes) at all of these enterprises. Yet the classic Sinatra albums and the *Gershwin* and other songbooks did much to change all that. After hearing the magic that Fitzgerald and Riddle wrought on "But Not for Me" and "How Long Has This Been Goin' On," it was still possible to debate what kind of art this was, but there was no denying that it was, indeed, art.

Following the huge success of the Gershwin project, in 1960, the *Songbook* series took a year off. Fitzgerald's blockbuster release for the opening of the new decade was *Mack the Knife – Ella in Berlin*, her classic live concert album, taped in February at the Deutschlandhalle. Whereas the epic *Gershwin Songbook* had taken eight months and the services of dozens of musicians to record, for this album, Granz simply stuck a mic in front of the great lady and turned on the tape recorder. The results were both pure musical magic and cash register gold.

Then he resumed the Songbook project in 1961, with *Ella Fitzgerald Sings the Harold Arlen Songbook*, featuring the audacious arrangements of Billy May in their only collaboration together. The final volumes in the series were both single disc packages under the baton of Riddle: *Jerome Kern* in 1963 and *Johnny Mercer* in 1964. From that point on, there were a number of addenda to the Songbook series: in 1981, she released *Ella Abraça Jobim* (subtitled *Ella Fitzgerald Sings the Antonio Carlos Jobim Songbook*), a two LP package of compositions by the innovative Brazilian composer, whose work Fitzgerald had long exalted. There was also *Ella Loves Cole*, from 1972 (reissued as *Dream Dancing*), in which the new arrangements by Nelson Riddle made it a major improvement over the original 1956 *Cole Porter Songbook* arrangements by Buddy Bregman.

And finally, there was *Nice Work If You Can Get It* from 1983. This third and final Ella-Gershwin project grew out of the admiration that pianist (and conductor and composer) André Previn felt for Fitzgerald; in 1979, she had been a guest on his PBS TV series, *Previn and the Pittsburgh*, on which he spoke at length of his love for the *Songbook* albums. She sang some Cole Porter ("Dream Dancing"), some Ellington ("I'm Just a Lucky So and So"), some Rodgers and Hart ("Glad to Be Unhappy"), and naturally, some Gershwin ("They Can't Take That Away from Me"). This also was the only occasion I know of when Fitzgerald sang both versions of "Oh, Lady Be Good," the uptempo arrangement with the wild scat solo and the slow ballad version with the verse. As Fitzgerald explained to the host: "Andre, I'd like to say that this was Norman Granz's idea to try it slow. I think that a lot of people never realized what a beautiful song it is. You understand the lyrics this way!"

Nice Work If You Can Get It was formally subtitled Ella Fitzgerald and Andre Previn Do Gershwin. As with the 1950 Ella Sings Gershwin, it is a more intimate project than the 1959 Songbook, and it is even more of a full-scale collaboration with a major pianist than the 1950 album. Recorded nearly twenty-five years after "the big one," Fitzgerald's voice has notably aged, but she is still in excellent shape, vocally, overall. All eight tracks (one of which is a three-song medley) are also in a decidedly medium tempo. It could be that this is a tempo that better suits Gershwin's melodies than say, those of Cole Porter or Irving Berlin; some are slightly faster or slower, but there is nothing of the crawl-tempo ballads or the horserace tempo swingers. In this case, however, the extreme tempos were likely avoided because the middle speeds were easier on Fitzgerald's aging voice.

Granz could have looked around for songs that Fitzgerald had missed in 1950 or 1959, or even some of the Porgy and Bess songs that Louis Armstrong had sung on his album with her, but no. These are all, so to speak, remakes of songs Ella had done before. Granz apparently conceived the album as a kind of last hurrah for both Fitzgerald and Ira Gershwin; Ella would make two more studio albums for Granz, but this is the best of her later projects, and Ira would live long enough for the sessions (in May 1983) but passed away (on August 17) just a few weeks before the album's release. In these recordings, Ella does not hold back. Her melodic inventiveness, particularly on the many embellishments on "Nice Work If You Can Get It," is greater than ever, while the melancholy mood she spins on "But Not for Me" is even more convincing than on her 1950 and 1959 versions. She also benefits greatly from the brilliant keyboard work of Previn, who ranks alongside Hank Jones, Tommy Flanagan, Lou Levy, Paul Smith, and Jimmy Jones, as among the finest of Fitzgerald's keyboard collaborators. Fitzgerald and Previn, relate marvelously both to the material and to each other. Nice Work is not so much an improvement as an addendum to her earlier Gershwin recordings. Nonetheless, the album is fairly essential to her overall output.

Unlike nearly every singer of any generation, by the third or fourth decades of her career, Fitzgerald was no longer singing her biggest hit singles; there are very few live versions of "A-Tisket, A-Tasket" from the 1960s. Her whole focus was on what was increasingly known as "The Great American Songbook," and it is worth noting that her other albums were filled with classic tunes by worthy composers – like Harry Warren, Frank Loesser, and Rodgers and Hammerstein – who never, alas, were awarded a songbook of their own.

In all three of her Gershwin projects (1950, 1959, and 1983), Fitzgerald exalted this music by singing it as close to what the composer intended as possible. While she was the greatest scat singer ever (no arguments, please), she also could make the original melodies sound supremely beautiful without changing them at all, and when she did make alterations, they were so subtle that the composers themselves barely noticed, and if they did, fully approved of them. Small wonder that Ira Gershwin spoke for the whole profession of songwriters when he said, "I never knew how good our songs were until I heard Ella Fitzgerald sing them."

Notes

1. Frank Sinatra, introducing the "Gershwin Finale," in his Timex-sponsored TV special, *An Afternoon with Frank Sinatra*, broadcast live on ABC TV, November 25, 1959.
2. More mysteriously, one song with lyrics by Ira Gershwin but music by Harry Warren, "Cheerful Little Earful," was also tackled during the January sessions. Both "bonus tracks" were left off the original issues of the *Gershwin Songbook* and instead used on the 1959 Fitzgerald album *Get Happy!* The only significant George and Ira Gershwin songs not included are the ones they wrote for *Porgy and Bess*, which Fitzgerald had recorded two years earlier in a classic double album with Louis Armstrong.

14 The Afterlife of *Rhapsody in Blue*

RYAN RAUL BAÑAGALE

> George Gershwin died on July 11, 1937, but I don't have to believe that if I don't want to.[1]
> JOHN O'HARA (1940)

Every story needs a beginning, and ours starts with the death of George Gershwin in Los Angeles, California at the age of thirty-eight. Although the reception of *Rhapsody in Blue* extends from the moment of its debut on February 12, 1924, the seminal positioning of the piece in the career of Gershwin became forever sealed when he died suddenly and unexpectedly; thirteen years and three thousand miles away from Aeolian Hall in New York City, where the work premiered. Gershwin's entire professional career encompassed just two decades, a length of time comparable to a "period" in the lives of other composers. In this context – and assuming a life lived as long as figures such as Aaron Copland (1900–1990) or Leonard Bernstein (1918–1990) – might his move to Hollywood just eleven months prior to his passing have demarcated a new chapter? Perhaps the end of his "theater phase" and the start of his "screen phase." Would there have been another opera after *Porgy and Bess*, or additional symphonic works?

Such hypotheticals betray a reality that affords a fascinating exploration of how Gershwin's musical legacy – and particularly that of *Rhapsody in Blue* – has been shaped as a result of his early passing. Gershwin's death on July 11, 1937 sent shock waves across the nation, and his memorialization through performances of the *Rhapsody* began almost immediately. Radio responded first, with tributes broadcast coast-to-coast. The evening after Gershwin's death, David Broekman's orchestra along with Bing Crosby and Victor Young appeared on the Mutual Broadcasting System, originating from Los Angeles. Simultaneously, the NBC Blue Network in New York City featured a concert by Paul Whiteman and his Orchestra. The next day the Chicago Philharmonic Orchestra, under the direction of Richard Czerwonky, included *Rhapsody in Blue* in their CBS broadcast from Grant Park, reaching over one hundred stations. They followed their performance of the piece with Siegfried's funeral march from Richard Wagner's *Götterdämmerung*. The audience held its applause, "sealing with silence its appreciation of a composer of popular music whose influence knew no barriers either of musical caste or of national boundary."[2]

Just two days after Gershwin's death, the fate of his *Rhapsody in Blue* was sealed. It became a national anthem, celebrated for its combination of popular and classical traditions. It has since come to stand as a sonic manifestation of the American Dream. From the dramatic rise of its opening clarinet glissando to the constant reinvention of its repeating Ritornello theme as it builds to its final, most elevated iteration six measures from the end of the piece.[3] The "rags-to-riches" trope also neatly maps onto popular biographical conceptions of Gershwin. From an early age, he played in the streets of his immigrant parents' adopted home of New York City. As the story goes, he left behind his rough and tumble ways soon after discovering music. Then it was on to his first job, as a song plugger for Jerome H. Remick's publishing house; his first hit "Swanee"; *Rhapsody in Blue*; a host of musicals and other concert works that led him in the direction of operetta; and finally, *Porgy and Bess* – from Tin Pan Alley to the land of opera in the span of just eleven years.

Like the man himself, *Rhapsody in Blue* has taken on a mythical status in the history of American music. The piece was written quickly while Gershwin's attentions were focused elsewhere. The *Rhapsody* was a side project – a supposedly forgotten commission – that received intermittent attention while he prepared a musical called *Sweet Little Devil* for the Broadway stage. Despite its hasty creation, the *Rhapsody* remains his best-known work for the concert hall. One reason for this popularity remains the inherent flexibility of the piece. Leonard Bernstein famously quipped in the 1950s that the *Rhapsody* "is not a composition at all. It's a string of separate paragraphs stuck together – with a thin paste of flour and water."[4] Although many have taken this observation as a pejorative perspective for which to deride the compositional merit of the piece, for Bernstein – and countless others – its rhapsodic construction remains an important attribute. It has offered opportunities to explore personal, professional, and collective identities through performances of the work over the course of the twentieth century and into the new millennium.

On the surface, this chapter is a reception history of *Rhapsody in Blue* since World War II. But to consider the piece only on such a level – identifying who did what with the piece, where and when – misses the opportunity to ask, as Christopher Small might: "What's really going on here?"[5] When framed merely as a sonic personification of the American Dream, or as a pops-orchestra war-horse that has steadily worked its way toward the more stately subscription series of our world's most celebrated ensembles, the piece is static; it is stagnant. But even erudite critics such as

Anthony Tommasini from the *New York Times* acknowledge that the piece should not be "treated as sacrosanct."[6] The piece lives, it breathes, it evolves. The following exploration of *Rhapsody in Blue* assumes the work to be alive, to be constantly evolving as it adapts and is adapted to the needs of individual musicians, ensembles, and corporations. It does not pretend that the *Rhapsody* only inhabits the concert hall – or even that Gershwin would have wanted it that way, because such standing ultimately undermines its original experimental impulse. Accordingly, through the guise of arrangement studies, this chapter largely focuses on encounters with the *Rhapsody* that exist beyond its familiar symphonic presentation, providing a new set of perspectives on both the piece and those responsible for its legacy.

Rhapsody in Blue on Multiple Fronts

Music and war go hand in hand. One such example is the sonification of the Allied forces "V for Victory" campaign that emerged during World War II. Programmers for BBC radio realized that the Morse code for the letter V – dot, dot, dot, dash – rhythmically aligns with the first four notes of Beethoven's fifth symphony.[7] This simple melody became recognized by civilians throughout Europe as a sonic calling card for the Allies. Albeit in less strategic ways, *Rhapsody in Blue* was also deployed in support of the war effort.

The Music Branch of the United States Special Services Division created the "V-Disc" record label in October 1943, providing an ongoing series of 78 rpm recordings for the entertainment and diversion of troops around the globe. The music released on this label represented, by and large, the only new popular music recordings to emerge between the summer of 1942 and the fall of 1944 while the American Federation of Musicians held a strike against commercial recording companies over a royalty dispute.[8] *Rhapsody in Blue* appears twice in the "V-Disc" catalogue.

The first version of the *Rhapsody* released by the Music Branch's V-Disc series has its roots in Hollywood. In the summer of 1942, Warner Bros. Pictures began work on a biopic about the life of Gershwin, titled appropriately enough, *Rhapsody in Blue*. One ongoing critique of the film is that it misrepresents certain aspects of Gershwin's history, even as it attempted to interpolate real-life celebrities that had figured prominently in his career.[9] Nonetheless, *Variety* observed that "as cinematurgy, designed for escapism and entertainment, no matter the season, *Rhapsody in Blue* can't miss."[10] Bandleader Paul Whiteman – who originally had commissioned and introduced *Rhapsody in Blue* – found himself in Hollywood that summer making a new recording of the piece with pianist Oscar Levant for use in the cinematic restaging of its 1924 premiere.

Although the film *Rhapsody in Blue* exaggerates various elements of Gershwin's life, it manages to capture the spirit of the premiere of the *Rhapsody* – but probably not the look of the first performance. Appearing on a multiterraced stage set, the Whiteman Ensemble is enlarged to forty members from the twenty-two who originally performed the piece. This enlarged ensemble facilitated a transformation of the work, mirroring the shift in audience encounters with the piece. The original jazz ensemble accompaniment had been completely supplanted by a full symphony orchestra by the 1940s. There are two additional trumpets, trombones, and reed players as well as an enlarged string section that integrates violas and cellos – instruments not at all present in Ferde Grofé's original arrangement of the piece. Ray Heindorf, an Academy-Award-winning composer and arranger for Warner Bros. Studios, prepared this particular version. With this expansion of the ensemble came several cuts that brought down the running time of the piece in the film. It was also condensed to allow the recording to fit on two sides of a 12 inch, 78 rpm disc, which was the format upon which it was released by V-Discs.

Placing the piece in this particular filmic environment further re-casts the sonic landscape and narrative destiny of the *Rhapsody*. For example, during the well-known andantino Love theme section, there is no piano present. Rather the expanded ensemble, section by section comes to the sonic and visual foreground – the grandeur is enhanced by the elongated shadows of the musicians cast on the backdrop. As the Love theme repeats, the camera takes the viewer on a bird's-eye trip over the audience, capturing the emotional responses of individuals while Gershwin basks in the glory of the moment from the stage. Given that movie-goers already know the outcome of the film – Gershwin's early death – this out-of-body representation of the performance adds an extra level of emotional import to this pivotal moment in Gershwin's career at a pivotal moment in the history of the *Rhapsody*.

The recording of *Rhapsody in Blue* encountered in this film was released as V-Disc 139 (Series "E") in February 1944, more than a year ahead of the movie's June 1945 New York City premiere and eighteen months before its national release the following September. The primary reason for this delay between filming and release was the studio's increased focus on war-time propaganda, including a short film titled "I Won't Play" released by Warner Bros. in November 1944.[11]

Although not directly about George Gershwin or *Rhapsody in Blue*, "I Won't Play" reveals a great deal about the standing of both as the United States found itself ever more ensconced in World War II. The protagonist is Joe Fingers, a Marine Corps Private with seemingly endless show business connections. Fingers incessantly impresses and entertains with tales of his illustrious associations. He "gave George [Gershwin] a hand with his opus;" helped Frank Sinatra get his start with Tommy Dorsey; played piano with Benny Goodman; and "invented" Hollywood starlet, Kim Karol – the very pinup girl that adorns the wall of the character's barracks. The extravagance of his accounts – including his claim to have written a portion of *Rhapsody in Blue* – raises suspicion among his fellow marines, who unceremoniously declare him an impostor. To make a short story shorter, a fortuitous series of events reveals his genuine relationship with Kim Karol, which is good enough evidence for the boys that Joe Fingers is for real.

Of course, Joe Fingers is no more real than his connection to the *Rhapsody in Blue* – both are the invention of Hollywood screenwriters Laurence Schwab and James Bloodworth, who arrange both Gershwin and the *Rhapsody* on multiple levels. The most apparent type of arrangement occurs though the sonic manipulation of disparate portions of the *Rhapsody* while maintaining its fluidity and familiarity. Each of the three phrases of the piece that Fingers plays on screen in less than a minute comes from a different part of the *Rhapsody*, even incorporating a transpositional key change. At the same time, however, "I Won't Play" arranges Gershwin and his music into the narrative action, relying heavily on the associative value of both. The presence of the *Rhapsody* – often thought of as *the* quintessential piece of American music – provides a sense of familiarity that both the characters on screen and the movie-going audience would have craved in a time of war.

Concurrently, the film arranges perceptions of Gershwin and the creation of *Rhapsody in Blue* – and, in doing so, contributes to the mythology of both. The compositional abilities of Gershwin were questioned long before his death, and here such supposition sustains. The film highlights Mr. Fingers's apparent involvement in the development of the *Rhapsody*. To use a Latin phrase from early Christianity, the film situates him *dextera domini*: Fingers becomes the right hand of the divine spirit known as Gershwin. Of course, a moment's reflection reveals the arrant absurdity of this facet of "I Won't Play": the early twenty-something Marine Corps Private that we see on screen in 1944 would have been a young child when the *Rhapsody* was written and premiered in 1924. This detail may explain the deliberate wink offered by Fingers to the audience in the closing moment of the film.

Although the films "I Won't Play" and *Rhapsody in Blue* introduce arrangements of the *Rhapsody* closer to what audiences had come to expect of the piece – a work for orchestra and piano – the second instance of the

Rhapsody released on V-Disc reminds us that the flexibility of the work remained just as strong with respect to its musical pliability as it did when telling the story of George Gershwin. This second recording, by Elliot Lawrence and his orchestra, appeared in February 1947.[12]

Lawrence provides a spoken introduction prior to the performance – a common feature of the V-Disc series. He concludes his remarks by saying: "We've got an unusual arrangement of the *Rhapsody in Blue*. How about it men? Shall we play?" Following an affirmative group response, the full ensemble launches in with an introductory fanfare motive. Although it does not replicate the famous clarinet glissando, it immediately opens space for the playful arrangement that follows. For example, in the Shuffle theme, the rhythmic underpinnings shift toward what Jelly Roll Morton once called the "Spanish tinge," a habanera feel made even more exotic by upper-register trumpet flourishes. The rhythm is also transformed in the Train theme, where the steady churning of the snare drum is replaced by plodding floor toms.

This "unusual" arrangement was prepared by Nelson Riddle, who had just recently been discharged from the army himself. Riddle would go on to a decorated career in the music industry, particularly through his arrangements for some of the biggest names on Capitol Records: Nat King Cole, Frank Sinatra, and Judy Garland. But this version of *Rhapsody in Blue* represents one of his earlier "for hire" arrangements, prepared during his brief stint in New York as a freelancer during the summer and fall of 1946.[13] Shortly after this recording, Riddle relocated to Los Angeles, having secured employment with Bing Crosby.

By the end of the 1940s, the status of both Gershwin and his *Rhapsody* were secure enough that an increasing number of musicians felt comfortable re-arranging the piece to best suit their individual style and professional goals. Simultaneously, the non-traditional approach taken by arranger Nelson Riddle and band leader Elliot Lawrence might be read as an example of the new confidence of a victorious nation, forwarded by the young men returning to civilian life after war. By shedding expected conventions of the piece and recasting it in a new sonic light, their arrangement signaled the beginning of a long series of *Rhapsody* arrangements following World War II.

Riffing on *Rhapsody in Blue*

As the United States settled into a Cold War reality during the 1950s, with its high patriotism and accompanying economic and domestic stability, the performance status of *Rhapsody in Blue* remained a bit more turbulent. In the two decades previous, the *Rhapsody* had become a "go to" pops selection for ensembles such as the Boston Symphony Orchestra, which performed the piece fifty-four times in the 1930s and thirty-three times in the 1940s, usually with pianist Jesús María Sanromá under the baton of Arthur Fiedler. But soon after the conclusion of the World War II, the work began to fade from the sonic landscape of the nation's orchestras. The Boston Pops only performed the piece three times during the 1950s, each time during its summer residency at Tanglewood. The *Rhapsody* had become a staple of the midsummer season, appearing annually on the New York Philharmonic's all-Gershwin concert at Lewisohn Stadium. But by the 1960s, it appeared that the piece might have run its course even in that venue. The May 1961 installation omitted the *Rhapsody* for the first time in nearly four decades.[14]

And then there is Leonard Bernstein. Perhaps owing to the ubiquity of the *Rhapsody* during his youth in Boston during the 1930s, Bernstein provided a boost in symphonic encounters with the piece on two separate occasions during his career.[15] The first occurred shortly after he took the helm at the New York Philharmonic in 1957. The *Rhapsody* figured prominently both at home and abroad in his "root and branch exploration of American music" during the 1958–59 season.[16] The second occurred during the 1976 American bicentennial. That summer, Bernstein conducted and performed the *Rhapsody* with the New York Philharmonic twenty times leading up to the monumental Fourth of July celebration. But the piece was not heard again from the New York Philharmonic until 1990 and then only four more times until the end of the millennium.

Although concert performances of *Rhapsody in Blue* continued to dot the symphonic landscape of the United States sporadically during the 1950s, it also became a piece that was used for experimentation by musicians of all stripes. John Duffy recorded a version on the Mighty Columbia Square Wurlitzer in 1955, and Hammond organist Wild Bill Davis released a rendition with his trio the following year.[17] Most of these arrangements reduce the piece to under three minutes in duration – a medley of its famous themes. These include recordings by popular orchestra leaders such as Liberace (1956), Ray Coniff (1958), and Lou Busch (1958), as well as solo arrangements for instruments such as the banjo by Eddy Peabody (1958).[18]

Ultimately, jazz musicians played most freely with *Rhapsody in Blue*. From its earliest days, jazz has embraced innovation. That was part of the initial impulse of *Rhapsody in Blue* when commissioned in late 1923 by Paul Whiteman for his "Experiment in Modern Music" Concert. Ferde Grofé, the primary arranger and orchestrator for the Paul Whiteman Orchestra, was responsible for taking Gershwin's two-piano short score and preparing it for the performing powers of the Whiteman ensemble, a role he undertook out of a combination of convention and time constraints. In the process, Grofé installed a good amount of novelty and modern dance band scoring techniques into the original arrangement of the piece. In addition to arranging "inside the strain" – a technique where as much variation as possible was added within a given chorus – Grofé called for uncommon timbres such as a trumpet with a "kazoo mute" and unexpected instrumental pairings such as the baritone and sopranino saxophones. Much of this was smoothed out, however, as Grofé subsequently prepared the piece for its flexible, published stock arrangement and again in its eventual symphonic orchestration – this symphonic orchestration is the one that audiences encountered most often during the 1930s and 1940s, and it remains the one most familiar to audiences today.[19]

Jazz musicians of both traditional and modern styles turned to the *Rhapsody* during the late 1950s and early 1960s. In 1958, boogie-woogie pianist Sammy Price and Cab Calloway trumpeter Doc Cheatham included a duet rendition of the piece on an album of Gershwin music produced in France.[20] Although not released until 1966, a medley of Gershwin tunes recorded by band leader and celebrated drummer Art Blakey in the spring of 1957 (following their *Hard Bop* sessions) located the *Rhapsody* at the outset. Blakey later stated, "we often find crackpots who wrongly say that modern jazz musicians do not know how to play a melody. For that reason, the guys and I got together to put this Gershwin medley on wax."[21] In 1958, Ella Fitzgerald riffed on the Stride theme on her celebrated recording of Irving Berlin's "Blue Skies."[22] And while these jazz encounters with the *Rhapsody* were relatively brief, others took the opportunity to expand the bounds of the piece, including Calvin Jackson.

Despite an extensive career, Jackson remains virtually unknown.[23] He was born in Philadelphia in 1919, and his musical talents were recognized early on; he received a scholarship from the National Association of Negro Musicians before he turned ten years old. The young Jackson studied with Joseph H. Lockett, an African American pianist who performed regularly with the Philadelphia Civic Orchestra and made appearances in New York's Town Hall.[24] Jackson had already built enough of a reputation by the age of twenty that he caught the ear of a young Leonard Feather, who in 1940 wrote that Jackson is "quiet and modest about his ability on piano and organ, but plays anything from Brahms to the blues with a style and technique which more professionals would find hard to beat."[25] In the early 1940s, while studying in the graduate program at the Juilliard School, Jackson served as accompanist for dancer Paul Draper – a performer also well known for his improvisatory abilities.

Jackson relocated to Los Angeles to work for MGM Studios during the mid-1940s. In his work as an assistant music director to George Stroll, he provided orchestrations for films such as *Meet Me in St. Louis* (1944) and *Ziegfeld Follies* (1945). Jackson also composed music for *Anchors Aweigh* (1945) and *Holiday in Mexico* (1946), which featured pianist José Iturbi. Following his time in Hollywood, he toured with his small combo across North and South America, with New York City serving as his home base.

Even in the context of the more progressive and experimental 1950s jazz scene, Jackson knew that any reworking of the reified symphonic *Rhapsody* would be treading on sacred ground. He respected performances by figures such as Bernstein – those symphonic renditions that Jackson referred to as the "longhair interpretation" – but concluded, "if you love jazz and Gershwin as do I, you must have felt as though here was an enormously interesting and vital Huckleberry Finn being stifled in a boiled collar and tails." In other words, Jackson saw the piece as a free spirit that had become bound to the concert stage. Of his 1957 recording of *Jazz Variations on Gershwin's Rhapsody in Blue*, Jackson wrote that "to re-analyze a major work in any light other than that which focuses on the traditionally accepted treatment is to invite ridicule, risk censure, incite the faithful to an examination of hempen cord and strong oak with the avowed intention of stretching the neck of the offender." He concluded, "it was a challenge I could not ignore."[26] Although he blithely entertains the possibility of being lynched for his efforts, the prose is softened by the album cover, which features a blue-velvet portrait of Jackson at the piano.

From the start, it is clear that Jackson's 17 minute arrangement embraces what he identified as the "present-day standards of advanced harmonics and listenability."[27] The initial measures sound like the opening of a late 1950s television variety show, introducing a host that will help us navigate the rest of the sundry program. Here the Ritornello theme of the *Rhapsody* serves that function. For the first five minutes, the listener experiences other familiar melodic gestures such as the Train and Stride themes, adorned with big-band flourishes and shifted placement of accents. Then, with the entrance of the Shuffle theme, the piece enters new territory. In fact, even those familiar with the *Rhapsody* might not recognize Jackson's transformation of this bluesy melody. Just when the arrangement feels as if it has lost its way, Jackson grounds the listener by returning to one of Gershwin's notated piano cadenzas. But this quickly becomes a point of departure for the long, improvised piano solo that emerges just after the halfway-point of the recording. This meditation on the Shuffle and Stride themes begins with a fugue that transitions into a waltz before Jackson gestures sonically toward the inevitable entrance of the Love theme. Albeit orchestrally and rhythmically recast, the final third of the arrangement largely follows that originally recorded by Paul Whiteman in 1924, with an unexpected harmonic alteration at the final cadence. *Billboard* reported: "The first attempt at interpreting 'Rhapsody in Blue' in modern jazz could be more of an *artistic* than a *commercial* success ... Jackson stays within the confines of the original melodic lines while still displaying inventive and highly colorful jazz."[28]

Jackson's interpretation, though little known today, seems to have inspired a chain of jazz explorations of *Rhapsody in Blue*. The most immediate influence was on Billy Strayhorn, one of Jackson's contemporaries and an important Duke Ellington collaborator. In fact, Strayhorn prepared his own version of the *Rhapsody* for the 1963 Ellington album *Will Big Bands Ever Come Back?*[29] Ellington's ensemble had recently taken to riffing on the "classics" through its 1960 reworkings of music from Pyotr Ilyich Tchaikovsky's *The Nutcracker* and Edward Grieg's *Peer Gynt* – both arranged in large-part by Strayhorn.[30] David Schiff notes that "in both instances Ellington was reopening a dialogue that defined the boundaries of jazz history."[31] But in the case of *Rhapsody in Blue*, the dialogue began long before. Although historiography suggests that Ellington maintained a marked distance from the concert works of Gershwin, his ensemble played arrangements of the *Rhapsody* as early as 1925, with an additional version emerging in 1932.[32] The iteration that appears on *Will Big Bands Ever Come Back?* re-envisions the piece through musical choices such as instrumentation and improvisation. Scoring similarities between Jackson and Strayhorn's arrangements also emerge, particularly during the ensemble's presentation of the Love theme. The theme becomes a backdrop for an improvised tenor solo by Paul Gonsalves that weaves intricate and increasingly chromatic figures around the Love theme. It is followed by a clarinet solo by Jimmy Hamilton – an outmoded instrument playing in a 1920s style, running gracefully up and down scales according to the changes. The contrast between the modern tenor and the quaint clarinet reminds the listener of the ways that expectations of jazz had changed in the forty years that separated this *Rhapsody* from the original.

Jackson and Ellington were not the only bandleaders to introduce improvisation into *Rhapsody in Blue* in an effort to conform to modern expectations of jazz. In 1995 jazz pianist Marcus Roberts recorded a thirty-minute arrangement of the *Rhapsody* prepared by frequent Jazz at Lincoln Center arranger Robert Sadin. This re-envisioning of the *Rhapsody* features extended improvised solos not only by Roberts but also by other members of an ensemble consisting of a symphony orchestra and jazz trio. As Roberts conceived it, the goal was to offer a rendering of the *Rhapsody* that Gershwin might have offered had he experienced many of the later trends that form present-day conceptions of jazz. In a similar manner to that recorded by Ellington in 1963 – though on a much broader scale with respect to both instrumentation and duration – it serves as a primer on the history of jazz as envisioned by historicist-minded bandleaders of the 1990s.

The semantic chaining that occurs as a result of the number and variety of jazz-oriented arrangements of *Rhapsody in Blue* continues unabated. For example, the Jackson-Ellington-Roberts trajectory of the piece inspired Bay Area percussionist, ethnomusicologist, and bandleader, Anthony Brown to recompose his own rendition of the *Rhapsody* in 2005 for his Asian American Jazz Orchestra. This version reflects the international scene of his hometown of San Francisco and his status as a child of the 1960s, placing traditional instruments such as the Japanese shakuhachi and the Chinese yangqin alongside the electric guitar and rock percussion. Arrangements such as that by Brown represent the embrace of an increasingly global audience for the piece over the course of the twentieth century and into the present day – one that has been particularly amplified over the past two decades by United Airlines.

Rhapsody in Blue Becomes Safe

As anyone who has flown United in the past quarter-century knows, the company has a long-standing history with *Rhapsody in Blue*. The piece appears in its television advertisements, its airport terminals, and even its pre-flight announcements. The history of the airline's use of the piece, however, is far from straightforward. The company originally selected the piece in 1987 (just three years after its use in the opening ceremony for the 1984 Olympic Games in Los Angeles) because of its associations with the upwardly mobile image of the ascendant Gershwin – perfect imagery for an airline on the rise.[33] However, over the course of time – largely through United's advertising campaigns – the piece has accompanied a range of narratives about life in America, from job interviews and business meetings to childhood fantasies, retirement expeditions, and all manner of personal and professional relationships.[34]

Most recently, the company has made *Rhapsody in Blue* the sonic centerpiece of its "Safety Is Global" campaign.[35] In a world where people pay even less attention to the pre-flight safety announcements than they did before the ubiquity of the smart phone, airlines have turned increasingly to creating engaging and gimmicky videos for their federally regulated safety announcements. Designed to make passengers pay attention, even on repeat viewings, the trend toward humor began in 2013 with Air New Zealand's videos featuring nonagenarian comedian Betty White.

Delta soon thereafter followed suit with a 1980s-themed video featuring numerous cameos from celebrities of that decade.[36]

Under the banner "Safety Is Global," United produced its own such video in 2014, integrating arrangements of the *Rhapsody*'s familiar themes while culturally diverse members of the United flight crew provide instructions from a series of specific and generic international locales.[37] Certainly, the visuals play a key role in signaling our recognition of these surroundings: the Eiffel Tower and street corner café for Paris, a pagoda in front of Mt. Fuji for Japan, casinos and neon signs for Las Vegas, snow-covered peaks and a ski gondola for the Alps, kangaroos for Australia, a Vespa scooter and Mt. Etna for Italy, Chilean flamingos for the bird sanctuary, and palm trees and white-sands for the tropical beach.

But perhaps most important in drawing out the setting of each scene are the dramatic – if not clichéd – musical arrangements of *Rhapsody in Blue*. While in France a pair of accordions play the introductory bars of the piece as a pilot welcomes us aboard and reminds us to heed their instruction. A flight attendant hops a cab to Newark Airport (United's East Coast hub) to the strains of a jazz combo setting of the Love theme. A tenor saxophone improvises lightly around this most famous melody of the *Rhapsody* while the flight attendant provides instruction on how to use the seatbelt from the bumpy backseat. A gong signals a move to Asia, where the ritornello theme of the *Rhapsody* emerges from a plucked zither and bamboo flute. The bright-lights of the Las Vegas strip, which go dark to make passengers aware of location lights during power outages, and a James Bond-inspired depiction of the Swiss Alps, where the use of supplemental oxygen masks are introduced, are accompanied by the traditional symphonic arrangement of the *Rhapsody*. Curious kangaroos learn about life vests as the Ritornello theme is heard on a harmonica punctuated by a didgeridoo and a rain stick. A mandolin plucks out the Shuffle theme while a flight attendant extinguishes a volcano like a birthday candle, indicating that no smoking is allowed. Finally, steel drums transport the viewer to a tropical bird sanctuary just prior to the final beach location and the announcement that the final pre-flight checks will commence. A tenor saxophone plays the Stride theme to a laid-back, quasi-bossa nova groove to help passengers settle in and relax.

While the apparent appeal of this initial safety video has led to annual installments that follow a similar model, the subsequent success of these pre-flight announcements ultimately represents the culmination of a decades-long branding campaign. Yet the ongoing use of the *Rhapsody* surprises even those who have played an important part in the branding process. This group includes composer and arranger Gary Fry, who created the arrangement of *Rhapsody in Blue* (titled *Rhapsody Ambiance*) that has accompanied the neon-tunnel underpass at Chicago's O'Hare International Airport since 1988.[38] As someone with nearly four decades of commercial advertising experience, he notes that it is "very smart, but it is very rare in contemporary American business that they do not just revolve into new advertising campaigns with a totally different feel every few months."[39] When the airline first began to use *Rhapsody in Blue*, this may well have been the plan, but over time, in ways similar to that of musicians such as Paul Whiteman or Duke Ellington, the variable arrangement of the *Rhapsody* has allowed the company to adapt to changing markets and audience expectations. Although advertising executives were probably unaware of it when they first used the piece in 1987, the musical and conceptual adaptability of the piece has made it one of the most successful corporate musical campaigns of all time. In the process, United has transformed the *Rhapsody* from a national symbol of success into an internationally applicable anthem for exploration – one that quite literally encircles the globe, non-stop daily.

The Future of *Rhapsody in Blue*

As *Rhapsody in Blue* travels the world it remains in continuous flux. It appeared in the 2015 comedic film *Trainwreck* and the 2017 relaunch of the popular HBO series *Curb Your Enthusiasm*. Each encounter with the *Rhapsody* over the course of the twentieth century and into the new millennium reveals why and how Gershwin's legacy remains alive – his music is still ripe for interpretation and investigation because much of it was never designed to be heard in a specific way or a specific space. Unless an unexpected major revision of current copyright law appears, *Rhapsody in Blue* is set to enter the public domain in 2020 – ninety-five full years after its initial publication date according to current statutes. And with even fewer restrictions on its use, *Rhapsody* will surely continue to be interpreted in multifarious ways by a wide range of artists. What we have witnessed so far, through the lenses of film, jazz, and corporate branding, is likely just the first chapter in the posthumous reception history of the piece. There is no doubt still much to come in the ongoing life and legacy of *Rhapsody in Blue*.

Notes

1. John O'Hara, "An American in Memoriam," *Newsweek* (July 15, 1940), 34. Quotation on George Gershwin by John O'Hara. Copyright © 1940 by John O'Hara, used by permission of The Wylie Agency LLC.

2. Cecil M. Smith, "Park Concert Pays Tribute to Gershwin," *Chicago Daily Tribune* (July 14, 1937).
3. Throughout this chapter the five central themes of *Rhapsody in Blue* will be referred to using the names originally assigned by David Schiff, *Gershwin: Rhapsody in Blue* (Cambridge: Cambridge University Press, 1997), 13–25. See also, Ryan Raul Bañagale, *Arranging Gershwin*: Rhapsody in Blue *and the Creation of an American Icon* (New York: Oxford University Press, 2014), 8–9.
4. Leonard Bernstein, *The Joy of Music* (New York: Simon & Schuster, 1959), 57.
5. Christopher Small, *Musicking: The Meanings of Performing and Listening* (Middletown, CT: Wesleyan University Press, 1998), 10.
6. Anthony Tommasini, "Review: Lang Lang Opens Carnegie Season with a Gershwin Gimmick," *New York Times* (October 5, 2017).
7. Matthew Guerrieri, *The First Four Notes: Beethoven's Fifth and the Human Imagination* (New York: Knopf, 2012), 211.
8. Kathleen Smith, *God Bless America: Tin Pan Alley Goes to War* (Lexington, KY: University Press of Kentucky, 2003), 41–42.
9. Charlotte Greenspan, "*Rhapsody in Blue*: A Study in Hollywood Hagiography," in Wayne Schneider, ed., *The Gershwin Style: New Looks at the Music of George Gershwin* (New York: Oxford University Press, 1999), 145–59.
10. Don Rayno, *Paul Whiteman: Pioneer in American Music, Volume 2, 1930–1967* (Lanham, MD: Scarecrow Press, 2012), 258.
11. "I Won't Play," Crane Wilbur, dir., Warner Bros. Pictures, 1944. The film received an Academy Award for Best Short Subject in 1945.
12. *Rhapsody in Blue* appeared as the B-side on a disc featuring Andre Kostelanetz and His Orchestra playing "Souvenirs," V-Disc 728 (Series "OO"). Lawrence's recording session took place in late November 1946 at Liederkranz Hall in New York. Richard S. Sears, *V-Discs: A History and Discography* (Westport, CT: Greenwood Press, 1980), 561.
13. Nelson Riddle, *Arranged by Nelson Riddle* (New York: Alfred Music, 1985), 194.
14. "Gershwin Night to Omit The 'Rhapsody in Blue,'" *New York Times* (May 10, 1961).
15. Bañagale, *Arranging Gershwin*, 73–95.
16. Humphry Burton, *Leonard Bernstein* (New York: Doubleday, 1994), 291.
17. John Duffy, *John Duffy at the Mighty Columbia Square Wurlitzer*, Liberty LRP 3004, 1955; Wild Bill Davis, *Evening Concerto*, Epic LN 3308, 1956.
18. Liberace, *Sincerely Yours*, Columbia CL 800, 1956; Ray Coniff, *Concert in Rhythm*, Columbia CS 8022, 1958; Lou Busch, *Lazy Rhapsody*, Capitol Records T1072, 1958; Eddie Peabody, *Favorites by Mr. Banjo, Himself!*, Dot Records DLP-3052, 1958.
19. Bañagale, *Arranging Gershwin*, 14–46.
20. Sammy Price and Doc Cheatham, *Sammy Price and Doc Cheatham Play George Gershwin*, Club Français du Disque, J 142, 1958.
21. Blakey's remarks come from Max Roach/Art Blakey, *Percussion Discussion*, Chess 2ACMJ-405, 1976. The original version to which Blakey refers was recorded in 1957 and released as Art Blakey and the Jazz Messengers, *Tough!*, Cadet Records 4049, 1966.
22. Ella Fitzgerald, *Ella Fitzgerald Sings the Irving Berlin Songbook*, Verve 830-2, 1958.
23. Todd Decker, *Music Makes Me: Fred Astaire and Jazz* (Berkeley: University of California Press, 2011), 149–54.
24. Kenan Heise, "Organist, choir director Joseph H. Lockett Jr., 85," *Chicago Tribune* (October 28, 1993).
25. Leonard Feather, *Chicago Downbeat* (May 15, 1940). Cf. Decker, *Music Makes Me*, 149.
26. Calvin Jackson, *Jazz Variations on Gershwin's Rhapsody in Blue*, LRP-3071, 1957.
27. Ibid.
28. *Billboard* (November 18, 1957), 30. Emphasis added.
29. Duke Ellington, *Will Big Bands Ever Come Back?* Reprise 6168, 1963.
30. Duke Ellington and his Orchestra, *The Nutcracker Suite*, Columba CL 1641, 1960; Duke Ellington and his Orchestra, *Selections from Peer Gynt Suites Nos. 1 & 2 and Suite Thursday*, Columbia CL 1598, 1960.
31. David Schiff, *The Ellington Century* (Berkeley: University of California Press, 2012), 246.
32. Bañagale, *Arranging Gershwin*, 96–118.
33. Ibid., 6–7.
34. Ibid., 158–73.

35. An earlier version of this section of the chapter appeared on Oxford University Press's OUPblog. Ryan Raul Bañagale, "United Airlines and *Rhapsody in Blue*," posted August 28, 2014, https://blog.oup.com/2014/08/united-airlines-gershwin-rhapsody-blue.
36. Air New Zealand, "Betty White – Safety Old School Style," YouTube video, 4:12, posted October 9, 2013, www.youtube.com/watch?v=O-5gjkh4r3g; Global Airline Safety Videos, "Delta Safety Video," YouTube video, 5:21, posted May 1, 2014, www.youtube.com/watch?v=eTkSYWVk0GE.
37. Canal Plus Productions, "Safety Is Global – United Inflight Safety Video," YouTube video, 4:34, posted July 31, 2014, www.youtube.com/watch?v=dXsUrFJ3n6E.
38. Bañagale, *Arranging Gershwin*, 168–73.
39. Ibid., 172–73.

15 Broadway's "New" Gershwin Musicals: Romance, Jazz, and the Ghost of Fred Astaire

TODD DECKER

Beginning in the mid-1980s, musicals with Gershwin scores returned to Broadway for the first time in half a century. Four "new" Gershwin musicals – widely distributed across almost a quarter century with none created or produced by the same individuals or organizations – put Gershwin songs (and sometimes his concert music) into brand new or greatly revised narratives. These shows effectively sidestepped the prohibitive commercial challenge of reviving Gershwin's musical comedies and operettas of the 1920s and 1930s in their original form. No other songwriter of Gershwin's era has enjoyed a similar pattern of book-show reinvention on the late twentieth- and early twenty-first-century Broadway stage.[1]

The "new" Gershwin musical begins with *My One and Only* (1983, 767 performances), a tap dance-laden show set in the 1920s starring Tommy Tune (who directed and choreographed with Thommie Walsh) and Twiggy. Inclusion of African American tapper Charles "Honi" Coles in the cast lent the production a living connection to show business history, and racially defined casting in the dancing chorus (black men; white women) put *My One and Only* in constant dialogue with issues of race and music and dance style in a manner unlike any of the subsequent "new" Gershwin musicals.

A defining hit of the 1990s, *Crazy for You* (1992, 1,622 performances) riffed on the 1930 Gershwin show *Girl Crazy* (as well as the 1943 MGM movie version) in a celebration of show business as a performer's craft marked by hard work and endless energy. *Crazy for You* was broad and comic, with full-out physical commitment in the book scenes (directed by Mike Ockrent) and several lengthy and memorable production numbers (by choreographer Susan Stroman).

The 2012 musical *Nice Work If You Can Get It* (478 performances), a modest book musical, relied on star performers Matthew Broderick and Kelli O'Hara and evoked the Jazz Age musical comedy of Gershwin's era quite closely. Broderick's star power fueled the success of the show: he played the production's entire thirteen-month run. Joe DiPietro's book effectively recreated the milieu and mood of Gershwin's 1920s musical comedies such as *Oh, Kay!* and *Lady, Be Good!*, if with a more frankly sexual tone.

Taking a different tack from the above three decidedly comic shows, *An American in Paris* (2015, 623 performances) opted for a serious approach to both story and dance. This very free adaptation of the 1951 MGM musical film starring Gene Kelly – which itself repurposed existing Gershwin songs and concert music for an original narrative – brought ballet to the fore. Developed at Paris's Théâtre du Châtelet, with classically trained leads and chorus and choreography and direction by ballet choreographer Christopher Wheeldon, *An American in Paris* included in its romance plot a French family grappling with the legacy of the Nazi occupation, yielding an aesthetically and thematically serious "new" Gershwin musical.

This chapter explores themes and approaches that run across these four disparate Broadway shows: each reliant on the power of the Gershwin name and the resilient charm of his songs; each a hit in its season.[2] All four borrow songs from Gershwin's film musicals as well as his Broadway scores. As a result, the ghost of Fred Astaire – for whom Gershwin wrote two films: *Shall We Dance* and *A Damsel in Distress* (both 1937) – and the romantic film musical as a genre hovers over each show to a greater or lesser extent. *My One and Only*, *Crazy for You*, and *Nice Work* draw explicit connections to Astaire's film dances. *An American in Paris* does so with lesser resonance, given that Kelly appeared in and co-directed the film. Still, it evokes Astaire repeatedly by way of song choices. All four shows attach Gershwin songs to sharply drawn period settings – 1920s (*My One and Only*, *Nice Work*), 1930s (*Crazy for You*), 1940s (*An American in Paris*) – and old-fashioned notions of love-at-first-sight romance. The dramaturgical method of each, however, is decidedly if differently contemporary, using musical and theatrical techniques to create a continuity of musical and dramatic action. In this, Gershwin's old-style theater songs are refreshed by later Broadway storytelling techniques. Three of the four also weave Gershwin's concert music into their scores, rewarding theatergoers with broader knowledge of the composer's output.

An American in Paris begins with the sound of a Victrola playing, in the words of Craig Lucas's book, "a recognizable Gershwin tune." Which Gershwin tunes qualify? The song choices in each of the four "new" Gershwin musicals offer one answer to this question. Most of the songs in the "new" shows come from Gershwin's catalog of song "hits" – tunes written to be marketed as sheet music in addition to being part of a given show or film score. None of the "new" shows dive very deeply into the obscure reaches of Gershwin's output, although *Crazy for You* and *Nice Work* draw selectively on cut or unused numbers. One song – "'S Wonderful" from the 1927 show

Funny Face – is heard in three of the four. Eleven tunes show up in two "new" shows: five of these come from Gershwin's Hollywood films and a further three, plus "'S Wonderful," while originating on Broadway were also interpolated into well-known MGM musicals.[3] Indeed, the "new" Gershwin shows all draw substantially from Gershwin's small corpus of film songs: one-third of the tunes in *Crazy for You* and *An American in Paris* and just under one-third in *Nice Work* originated on the screen. Only two of the sixteen songs in *My One and Only* come from Hollywood, but the show's inclusion of "Funny Face" (associated with the 1957 Astaire film of the same name) and "High Hat" (a number from the show *Funny Face* staged in *My One and Only* in a manner that directly evokes several Astaire film routines) heightens that show's links to Astaire. *An American in Paris* includes three tunes from the eponymous film (two associated with Kelly) and three introduced on the screen by Astaire, bringing the latter dancing star strongly into the putative stage version of the former's magnum opus. Taking the four "new" shows together, every song in *Shall We Dance* and all but one in *A Damsel in Distress* has been staged in a Broadway musical. In short, the "new" Gershwin musicals collectively tilt toward the screen legacy and strong audience memory of Fred Astaire: his spirit hovers over the "new" Gershwin musical. Astaire's films and star persona – something the makers of these shows and some in the audience carry with them into the theater – resonates across these shows along two tracks: the thrill of romance and the power of jazz. The latter, inevitably, raises issues of race. Before exploring how Astaire's screen musicals inform the romantic and rhythmic content of the "new" Gershwin musicals, the form of these shows' scores – built, as they are, on songs – is considered.[4]

Songs into Scores

The "new" Gershwin shows adopt several common dramaturgical and musical techniques to turn the old-fashioned materials offered by Gershwin's thirty-two-bar tunes into larger structures and forms that will satisfy later generations of Broadway audiences for whom the memory of the Jazz Age dramaturgy of this music is entirely unknown. The overarching formal strategy of the "new" Gershwin shows is continuity, identifiable in the domains of staging and storytelling, musical arranging, and clever integration of familiar and unfamiliar song lyrics in new dramatic contexts.

Gershwin's 1920s musicals employed limited changes of scenery, usually just one set per act. The "new" Gershwin musicals utilize a more flexible approach, refreshing the eye with constant changes of scene. *My One and Only* begins in what Peter Stone and Timothy S. Mayer's script calls "Limbo," an abstract blue space. During the opening number, a storm (made with projections) cues the appearance of umbrellas in the hands of the dancers, then a railroad station "forms around" the already singing and dancing cast. Easy and visible movement between stylized locales characterizes the entire production. The opening scenes of *Crazy for You* transition freely from onstage to backstage to the street in front of the fictitious Zangler Theatre, which has the characteristic curved façade of the Ziegfeld Theatre on 54th Street (demolished 1966). This approach to setting continues after the story moves to Deadwood, Nevada where, over the course of a song and dance, "evening falls." *Nice Work*, closest to Jazz Age practices in story and dialogue, moves flexibly from room to room, inside and outside a Long Island mansion. In this case, the many changes of scene are accompanied by musical interludes drawing on Gershwin's concert music (some are included on the cast recording). *An American in Paris* took flexibility of locale to an extreme. At the start of the show, the main character, Jerry Mulligan (an American GI turned artist), "looks at the city, begins to sketch, and as HE does, we see it come to life." The entire production used dynamic, colorful projections, often against moving set pieces, to suggest an artist at work on an artistic representation of Paris. In all four shows, contemporary sets and lighting concepts insured that the period setting and songs moved with an up-to-date sophistication.

Continuity in the musical domain engendered surprising juxtapositions of well-known tunes and rewarded theater-goers familiar with the Gershwin song catalog. In a profligate use of great tunes, *Crazy for You* transitions directly from "Could You Use Me?" to "Shall We Dance" in Act I, when Bobby and Polly fall in love, and from "They Can't Take That Away from Me" to "But Not for Me" in Act II when they part. A similar pairing occurs in *My One and Only*, when a chorus of "Funny Face" erupts joyfully in the middle of Billy and Edith's long romantic routine to "He Loves and She Loves." Select cutting and pasting on a smaller scale melds two numbers into one: the chorus girls in *Crazy for You* stride in silhouette into Deadwood to the jazzy strains of "I'll Build a Stairway to Paradise," but when the lights come up they sing the verse of "Bronco Busters" from *Girl Crazy*. (The cowboys on the scene in *Crazy for You* did not, however, sing the chorus, which carries ironic and reflexive lyrics that would have pulled the "new" show out of its more firmly Western locale. The cowboys in *Crazy for You* are – as befits a much later musical comedy – more like real cowboys than the chorus "boys" in *Girl Crazy* ever were.) *Nice Work* gives its star-featured role, the militant Prohibitionist Duchess Estonia Dulworth, an appropriately grand instrumental entrance: the opening measures of Gershwin's Concerto in F herald the obscure song "Demon Rum."

Three "new" Gershwin musicals include mashups that put unrelated tunes into direct relationship. This happens early on in *My One and Only*: Edith sings "Boy Wanted," Billy sings "Soon," then both sing their respective songs together in an arrangement that favors the latter but that sounds convincingly contrapuntal, evoking duets by Irving Berlin such as "Just in Love" and "I Love a Piano." *Nice Work* deploys a mashup of "By Strauss" and "Sweet and Low-Down," pitting the haughty, high soprano Duchess against Cookie, a bootlegger disguised as a butler. He answers her coloratura with tap breaks. The number captures in a new form the enduring Gershwin theme of highbrow versus lowbrow. With a more psychological bent, the complexities of *An American in Paris*'s five-person love story are expressed musically in a four-song mashup. Determined to forget their romantic disappointments, Milo and Henri sing "Who Cares?" followed by a chorus of "For You, For Me, Forevermore" passed among the principals arrayed in isolation from each other. The intensity of the moment builds on a quick transition into the ballad "But Not for Me," begun by Adam, with Milo contributing bits of "Shall We Dance" (a reprise from Act I) in counterpoint. At the midpoint of "But Not for Me," Adam and Milo exchange roles: she takes up "But Not for Me" and Adam sings fragments of "Who Cares?" – the song that started the number. For knowledgeable listeners, this sequence packs four Gershwin tunes into a tight, overlapping space – matching in the musical domain the setting, which the script describes as combining "Three Locations at Once." Arranger Rob Fisher builds a sophisticated musical theater dramaturgy – a quasi-operatic ensemble – with melodic materials Gershwin never intended to go together.

Constructing an *ex post facto* continuity between a "new" musical's plot and characters and the Gershwins' catalog proves an important strategy, at times served by resurrecting very obscure selections. The tune "What Causes That?," cut in tryouts from the 1928 flop *Treasure Girl*, perfectly serves as a duet for two men at a key juncture in *Crazy for You*. In context, it sounds purpose-composed for the "new" show, but it is, instead, evidence of a deep dive into the Gershwin trunk. Three similarly obscure works serve important structural purposes as Act II openers: "In the Swim" (from *Funny Face*) for a novelty dance in *My One and Only*; "The Real American Folk Song is a Rag" (a song for the show *Ladies First* and Ira Gershwin's first Broadway lyric dating to 1918) sung to entertain English visitors to Deadwood in *Crazy for You*; and the posthumous instrumental "For Lily Pons" as accompaniment for an artsy ballet in *An American in Paris*.

But familiar Gershwin tunes are also candidates for such integrated use, whether by fitting a known lyric to a new situation or by simple substitution of words, just as Ira sometimes did in the 1920s. "Let's Call the Whole Thing Off," a combative duet from *Shall We Dance*, is expanded into an unlikely trio in *Nice Work*. Jimmy and Billie, pretending to be newlyweds on their wedding night, feign linguistic disagreement to keep Police Chief Berry off Billie's trail (she's a bootlegger). Eventually, Berry gets involved in the dispute and sings a few lines himself. (Underscoring in the scene draws on the instrumental "Walking the Dog," also from *Shall We Dance*.) Small changes to key words integrate songs in *My One and Only* (a "race" rather than a "war to be won" in "Strike Up the Band") and *Crazy for You* (come to "Polly" rather than "papa" in "Embraceable You"). On her wedding day in *Nice Work*, Eileen's fantastic self-regard – as big as her endless bridal veil is long – gets lyrical expression when she sings "I've Got a Crush on You" to her groom as "you've got a crush on me." The most substantial such integration came about by chance: the French heroine's name in the film *An American in Paris* is Lise; the stage version uses the song "Liza (All the Clouds'll Roll Away)" to recast Lise as an imagined American when in company with Jerry. The racial implications of this fortuitous similarity are discussed below.

But integration is not, in the end, what the "new" Gershwin musicals sell, and there are plenty of moments when a Gershwin tune is simply sung for the audience's pleasure. Ballads, sung by the heroine, come in for straightforward treatment similar to their original Broadway uses. See, for example, "Nice Work If You Can Get It" (*My One and Only*) and "But Not for Me" (*Nice Work*), identically placed just after a rousing Act II opening dance number. "Someone to Watch Over Me" serves two shows in the same way: midway through Act I, the heroines of *Crazy for You* and *Nice Work*, Polly and Billie, alike pause to opine about the love they are looking for, in the process revealing the romantic heart concealed behind their respective "denim and rawhide" and "toughest bootlegger in the business" exteriors.

Romance in the Manner of Astaire

Like most 1920s musical comedies, the "new" Gershwin musicals end with a stage full of couples. *Crazy for You* and *Nice Work* sort their casts into four pairs; *An American in Paris* resolves into three (counting Adam: alone at the close, he tells the audience he "got the girl" by "[putting] her in the music where she belongs, for me at least."). *My One and Only* ends with the show's two dancing choruses – black men, white women – pairing off as couples after a lengthy dance to "Kickin' the Clouds Away" (with two more men than women, the last couple to pair off is two black men, a moment taken in good fun).

All four "new" Gershwin musicals invest in the notion of love at first sight – often music marks the crucial moment. Billy and Edith react identically to their first sights of each other: each sings "Blah, Blah, Blah" as all other stage action freezes with the lovers spotlighted. *Crazy for You* adopts a similar strategy: Bobby takes one look at Polly and starts to sing "Things are Looking Up" while "in a cloud of adoration." Bobby completes the AABA tune to end the scene, with stretches of dialogue between each phrase. Given the convoluted plot of *Crazy for You*, Polly has no similar moment, but near the end of the show her father takes one look at Bobby's mother and launches into "Things Are Looking Up," demonstrating the comic economy of the love-at-first-sight-to-a-Gershwin-tune trope. With its dance-driven dramaturgy, *An American in Paris* uses an expansive opening ballet set to the Concerto in F to show Lise and Jerry's string of brief encounters on the streets of Paris: he pursues; she retreats.

Given the inevitability of Broderick/Jimmy and O'Hara/Billie's star pairing, *Nice Work* holds off on love at first sight. In their first scene together, she lobs sarcastic replies at his always slightly naïve come-ons.

JIMMY: Oh no, you're falling in love with me, aren't you?
BILLIE: Oh yeah, I never knew it could be this good.
JIMMY: Oh, please don't fall in love with me –
BILLIE: Hey, love is for suckers.

The pair's first dance duet follows: Jimmy, close to drop dead drunk, sings "Nice Work If You Can Get It," then pulls her into a dance. Billie says, "Hey, I don't know nothin' about no dancin'," Jimmy replies, "Me neither – then just follow along." In the dance, Jimmy "keeps nearly toppling over, forcing BILLIE to come to his rescue, which eventually has the effect of sweeping her into the loose-limbed, carefree dance." Executed by a comic male star and a singing female star, the dance points in a humorous way toward the drunk dance from Astaire's 1941 film *Holiday Inn*. The drunk Astaire, with Marjorie Reynolds as a more solicitous partner than Billie in *Nice Work*, combines comedy with dance and concludes the routine flat on his face on the floor, as does Jimmy. The motif of Broderick and O'Hara re-enacting moments from Astaire's films in their less accomplished, more relatable (to the audience) skills is established. (Broderick, attired à la Astaire in top hat, white tie and tails, even tosses his hat into the air at one point: failing to catch it, he kicks it instead.)

But the pleasure of *Nice Work*, as in any Astaire and Rogers film, comes from knowing that despite her protestations, the woman in the story *is* a sucker for love. In the next scene, Billie even lets Jimmy kiss her, merely as a demonstration, and a familiar bit of Gershwin scores the moment. Billie calls kissing "Five seconds of nothin'." The five seconds of *Rhapsody in Blue* that burst forth from the orchestra pit when Jimmy kisses Billie suggest otherwise; as does a second kiss, similarly accompanied, initiated by Billie. By this point, the script reads, "There is electricity between them."

My One and Only, Crazy for You, and *Nice Work* all feature lengthy romantic partner dances for their respective principal couples about half way through Act I. In *My One and Only*, the dance begins in response to Billy and Edith's first kiss, led up to by a vocal version of "He Loves and She Loves," the tune that accompanies the dance, which, as with most Astaire–Rogers routines, also includes tap. (Michael Gibson's orchestration incorporates the two-piano sound of Arden and Ohman, central to Gershwin's 1920s shows.) The routine ends with the couple in silhouette, posed inside the full moon which hangs over the entire number. A full moon also attends Polly and Bobby's long dance to the tune "Shall We Dance." With no tap, Stroman's choreography does not evoke as directly Astaire and Rogers's style. Still, Polly and Bobby finish *Crazy for You* with her in a flowing white gown and him in a tux, posed in a manner that evokes Astaire and Rogers (even as the surrounding chorus girls in elaborate costumes recreate Broadway revues such as the *Ziegfeld Follies*, another persistent point of reference in the show).

Nice Work proves the most invested in recreating Astaire and Rogers. In their lengthy dance to "'S Wonderful," Broderick and O'Hara reenact several combinations taken directly from the screen. Dancing in the living room of a mansion, they bound over and on the sofa and step in closed partner position up and over a square table and two chairs, exactly as Astaire and Rogers do twice in their celebratory dance at the close of *The Gay Divorcee* (1934). "'S Wonderful" also includes the pair sliding down the curving bannister and taking up the tango. This ambitious dance number for two putative non-dancers works to tremendous effect: Broderick and O'Hara are at once cautious and committed. With O'Hara in pants – as Rogers often was for partner dances – and frequently matching each other move for move and stunt for stunt, the pair performs romantic love as an equal partnership. The exuberant charm of the Gershwins' slangy song, with its many made-up words as well as the gushing line "you've made my life so glamorous," supports these silly, regular folks – also Broadway stars, of course – who dance and dance, as the script says, "buoyantly and joyfully – two people in love."

Jazz (and Race in Casting)

The principal lovers in *An American in Paris* follow a tortured path toward dancing together. Lise (tacitly given to Henri, whose family hid her during the war) and Jerry initially agree to meet daily near the Seine river as strictly friends: "In America," Jerry explains, men and women "do it all the time." But given Jerry's dogged pursuit of Lise to this point, the romantic subtext to their time together – and their first dance together – is clear. Jerry re-christens Lise as Liza, a strategy designed to help her escape "that sad girl" and become "that brash happy crazy girl no one but us knows about." The fortuitous proximity of the name Lise (taken from the film) to Liza (among Gershwin's only tunes titled with a first name) opened the way for *An American in Paris* to use the rarely heard "Liza (All the Clouds'll Roll Away)" as the key song for these stage lovers. Indeed, at the close of the show, when Lise chooses Jerry over Henri, the pair dances a short final partner routine to seal their love to a reprise of "Liza." This ending, a romantic victory dance of sorts, echoes several Astaire films.[5]

The use of "Liza" (from the 1929 show *Show Girl*) raises the question of how race inheres in the Gershwins' songs and their reuse. According to George, "Liza" was composed at the request of Florenz Ziegfeld, producer of *Show Girl*, who wanted "a minstrel number in the second act with one hundred beautiful girls seated on steps that cover the entire stage."[6] The sophisticated tune Gershwin delivered – its chromatic rising bass line quickly making it a favorite of jazz improvisers – was conceived for a racially defined routine deeply familiar to its original audience. Ira's lyric includes black dialect and implies a black voice. Evocations of nature, such as "moonlight shinin' on the river," locate the song in the American South as imagined in popular music from the late nineteenth century. The insistently named love object carried black connotations linked to the character Eliza in *Uncle Tom's Cabin*, and phrases like "I get lonesome, honey" would have been heard in 1929 as old-fashioned, ragtime sentiments (echoing use of the endearment *honey* in songs like "Alexander's Ragtime Band" [1915] and "Hello! Ma Baby" [1899]). Ruby Keeler introduced the song in *Show Girl*, and her then husband Al Jolson rose from his seat in the audience to sing it with her at more than a few performances. Jolson's association with blackface performance also shaped the legacy of "Liza." As used in *An American in Paris*, "Liza" is stripped of all these associations. The river in question becomes the Seine and the overdetermined racial elements of the lyric sound, in Jerry's mouth, as simply the way (white) Americans talk. The absorption of black culture as filtered through mass popular culture into whiteness – a process also performed by the Gershwins' musical comedies in the latter 1920s – is here re-enacted in a twenty-first-century context, where few in the audience likely have any awareness of the racial borrowing going on.

The complete elision of blackness as an element that informs the Gershwins' Broadway output carries across *An American in Paris*, including in the show's two rhythm tune production numbers expressing the exuberance of the American spirit: "I Got Rhythm" and "Fidgety Feet." The reawakening of jazz in the city shortly after the end of the Nazi occupation proves a theme in both numbers, as described in the script: in the former, the dance involves "PEOPLE exploding with pent-up energy – drunk, sexualized, perhaps some physical violence;" in the latter, "JERRY's impulsive rhythms and movements begin to infect OTHER GUESTS," engulfing and ending the pretentious ballet being performed. The narrative context for "I'll Build a Stairway to Paradise" – an elaborate Act II production number and the show's most explicit example of Broadway brashness – explicitly raises the specter of jazz. The number represents Henri's imagined debut at Radio City Music Hall in New York City. Adam, his war-wounded leg restored, joins Henri and both lead the chorus in a tap dance that includes the names of specific tap steps, such as the eagle rock (originally an African American dance move). Framing this fantasy is Henri's actual, less extravagant performance in a Montmartre cabaret where the master of ceremonies, the "VOODOO LADY," sings the Gershwins' "Clap Yo' Hands" (another of Ira's black dialect lyrics) with her trio. Henri's staid parents, members of the Resistance during the war, show up at the cabaret unexpectedly, and their son's performance breaks open the family's agreement "to *say* we dislike jazz while under [Nazi] Occupation." To Henri's surprise, his parents encourage his pursuit of the stage. Jazz is freedom and release in *An American in Paris*: using Gershwin tunes, both familiar and unexpected, the show presents the category of jazz as the expressive property of white Americans and as irresistible to the French returning to life after what Jerry calls "that whole filthy war."

An American in Paris included no visibly non-white performers in its opening night cast, a conventional choice for a period show that deals in serious terms with the past. *Crazy for You* and *Nice Work*, alike shows with no intentions beyond entertainment, both incorporated performers of color in a context where their blackness had no dramatic resonance within the show but offered an image of inclusiveness to the audience watching in the theater.[7] *Nice Work*'s featured roles even included cross-racial casting: the experienced African American actor Stanley Wayne Mathis as Chief Berry of the Long Island police, a comic character who sings a trio with the white romantic leads and is paired off at show's close with Eileen (played by white actress Jennifer

Laura Thompson). Indeed, when Eileen kisses Chief Berry, "*Rhapsody in Blue* plays" – and everyone knows what that means.

Only *My One and Only*, hailing from the early 1980s, attempts to explicitly stage the racial context for Gershwin's (and Astaire's) jazz-inflected Broadway and Hollywood music. The show's interracial cast allows for the white act of slumming to be represented as a crossing of the color line. Segregation in American life and culture, as well as the white urge to emulate black culture, is put on the Broadway stage to the music of Gershwin. The show opens in "Limbo" with jazzy vocal stylings by the young, black New Rhythm Boys. A vocal counterpart to this snazzy group is provided by periodic comic crossovers by the Ritz Quartette, four old rich white men described in a line as "from downtown – <u>way</u> downtown. When our beloved President says 'The business of America is <u>business</u>,' it is these very men who are <u>giving</u> America the business." The white female dancing chorus plays various objectified female types: fanciful nightclub dancers dolled up as suggestive Latin American products (sugar, a bunch of bananas, a cigar); aquacade swimmers dressed as fish; veiled harem girls in Morocco. The leading lovers – Tune and Twiggy – are Texan and British respectively but the central supporting roles of Deacon Montgomery (he runs a mission by day, a nightclub by night) and Mr. Magix are black. The Deacon enters seeking to lure Billy to his uptown club (understood to be in Harlem). Billy asks for help escaping his "hick" appearance and manner, so the Deacon sends him to Mr. Magix's Emporial, a barber shop (also in Harlem) where Charles "Honi" Coles as Magix dispenses comic romantic advice.

Billy visits Magix once in each act. In the second act, Coles and Tune dance a shared tap routine, with Coles as teacher. Coles was a tap legend. His career reached back to Harlem's Cotton Club in 1940. For many years part of a double act with Charles "Cholly" Atkins, Coles frequently played the Apollo Theatre and was among the first black dancers on network television. As a solo performer, Coles influenced the growth of tap on the concert stage in the 1970s, especially as spearheaded by the white dancer Brenda Buffalino. As described by tap historian Constance Valis Hill, "Coles had a polished style that melded high-speed tapping with an elegant yet close-to-the-floor style where the legs and feet did the work; his specialty was precision."[8] Coles's only previous Broadway credits were a featured number with Atkins in *Gentlemen Prefer Blondes* (1949) and as a replacement lead in the retrospective black musical theater show *Bubbling Brown Sugar* (1976). *My One and Only* made Coles – after decades in show biz – a Broadway star. He won the Tony Award for Best Featured Actor in a Musical in a role that put a black man in the position of instructing a white star – and an unusual one at that: Magix comments when Tune walks in, "we don't get too many 6-foot-6 white tap dancers in here." Coles's dance was credited to him as special material in the program. The original and enduring ownership of Coles's brand of "class" tap as black was reinforced again and again. In a role created to feature a performer with an aura of the legendary about him, Coles, at age seventy-two, played Magix for *My One and Only*'s entire twenty-two month run.

Coles does not dance in the Act I Magix scene. Instead, he leads Tune's hick character toward a new, more sophisticated persona that directly evokes Astaire and, by analogy with Tune's homage to the white film star, represents Astaire's debt to black male tap dancers. The song "High Hat," introduced by Astaire with white male chorus in the show *Funny Face*, features Tune with the black men of *My One and Only*. Tune and Walsh's staging of "High Hat" recalls Astaire's film number "Top Hat, White Tie, and Tails" (*Top Hat*, 1935). Indeed, Astaire's "Top Hat" routine is a screen version of his earlier stage routine to "High Hat." Thus, Tune recycles the concept one more time and returns it to the stage – this time with an explicit racial dimension. Most of Tune's "High Hat" is done in unison: white star, black chorus moving together. Astaire's often aggressive interaction with the men dancing in lines behind him – he shoots them down one by one in "Top Hat" – is omitted. Nodding toward Astaire's many special effects dances, "High Hat" includes a section using black light, during which only the dancers' white gloves, ties, canes, and spats are visible – rendering racial difference briefly invisible. In a Broadway trope that practically demands applause, Tune and the black male chorus close the number with a kick line (something Astaire never did and likely never thought of doing). The entire number can be read as a racial coming together among the men in the cast, much as the interracial couples in the finale dance to "Kickin' the Clouds Away" described above.

Still, the racial politics of *My One and Only* are naïve at best. The plot and musical numbers reproduce in the happiest of tones the Jazz Age reality of African American musicians teaching and modeling new music, dance, and style for white performers who, rather quickly, absorb black style into a new, updated brand of whiteness. The inclusion of a black "legend" (Coles) and the racially sorted cast telling a tale of slumming represents the color line of the period but not in a critical spirit. Indeed, *My One and Only* concludes with a big patriotic production number, including the old white men of the Ritz Quartette parading with American flags. This show – like all Gershwin's musical comedies, whether from the 1920s or "new" – is a feel-good song-and-dance extravaganza.

Brief mention of Gershwin in the black-cast 2016 musical *Shuffle Along, or the Making of the Musical Sensation of 1921 and All That Followed* calls out white musicians – specifically Gershwin – for stealing from African Americans in the 1920s. The brief, dismissive number '"Till Georgie Took 'Em Away" explicitly accuses Gershwin of taking the melody for "I Got Rhythm" from William Grant Still, a well-known African American composer, who played in the pit for the original *Shuffle Along* (1921). As described in George C. Wolfe's script, "Lights reveal STILL, dancing as he plays a jazz solo on his clarinet, the dancing/music pulses with theatricality, vibrancy and rage." The angry number twists Gershwin's familiar tune (which was apparently not licensed by the production) and turns Ira's lyrics into a description of racial theft: "STEAL THOSE BLACK NOTES! / STEAL THAT RHYTHM! / WRITE A HIT SONG! / WHO COULD ASK FOR ANYTHING – "[9] Blackout.

But for Broadway's strongly and enduringly white audience, the "new" Gershwin musicals do not offer the historical critique of *Shuffle Along . . . and All That Followed*. Instead, Gershwin is tied to glamorous romance, often evoking screen memories, jazzy rhythms and bluesy tunes freed of racial conflict, an optimistic realm where kisses spark a song in the heart and infectious, fascinating rhythms are a welcome guest. In typical fashion for all Gershwin musicals, *Crazy for You* forecloses any deeper matters with a familiar line: Polly asks, "You wanta dance, Bobby?" and he replies, "Who could ask for anything more?"

Notes

1. *Irving Berlin's White Christmas* played seasonal Broadway engagements in 2008 and 2009, launching annual seasonal national tours of the show. *Holiday Inn: The New Irving Berlin Musical* had a short run in 2016. A stage version of Jerome Kern's *Swing Time* (1936) titled *Never Gonna Dance* closed after eighty-four performances in 2003.
2. This chapter draws on the Broadway scripts and videotapes of the original Broadway casts in performance (all in the collection of the New York Public Library for the Performing Arts) and the original cast recordings.
3. Songs in two "new" shows are: from Broadway – "I'll Build a Stairway to Paradise" (*George White's Scandals of 1922*), "Sweet and Low-Down" (*Tip-Toes*), "Someone to Watch Over Me" (*Oh, Kay!*), "I Got Rhythm" and "But Not for Me" (*Girl Crazy*), "Who Cares?" (*Of Thee I Sing*); from Hollywood – "Blah, Blah, Blah" (*Delicious*), "Shall We Dance" and "They Can't Take That Away from Me" (*Shall We Dance*), "I Can't Be Bothered Now" and "Nice Work If You Can Get It" (*A Damsel in Distress*).
4. *An American in Paris* builds substantial dances, each with significant narrative content, on the Concerto in F, the *Second Rhapsody* combined with the *Cuban Overture*, *An American in Paris*, and the second of the Three Preludes for piano.
5. *The Gay Divorcee*, *Top Hat* (1935), *You Were Never Lovelier* (1942), and *Daddy Long Legs* (1955) end with similar moments.
6. Cf. *The Complete Lyrics of Ira Gershwin*, ed. Robert Kimball (New York: Alfred A. Knopf, 1993), 143.
7. Todd Decker, "The Multiracial Musical Metropolis: Casting and Race after *A Chorus Line*," in Jessica Sternfeld and Elizabeth Wollman (eds.), *The Routledge Companion to the Contemporary American Stage Musical* (New York: Routledge, 2019).

8. Constance Valis Hill, *Tap Dancing America: A Cultural History* (New York: Oxford University Press, 2010), 161.
9. *Shuffle Along, or the Making of the Musical Sensation of 1921 and All That Followed* (2016 typescript libretto), New York Public Library for the Performing Arts, Lincoln Center, New York.

16 Gershwin and Instrumental Jazz

NATE SLOAN

More than eight decades after his death, George Gershwin remains an outsize figure in the story of instrumental jazz. "I Got Rhythm" (1930), a popular hit from the musical *Girl Crazy*, provided an essential template over which swing musicians such as Lester Young etched free-wheeling improvisations during the 1930s. "I Got Rhythm" continued its prominence in the 1940s, when its melody and harmonies were reworked by the likes of Thelonius Monk and Charlie Parker. Over time, musicians streamlined Gershwin's original composition into a standard form known as "rhythm changes." This thirty-two-bar, AABA chord progression became a template to rival the twelve-bar blues as a jam-session cornerstone. In the 1950s, Gershwin's compositions spurred explorations of modal jazz, as on Miles Davis's and Gil Evans's album-length reinterpretation of the opera *Porgy and Bess* (1958). Even the avant-garde jazz of John Coltrane and Ornette Coleman in the 1960s expressed a debt to Gershwin: "Embraceable You" (1928) was one of the only cover songs that Coleman recorded among his path-breaking original compositions. In the intervening years, Gershwin has not galvanized the same kind of innovation in jazz but remains a reliable font for musicians of all levels, his works continually renewed and re-inscribed. Herbie Hancock's 1998 album *Gershwin's World* begins by reimagining "Fascinatin' Rhythm" (1924) as a samba, while jazz students around the world continue to woodshed their "rhythm changes" in all twelve keys, if they are serious about mastering the art.

Despite the centrality of Gershwin's work to the jazz tradition, certain aspects of his style and legacy still sit uncomfortably within it. The question of whether Gershwin's work deserves the appellation of "jazz" at all has occupied musicians and critics since the debut of *Rhapsody in Blue* in 1924. Gershwin's contentious status – between jazz, popular music and concert music – indexes wider disciplinary tensions surrounding the interplay of commerce, artistic autonomy and race in popular music. Gershwin's identity has also proven confounding in this respect. Although Gershwin was open to charges of appropriation as an outsider among jazz's African American progenitors, there remains a long-standing perception of him as being especially "in" with contemporary jazz musicians when compared to other Tin Pan Alley songsmiths. Gershwin merited insider status in part because of his own, Jewish outsider identity – a resilient bit of mythos that merits closer interrogation.

This chapter highlights Gershwin's foundational contributions to the development of jazz through selected compositions and performances, then unpacks his complex role in the music's history through a lens of labor politics and critical race theory. In order to better understand Gershwin's jazz legacy, I place his song-texts in dialogue with musicians who used his material as a catalyst for innovation, recognizing that jazz musicians did not "shield" themselves from Tin Pan Alley but deliberately *engaged* with popular song.[1] Studying Gershwin in this way shines new light on an American original and provides fresh heuristics for better understanding both his work and that of his greatest jazz interpreters.

Why Gershwin?

Before proceeding further, it is worth posing a central question: Why, out of all the Golden Age songsmiths whose work has inspired jazz musicians – Cole Porter, Richard Rodgers, Harold Arlen, Jerome Kern, Irving Berlin – does Gershwin occupy such a singular role in the jazz firmament? C. Andre Barbera offers one direct explanation: Gershwin's compositions were popular with jazz musicians because they were popular songs, period.[2] This is certainly true by any metric. Richard Crawford tallies eighty-one recorded covers or reharmonizations of "I Got Rhythm" between 1930 and 1942, and Ted Gioia counts over four hundred jazz covers of "Summertime" (1935) during the 1950s and 1960s.[3] Such staggering statistics act as a potent reminder that despite jazz's gradual drift toward "art music" following World War II, in the first half of the century jazz was indivisible from popular music.[4]

Still, popularity alone cannot account for Gershwin's central presence in the history of instrumental jazz, and from the start of his career critics have sought to categorize elements of his style as distinctly and inherently "jazzy" in nature. Initially, these were located into two particularly audible aspects: 1) an emphasis on blue notes and 2) an interest in intensely syncopated phrases inspired by ragtime rhythms. "The Man I Love" (1924) offers an example of Gershwin's blue notes (i.e. playing a minor third, diminished fifth, or minor seventh over a major chord), as the opening melody fixates on the minor seventh scale degree. "Fascinating Rhythm" (1924) has been hailed as a masterpiece of syncopation, in which Gershwin imposes a rhythmic pattern of seven quarter notes onto a 4/4 meter (Example 16.1).[5] In these instances, Gershwin's blue notes and

Example 16.1 "Fascinating Rhythm," chorus, mm. 1–4

syncopation have been cited as distinctive and daring, but as Larry Starr has shown, both techniques already appear in a song that predates Gershwin's efforts: "Everybody Step" (1921) by Irving Berlin.[6]

If Gershwin's blue notes and metric displacement were "virtually clichés" of 1920s popular song, neither were they particularly daring in a jazz context. Stride pianists in New York City like Willie "the Lion" Smith had been experimenting with metric displacement since the beginning of the decade, infusing ragtime rhythms with an up-tempo verve. A few years after "Fascinating Rhythm" was published, Louis Armstrong began bulldozing those same stride and ragtime rhythms in Chicago cabarets. Although Gershwin's inventiveness electrified white audiences, his cellular approach to rhythm appeared passé to jazz musicians once Armstrong, in collaboration with innovative, "eccentric" dancers, popularized a more propulsive, linear rhythmic concept.[7] Amongst prominent Tin Pan Alley composers, Harold Arlen more seamlessly assimilated contemporary jazz practice into his work than Gershwin. As Walter Frisch has shown, not only did Arlen cut his teeth as a jazz pianist in bands like The Buffalodians (Can readers guess Arlen's hometown?), but he also incorporated lessons from the bandstand into his popular songs. An excellent example is the hit "Stormy Weather" (1933), which uses two-bar "breaks" drawn from jazz in its form, and whose melody begins on a blue third.[8]

The Many Lives of "I Got Rhythm": Gershwin and Jazz from the 1920s to the 1940s

If Gershwin's patented blue notes and syncopations have proven to be less distinctive than once thought, scholars like Barbera, Crawford and Scott DeVeaux have identified subtler aspects of harmony and form that made his work especially appealing to jazz interpreters. "I Got Rhythm" offers an excellent site for understanding these aspects of the composer's craft. For one, "Rhythm" indicates that Gershwin's popular songs, composed for Broadway and Hollywood musicals, made up the section of his oeuvre most valuable to jazz improvisers. By contrast, Gershwin's celebrated concert works like *Rhapsody in Blue* were largely ignored.[9] Of the

Example 16.2 "I Got Rhythm," chorus, mm. 1–4

Gershwin songs that have reached jazz standard status, "I Got Rhythm" stands out for its ubiquity and durability. Successive generations of jazz musicians re-composed the song so many times that the composition must be seen as one of the great palimpsests in American musical history. While some interpretations would keep the song's original melody intact, most jazz musicians chose to forego it and instead hang their own melodies and improvisations on Gershwin's harmonic scaffolding. In part, this rejection of the "I Got Rhythm" melody may be due to the song's use of a dated ragtime syncopation similar to that found in "Fascinating Rhythm." As Allen Forte points out, the pairs of dotted quarter notes in "I Got Rhythm" reference the Charleston, a dance that was going out of fashion by 1930 and being replaced with the forward drive of the Lindy Hop (Example 16.2).[10] Musicians exploited the harmony and form of "I Got Rhythm" and increasingly left the song's melody behind, until "rhythm changes" became part of the lingua franca of jazz from New York to Kansas City, its chords presenting an ideal template for all-night jam sessions. By simplifying or complicating the harmonic progression, musicians could spontaneously and non-verbally create extended improvisations based on a mutually understood harmonic lexicon.

The swing-era approach to "I Got Rhythm" is well illustrated in two takes of the song recorded by Lester Young in 1944 and reissued by Commodore in 1997.[11] Together, they give rare insight into the process by which musicians reworked Gershwin's original tune in loosely structured "head arrangements." Though these recordings keep the song's title rather than renaming it, Gershwin's melody is never heard. Instead, listeners are privy to a group of musicians generating a new arrangement of the song on the fly. Such extemporaneous head arrangements were not always without obstacle. On one take (titled "I Got Rhythm #3" on the reissue), Young unexpectedly starts the song in minor, rather than major. Pianist Joe Bushkin takes a few measures to realize that Young has switched the mode, and a cat-and-mouse drama ensues between the piano accompaniment, which keeps attempting to modulate to major, and saxophone solo, which stubbornly insists on staying in minor. The next soloist, trumpeter Bill Coleman, continues the game, toying with major but staying mostly in minor. Trombonist Dickie Wells improvises using the major mode during his solo, which Bushkin continues in his

Example 16.3 Transcription of Lester Young's solo on "I Got Rhythm," 1944, Take 2, 00:20–00:25

ensuing piano solo. Following Bushkin's solo, all the horns re-enter for some collective improvisation over the last eight measures of the form, but the question of mode, temporarily resolved in favor of major, turns out to be still open for debate. Pianist Bushkin, bassist John Simmons and trombonist Wells all play in major, while Young and trumpeter Coleman play in minor. The resultant cacophony ensures this take will never become a jazz classic, but the recording does an excellent job of revealing the extent to which the skeleton of "I Got Rhythm" was open to radical, real-time reinvention.

On the next take, "I Got Rhythm #2," Young and his bandmates try again. This time, Young starts the song in the major mode, and the ensemble seems to catch fire as they lock into the song's form. Once they do, Young launches into a series of riffs that demonstrate why "rhythm changes" proved so adaptable for swing musicians. Though Gershwin's chord progression moves at a rapid pace, changing harmonies every two beats, its simplicity permits a range of improvisational approaches. The song's A section begins with the sequence (B♭maj7 Gm7 | Cm7 F7), and then repeats those two measures verbatim, an approach Crawford calls "elemental" and presenting a "bare, abstract quality" of which soloists were primed to take advantage.[12] Young sounds the "elemental" aspects of rhythm changes when, during the second chorus of his solo, he unravels a blistering series of repeated notes over the first five measures of the B section (Example 16.3).

In doing so, Young effectively flattens the song's shifting harmonies into a single tone, sublimating melody into pure rhythmic motion. Gershwin's original melody is long gone, replaced with the driving, forward propulsion of swing rhythm.[13] During this era of the 1930s and early 1940s, when jazz bands were often required to play from early evening until dawn, the elemental qualities of "rhythm changes" provided a template that could be endlessly rewritten and retrofitted to the needs of the crowd and musicians.

If Young and his fellow swing musicians valued "I Got Rhythm" for its harmonic simplicity, the generation of bebop musicians that followed discovered in Gershwin's songs ideal sites for their interest in complexity: harmonic substitutions, chromatic melodies, and angular rhythms. Although bebop's innovators have been described as representing a radical break from their swing-era predecessors, the musicians still drew from the same well of raw material. Parker, Dizzy Gillespie, Tadd Dameron, and their peers in post-war New York City continued the practice of adapting "I Got Rhythm" and other Tin Pan Alley numbers for their own purposes. "Rhythm changes" provided the foundation for key Parker compositions like "Anthropology" (1945) and "Moose the Mooche" (1946). In certain cases, entirely different Gershwin numbers were smashed together in a kind of harmonic collage. Guy Ramsey identifies one of these "Frankenstein" compositions in pianist Bud Powell's "Webb City" (1946), which features an A section built on "rhythm changes" and a B section employing chord changes from another Gershwin tune, "Oh, Lady Be Good!" (1924).[14]

Thelonious Monk took an especially keen interest in Gershwin material. Scott DeVeaux argues that Monk's predilection for the Gershwins' "Nice Work If You Can Get It" (1937) lay in the song's use of a series of augmented dominant-seventh chords, which resonated with Monk's "weird," "tritone-based, whole-tone idiom."[15] Like his peers, Monk also adapted "rhythm changes" to his own purposes, as on "Rhythm-a-ning," one of his most-recorded songs. First released in 1958 on the Atlantic LP *Art Blakey's Jazz Messengers with Thelonius Monk* but composed some time before, "Rhythm-a-ning" offers insight into how the famed bop pianist went about recomposing Gershwin. Robin D.G. Kelley notes that the song uses a typical "rhythm changes" harmonic scheme but interpolates the melody of its opening four bars from a 1936 big-band chart that Mary Lou Williams wrote for Andy Kirk, "Walking and Swinging."[16] One can imagine Monk's title as adding a neologism to Williams's pair of verbs: "*Rhythmaning*: the act of improvising or composing over 'rhythm changes.' Orig. c. 1940s, Harlem." While the harmonic changes in "Rhythm-a-ning" may be straightforward, its melody moves in surprising directions. Monk follows his quotation of Williams with four measures all his own, an off-kilter, repeated three-note riff (f′–g′–ab′). In the B section of the song, Monk reuses this rhythm from the A section (Example 16.4). Monk modulates the phrase to D major (d′–e′–f♯′) in keeping with the first harmony of the B section. But then, on the fifth bar of the bridge, when the harmony has moved to a C7 chord, Monk keeps the phrase in D major, creating a pungent dissonance between harmony and melody. Monk ends this second statement of the phrase with an added extension, continuing the (d′–e′–f♯′) cell with (g♯′–bb′–c′) and turning the three-note riff into a complete whole-tone scale.

As challenging and modern as Monk's melody sounds, it shares Gershwin's interest in metric displacement. Monk creates a polymetric effect with the B section's repeated phrase, similar to what Gershwin does

Example 16.4 "Rhythm-a-ning," B section, mm. 17–24

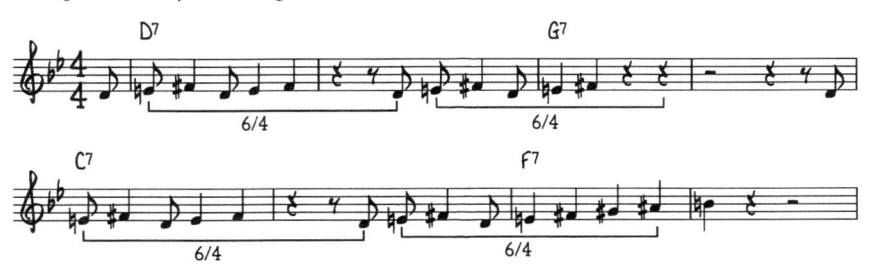

in the chorus of "Fascinating Rhythm." Where "Fascinating" imposed a seven-beat phrase over common (cut) time, Monk's "Rhythm-a-ning" imposes a six-beat phrase over common time. If the ragtime syncopation of Gershwin's melodies proved rhythmically underwhelming for jazz musicians, "Rhythm-a-ning" shows that the composer's metric superimpositions were still viable, just in need of updating.

Gershwin and Experimentation in the 1950s and 1960s

While Gershwin's influence on stylistic developments during the swing and bebop eras is widely accepted, the composer appears to exert less sway over avant-garde jazz that emerged in the late 1950s and early 1960s. Nevertheless, Gershwin compositions appear on pivotal recordings during this period. In 1958, with a movie version of *Porgy and Bess* forthcoming, and having just released a successful big-band album arranged by Gil Evans, *Miles Ahead* (1957), Miles Davis and his record label Columbia decided to record selections from Gershwin's opera for the trumpeter's next project with Evans. *Porgy and Bess* (1959) went on to become one of Davis's best-selling albums and was met with critical acclaim for the trumpeter's lyrical playing and Evans's ethereal arrangements. The album was significant in Davis's career for another reason: it helped refine his burgeoning interest in modal jazz. Davis had explored this modal approach – improvising over static harmonies using pitches drawn from a single scale, or *mode* – on earlier tracks like "Milestones" (1957), and he crystallized it on the landmark album *Kind of Blue* (1959). Mark Tucker argues that the version of "I Loves You, Porgy" on *Porgy and Bess* represents a transitional moment in Davis's development of modal technique. Evans's arrangement of the song erases Gershwin's original harmonic structure, keeping only the incipit of the song's melody. As the bass alternates pedaling F and C, brass and strings sound coruscating harmonies drawn from the A Phrygian mode, while Davis solos using the same. For Tucker, the result is a "painterly effect"

Example 16.5 a) Gershwin chord changes, "But Not for Me," chorus, mm. 1–4

Eb6	Cm7	| Fm7	Bb9	| Ebmaj7	Cmi7	| Fm7		Bb7 |
F9		| Bb7		| Ebmaj7		| Bbmi7		Eb7 |

b) Coltrane reharmonization, "But Not for Me," chorus, mm. 1–4

Ebmaj9/Bb	Gb13/Ab	| Bmaj9/F#	D9/E	Gmaj9/D	Bb13/C	| Ebmaj9/Bb	Bb7 |
Ebmaj9	Gb13/Db	| Bmaj9	D9/A	Gmaj9	Bb13/F	| Bbmi7	Eb7 |

that "conveys the fresh possibilities for freedom and open space offered by modal jazz."[17] It can be added that the "open space" Davis and Evans discovered in "I Loves You, Porgy," was likely inspired by the open nature of Gershwin's melody, a series of rising and falling thirds that lands on every note in the A Phrygian scale over eight measures.

Gershwin continued to provide instrumentation for jazz experimentation in the following decade. In 1960 Coltrane recorded the album *My Favorite Things* (1960), which applied his "sheets of sound" improvisational approach and interest in harmonic motion by major thirds to a set of Tin Pan Alley standards. Lawrence Kramer hears Coltrane developing "a new American songbook" with this album by "going against the grain" of the original material.[18] Of the four songs on *My Favorite Things*, the two on Side B are both composed by Gershwin. Coltrane's version of "Summertime" is raucous and raw, a far cry from its intended function as a lullaby in the *Porgy and Bess* opera. This "Summertime," by contrast, is explosive, searching and anguished, presaging the spiritual meditations still to come on *A Love Supreme* (1964). Coltrane ends the LP with Gershwin's "But Not for Me" (1930), like "I Got Rhythm" originally composed for the Broadway musical *Girl Crazy*. Coltrane reharmonizes Gershwin's original chord progression with his own third-based "Coltrane changes" (Examples 16.5 and 16.6). Pianist McCoy Tyner and bassist Steve Davis avoid playing the root note of each chord, and instead sound out a descending whole-tone scale bass line [Bb–Ab–F#–E–D–C] beneath each harmonic change. In the next four measures of the song, Coltrane repeats the same set of chord changes, but Tyner and Davis play a new bass pattern, this one tracing another whole-tone scale [Eb–Db–B–A–G–F]. With these twin descending whole-tone bass lines, Coltrane's rhythm section collects all twelve pitches of the chromatic scale over the course of eight bars.

Coltrane located an ideal vessel for his experiments with harmony and improvisation in "But Not for Me." Like "I Got Rhythm," it expresses the "elemental" aspect of Gershwin's popular songs in its formal symmetry and pliable, three-note opening melody. Coltrane's re-arrangement of the song's first eight measures leads his quartet to scalar possibilities that would not have been possible using Gershwin's original voicings. And if the version of "But Not for Me" on vinyl sounds impressive, one can only imagine what it was like when Coltrane's quartet performed the song live. Ben Ratliff describes an unreleased, reel-to-reel recording from the early 1960s, in which Coltrane and his quartet unravel a thirty-six-minute version of the tune.[19]

Even Ornette Coleman, the most controversial jazz musician of the twentieth century, owed much to Gershwin's music. Coleman posed as stark a challenge to the norms of jazz as John Cage had to Western art music, stretching the harmonic innovation of Davis and Coltrane even further, beyond modes and chords altogether to a world of "free" improvisation. Still, Coleman anchored his work to jazz tradition by including the Gershwin composition "Embraceable You" (1928) on his 1960 LP *This Is Our Music*. Coleman's quartet starts the song with a new introduction, a moody series of descending riffs played by Coleman's alto sax and Don Cherry's trumpet while bassist Charlie Haden bows long tones underneath. Coleman then plays a deconstructed version of Gershwin's original melody over a sparse accompaniment from Haden's bass and Ed Blackwell's drums, gradually trailing away from the original melody and chords until he enters a "harmolodic" world all his own. For Iain Anderson, Coleman "changed the entire sound of jazz" with this recording, since unlike Coltrane, Davis and Monk, Coleman does not reharmonize or embellish Gershwin's original composition but turns it into a blank slate for his avant-garde explorations by gradually erasing its harmony, form, and melody entirely.[20] "Embraceable You" was one of the only pieces recorded by Coleman over his long career that was not an original, indicating that Gershwin occupied a special role in Coleman's practice. Coleman's relationship to Gershwin extended beyond covers, as well. Like his bebop predecessors, Coleman composed new tunes based on "rhythm changes," including "Chronology" off his explosive album *The Shape of Jazz to Come* (1959).

Beyond the 1960s: Rethinking Gershwin

From Coleman to the present day, Gershwin has remained a constant presence in instrumental jazz, though his music ceased to provide the same galvanizing force for innovation that it did from the 1930s to the 1960s. In the 1970s and 1980s, Gershwin and other Tin Pan Alley composers held less relevance for jazz musicians bent on melding rock and funk into new genres like fusion.[21] In the late 1980s and 1990s, Gershwin once again emerged as a significant figure with the rise of neoclassical "Young Lions" such as Wynton Marsalis. Marsalis's conservative approach to jazz rebuked the pop leanings of fusion and insisted jazz's future could be discovered in its past. Marsalis won the Grammy Award for Best Jazz Instrumental Performance with his 1987 album *Marsalis Standard Time, Vol. 1*, which contained two original compositions and ten jazz standards, including Gershwin's "A Foggy Day" (1937). Smooth jazz also leaned on Gershwin to establish itself as a genre in the 1990s: Kenny G's hit album *Classics in the Key of G* (1999) opens with a cover of "Summertime."

Toward the end of the 1990s, Herbie Hancock released a Grammy-winning tribute album to the composer, *Gershwin's World*. Featuring guest vocals from Joni Mitchell and Stevie Wonder, *Gershwin's World* represents Hancock's attempt to situate Gershwin's music in its historical context while updating his sound to the present. Hancock includes songs written by African American contemporaries of Gershwin, such as W.C. Handy's "St. Louis Blues" (1914) and Duke Ellington's "Cotton Tail" (1940) (which is also based on "rhythm changes"). Despite the album's critical and commercial success, Hancock's motivations for making the record were largely obscured, and his thoughts on the album's genesis are worth quoting in full:

> [Verve] wanted me to do a tribute album to one of the Great American Songbook composers . . . These were all great American composers, but why should I make a record celebrating a great white American musician? Especially when that musician had gained fame by creating music in a style that was actually founded by black musicians – who never got the credit, the fans, or the money they so richly deserved. Gershwin's music was obviously infused with the influence of the African American cultural tradition, which became the American cultural tradition in the '20s and '30s "jazz age," through tap dancing, shimmying, the Charleston, and other popular artistic movements. I knew I'd get flak for it from the black community, and understandably so. What message would it send for me, a black musician who'd managed to achieve a certain degree of stature, to use whatever capital I had to celebrate white composers? And yet . . . was there a way I could approach it from another perspective, a way that would allow me to make such a record in good conscience? I didn't want to buy into the distorted view that made it look like George Gershwin was an inventor of jazz.[22]

Hancock's candid account of his complex relationship toward Gershwin's legacy exposes latent tensions in the history of Gershwin and instrumental jazz. The remarkable story of Gershwin and his jazz interpreters recounted above has been hailed as a uniquely American project, an artistic collaboration only possible in a tolerant and forward-looking society. The Jewish, immigrant backgrounds of Gershwin and other Tin Pan Alley composers have only added to the mythos of American popular music as a valiant, cross-cultural exchange, in which "song provided a haven for two marginalized ethnic groups before integration became the law of the land."[23] This heroic narrative emerged at the beginning of Gershwin's career, and it was encouraged by the composer himself, who in 1926 wrote an article titled "Jazz Is the Voice of the American Soul," wherein he stated: "the American soul . . . is black and white. It is all colors and all sounds unified in the great melting pot of the world."[24] Touted as the foremost jazz composer in America, Gershwin was lauded by critics for "elevating" jazz, as in a review of Gershwin's 1934 concert tour: "Jazz, with its not so very distant heritage of primitive savages beating drums, has become the real music of today. An occasional composer has attempted to lift jazz toward the realm of good music and Gershwin has probably done more of this than any other individual."[25] That critics saw Gershwin as the savior of jazz only added insult to injury for black composers. After all, this was the same composer who held up a blackface performer like Al Jolson as a paragon of jazz singing.[26]

The more Gershwin was fêted for elevating jazz from its "primitive" roots, the greater the backlash from black jazz musicians and "hip" white critics alike. In 1933 the British musician Spike Hughes dismissed Gershwin as an inauthentic interlocutor, expressing his bewilderment at "the almost universal and distressing acceptance of the 'Rhapsody in Blue' as the apotheosis of jazz . . . the mere fact that a Gershwin 'number' is incidentally used for dancing does not mean that it is jazz."[27] Hughes went on to express his pleasure that "the arrival of Duke Ellington and his orchestra to these shores means that, at long last, the British public will have an opportunity to hear what jazz is really all about."[28] As a result of such reception, Gershwin's music gradually became "decidedly not jazz," as Ryan Bañagale succinctly puts it.[29] If Hughes was skeptical of Gershwin in 1933, by the 1960s the thought of Gershwin as jazz was outright anathema. Bañagale quotes a 1963 critic who wrote: "*Rhapsody in Blue* seems to be traditional music dressed in jazz costume and coloring – Liszt, as it were, in blackface, a rented tuxedo, and battered top hat."[30]

It is important to note, though, that black musicians' enmity toward Gershwin often was not directed at the composer specifically, but at how Gershwin's success symbolized the larger inequity of an entertainment industry that rewarded the white composer's "jazz mastery" with symphony and opera commissions, critical plaudits, and commercial gain, whereas black musicians rarely had access to such opportunities. Amiri Baraka stated the case in raw terms: "People like George Gershwin, who literally learned at the feet and elbows of Willie "The Lion" Smith, James P. Johnson, and Fats Waller, could be named Great Composers and live sumptuously, while his teachers always struggled for recognition, even survival!"[31]

Baraka's plaint echoes Hancock's concern that "black musicians ... never got the credit, the fans, or the money they so richly deserved," and points to critical gaps in the history of popular song and instrumental jazz.[32] Many appraisals of Gershwin's role in jazz history frame his work along a binary of authenticity and artifice. Instead, a more fruitful lens to study Gershwin's jazz legacy is through the politics of race, labor, and power in the American entertainment industry. Metrics of "authenticity" serve to obscure both the heterogeneous quality of early jazz and the structural inequities that catapulted Gershwin to success while leaving his black peers on the margins.[33] Rather than connecting Gershwin's musical creativity to race, ethnicity or religion, scholars must consider the economic and political forces that shaped his reception. Cultural exchange between Jewish songwriters and black jazz musicians may have offered a "haven" for the two marginalized groups – but how equal was that exchange? For instance, in the 1920s and 1930s, Gershwin was free to go out for a night on the town in Harlem to hear Duke Ellington or Cab Calloway perform at the Cotton Club, but black patrons were not allowed through that venue's doors. Although marked as a racial other, Gershwin was clearly afforded a different level of freedom in Jim Crow America than his black peers.

An example of how labor, race, and politics can inform Gershwin studies lies in the bebop era and the "rhythm changes" compositions of Monk, Parker, and others. The link from Tin Pan Alley to jazz has been hailed as testament to the unique melting pot of American culture, but the melodic re-compositions of the bebop era were as much a way of avoiding copyright royalties as they were an inevitable musical engagement. Bebop musicians' desire to re-compose their own material was not without political edge, since "black musicians noticed the royalties were going back to these people, like ASCAP, the Jerome Kerns, the Gershwins," according to drummer Max Roach, and "the only reason that the music of the Gershwins and all these people lived during that period was because all the black people, the Billie Holidays, Ella Fitzgeralds, Dizzy Gillespies, Charlie Parkers, the Monks, the Coleman Hawkinses projected this music, used this music and kept it alive."[34] Roach had good reason to complain that Gershwin and other white songwriters benefited from an unequal system. As Marc Myers relates, the performing-rights group ASCAP maintained a tiered system in which "high-profile members like Cole Porter and George Gershwin earned significant sums writing catchy songs for Broadway and the movies, which meant sizeable royalties" while "restrictive rules ... all but barred a growing number of composers" of jazz and blues.[35] Although Gershwin and his estate continually profited from recordings of his music, a jazz composer like Jelly Roll Morton – whose "King Porter Stomp" (1922) became a massive hit for Benny Goodman and other swing orchestras in the 1930s – only earned ASCAP membership in 1939 after five years of unsuccessful applications. Having witnessed their older peers endure this system, bebop musicians signed with rival publisher BMI, determined to rewrite Tin Pan Alley melodies rather than see their labor redound to already-wealthy composers.

Herbie Hancock kept these realities in mind when recording *Gershwin's World*, and his consciousness has been sustained by twenty-first-century jazz musicians. Echoing Hancock's discomfort with the hagiography of white composers from the Jazz Age, modern musicians like Jason Moran have chosen to celebrate figures from the margins of that era. Moran's 2014 album *All Rise: An Elegy for Fats Waller* does not aim to recreate the 1920s and 1930s jazz milieu, but instead captures the spirit of that moment by merging it with the sound of contemporary hip hop and R&B. In this way, Moran re-sounds Waller's music for its original locales: the city streets, nightclubs, and house parties that once provided the soundtrack to dizzy evenings of dancing and socializing. Gershwin will benefit from similar treatments in the new millennium. Modern audiences can handle hearing a messier Gershwin in new interpretations that reflect his fascinatingly messy role in the history of instrumental jazz.

Notes

1. Scott DeVeaux, "'Nice Work If You Can Get It': Thelonious Monk and Popular Song," *Black Music Research Journal* 19/2 (1999), 183.
2. C. Andre Barbera, "George Gershwin and Jazz," in Wayne Schneider (ed.), *The Gershwin Style* (New York: Oxford University Press, 1999), 201.
3. Richard Crawford, *The American Landscape: The Business of Musicianship from Billings to Gershwin* (Berkeley, CA: University of California Press, 2000), 158–60; Ted Gioia, *The Jazz Standards: A Guide to the Repertoire* (New York: Oxford University Press, 2012), 412.
4. Bernard Gendron, "Moldy Figs and Modernists: Jazz at War (1942–1946)," *Discourse* 15/3 (1993).
5. Steven Gilbert, *The Music of George Gershwin* (New Haven, CT: Yale University Press, 1995), 32.
6. Larry Starr, *George Gershwin* (New Haven, CT: Yale University Press, 2010), 48; Jeffrey Magee, "Everybody Step: Irving Berlin, Jazz, and Broadway in the 1920s," *Journal of the American Musicological Society* 59/3 (2006), 697–732.
7. Brian Harker, "Louis Armstrong, Eccentric Dance, and the Evolution of Jazz on the Eve of Swing," *Journal of the American Musicological Society* 61/1 (2008), 67–121.
8. Walter Frisch, "Arlen's Tapeworms: The Tunes That Got Away," *The Musical Quarterly* 98/1 (2015), 10–13.
9. There are notable exceptions when jazz musicians tackled *Rhapsody in Blue*, such as Louis Armstrong's quotation of the *Rhapsody* in a trumpet solo on Fats Waller and Andy Razaf's "Ain't Misbehavin'" (1929), reissued on Louis Armstrong, *Portrait of the Artist as a Young Man (1923–1934)*, Legacy/Columbia (1994), CD/MP3. Duke Ellington and Billy Strayhorn also made brilliant arrangements of *Rhapsody*. Ryan Raul Bañagale, "Rewriting the Narrative One

Arrangement at a Time: Duke Ellington and *Rhapsody in Blue*," *Jazz Perspectives* 6/1–2 (2012), 5–27.
10. Allen Forte, *The American Popular Ballad of the Golden Era, 1924–1950* (Princeton, NJ: Princeton University Press, 1995), 20.
11. Lester Young, "I Got Rhythm #3" and "I Got Rhythm #2," *The Kansas City Sessions*, Commodore CMD 402 (1997), CD/MP3.
12. Crawford, *The American Landscape*, 226. Most "rhythm changes" jam sessions cut the extra two-bar "tag" at the end of Gershwin's original song.
13. John McDonough, "Streamlining Jazz: Major Soloists of the 1930s and 1940s" in Bill Kirchner (ed.), *The Oxford Companion to Jazz* (New York: Oxford, 2000), 211.
14. Guthrie Ramsey, *The Amazing Bud Powell: Black Genius, Jazz History, and the Challenge of Bebop* (Berkeley, CA: University of California Press, 2013), 179.
15. DeVeaux, "Nice Work If You Can Get It," 176.
16. Robin D.G. Kelley, *Thelonious Monk: The Life and Times of an American Original* (New York: Simon & Schuster, 2010), 74.
17. Mark Tucker, "Porgy and Miles," *Current Musicology* 71–73 (2001), 18.
18. Lawrence Kramer, *Musical Meaning: Toward a Critical History*, Volume 1 (Berkeley, CA: University of California Press, 2002), 255. For his analysis of Coltrane's "Summertime," 247–54.
19. Ben Ratliff, *Coltrane: The Story of a Sound* (New York: Macmillan, 2007), 136.
20. Iain Anderson, *This Is Our Music: Free Jazz, the Sixties, and American Culture* (Philadelphia, PA: University of Pennsylvania Press, 2007), 1.
21. Kevin Fellezs, *Birds of Fire: Jazz, Rock, Funk, and the Creation of Fusion* (Durham, NC: Duke University Press, 2011), 82.
22. Herbie Hancock with Lisa Dickey, *Possibilities* (New York: Viking, 2014), 296.
23. David Yaffe, *Fascinating Rhythm: Reading Jazz in American Writing* (Princeton, NJ: Princeton University Press, 2005), 17.
24. George Gershwin, "Jazz Is the Voice of the American Soul," *Theatre Magazine* (1926), reprinted in *The George Gershwin Reader*, ed. Robert Wyatt and John Andrew Johnson (New York: Oxford University Press, 2007), 92.
25. Cf. Wayne Schneider, "Gershwin in the Heartland: Critical and Public Reception of the 1934 Leo Reisman Tour," *The Musical Quarterly* 94/1–2 (2011), 76.
26. George Gershwin, "Does Jazz Belong to Art?" *Singing* (1926), reprinted in *The George Gershwin Reader*, 97.
27. Spike Hughes, "Meet the Duke," Daily Herald London (June 13, 1933), reprinted in The Duke Ellington Reader, ed. Mark Tucker (New York: Oxford University Press, 1995), 74.
28. Ibid.
29. Ryan Raul Bañagale, *Arranging Gershwin: Rhapsody in Blue and the Creation of an American Icon* (Oxford: Oxford University Press, 2014), 110.
30. Ibid.
31. Amiri Baraka, "'Jazz and the White Critic' Twenty Years Later," in *Digging: The Afro-American Soul of American Classical Music* (Berkeley, CA: University of California Press, 2009), 148.
32. Hancock, *Possibilities*, 296.
33. As Catherine Parsons, *William Grant Still: A Study in Contradictions* (Berkeley, CA: University of California Press, 2000), 136–41, explains, Gershwin may have taken the melody to "I Got Rhythm" from African American composer William Grant Still.
34. Dizzy Gillespie and Al Fraser, *To Be or Not to Bop: Memoirs of Dizzy Gillespie* (New York: Da Capo Press, 1985), 209.
35. Marc Myers, *Why Jazz Happened* (Berkeley, CA: University of California Press, 2013), 118–19.

Epilogue: The Gershwin I Knew, and the Gershwin I Know

MICHAEL FEINSTEIN

All of us experience moments that permanently change the course of our lives. Mine came when I met Ira Gershwin in 1977. I was twenty, and he was eighty. For years, I had been reading about and collecting everything I could get my hands on regarding the Gershwin brothers. When I finally met Ira, I was well prepared for the encounter.

For the next six years I became blissfully immersed in a long-vanished era, channeled through a survivor with whom I vicariously relived a time that looms large in cultural history. George had died forty years before, but he was still alive and well in Ira's house. Surrounded by George's everyday items – his pipe, tie clip, self-portraits, tune notebooks, grand piano, gold bracelet, photos, letters, and passport – I soaked up a sense not only of him, but also of his music and how it evolved and changed through the years. Countless stories were told by Ira and his friends.

As a testament to the inspiration, resonance and durability of his work, George Gershwin's music still inspires and galvanizes the hearts of many around the world. Curiosity about the man has generated countless pages of biographical material, filling bookshelves year after year. Keeping apace have been the published analyses of his music; and reprintings of the numerous compositions have surfaced, often purporting to be definitive editions reflecting his original intentions. New productions of his musicals are routinely mounted, and occasionally trumpeted as reconstructions using original orchestrations. Among the legions of sound recordings are those offered as authentic emulations of the Gershwin style, sometimes purveyed with the help or blessings of his associates, acquaintances, friends and experts. Many of these efforts are noble and well intentioned, yet there is too much chaff among the wheat. Gershwin factoids and anecdotes have been so long misspoken that as far back as 1945, his friend and musical champion Oscar Levant stated: "Even the lies about him are being distorted."

What is a Gershwin fan to do?

Granted, it is not the balance of the world that depends on assiduous truth in these matters, but the hunger for the essence of what made Gershwin and his music tick is important to many. In this era of

Wikipedia, the distortions of fact and fiction will not permanently dent the halo around George Gershwin's legacy. But for those, like me, who care about the heart of preservation, it is nettling to see falsehoods about his life and music perpetuated.

In the years I spent working with Ira Gershwin, I met many of Gershwin's friends. They all carried a little piece of the puzzle, a shard of the full portrait, and I have come to understand certain things about him that have helped me shape my own conception of who he was and how his fundamental nature as a man was tied to his work. Despite all that has been written about him, George Gershwin is still, at his essence, a shadowy figure. Even the biographies, especially the more recent, well-intentioned and wonderfully scholarly ones, do not give readers a full sense of who he was as a man. Thus, the question arises: Why has describing Gershwin proven so difficult? Is it because he was a chameleon? Was he hiding a part of himself? Was he misrepresented by many of his contemporaries because of personal agenda or bias? Is it faulty memory? Or is it simply impossible to contain in any way a force so combustible and vital without his corporeal presence?

All these answers are true in some sense. And since the birth of the internet, and the easy proliferation of information, both true and false, the image of Gershwin the man has become all the more shadowy and indistinct. Even his birthdate is in question. Although his official birth certificate, registered with the State of New York on October 6, 1898, gives his date of birth as September 26, 1898, his mother Rose remembered it differently. In the mid-1940s she claimed that he was born near the stroke of midnight on the 25th, not the 26th. She must have told this to her son, because when he registered for the draft in 1918 he listed his birthday as the 25th.[1] His sister Frankie, born eight years later, lovingly disagreed with her mother and brother. But she was not there, was she? Neither were we. So, it is the birth certificate versus a mother's memory.

His name has been given as Gershovitz, Gershwine, Gershvin and so on, and even Ira could not remember exactly what the chronology of the names had been before Gershwin permanently became the official family name.

Because Gershwin died unexpectedly, at a relatively young age, his legacy was left in the hands of family members, friends, and collaborators. Although these were the people who undoubtedly knew him best during his lifetime, their memories have often created more confusion than clarity.

Gershwin's first hit "Swanee" was remembered variously by lyricist Irving Caesar as having been written in about an hour, in forty-five minutes, in twenty minutes, and in only a few minutes. Caesar was even once emboldened to state that George just played a vamp on the piano and Caesar himself came up with the melody that became Gershwin's first hit song, proving that those who live the longest often end up not only shaping history but also changing it along the way.

Rhapsody in Blue was the musical shot fired around the world, and the debate over the specifics of its fundamental creation is ongoing. Paul Whiteman gave many conflicting interviews through the years and, like Irving Caesar, came to take more and more credit as the ghost of Gershwin receded and legend loomed larger than life. But to be fair, it was that same braggadocio that led to the work's creation, when Whiteman stated in an interview that Gershwin was writing a piece for the orchestra, taking the young songwriter by surprise when he read it in the newspaper. Ira remembered the story as George told it and said that Whiteman was merely riffing for the press, even announcing that Irving Berlin was also writing a piece for the orchestra, a challenge that Berlin, sadly, did not embrace.

The opening clarinet glissando in *Rhapsody in Blue* is often credited as being the inspiration of Ross Gorman, Whiteman's clarinetist. Ira, however, remembered when George came up with the idea for that clarinet glissando, which happened after hearing clarinetist Gorman improvising riffs at a rehearsal.

Credit about the addition of the iconic slow theme is another bone of contention. It was added later in the composing process and was not included in the early draft of *Rhapsody in Blue*. Ferde Grofé said that he was the one who initially suggested that George include the famous E major Andante motif. But Ira insisted it was his idea and hummed it for George to remind him of it. Ira had remembered the insistent theme, which had been written two years earlier, and felt it was needed for contrast to break up all the syncopated stuff in the score. Perhaps Ira and Ferde were both involved, for each remembered the other's presence in the workroom on 110th Street.

The first Gershwin biography, published by Isaac Goldberg in 1931, offered an engaging narrative that was read and approved by George, and thus subject to the pros and cons of being vetted by its subject. Ira always felt that editor Merle Armitage compiled the most accurate representation of his brother in the 1938 memorial anthology simply titled *George Gershwin*. The next major book about Gershwin, David Ewen's *George Gershwin: His Journey to Greatness*, appeared in 1956. Ewen was an early proponent of Gershwin's work, and he had desired to write a book about George while he was alive, but George politely declined. Unfortunately, Ewen's eventual biography was so riddled with errors that Ira anonymously edited a new edition in 1970. But this did not stop the proliferation of misinformation. Ewen also wrote a biography about Jerome Kern, published shortly before his passing in 1945. Kern once related to Ira a passage from the book, which described how a young George Gershwin used to stand outside the window of Kern's dwelling to listen to him play the piano. Upon hearing the tale, Ira gently reminded Kern that he lived in a high rise and that George could not possibly have heard him playing. With no small amount of irritation Kern shot back: "But it says so in the book!"

While much misinformation about the composer is spread unwittingly by writers, two biographers, Charles Schwartz and Joan Peyser, engaged in salacious rumor. Both seem to have had unfriendly agendas and played loose and fast with history. This is most clearly seen in their attempts to prove that Albert Schneider (aka Alan Gershwin) was the illegitimate son of George. Schneider bore a striking resemblance to the composer, even giving pause to some of George's friends. Consequently, he became convinced that Gershwin was his father, and after the composer's death, he began to make statements that were later disproved. Schwartz and Peyser embraced these claims, despite testimony from friends and family that Schneider's beliefs were unfounded. Schneider claimed to remember Gershwin taking him to a rehearsal of *Porgy and Bess*. Todd Duncan, the original Porgy, said that certainly he, or someone, *anyone*, would have remembered George coming to a rehearsal with a little boy. This back and forth over Schneider's paternity went on for years until DNA evidence conclusively proved that Schneider was not the son of George Gershwin. End of wild goose chase.[2]

The theories about the cause of George Gershwin's illness and death have also engendered fanciful embellishment. Lillian Gish remembered warning George about an electronic contraption worn on the cranium to prevent hair loss and insisted that it caused his brain tumor. Another stated that hitting his head while escaping from a 1933 hotel fire in Chicago had damaged his brain. In 1937 the songwriter Harold Spina had occupied the bungalow at Goldwyn Studios, recently vacated by George where he had labored over his final film score. Spina concluded that the bungalow was so drafty that it caused Gershwin to contract pneumonia, and that that was the illness, not a brain tumor, that eventually felled the composer. Memory is treacherous. Mickey Rooney vividly recalled George Gershwin visiting the set during his filming of *Girl Crazy* with Judy Garland. When I gently told him that Gershwin had died six years earlier, Rooney bellowed "He was there, God damn it. He was there!"

Gershwin's last song, "Love Is Here to Stay" has dueling narratives about its creation, one offered by composer Vernon Duke, who claimed he helped compose it, a mistruth that has been propagated as fact. According to Ira, what happened was this: George died before he could fully notate the chorus of the song or write the verse music, leaving it partially unfinished. Oscar Levant was able to notate the chorus of the song from memory, and Duke claimed credit for composing the verse. Ira rebuked that notion, stating that he himself composed the verse music in addition to writing the words, and that Vernon had only written it down. His proof of such was simple. He said: "It has to have been composed by me, because it's so undistinguished."

In those final days of George's illness, it was hell for everyone. Some, like Irving Berlin, insisted that he was only psychosomatically sick. Berlin said: "There's nothing wrong with George that a song hit can't cure." Perhaps that is why Irving's posthumously written tribute was particularly affecting, to assuage his feelings of guilt. Ira, who was the most affected of anyone, has been described as recovering relatively soon after his brother's sudden passing, or at least feeling the clouds lifting and getting on with it. Not true. He was in such deep shock that he was not even able to cry until he was face to face with Fred Astaire, whose own grief so overcame Ira that he finally released his own flood of tears. George's last words to Ira were about Fred, and in the dark days after his loss, it was Astaire's recordings of their songs that brought Ira a sense of continuum and the understanding that he must go on. But he remained in a deeply depressed state for three years after George died and could suddenly lapse back into the doldrums at any moment if something reminded him of George's unfair exit at such a young age. Forty years later, it never got easier, even when Ira, who never believed in God, confided that he actually saw George once, but it did not bring a sense of peace or closure.

The Gershwin ego is perhaps the most grossly misunderstood aspect of his personality. Often Gershwin has been described as a self-absorbed, egocentric bore. There was self-absorption, but it was because of his own wonder and fascination with his achievements, almost as if it were an out-of-body experience. There was no false humility. If you were to tell him how much you admired, say, *Porgy and Bess*, he would tell you that he admired it too. He was a vessel through which the music poured, and he could not explain how it happened, thus he sometimes referred to himself in third person. At the same time, he was a kind man and doggedly faithful to his friends, non-competitive with his co-workers, and often championing the work of other songwriters. His closest friends, though, well understood that he had no contrived modesty, because he was himself as impressed by his creative achievements as others.

It was perhaps the feeling of being a musical channel that got Gershwin interested in metaphysics, having readings by the famous "sleeping prophet" Edgar Cayce and the palmist Nellie Simmons Meier. He named his publishing companies New World and later New Dawn Music and was fascinated with New Age thought, something he shared with his talented paramour, composer Kay Swift. Both were interested in the Theosophical Society, and George befriended the famed Theosophist Walter Russell, who later created a beautifully wrought sculpture of him.

A picture of happiness and joy is ascribed to Gershwin in his early days, playing piano for hours and living life fully and furiously. That too, while accurate on the surface, belies a confused soul who was conflicted. On the one hand he had the singular ability to express the aspirations and times of a generation; on the other he was unsatisfied emotionally and confused romantically, which became a more serious issue as time progressed. He was prudish with his innocent sister, telling her to pull down the hemline of her skirt, while at the same time attracted to the opposite kind of woman. When it came to marriage, however, only a certain type of woman would do. Proposing to Kitty Carlisle seemed like a perfect solution, because she was Jewish and in the eyes of his mother the right woman for her famously eligible son. Kitty knew he did not love her though and doubted that he understood what love was, citing his rather juvenile and non-romantic "love" letters. The irony of George writing some of the world's greatest love songs was not lost on her.

Cecelia Ager, close friend of George and wife of songwriter Milton Ager, insisted that George was homosexual. Milton sputtered that such a claim was absurd. Irving Caesar also insisted that George was gay, at least in the early days, and there exists a photo of him in drag from around 1918. Kay Swift described him as the best lover she ever had. Tom Van Dycke, along with a jolly group of drunken friends, claimed to have watched through a keyhole as a "mechanical" George had sex with a French prostitute in Paris in 1928. Simone Simon, a great beauty, later went to bed with George in 1937 and said that he never laid a hand on her. Yet he was also thought to be prolific with females, and in response to the suggestion that he was with so many girls because he was trying to prove he was a man, Oscar Levant retorted: "What a wonderful way to prove it."

One could use these vignettes to bolster any theory, but that is a dangerous path to take. The complexity of his inner life cannot be revealed in these few stories, and they are shared here simply for the sake of poignant contrast to the rich and clear path he traversed artistically. Perhaps the only conclusion to be drawn from our attempts to know George Gershwin is that his true mistress was music, illustrated by the story of a showgirl sitting on his lap at a party, and when he was asked to play the piano, got up so quickly that the unfortunate chorine was knocked to the ground.

Unfortunately, the reception of some of his compositions has been affected by storytelling, too. The distortions of his music started with Paul Whiteman shortly after conducting the premiere of *Rhapsody in Blue* in 1924. Whiteman decided to add a "luft" pause to the Andante section of the Rhapsody that angered George greatly. It all reached a boiling point at the 1927 recording session for the composer's second waxing of the work with Whiteman conducting. They got into such an argument that the session was concluded with Nathaniel Shilkret taking the baton from Whiteman in order to finish the recording. Whiteman's continued distortions of the work included a recording in the 1940s featuring a vocal chorus wordlessly intoning the hymn-like E major theme. After that, a best-selling recording of the *Rhapsody* made in the 1950s mistakenly trumpeted the name of Whiteman as conductor along with his picture on the record jacket, although Roy Bargy served as the actual conductor. Leonard Pennario, the piano soloist, never met Whiteman.

There are various orchestrations of *Rhapsody in Blue* mirroring the work's evolution from its start as a Whiteman band specialty to concert hall staple. Most orchestras today play the 1942 Grofé arrangement for classical instrumentation. More recently the practice of playing Grofé's original 1924 jazz band instrumentation has gained traction as being the way Gershwin intended it. While it is exciting to hear the original smaller, jazzier lean and mean version, one should note that Gershwin himself always performed the composition in Grofé's 1926 expansion for concert orchestra, save for an occasional necessary reunion with Whiteman, when, according to Ira, he would grit his teeth and dig into the piano and endure the distortions that "Pops" wrought. Whiteman's recording of Gershwin's Concerto in F was equally disliked by the composer, and he was loath to autograph a copy of it for Alfred and Elizabeth Simon, relenting at the last minute, uttering: "What the hell."

A later recording of *Rhapsody in Blue*, released in the 1970s, had another secret. The idea was a fun one: recreate the original 1924 Grofé arrangement for the Whiteman band and use the Gershwin piano roll to reunite composer and jazz band orchestration in modern sound. The only problem was that the piano roll was too erratic to properly synchronize with the orchestra, and so virtuoso Stan Freeman was secretly brought in to play various passages of *Rhapsody*. The attractive cover of the LP features a Hirschfeld caricature showing a ghosted image of George Gershwin at the keyboard with a lithe Michael Tilson Thomas conducting the band. It should have also depicted Stan Freeman at the keys.

One day in 1982, I brought Michael Tilson Thomas to meet Ira Gershwin. He wanted to play for him a cadenza he had crafted for the *Second Rhapsody*.

On Gershwin's own 1931 demonstration recording of the work, at the passage in question, the composer plays a fragment of a cadenza, perhaps indicating that he included one in his live performances of the work, but which has never been verified. Ira enjoyed the virtuosity of Tilson Thomas's cadenza, but told him that it should not be included in the recoding he was about to make of the work. Tilson Thomas abided by Ira's wishes and did not record his cadenza. In 1998, fifteen years after Ira's passing, Tilson Thomas re-recorded the *Second Rhapsody* and this time included the cadenza, claiming in the liner notes that Ira had heard and approved of its addition. Since I was present at the meeting in question, I can definitively say: "It ain't necessarily so."

There have been recordings and a publication of the complete "lost" Gershwin Preludes that never would have been sanctioned by Ira were he alive. While it is irresistible to want to bring to light any rare and precious piano music by Gershwin, especially since his only published classical piano music consists of Three Piano Preludes, it is a disservice to the memory of the composer to release incomplete works as if they were intended to be heard in such a state.

The "authentic" recreations of many of the Gershwin musicals have contained a great deal of conjecture and guesswork where original materials were not available. This is not necessarily a bad thing, especially if it means the difference between making a score viable and available once again or staying sequestered; and most of these recreations are musically rich and entertaining. It would be appreciated, however, if the new editions fully revealed what is original and what is not. Kay Swift has never been properly credited for ghosting the verse and half of the chorus of "First Lady and First Gent" from *Let 'Em Eat Cake*. Ditto her harmonization from a lead sheet for "Union League" from the same show. Burton Lane never received credit for newly composing the lost verse music for "Meadow Serenade" from *Strike Up the Band*, and at the time the producers made a conscious decision not to reveal his contribution.

The question of *Porgy and Bess*, and what is the authentic performing version, begets another great bone of contention. It was famously shorn of forty-five minutes during the initial 1935 tryout in Boston before coming to Broadway, and some claim that George never got to hear his full masterpiece. Actually, he did hear it, because it was heard in its entirety before the shears started snipping. Director Rouben Mamoulian worked closely with George to make the cuts, and while George was not always happy with them, he was a man of the theater who realized that they were necessary to make his work stronger and more effective. By the time *Porgy and Bess* opened in New York, Gershwin was happy with it, even though it was a financial failure. Seeing the bigger picture, Gershwin predicted that one day it would be acclaimed as a great work, and he was more than prescient in that proclamation. The many revivals of *Porgy and Bess* have altered the opera dramatically, firstly in 1942, when it was revived on Broadway as a musical play minus much of the recitative, and in that form, it first started to achieve immortality. The 1950s revival with Leontyne Price and William Warfield also drastically changed the work, but also brought it back into pure operatic form. The 1973 Houston Grand Opera production restored the work to its full running time to great acclaim, and exhaustion of others. Ira, who became the guardian of George's work after his death, had cannily and carefully approved all of these various permutations of *Porgy and Bess*, and late in life he insisted that it be performed uncut. He also removed the "N" word from the text, privately stating that if they had initially realized the truly painful connotation of the word, they never would have used it.

Coming full circle, one of the most recent recordings of *Porgy and Bess*, conducted by John Mauceri, has gone back to the version first performed on Broadway in October 1935, claiming it to be (here we go again) the "definitive" version. I cannot agree. That was a specific moment in time, and had Gershwin lived he would surely have revised the opera yet again, recognizing the need to do so, minus the pressure and deadline of a Broadway opening. He would have tightened and clarified the musical and dramatic arc. But since he is not here, we will never know what his mature vision might have been. Or know any of the other works that were waiting in the wings.

George Gershwin's mystery, his aura, his lifeblood has imbued a mere twenty years of creative work with an immortality that cannot diminish with time. Regardless of the ever-expanding and wanton liberties currently affecting all art in this digital age, it is odd that on one level it does not matter; for even in its most diluted state, Gershwin's music is still magic. The mysteries of the man are as unknowable as the sphinx and as inscrutable as Mona Lisa's smile, but the openhearted gift that came from his soul through his music is for everyone, for all time. The Gershwin I knew was Ira – a trusted friend, mentor, and colleague, whose words of wisdom are as fresh in my mind now as the day he uttered them. The Gershwin I know – not personally, but through his music – is George. If there is such a thing as an American soundscape, it is infused with his spirit. I think that would have made him very happy.

Notes

1. George Gershwin's Draft registration card, dated September 10, 1918. The National Archives at Atlanta www.archives.gov/atlanta/wwi-draft/gershwin.html?fbclid=IwAR06uSodxlRR8-C-_SWr3TKFp0ZYpbTeQ4SRgq20K6gEPVd0vSqfGWpySS4.
2. David Margolick, "Alan Gershwin, Who Claimed a Famous Father, Is Dead at 91," *New York Times* (March 7, 2018), A24.

Guide to Further Reading

André, Naomi. *Black Opera: History, Power, and Engagement* (Urbana, IL: University of Illinois Press, 2018).
  "From Otello to Porgy: Blackness, Masculinity, and Morality in Opera," Karen M. Bryan and Eric Saylor (eds.) *Blackness in Opera* (Urbana, IL: University of Illinois Press, 2012).
Armitage, Merle (ed.), *George Gershwin* (London: Longmans, Green & Co. 1938).
Bagatti, Davide. "Music and Medicine: The Tragic Case of Gershwin's Brain Tumor and the Challenges of Neurosurgery in the First Half of the 20th Century." *World Neurosurgery* 85 (January 2016), 298–304.
Bañagale, Ryan Raul. *Arranging Gershwin: Rhapsody in Blue and the Creation of an American Icon* (Oxford: Oxford University Press, 2011).
  "Rewriting the Narrative One Arrangement at a Time: Duke Ellington and *Rhapsody in Blue*," *Jazz Perspectives* 6/1–2 (2012), 5–27.
Botkin, B.A. "Self-Portraiture and Social Criticism in Negro Folk Song," *Opportunity: A Journal of Negro Life* V (February 1927), 38–42.
Brooks, Noel. "A Schillingerian and Schenkerian Approach to George Gershwin's '*I Got Rhythm*' Variations," M.M. thesis, University of Western Ontario (1998).
Clague, Mark. "An American in Paris: A Gershwin Manifesto," in Mark Clague (ed.), *George Gershwin, An American in Paris: A Tone Poem for Orchestra*, The George and Ira Gershwin Critical Edition (Mainz and New York: Schott International/European American Music, 2019).
Crawford, Richard. *The American Landscape: The Business of Musicianship from Billings to Gershwin* (Berkeley, CA: University of California Press, 2000).
  America's Musical Life: A History (New York: W.W. Norton, 2001).
  Summertime: George Gershwin's Life in Music (New York: W.W. Norton, 2019).
Davis, Andrew and Howard Pollack. "Rotational Form in the Opening Scene of *Porgy and Bess*," *Journal of the American Musicological Society* 60/2 (2007), 373–414.
Decker, Todd. *Music Makes Me: Fred Astaire and Jazz* (Berkeley: University of California Press, 2011).
Duke, Vernon Duke. "Gershwin, Schillinger, and Dukelsky: Some Reminiscences," *The Musical Quarterly* 33/1 (January 1947).
Ewen, David. *A Journey to Greatness: The Life and Music of George Gershwin* (New York: Henry Holt, 1956).
Feinstein, Michael. *The Gershwins and Me: A Personal History in Twelve Songs* (New York: Simon & Schuster, 2012).
Gershwin, George. Introduction to *George Gershwin's Song-book* (New York: Simon & Schuster, 1932).

Gershwin, Ira. *The George and Ira Gershwin Song Book* (New York: Simon & Schuster, 1960).
  Lyrics on Several Occasions (New York: Knopf, 1959).
Gilbert, Steven E. *The Music of George Gershwin* (New Haven, CT: Yale University Press, 1995).
Goldberg, Isaac. *George Gershwin: A Study in American Music* (New York: Simon & Schuster, 1931).
Greene, Harlan (ed.), *Porgy & Bess: A Charleston Story* (Charleston, SC: Home House Press, 2016).
Handy, W.C. *Blues: An Anthology* (New York: Albert and Charles Boni, 1926).
Heyward, DuBose. *Porgy* (New York: Grosset & Dunlap, 1925).
Horowitz, Joseph. *"On My Way": The Untold Story of Rouben Mamoulian, George Gershwin, and* Porgy and Bess (New York: W.W. Norton, 2013).
Hutchisson, James M. *DuBose Heyward: A Charleston Gentleman and the World of* Porgy and Bess (Jackson: University of Mississippi Press, 2000).
Hyland, William G. *George Gershwin: A New Biography* (Westport, CT: Praeger, 2003).
Jablonski, Edward. *Gershwin* (New York: Doubleday, 1987).
  "Gershwin on Music," *Musical America* 82/7 (July 1962), 33.
  Gershwin Remembered (Portland, OR: Amadeus Press, 1992).
Jablonski, Edward and Lawrence D. Stewart, *The Gershwin Years* (Garden City, NY: Doubleday, 1958).
Kimball, Robert, Alfred Simon, and Bea Feitler. *The Gershwins* (New York: Atheneum, 1973).
Krasker, Tommy. *Catalog of the American Musical: Musicals of Irving Berlin, George & Ira Gershwin, Cole Porter, Richard Rodgers & Lorenz Hart* (Washington, DC: National Institute for Opera and Musical Theater, 1988).
Maisel, Arthur. "Talent and Technique: Gershwin's *Rhapsody in Blue*," in Allen Cadwallader (ed.), *Trends in Schenkerian Research* (New York: Schirmer, 1979), 51–70.
Margolick, David. "Alan Gershwin, Who Claimed a Famous Father, Is Dead at 91," *New York Times* (March 7, 2018), A24.
Monod, David. "Disguise, Containment and the *Porgy and Bess* Revival of 1952–1956," *Journal of American Studies* 35 (2001), 275–312.
Nahshon, Edna (ed.), *New York's Yiddish Theater: From the Bowery to Broadway* (New York: Columbia University Press, 2016).
Nauert, Paul. "Theory and Practice in *Porgy and Bess*: The Gershwin-Schillinger Connection," *The Musical Quarterly* 78/1 (Spring 1994).
Neimoyer, Susan. "After the *Rhapsody*: George Gershwin in the Spring of 1924," *Journal of Musicology* 31/1 (Winter 2014).
  "George Gershwin and Edward Kilenyi, Sr.: A Reevaluation of Gershwin's Early Musical Education," *The Musical Quarterly* 94/1 and 2 (Spring/Summer 2011).
  "*Rhapsody in Blue*: The Culmination of George Gershwin's Musical Education," Ph.D. dissertation, University of Washington (2003).
Noonan, Ellen. *The Strange Career of* Porgy and Bess: *Race, Culture and America's Most Famous Opera* (Chapel Hill: University of North Carolina Press, 2012).

Oja, Carol J. "Gershwin and the Modernists of the 1920s," *The Musical Quarterly* 78/4 (Winter 1994), 646–68.
  Making Music Modern: New York in the 1920s (Oxford: Oxford University Press, 2000).
Pollack, Howard. *George Gershwin His Life and Work* (Berkeley, CA: University of California Press, 2007).
Reynolds, Christopher A. "*Porgy and Bess*: 'An American *Wozzeck*,'" *Journal of the Society for American Music* 1/1 (February 2007), 1–28.
Rimler, Walter. *George Gershwin: An Intimate Portrait* (Urbana and Chicago: University of Illinois Press, 2009).
Rosenberg, Deena. *Fascinating Rhythm: The Collaboration of George and Ira Gershwin* (Ann Arbor, MI: University of Michigan Press, 1991).
Sandifer, James. *Porgy and Bess: An American Voice* (Princeton, NJ: Films for the Humanities & Sciences, 1999).
Schiff, David. *Gershwin*: Rhapsody in Blue (Cambridge: Cambridge University Press, 1997).
Schneider, Wayne. "Gershwin in the Heartland: Critical and Public Reception of the 1934 Leo Reisman Tour," *The Musical Quarterly* 94/1–2 (2011).
  (ed.), *The Gershwin Style: New Looks at the Music of George Gershwin* (New York: Oxford University Press, 1990).
Schwartz, Charles. *Gershwin: His Life and Works* (Indianapolis, IN: Bobbs-Merrill, 1973).
Starr, Larry. *George Gershwin* (New Haven, CT: Yale University Press, 2011).
Suriano, Gregory R. (ed.), *Gershwin in His Time: A Biographical Scrapbook, 1919–1937* (New York: Gramercy Books, 1998).
Thompson, Robin. *The Gershwins' Porgy and Bess: A 75th Anniversary Celebration* (Milwaukee, WI: Amadeus Press, 2010).
Thomson, Virgil. "George Gershwin," *Modern Music* 13/1 (November–December 1935).
Tucker, Mark. "Porgy and Miles," *Current Musicology* 71–73 (2001).
Wierzbicki, James. "The Hollywood Career of Gershwin's Second Rhapsody," *Journal of the American Musicological Society* 60/1 (Spring 2007).
Wodehouse, Artis. "Tracing Gershwin's Piano Rolls," in Wayne Schneider (ed.), *The Gershwin Style: New Looks at the Music of George Gershwin* (Oxford: Oxford University Press, 1999).
Wyatt, Robert and John Andrew Johnson (eds.), *The George Gershwin Reader* (Oxford: Oxford University Press, 2004).

Index

Aarons, Alex, 7
Ager, Cecelia, 294
Ager, Milton, 294
Albee, Edward, 67
Alberts, Charles S., 138
Alda, Robert, 134
Alexander III, Czar of Russia, 5
Allen, Gracie, 207, 212, 213
Americana (1928) musical, 10
An American in Paris (1951) film, 214, 240, 262
An American in Paris (2015) musical, 262, 264, 265, 266, 267, 269, 270
Anchors Aweigh (1945) film, 254
Anderson, Marian, 191
Antheil, George, 155–56, 229
   Ballet mécanique, 155, 156
   Jazz Symphony, 156
Anything Goes (1936) film, 200
Arcadelt, Jacques, 36
Arden, Victor, 93, 97, 268
Arlen, Harold, 9, 47, 49, 199, 276, 277
   "Stormy Weather," 277
Arlen, Michael, 154
Armitage, Merle, 48, 53, 291
Armstrong, Louis, 244, 277
Arvey, Verna, 25
Asian American Jazz Orchestra, 256
Askins, Harry, 132
Astaire, Adele, 7, 86, 88, 89, 96–97, 98–99, 199
Astaire, Fred, 7, 45, 46, 47, 53, 82, 86, 88, 93, 96–97, 98–99, 197, 198, 199, 200, 201, 202, 203–6, 207, 208–9, 210, 211, 212, 213, 216, 236, 239, 262, 263, 266–68, 271, 272, 293
"A-Tisket, A-Tasket," 235, 240, 245
Atkins, Charles "Cholly," 271
Atkinson, Brooks, 177
Auner, Joseph, 231
Auric, Georges, 160
Austin, William, 223, 224, 225–26
Avakian, George, 236

Bach, Johann Sebastian, 32, 35, 36
   Toccata and Fugue in E Major, 37
Baker, Kenny, 213
Balakirev, Mily, 36
Banfield, Stephen, 229
Baraka, Amiri, 285–86
Barber, Samuel, 223
Bargy, Roy, 123, 295

Barkleys of Broadway (1949) film, 206, 214
Bartók, Bela, 119
"Battle Hymn of the Republic," 36
Bauer, Marion, 222
"Beale Street Blues," 238
Beethoven, Ludwig van, 9, 35, 76, 225
   Rondo a Cappricio, Op. 129, 37
   Sonata in F Minor, Op. 57 ("Appassionata"), 37
   Sonata Op. 110, 37
   Sonata Op. 81, 37
   String Quartet, Op. 18, No. 4, 37
   Symphony No. 3 ("Eroica"), 37
   Symphony No. 5, 248
   Symphony No. 7, 37
Bennett, Robert Russell, 47, 199, 201, 211, 212, 214, 216
Bennett, Tony, 238
Benton, Thomas Hart, 162
Berg, Alban, 162, 225, 229
   Lyric Suite, 33, 162
   Wozzeck, 231
Bergere, Valerie, 72
Berkeley, Busby, 45
Berlin, 161
Berlin, Irving, 44, 48, 53, 61, 64, 68, 69, 93, 154, 225, 239, 244, 276, 291, 293
   "Alexander's Ragtime Band," 68, 269
   "Blue Skies," 240, 253
   "Everybody Step," 277
   "Everybody's Doing It Now," 87
   "I Love a Piano," 265
   "Just in Love," 265
   Stop! Look! Listen!, 75
   Watch Your Step, 69, 96
Berliner, Paul, 31–32
Berman, Pandro, 206
Bernstein, Leonard, 223, 225, 246, 247, 252, 254
Beverly Hills, 12, 13, 44, 199
Biddle, George, 170
Bizet, Georges, 35
   Carmen, 73
Blackwell, Ed, 283
Blake, Eubie, 23, 25, 34
   Shuffle Along, 25, 72, 73, 273
Blakey, Art, 253
   Art Blakey's Jazz Messengers with Thelonius Monk, 280

Blitzstein, Marc, 223, 225
Bloch, Ernst, 227
Bloodworth, James, 250
Boas, Franz, 159
Bok, Mary Curtis, 155
Borel-Clerc, Charles
  "La Mattchiche," 156
Borroff, Edith, 226
Boston, 45, 51, 114, 143, 144, 145, 146, 149, 152, 162, 182, 252, 296
Boston Pops, 252
Boston Symphony Orchestra, 45, 114, 252
Botkin, Benjamin A., 153, 158–59, 164–66, 168, 169, 171, 172, 173
  Folk-Say, 164–66, 172
  "Self-Portraiture and Social Criticism in Negro Folk Song," 164
  Treasury of American Folklore, 175
Botkin, Harry. *See* Botkin, Henry
Botkin, Henry, 153, 154, 162–63, 164, 171, 173, 177
Boulanger, Nadia, 33, 160
Braggiotti, Mario, 161
Brahms, Johannes, 35, 253
  Three Hungarian Dances, 145
  Variations on a Theme of Paganini, 37
  Zigeunerlieder, 37
Braque, Georges, 162
Bregman, Buddy, 243
Bristow, George, 75
Broderick, Matthew, 261, 267, 268
Broekman, David, 246
Brown, Anne, 172, **183**, 190
Brown, Anthony, 256
Brown, Lew, 44
Bruskin, Rosa. *See* Gershwin, Rose
Bubbling Brown Sugar (1976) musical, 271
Buffalino, Brenda, 271
Buffet, Bernard, 242
Burkholder, J. Peter, 224
Burns, George, 207, 212, 213
Busch, Lou, 252
Bushkin, Joe, 278–79
Busoni, Ferrucio, 35
Butler, David, 198

Caesar, Irving, 7, 136, 138, 139, 290–91, 294
Cage, John, 283
Calloway, Cab, 99, 253, 286
Calvin, Jackson
  Jazz Variations on Gershwin's Rhapsody in Blue, 254
Campbell-Watson, Frank, 106, 114, 118
Cantor, Eddie, 199
Capitol Revue (1919) musical, 81
Capra, Frank, 48, 216
Carlisle, Kitty, 294

Carpenter, John Alden, 140, 157, 225, 229
  Skyscrapers, 229
Carter, Desmond, 98
Carter, Elliott, 226
Caruso, Enrico, 6
Caryll, Ivan, 61
Castle, Irene, 96
Castle, Vernon, 96
Castro Brothers Orchestra, 166
Cavendish, Charles, 99
Cayce, Edgar, 293
Cedars of Lebanon Hospital, 51, 52
Cerf, Bennett, 166
Cezanne, Paul, 154
Chabrier, Emmanuel, 36
Chadwick, George, 140
Chagall, Marc, 163
Chaplin, Charlie, 47, 49
Charleston, SC, 153, 169–74, 176
  Etchers Club, 170
  Macedonia Church, 171
  Poetry Society of South Carolina, 170
  Society for the Preservation of Old Spirituals, 170, 171
Chase, Gilbert, 223–24
Cheatham, Doc, 253
Cherry, Don, 283
Chicago Philharmonic Orchestra, 246
Chopin, Frédéric, 32, 35
  Ballades (nos. 1 and 3), 37
  Scherzo No. 2 in B♭ Minor, 37
  Sonata No. 3 in B Minor, 37
City for Conquest (1941) film, 215
Clague, Mark, 192
Clarke, Hugh A., 61
Clef Club Orchestra, 68
Coburn, Charles, 134
Cocteau, Jean, 155
Coffee, Lenore, 215
Cogdell, J., 70
Cohan, George, 53, 61
Cole, Nat King, 238, 240, 251
Coleman, Bill, 278–79
Coleman, Ornette, 283
  "Chronology," 283
  The Shape of Jazz to Come, 283
  This Is Our Music, 283
Coles, Charles "Honi," 261, 271–72
Coltrane, John, 275, 283
  A Love Supreme, 282
  My Favorite Things, 282–83
Columbia University, 38, 158
Confrey, Zez, 224
Coniff, Ray, 252
Connor, Chris, 237
Conrad, Con
  "Singin' the Blues," 103

Cook, Will Marion, 60, 63–64, 73
　Clorindy, 63
　In Dahomey, 63
Copland, Aaron, 29, 140, 222–23, 224, 225, 227, 228, 229, 230, 246
　Piano Concerto, 222
Corelli, Archangelo, 36
Cortot, Alfred, 161
Cowell, Henry, 33, 38, 39, 228
Crawford, Richard, 221, 226, 229–30
Crazy for You (1992) musical, 261, 262, 263, 264, 265, 266, 267, 268, 270, 273
Crosby, Bing, 200, 246, 251
Cuban Love Song (1931) film, 166
Cugat, Xavier, 13
Cullen, Countee, 169
　Color, 164
Curb Your Enthusiasm, 258
Cushing, Edward, 145
Cushing, Harvey, 52
Czerwonky, Richard, 246

Daintyland, 10
Daly, William, 146, 148
Dameron, Tadd, 280
Damrosch, Walter, 7, 53, 106, 140, 142, 149, 163
Damrosh, Alice, 140
Dandy, Walter, 52
Darnton, Charles, 75
Davis, "Wild" Bill, 252
Davis, Miles, 275, 281–82, 283
　Kind of Blue, 281
　Miles Ahead, 281
　"Milestones," 281
　Porgy and Bess, 281–82
Davis, Steve, 282
Dawson, Mary Cardwell, 190
De Forrest, Muriel, 137
De Koven, Reginald, 61
Debussy, Claude, 32, 140, 149, 154, 225
　Estampes, 119
　Préludes, 33
Delius, Frederick, 225
　Koanga, 184
Demi-Tasse Revue (1919) musical, 137
Derain, André, 162
Deri, Otto, 224
Dessalines, Jean-Jacques, 184
DeSylva, Buddy, 44, 72, 81, 84, 135, 153
　"Chloe," 135
　"I'll Say She Does," 135
　"I'll Tell the World," 135
Dett, Nathaniel, 189, 193
Diaghilev, Sergei, 154, 161, 188
Dietrich, Marlene, 47
Dillingham, Charles, 64, 65–66, 132
DiPietro, Joe, 261

Don Juan (1926) film, 44
Donizetti, Gaetano, 225
Dorsey, Jimmy, 93, 201
Dorsey, Tommy, 250
"Down Where the Swanee River Flows," 138
Drake, Alfred, 238
Draper, Paul, 253
Drdla, Franz, 70
Dresser, Louise, 132
Dreyfus, Max, 48, 132, 134–35, 148
DuBois, W. E. B.
　The Souls of Black Folk, 188, 189
Duffy, John, 252
Duke, Vernon, 9, 30, 53, 62, 221, 225, 240, 292
Dukelsky, Vladimir. *See* Duke, Vernon
Dumas, Abe, 172
Dunayevsky, Isaak, 225
Dunbar, Paul Laurence, 189
Duncan, Todd, 50, 190, 292
Durante, Jimmy, 146
Dushkin, Samuel, 48
Dvořák, Antonín, 35
　"Humoresque," 72

Edwards, Cliff, 89, 95
Edwards, Julian, 61, 73
　The Patriot, 73
Elgar, Edward, 140
Ellington, Edward Kennedy "Duke," 18, 19, 33, 34, 146, 225, 255, 258, 284, 285, 286
　"Cotton Tail," 284
　Harlem Air Shaft, 18
　"I'm Just a Lucky So and So," 244
　Will Big Bands Ever Come Back?, 255
Elman, Mischa, 71
Emerson, Lake, and Palmer, 228
Engles, George, 140
Epstein, Julius, 215
Europe, James Reese, 68, 69
Evans, Gil, 275, 281–82
Evans, Walker, 170
Ewen, David, 291–92

Farmer, Art, 33
Faulkner, Anne Shaw, 70
Feather, Leonard, 253
Feinstein, Michael, 237
Ferris, Jean, 228
Fiedler, Arthur, 252
Finkelstein, Sidney, 227
Fisher, Rob, 265
Fitzgerald, Ella, 235–45, 253, 286
　Ella Abraça Jobim, 243
　Ella Fitzgerald Sings the Irving Berlin Songbook, 240
　Ella Fitzgerald Sings the Cole Porter Song Book, 237, 243

Fitzgerald, Ella (cont.)
　Ella Fitzgerald Sings the Duke Ellington Song Book, 237
　Ella Fitzgerald Sings the George and Ira Gershwin Songbook, 239, 240–43
　Ella Fitzgerald Sings the Harold Arlen Songbook, 243
　Ella Fitzgerald Sings the Irving Berlin Song Book, 237
　Ella Fitzgerald Sings the Jerome Kern Songbook, 243
　Ella Fitzgerald Sings the Johnny Mercer Songbook, 243
　Ella Fitzgerald Sings the Rodgers & Hart Song Book, 237
　Ella Loves Cole, 243
　Ella Sings Gershwin, 235, 236, 237–38, 244
　Lullabies of Birdland, 236, 240, 241
　Mack The Knife – Ella In Berlin, 243
　Nice Work If You Can Get It, 243, 244
Fitzgerald, F. Scott
　"May Day," 97
Flagler, Harry Harkness, 140
Flanagan, Tommy, 244
Florida, 170, 184
Flotow, Friedrich von
　Martha, 211
Folly Island, SC, 51, 171–72, 189
Fontaine, Joan, 46, 47, 207, 208–9
Foster, Stephen, 221
　"Old Folks at Home," 138
Four Daughters (1938) film, 215
Francis, Arthur. *See* Gershwin, Ira
Fray, Jacques, 161
Freed, Arthur, 44
Freeman, Harry Lawrence, 73, 190
　VooDoo, 184
Freeman, Stan, 295
Friml, Rudolf
　The Student Prince in Heidelberg, 92
Fry, Gary, 257
Fry, William Henry, 75
Funny Face (1957) film, 238, 239

Gabler, Milt, 235
Gann, Kyle, 228, 229
Garbo, Greta, 241
Garland, Judy, 251, 292
Geller, Gertrude, 3
Gentlemen Prefer Blondes (1949) musical, 271
Geraty, Virginia Mixson, 190
Gershovitz, Morris. *See* Gershwin, Morris
Gershwin Collection at the Library of Congress, 35, 38

Gershwin Initiative, 192
Gershwin, Aaron, 3
Gershwin, Alan. *See* Schneider, Albert
Gershwin, Arthur, 3, **4**, 9–10, 12–13, 146
　"Invitation to the Blues," 13
　A Lady Says Yes, 13
　"Slowly but Surely," 9
Gershwin, Frances, 3, **4**, 9, 10, 12, 13–14, 30, 32, 43, 51, 159, 160, 290, 294
　For George and Ira, 14
Gershwin, George, **4**, **5**, **50**, **175**
　as businessman, 130
　as concert pianist, 120–27
　as conductor, 145, 149
　classical music appreciation, 34
　connection to Yiddish theater, 24–25
　death of, 12, 13, 43, 51–53, 127, 214, 215, 246, 249, 250, 290, 293
　film industry, 43–45
　formative years in New York, 16–24
　interest in visual art, 49, 162–63
　"Jazz Is the Voice of the American Soul," 285
　Music by Gershwin (radio show), 9
　music theory studies, 38–40
　musical education, 29–41
　perceptions of ragtime and jazz, 66–67, 70–71, 161, 284–85
　Portrait of Grandfather, 49
　representation in music history texts, 221–32
　rumored sexual orientation, 294
　scrapbooks of, 35
　source for instrumental jazz, 275
　work as song plugger, 23–24, 32
　Works
　　135th Street. See Blue Monday
　　The Ambulatory Suite, 242
　　An American in Paris, 82, 114, 131, 141–49, 150, 153, 156–57, 160, 161, 163, 168, 199, 207, 215, 222, 231, 242
　　"Baby!," 90
　　"Bess, You Is My Woman Now," 182, 215, 228
　　"Blah, Blah, Blah," 267
　　Blue Monday, 39, 44, 60, 72–77, 157, 228
　　"Boy Wanted," 265
　　"Boy! What Love Has Done to Me," 89, 99
　　"Bride and Groom," 88
　　"Bronco Busters," 87, 88, 264
　　"But Not for Me," 199, 239, 243, 244, 264, 265, 282, 283
　　"Buzzard Song," 184
　　"By Strauss," 46, 80, 240, 265
　　"Clap Yo' Hands," 95, 270

Index

"Come to the Moon," 137
Concerto in F, 30, 50, 51, 59, 61, 98, 102, 106–13, 118, 122, 124, 126, 127, 131, 140–41, 149, 150, 155, 157, 215, 216, 222, 223, 230, 264, 267, 295
"A Corner of Heaven with You," 133
"Could You Use Me?," 264
Cuban Overture, 45, 153, 167–68, 240
A Damsel in Distress, 43, 46, 47, 82, 197–98, 206–13, 216, 239, 262, 263
"Dear Little Girl," 88
Delicious, 43, 45, 114, 197, 198–99, 202, 215
"Demon Rum," 264
"Don't Ask," 90
"Down with Everything That's Up," 92
"Embraceable You," 8, 199, 266, 275, 283
"End of a String," 88
"Fascinating Rhythm," 88, 89, 91, 96–97, 211, 240, 275, 276, 277, 278, 281
"Fidgety Feet," 242, 270
"A Fine Romance," 200
"First Lady and First Gent," 296
"Florida," 87
"A Foggy Day," 47, 208, 209, 284
"For Lily Pons," 265
"For You, For Me, Forevermore," 265
Funny Face, 85, 93, 199, 239, 263, 264, 265, 272
George Gershwin's Song-Book, 123, 223
Girl Crazy, 8, 83, 86, 87, 89, 90, 93, 99, 118, 199, 210, 261, 264, 275, 282
"The Half of It, Dearie, Blues," 97, 157
"Hang on to Me," 88, 98
"He Loves, and She Loves," 242, 264, 268
"Heaven on Earth," 96
"High Hat," 272
"Hoctor's Ballet," 46, 47
"How Can I Win You Now?," 90
"How Long Has This Been Going On?," 238, 243
"I Can't Be Bothered Now," 207, 209
"I Got Plenty o' Nuttin'," 182
"I Got Rhythm," 89, 203, 224, 240, 270, 275, 276, 277–80, 282
"I Was Doing All Right," 241
"I Won't Play," 249–50
"I'd Rather Charleston," 89, 98, 99
"I'll Build a Stairway to Paradise," 76, 264, 270
"I've Got a Crush on You," 92, 238, 266
"I've Got Rhythm," 210
"In Sardinia," 89

"In the Mandarin's Orchid Garden," 10, 239
"In the Swim," 265
"It's a Great Little World," 96
"The Jolly Tar and the Milk Maid," 47, 210, 239
"Juanita," 89
"Just Another Rhumba," 240
"Kickin' the Clouds Away," 95, 266, 272
Lady, Be Good!, 7, 11, 67, 76, 81, 83, 84, 85, 86, 87, 88, 89, 90, 92, 93, 95, 96–98, 141, 154, 157, 199, 212, 239, 262
La-La-Lucille!, 80, 81, 135
Let 'Em Eat Cake, 45, 81, 92, 296
"Let's Call the Whole Thing Off," 46, 200, 201, 207, 266
"Linger in the Lobby," 87, 88
"Little Jazz Bird," 89, 95
"Little Sunbeam," 71
"Liza," 146, 266, 269
"Looking for a Boy," 90
"The Lorelei," 99
"Love Is Here to Stay," 53, 213, 239, 242, 292
"Love Is in the Air," 87
"Love Is Sweeping the Country," 242
"Love Walked In," 213, 242
"Loving Makes Living So Sweet," 133
Lullaby for String Quartet, 39, 72, 74, 228
"Making of a Girl," 80, 132
"The Man I Love," 239, 276
"March of the Swiss Soldiers," 242
"Meadow Serenade," 296
"Mischa, Jascha, Toscha, Sascha," 71
"The Moon Is on the Sea," 87
"My Cousin in Milwaukee," 100
"My Fair Lady," 88
"My Man's Gone Now," 182
"My One and Only," 238
"Never Gonna Dance," 204
New York Concerto. See Concerto in F
New York Rhapsody. See Second Rhapsody
"Nice Baby! (Come to Papa!)," 90
"Nice Work If You Can Get It," 47, 210, 244, 266, 280
Novelette in Fourths, 72
Of Thee I Sing, 8, 81, 82, 83, 85, 92
"Oh Lawd, I'm On My Way," 182
Oh, Kay!, 82, 83, 86, 87, 88, 90, 91, 93, 95, 96, 157, 262
"Oh, Lady Be Good!," 87, 91, 240, 241, 244, 280

Gershwin, George (cont.)
  Pardon My English, 45, 81, 83, 99, 100
  "Pick Yourself Up," 201, 209
  Porgy and Bess, 29, 40, 45, 46, 50, 51, 59, 73, 76, 80, 81, 82, 83, 150, 153, 159, 168, 171, 173, 174, 176, 177, 182–95, **185**, 197, 202, 223, 224, 225, 226, 227, 228, 229, 230, 231, 244, 246, 247, 275, 281, 282, 292, 293, 296–97
  Primrose, 81
  Promenade, 46
  "Ragging the Traumerei," 69
  "The Real American Folk Song (is a Rag)," 69, 70, 93, 239, 265
  Rhapsody in Blue, 7, 26, 30, 34, 38, 39, 44, 46, 50, 59, 60, 67, 72, 74, 75, 76, 82, 92, 96, 98, 102–6, 107, 112, 113, 114, 117, 118, 119, 120, 122, 123, 124, 125, 126–27, 131, 140, 141, 143, 145, 149, 150, 155, 156, 157, 158, 160, 162, 199, 203, 215, 216, 221, 222, 223, 224, 227, 228, 229, 242, 246–58, 268, 271, 275, 277, 285, 291, 295
  Rhumba. See Cuban Overture
  "'S Wonderful," 231, 262, 263, 268
  "Sam and Delilah," 89, 99
  Second Rhapsody, 8, 40, 44, 45, 102, 113–17, 118, 119, 122, 198, 229, 295, 296
  Shall We Dance, 43, 46, 47, 82, 197–206, 207, 210, 211, 213, 214, 216, 239, 262, 263, 264, 266, 268
  "Shopgirls and Mannequins," 87
  Show Girl, 145–48, 149, 269
  "Sing of Spring," 47, 210
  "Six Simultaneous Prayers," 174, 182
  "Slap That Bass," 201–2, 211
  "Somebody from Somewhere," 241
  "Someone to Watch Over Me," 238, 239, 266
  Song of the Flame, 81
  "Soon," 92, 265
  "Stiff Upper Lip," 211, 212, 213
  Stop Flirting, 7
  Strike Up the Band, 83, 84, 92, 93, 241, 296
  "Summertime," 182, 276, 282, 284
  "Swanee," 4, 7, 10, 81, 131, 134–40, 148, 149, 247, 290
  "Swanee Rose," 139
  "Sweet and Low-Down," 94, 95, 265
  Sweet Little Devil, 81, 84, 247
  Swing Time, 201, 204, 209
  "Swiss Miss," 89, 98, 212

  Tell Me More, 84, 86, 87, 88, 89, 90, 91, 95, 154
  "That Certain Feeling," 91
  "There's More to a Kiss," 133
  "They All Laughed," 207
  "They Can't Take That Away from Me," 46, 47, 203–6, 244, 264
  "Things Are Looking Up," 208, 209, 267
  "Three Preludes," 223, 225, 242, 296
  Tip-Toes, 84, 86, 87, 88, 89, 90, 91, 93, 94, 95, 96
  "Tomalé (I'm Hot for You)," 139
  Treasure Girl, 92, 93, 265
  "Treat Me Rough," 90
  "Union League," 296
  Variations on "I Got Rhythm," 40, 45, 102, 117–20, 122, 124, 223
  "Waiting for the Sun to Come Out," 11
  "Walking the Dog," 46, 203, 242, 266
  "The Way You Look Tonight," 209
  "We're Here Because," 90
  "We're Six Little Nieces of Our Uncle Sam," 71
  "What Causes That?," 265
  "When Do We Dance?," 88
  "When the Debbies Go By," 88
  "When You Want 'Em, You Can't Get 'Em, When You've Got 'Em, You Don't Want 'Em," 131
  "Who Cares?," 265
  "A Woman's Touch," 87
  "A Wonderful Party," 87, 88
  "Yan-Kee," 71
  "Yankee Doodle Blues," 71
Gershwin, Ira, 3, **4**, **5**, 6, 7, 8, 9, 10, 11, 12, 13, 17, 20, 21, 22, 30, 31, 35, 38, 39, 41, 42, 44, 46, 47, 48, 52, 53, 69, 70, 71, 81, 82, 84, 88, 90, 91, 93, 94, 95, 96, 97, 100, 146, 147, 148, 158, 159, 160, 161, 162, 164, 168, 177, 184, 190, 193, 197, 198, 199, 200, 202, 211, 213, 224, 230, 235, 239, 240, 244, 245, 265, 266, 269, 270, 273, 289, 290, 291, 292, 293, 295, 296, 297, 300
  Lyrics on Several Occasions, 13
  Works (with a collaborator other than George)
    The Firebrand of Florence, 13
    "Island in the West Indies," 240
    Lady in the Dark, 13
    "Long Ago and Far Away," 13
    "The Man That Got Away," 13
    Park Avenue, 13
    Two Little Girls in Blue, 11

Gershwin, Leonore, 48, 53, 83, 159, 160
Gershwin, Morris, 3, 4, 5, 6, 7, 8, 9, 11, 12, 14, 17, 24, 247
Gershwin, Rose, 3, 4, **5**, 6, 9, 10, 11, 12, 17, 20, 171, 214, 247, 290, 294
Gershwine, Jacob. *See* Gershwin, George
Gibson, Michael, 268
Gilbert, Steven, 230
Gilbert, W.S., 47, 71, 81, 92, 210
   Mikado, 71
Gilbreth Jr., Frank, 172
Gillespie, Dizzy, 280, 286
Gingold, Hermione, 242
Girl Crazy (1943) film, 292
Gish, Lillian, 292
Glaenzer, Jules, 153, 154
Glazunov, Alexander, 36, 221, 226
Glière, Reinhold, 36
Goddard, Paulette, 49
Godfrey Wetterlow Company, 142
Godowsky, Frances Gershwin. *See* Gershwin, Frances
Godowsky, Jr., Leopold, 10, 12, 13
Godowsky, Leopold, 8, 36
Goetschius, Percy, 38
Goldberg, Isaac, 3, 19, 20, 21, 30, 61, 81, 291
Goldman, Richard Franko, 227
Goldmark, Rubin, 38, 39
Goldwyn, Samuel, 43, 47, 214
   The Goldwyn Follies, 43, 53, 213–14, 239, 240
Gone with the Wind (1939) film, 215
Gonsalves, Paul, 255
Goodman, Benny, 93, 250, 287
Gorman, Ross, 291
"Gotta Pebble in My Shoe," 235
Gounod, Charles, 36
Granz, Norman, 235, 236–37, 238, 239, 240, 242, 243, 244
Greenhalgh, Herbert S., 76
Grieg, Edvard, 35, 127
   Peer Gynt Suite, 255
   Piano Concerto in A Minor, 37
Griffiths, Paul, 231
Grofé, Ferde, 103, 104, 127, 249, 252–53, 291, 295
Gromaire, Marcel, 162
Grout, Donald Jay, 224–25

Habanero Sextet, 167
Haden, Charlie, 283
Hailstork, Adolphus, 193
Hambitzer, Charles, 32, 35, 36, 108
Hamilton, Harry
   "My Swanee Home," 138
Hamilton, Jimmy, 255
Hamm, Charles, 227–28
Hammerstein II, Oscar, 51, 53, 81, 132, 245

Oklahoma!, 51
Show Boat, 146
Hancock, Herbie, 284, 286
   Gershwin's World, 275, 284, 287
Handel, George Frideric, 36
Handy, W. C., 53, 98, 156, 157, 284
   Blues: An Anthology, 98, 157
   "St. Louis Blues," 98, 284
Hannenfeldt, Zenna, 49
Harburg, Yip, 6, 47, 52, 199
Harms Music Publishing Co., 132–34
Harris, Roy, 223, 227, 228
Hart, Lorenz, 239
   "Glad to Be Unhappy," 244
Hart, Moss, 13, 48
Harvard University, 158
Hassam, Childe, 170
Havana, 153, 166–68, 176
   Almendares Hotel and Golf Club, 166
Hawkins, Coleman, 286
Haydn, Franz Josef, 35
   Quartet No. 8, 37
   Symphony No. 13, 37
Heifetz, Jascha, 71
Heindorf, Ray, 249
Henderson, NC, 173–74
Henderson, Ray, 44
Herbert, Victor, 61, 64–66, 75
   Babette, 65, 66
   The Magic Knight, 75
Heyman, Edward, 9
Heyward, Dorothy, 174, 183, 190, 193, 230
   Porgy (1927) play, 169, 170, 183, 184–85, 187, 188, 190, 202
Heyward, DuBose, 51, 157, 169, 170, 172, 177, 183, 184, 185, 189, 190, 193, 230
   Porgy (1925) novel, 157–58, 169, 170, 171, 173, 183, 184, 185–88
   Porgy (1927) play, 169, 170, 183, 184–85, 187, 188, 190, 202
The HiLos, 242
Hirschfeld, Al, 295
Hitchcock, H. Wiley, 226
Hitler, Adolf, 173
Hoctor, Harriet, 46, 147, 206
Hogan, Ernest, 67
Holiday in Mexico (1946) film, 254
Holiday, Billie, 286
Hollywood, 43–54
Holtz, Lou, 89
Honegger, Arthur, 161
   Les Aventures du Roi Pausole, 33
Hoogstraten, Willem van, 145
Hopper, Edward, 170
Horowitz, Joseph, 230

Horowitz, Vladimir, 161
Houston Grand Opera, 297
Howard, John Tasker, 221–22
Howells, William Dean, 19
Hughs, Spike, 285
Humperdinck, Engelbert, 36

"I Found My Yellow Basket," 235
Ibert, Jacques, 160
Ippolitov-Ivanov, Mikhail, 36
Iturbi, José, 254
Ives, Charles, 223, 224, 230

Jablonski, Edward, 231, 238
Jackson, Calvin, 253–55
    Arrangement of *Rhapsody in Blue*, 254–55
Jacobs, Everett, 166
Jacobsen, Sascha, 71
Jenkins, Edmund, 76
Jenkins' Orphanage Band, 169, 170, 174
Jerome H. Remick and Co., 23, 32, 34, 131, 132, 133, 199, 247
Jessye, Eva, 189
Jim Crow, 67, 188, 286
Johnson, Hall, 189
Johnson, James P., 23, 25, 26, 34, 106, 170, 190, 285
    "The Charleston," 170, 284
    Runnin' Wild, 106, 170
Johnson, John Rosamond, 60, 193
Jolson, Al, 7, 81, 134–38, 139, 146, 149, 151, 269, 285
Jones, Hank, 244
Jones, Jimmy, 244
Joplin, Scott, 67
    Treemonisha, 184
Jordan, Louis, 236
Joyce, James, 154, 155

Kahn, Gus, 146
Kálmán, Emmerich, 161, 164
    Die Herzogin von Chicago, 161
Karol, Kim, 250
Kaufmann, George S., 81
Keeler, Ruby, 146, 269
Keith, B. F., 67
Kelly, Gene, 262, 263
Kenny G
    Classics in the Key of G, 284
Kerker, Gustave
    Burning to Sing or Singing to Burn, 73
Kern, Jerome, 32, 46, 48, 49, 80, 85, 132, 199, 225, 238, 276, 286, 292
    Miss 1917, 132
    Show Boat, 146
Khachaturian, Aram, 226
Kilenyi, Sr., Edward, 35, 38–39, 40

King of Jazz (1930) film, 44
Kingman, Daniel, 227
Kirk, Andy, 280
Kneisel Quartet, 37
Knopf, Edwin H., 154
Koemmennich, Louis, 61
Kolish, Rudolf, 161, 162
Koussevitzky, Serge, 45, 114
Krasker, Tommy, 84
Kreisler, Fritz, 7, 161
Krenek, Ernst, 164
    Jonny spielt auf, 161
Krupa, Gene, 93

L'Ouverture, Toussaint, 184
La Touraine Coffee Concerts, 143
Ladies First (1918) musical, 93, 265
Landis, Carole, 13
Lane, Burton, 296
Lane, Judy, 13
Larkins, Ellis, 237, 238
Lawford, Peter, 242
Lawrence, Elliot, 251
Lawrence, Gertrude, 99
Lecuona, Ernesto, 161, 166
Léger, Fernand, 155
Lehár, Franz, 161, 226
Leith, Ernest. *See* Milne, Frank
Leo Reisman Orchestra, 117
Leoncavallo, Ruggiero, 36
    Pagliacci, 74
Lerner, Alan Jay, 132
Levant, Oscar, 32, 48, 53, 134, 199, 203, 214, 215, 249, 289, 293, 294
Levy, Lou, 244
Lhevinne, Josef, 36
Liberace, 252
Liszt, Franz, 32, 35, 105, 225, 285
    Hungarian Rhapsody No. 12, 37
    Hungarian Rhapsody No. 6, 37
    Legende (St. Francis Walking on the Waves), 37
    Les Préludes, 37
    Sonata in B Minor, 37
Livingston, Alan, 236
Livingston, Fud, 47
Locke, Alain
    The New Negro, 188
Lockett, Joseph H., 253
Loeffler, Charles Martin, 140
Loesser, Frank, 245
Loewe, Frederick, 226
London, 7
Los Angeles, 43–54, 166, 246, 251, 254
    1984 Olympic Games, 256
    Temple B'nai B'rith, 53
Los Angeles Philharmonic, 50, 51

Lucky Strike Hit Parade, 243
Lurçat, Jean, 162
Lyons, Arthur, 50

MacDonald, Jeanette, 45
MacDowell, Edward, 36
Machlis, Joseph, 224–25
Mack, Cecil
   Runnin' Wild, 106
Mahler, Gustav
   Symphony No. 4, 140
"Mairzy Doats," 243
Mamoulian, Rouben, 48, 202, 296
   Love Me Tonight (1932) film, 202
Man Ray, 161
Marie Harriman Gallery, 53
Marsalis, Wynton, 283–84
   Marsalis Standard Time, Vol.1, 284
Marx Brothers, 200, 210
   A Night at the Opera, 200
Marx, Harpo, 215
Mascagni, Pietro, 36
Mason, Daniel Gregory, 140, 221
Mathis, Stanley Wayne, 270
Matisse, Henri, 154, 162
Mauceri, John, 297
May, Billy, 237, 243
Mayer, Timothy S., 263
McBride, Robert, 114, 118
McCarron, Charles K., 138
McEvoy, J. P., 146
McGlinn, John, 83
Meet Me in St. Louis (1944) film, 254
Meier, Nellie Simmons, 293
Melinda the Mousie, 235
Mellers, Wilfrid, 224, 225
Mendelssohn, Felix, 35
   Piano Concerto No. 1, 37
   Symphony No. 4, 37
   "Wedding March," 74
Menotti, Gian Carlo, 225
Merman, Ethel, 86, 89, 99, 224, 238
Merry-Go-Round (1927) Broadway revue, 10
Metropolitan Opera, 168, 191, 193
Mexico, 12
Miami Beach, 9
Milhaud, Darius, 33, 140, 161, 188
   Creation of the World, 222
Miller, Glenn, 40, 93
Mills, Florence, 25
Milne, Frank, 143
Minnelli, Vincente, 46, 240
Mitchell, Joni, 284
Modern Times (1936) film, 49
Modigliani, Amedeo, 162
Molnár, Ferenc, 161
Monk, Thelonius, 275, 280–81, 283, 286

"Rhythm-a-ning," 280–81
Monteux, Pierre, 37
Moore, Tom, 67
Moore, Undine Smith, 189, 193
Moran, Jason, 287
Morgan, Robert P., 228
Morton, Jelly Roll, 251, 287
   "King Porter Stomp," 287
Mosbacher, Emil, 52, 166
Mozart, Wolfgang Amadeus, 35, 225
Mueller, Paul, 51, 171, 173
Murrow, Edward, 225
Music Branch of the United States Special
   Services Division, 248
"My Happiness," 236
My One and Only (1983) musical, 261, 262, 263,
   264, 265, 266, 268, 271, 272

Naffziger, Howard, 52
National Association of Negro Musicians, 253
Nero, Peter, 228
Nevin, Ethelbert, 221
New World Music Corporation, 148
New York, 3, 6, 7, 11, 12, 37, 45, 51, 59, 102, 103,
   105, 114, 116, 117, 118, 141, 143, 145,
   156, 170, 171, 177, 183, 215, 247, 280,
   296
   Temple Emamu-El, 53
New York Philharmonic, 37, 53, 141, 144, 145,
   149, 163, 252
New York Philharmonic Society, 141
New York Symphony, 141
New York Symphony Society, 140
Nice Work If You Can Get It (2012) musical, 261,
   262, 263, 264, 265, 266, 267, 268, 270
Nichols, David, 228
Nichols, Red, 93
Niles, Abbe, 157, 163
Noble, Ray, 210
Nothing Sacred (1937) film, 215

O'Day, Anita, 237, 238
O'Hara, Kelli, 261, 267, 268
Ockrent, Mike, 261
Ohman, Phil, 93, 97, 268
Oja, Carol, 228, 230
Ornstein, Leo, 35, 36
Ossining, New York, 162

Packer, Chauncey, 194
Palais Royale Orchestra, 76
Palastrina, Giovanni Pierluigi da, 36
Palau Brothers Hollywood Orchestra, 166
Paley, Emily, 154, 157, 173
Paley, Lou, 154
Palisca, Claude, 224
Pallay, George, 52, 167
Pan, Hermes, 211, 213

Paris, 153–63, 171, 176
Parker, Charlie, 275, 280, 286
    "Anthropology," 280
    "Moose the Mooche," 280
Partch, Harry, 228
Passing Show of 1916, 80
Patterson, Willis, 193
Peabody, Eddy, 252
Pennario, Leonard, 295
Pennsylvania, 9
Peyser, Joan, 292
Picabia, Francis, 155
Picasso, Pablo, 49, 154, 155, 162, 188
    Absinthe Drinker, 49
Piñeiro, Ignacio, 167
Piston, Walter, 223, 226
Porter, Cole, 10, 90, 132, 238, 241, 244, 276, 286
    "Dream Dancing," 244
    Les Revue Des Ambassadors, 10
Poulenc, Francis
    Les Biches, 226
Pound, Ezra, 154, 155
Powell, Bud
    "Web City," 280
Powell, John, 76
Previn, André, 243, 244
    Previn and the Pittsburgh, 243
Price, Leontyne, 297
Price, Sammy, 253
Pringle, Aileen, 49
Prokofiev, Sergei, 161, 225
    Piano Concerto No. 3, 33
Prowse, Juliet, 242
Puccini, Giacomo, 36, 225
    Tosca, 193

Rachmaninoff, Sergei, 35
    Piano Concerto No. 2, 37
Rameau, Jean-Phillippe, 36
Ramsey, Guy, 280
Rand, Carl, 52
Rasch, Albertina, 147
Ravel, Maurice, 33, 130, 154, 160, 161, 225, 228, 229
Ray, Man, 155
Reiner, Fritz, 144
Rhapsody in Blue (1945) film, 6, 134, 136, 139, 214, 248–51
Rhené-Baton, Emmanuel, 161
Rice, Thomas Dartmouth, 185
Riddle, Nelson, 238, 240, 241, 242, 243, 251
Riegger, Wallingford, 33, 38
Riggs, Lynn, 51
    "Green Grow the Lilacs," 51
Rimsky-Korsakov, Nikolai, 36
    Scheherezade, 37
Roach, Max, 286

Roberti, Lyda, 100
Roberts, Luckey, 23, 34, 224
Roberts, Marcus, 255
Robinson, Edward G., 12
Robinson, J. Russel
    "Singin' the Blues," 103
Robinson, Morris, 193
Rodgers, Richard, 132, 239, 245, 276
Roemheld, Heinz, 215
Rogers, Alex, 63
Rogers, Ginger, 45, 46, 47, 49, 197, 198, 199, 200, 201, 203–6, 207, 209, 210, 267, 268
Rogers, Richard, 53
    "Glad to Be Unhappy," 244
    Oklahoma!, 51
Romberg, Sigmund, 88
Rooney, Mickey, 292
Rosenfeld, Paul, 221
Ross, Alex, 231
Rossini, Gioachino, 36
Roth, Murray, 131
Rouault, George, 154, 162, 163
Rousseau, Théodore, 49
    L'Île de la Cité, 49
Rubinstein, Anton, 35, 107, 225
    Melody in F, 21
    Piano Concerto No. 4, 108, 109
Rudhyar, Dane, 29
Ruggles, Carl, 224
Russell, Walter, 294
Russia, 36
    St. Petersburg, 5, 6, 17
Ryskind, Morrie, 81

Sadin, Robert, 255
Saint-Saëns, Camille, 35
Salten, Felix, 161
Salzman, Eric, 226
Saminsky, Lazare, 221
Sandburg, Carl, 158
Sandrich, Mark, 198, 200, 201, 207
Sanromá, Jesús María, 252
Satie, Erik, 154
Savoy, Bert, 97
Sawyer, Charles Pike, 76
Scheff, Fritzi, 65, 66
Schiff, David, 230
Schillinger, Joseph, 38, 40, 119, 168, 225, 229
Schirmer, Mabel, 35, 43, 50, 141, 154–55, 156, 159, 160
Schirmer, Robert, 141, 154–55, 156, 160
Schneider, Albert, 292
Schneider, Wayne, 231
Schoenberg, Arnold, 33, 36, 48–49, **50**, 161, 199, 215, 223, 225
    Harmonielehre, 39
    Pierrot Lunaire, 37

Schoenfeld, William, 118
Schoppe, Palmer, 170
Schubert, Franz, 35, 76, 161
   Quintet in A Major, Op. 114, 37
   Symphony No. 8 ("Unfinished"), 37
Schumann, Robert, 35
   Kinderscenen, 37
   Vogel als Prophet, 37
Schwab, Laurence, 250
Schwartz, Charles, 292
Secunda, Sholom, 63
   "Bei mir Bist du Schön," 63
Seidel, Toscha, 71
Septeto Nacional, 167
Sessions, Roger, 223, 224, 226, 228
Shilkret, Nathaniel, 47, 143, 199, 201, 214, 295
Shirley, Wayne, 192, 227, 231
Shostakovich, Dimitri
   Symphony No. 1, 33
Show Is On, The (1936) musical, 80, 240
Shuffle Along, or the Making of the Musical Sensation of 1921 and All That Followed (2016), 273
Silberberg, Daniel, 166
Simmons, John, 279
Simms, Bryan R., 228
Simon, Alfred, 295
Simon, Elizabeth, 295
Simon, Simone, 49, 294
Simons, Moisés
   "The Peanut Vendor (El manisero)," 166, 167
Sinatra, Frank, 235, 236, 238, 242–43, 250, 251
   Songs for Swingin' Lovers, 242
Sinbad, 7, 135, 136, 139
Sinding, Christian, 36
Sissle, Noble, 25
   Shuffle Along, 25, 72, 73, 273
Smith, Paul, 244
Smith, Queenie, 89
Smith, Willie "The Lion," 24, 26, 34, 277, 285
Spina, Harold, 292
Stanley, Aileen, 104
Starr, Larry, 29, 229, 231
Steamboat Willie (1928) short film, 44
Steiner, Max, 215
Stern, Maurice, 162
Stevens, George, 198, 207, 208–9
Stewart, Lawrence D., 238, 239, 242
Still, William Grant, 25, 190, 225, 273
   Levee Land, 25
"Stone Cold Dead in the Market," 236
Stone, Peter, 263
Stoney, Thomas P., 170
Stothart, Herbert, 81
Strauss, Richard, 140

Stravinsky, Igor, 12, 47, 119, 130, 140, 154, 160, 188, 225, 227, 229
   "Les Noces," 33
   Pulcinella, 226
   Symphonie des Psaumes, 33
Strayhorn, Billy, 255
   Arrangement of *Rhapsody in Blue*, 255
Stroll, George, 254
Stroman, Susan, 261, 268
Struble, John Warthen, 228, 229
Sublett, John William "Bubbles," 190
Suesse, Dana, 9
Sullivan, Arthur, 47, 71, 81, 92, 210
   Mikado, 71
Sunny Side Up (1929) film, 44
Suppé, Franz von, 36
Swift, Kay, 9, 31, 34, 49, 53, 97, 142, 294, 296
Swing Time (1936) film, 46
Szirmai, Albert, 161

Tartini, Giuseppe, 36
Taruskin, Richard, 230
Tawa, Nicholas E., 221
Taylor, Deems, 8, 140, 143, 163
Tchaikovsky, Pyotr Ilyich, 35, 127
   Nutcracker Suite, 255
   Piano Concerto No. 1, 37
   Symphony No. 4, 37
Teagarden, Charlie, 93
Teagarden, Jack, 93
Temple, Shirley, 45
The Jazz Singer (1927) film, 44
Theodore Drury Grand Opera Company, 190
Thompson, Jennifer Laura, 271
Thomson, Virgil, 29, 123, 223, 226, 228
   Four Saints in Three Acts, 226
Tilson Thomas, Michael, 83, 295, 296
Tiomkin, Dimitri, 161, 215–16
   Lost Horizon (1937) film, 216
Tischler, Barbara L., 227
Toch, Ernst, 161
   Die Reise Benjamins des Dritten, 161
Todd, R. Larry, 228
Trainwreck (2015) film, 258
Trevigne, Talise, 193
Tucker, Sophie, 131
Tune, Tommy, 261, 271, 272
Twiggy, 261, 271
Tyner, McCoy, 282

Uncle Tom's Cabin, 269
United Airlines's use of *Rhapsody in Blue*, 256–58

Van Dycke, Tom, 294
Van Eps, Fred, 136
Van Norman, Julia, 49

Van Vechten, Carl, 8
Varèse, Edgard, 161, 224, 228
Vaughan, Sarah, 237
Verdi, Giuseppe, 36, 69, 225
   Aida, 193
   Un ballo in Maschera, 191
Vienna, 161–62
Vieuxtemps, Henri, 35
   Violin Concerto No. 2, 37
Vodery, Will, 23, 60–61, 73
Von Tilzer, Albert, 138
"Voodoo," 184

Wagner, Richard, 35
   Götterdämmerung, 37, 246
   Die Meistersinger, 37
   Tristan und Isolde, 74
Walker, Arnetia, 100
Waller, Fats, 24, 26, 34, 285, 287
Walsh, Thommie, 261
Warburg, James, 49, 142
Warfield, William, 297
Warner, Russell, 83
Warren, Harry, 245
Waters, Ethel, 25
Watkins, Glenn, 228, 229
Wayburn, Ned, 132, 137
Webb, Chick, 241
Weber, Carl Maria von, 35
   Overture to *Der Freischutz*, 145
Weeks, Harold
   "Hindustan," 7, 139
Weill, Kurt, 13, 132, 161, 225
   Lady in the Dark, 13
Wells, Dickie, 278–79
Wheeldon, Christopher, 262
White, Betty, 256

White, Clarence Cameron, 190
   Ouanga!, 184
White, George, 7, 72, 73
   George White's Scandals, 7, 72, 76, 81, 93, 95
Whiteman, Paul, 53, 76, 96, 102, 104, 122, 123, 125, 127, 140, 156, 199, 246, 248, 252, 255, 258, 291, 295
   Experiment in Modern Music, 76, 103, 123, 252
Whiting, Margaret, 235
Whyte, Gordon, 73
Wiley, Lee, 235
Williams, Joe, 241
Williams, Mary Lou, 280
   "Walking and Swinging," 280
Wodehouse, P. G., 47, 197, 206, 207
   Damsel in Distress (1919) novel, 47, 206, 207
Wolfe, George C., 273
Wolpin, Kate, 3, 6
Wonder, Stevie, 284
Work III, John Wesley, 189
Work, Jr., John Wesley, 189

Yiddish theater, 24, 59, 63, 223
Youmans, Vincent, 11, 132, 148, 154
Young, Lester, 275, 278–79
Young, Victor, 246
Yvain, Maurice, 154
   Pas sur la Bouche, 155

Ziegfeld Follies (1945) film, 254
Ziegfeld, Florenz, 132, 145, 146, 147–48, 149, 269
   Ziegfeld Follies, 73, 137, 146
Zilboorg, Gregory, 49
Zimbalist, Efram, 36